The United States Air Force
in
Southeast Asia, 1961–1973:
An Illustrated Account

Edited by
Carl Berger

The Authors
Jack S. Ballard
Ray L. Bowers
Roland W. Doty, Jr.
R. Frank Futrell
William Greenhalgh
J. C. Hopkins
William B. Karstetter
Robert R. Kritt
Doris E. Krudener
Kenneth L. Patchin
Ralph A. Rowley
Jacob Van Staaveren
Bernard T. Termena

Revised Edition
OFFICE OF AIR FORCE HISTORY
UNITED STATES AIR FORCE
WASHINGTON, D.C.   1984

Library of Congress Cataloging in Publication Data

Main entry under title:

the United States Air Force in Southeast Asia.

Includes index.
1. Vietnamese Conflict, 1961-1975—Aerial operations, American. 2. United. Air Force—History.
I. Berger, Carl, Jan. 28, 1925- II. Ballard, Jack S. III. United States. Office of Air Force History.
DS558.8.U54   959.704'348   76-608038

For sale by the Superintendent of Documents,
U.S. Government Printing Office
Washington, D.C. 20402

United States Air Force
Historical Advisory Committee
(As of May 1, 1984)

Lt. Gen. Charles G. Cleveland,
USAF
Commander, Air University, ATC

Mr. DeWitt S. Copp
The National Volunteer Agency

Dr. Philip A. Crowl
Annapolis, Maryland

Dr. Warren W. Hassler, Jr.
Pennsylvania State University

Brig. Gen. Harris B. Hull,
USAF, Retired
National Aeronautics and Space
Administration

Dr. Alfred F. Hurley
Brig. Gen., USAF, Retired
North Texas State University

Gen. Bryce Poe II, USAF, Retired
Alexandria, Virginia

Lt. Gen. Winfield W. Scott, Jr.
Superintendent, USAF Academy

Dr. David A. Shannon *(Chairman)*
University of Virginia

Mr. Eugene R. Sullivan
The General Counsel, USAF

Foreword to Revised Edition

While United States' involvement in the Southeast Asian conflict extended back into the 1950's, this volume covers the years of active American participation from the early 1960's to 1973. From the outset American officials regarded the conflict basically as a land war, with the fighting in South Vietnam commanding top priority. As a result air power rarely played an independent role during the war, and air operations served primarily to assist troops on the ground. For example, as the communists moved men and supplies down the Ho Chi Minh Trail—under the jungle canopy and often at night—the Air Force developed reconnaissance aircraft and surveillance equipment to pierce the enemy's cover, and gunships to hinder his combat effectiveness. The Air Force also flew hundreds of thousands of sorties to close air support, interdiction, airlift, and battle illumination inside South Vietnam.

The most controversial periods for air operations occurred between 1965 and 1968, and later in 1972, over North Vietnam. When attacking the North, U.S. airmen faced a formidable air defense network. Detailed rules of engagement governed the conduct of all U.S. air operations throughout Southeast Asia, not only to prevent escalation but also to avoid civilian casualties, which would turn world public opinion against the war and alienate the citizens of the government which the U.S. was trying to help. At various times U.S. aircraft were not allowed to attack surface-to-air missile (SAM) sites, MIG airfields, and other targets judged too near to Hanoi and Haiphong, or considered especially sensitive for other reasons. The Air Force countered the North Vietnamese air defenses with formations flying evasive maneuvers that afforded both flexibility of action and adequate radar jamming from recently developed electronic counter measures. Bombing operations proved extremely complex, requiring coordination among several elements of air power. On a "typical" bombing run, escort aircraft fitted out for aerial combat or to attack radar sites, accompanied the strike group to protect the attackers from enemy SAMs and MIGs. Aerial tankers and airborne control centers contributed to the success of each day's operations, while rescue units stood by to recover downed airmen. Often support aircraft outnumbered the strike group.

The Office of Air Force History is reissuing this book in revised form because of demand for a single-volume history of air activity in the Vietnam War. Although a comprehensive and analytical one-volume history must await completion of the entire series on The United States Air Force in Southeast Asia, we hope that *An Illustrated Account* will help meet the present need. First published shortly after the end of the war, the chief merit of the volume lies more in depicting the complexity of the war than in offering dispassionate analysis. This edition corrects errors of omission, typography, or fact found in the original.

Jacob Neufeld, Chief of the Special Histories Branch in the Office of Air Force History, directed the work associated with this revised edition. Special thanks are due to several members of the office who reviewed the original text and recommended changes or corrections, including Maj. John F. Kreis, Lt. Col. Vance O. Mitchell, Mr. Bernard C. Nalty, Lt. Col. John F. Shiner, and Dr. Wayne W. Thompson. Others whose participation was most helpful included three authors of chapters in the book, Col. Ray L. Bowers (USAF, Ret.); Mr. J. C. Hopkins, History Office,

Strategic Air Command; and Mr. Jacob Van Staaveren. Col. John Schlight (USAF, Ret.) earlier contributed a detailed list of needed corrections. Finally, this volume owes much of its improvement to the expert scrutiny of several individuals serving throughout the USAF history program: Mr. Gerald T. Cantwell, Historian, Air Force Reserve; Capt. George W. Cully, History Office, Air Force Operational Test and Evaluation Center; Mr. Ben Goldman, Historian, Tactical Air Command; Mr. R. Cargill Hall, Chief, Research Division, USAF Historical Research Center; Dr. Charles O'Connell, History Office, Tactical Air Command; and Mr. David W. Shircliffe, Historian, Air Training Command. The editing tasks were ably performed by Mr. Lawrence J. Paszek and Ms. Bobbi Levien of the Office of Air Force History.

RICHARD H. KOHN
Chief, Office of Air Force History

Foreword

The year 1973 saw the end of direct American combat involvement in the Southeast Asia conflict—a conflict sometimes referred to as the Indochina War, the Vietnam War, and by other assorted sobriquets. This is an illustrated account of United States Air Force activities in that war from 1961 to 1973. It makes no pretense of being a comprehensive history of the war, or even of Air Force participation therein—not because it lacks historical authenticity (it contains *only* verifiable material), but simply because it is, by design, limited in scope and depth. Official, definitive histories are in progress but will not be widely available for several years. In the interim, this book can help fill a void in public knowledge of the Air Force's experience in Southeast Asia.

That experience was marked by great frustration--frustration flowing from the lack of a clear, definable, attainable objective and means for measuring success in achieving that objective—frustration arising from constraints that could only appear unreasonable to airmen—frustration from stringent rules of engagement which tended to offset advantages in skill and technology. This, however, should not be permitted to obscure the great dedication and zeal with which the men and women of the Air Force invariably carried out the job given them in Southeast Asia—despite the fact that missions, tactics, and targets frequently seemed inconsistent with their experience, training, and doctrine. The entire episode provides eloquent testimony to the disciplined professionalism of Air Force people. This effort to chronicle and depict some of their wartime activities should contribute to a broader understanding of the Air Force role in the Vietnam War.

DAVID C. JONES
General, USAF
Chief of Staff

Acknowledgements

Historians in the Office of Air Force History, Headquarters USAF and in such field organizations as the Strategic Air Command, Air Force Logistics Command, and Military Airlift Command wrote or otherwise contributed to the preparation of this narrative. Many civilian and military personnel of the Air Force, Army, Navy, Marine Corps, Office of the Joint Chiefs of Staff, and Office of the Secretary of Defense read and commented on the draft manuscript. Most of these reviewers possessed expert knowledge of specific aspects of the war, acquired through personal participation in it or years of research and writing on the subject. Their suggestions and criticisms were invaluable in eliminating errors of fact and correcting distortions.

General William M. Momyer (USAF, ret), who served as commander of the Seventh Air Force in Southeast Asia (1966-1968), provided an especially helpful commentary. Others who offered significant comments included Samuel A. Tucker, in the Office of the Secretary of Defense; Charles B. MacDonald, Chief, Current History Branch, U.S. Army, Center of Military History; and several faculty members of the Department of History, Air Force Academy. Special thanks are due to Capt. Robert H. Whitlow, U.S. Marine Corps, who kindly provided a portion of his manuscript dealing with attempts to recover several downed aircraft, which clarified an air rescue mission.

Work on this volume began in August 1973 under the direction of Brig. Gen. Brian S. Gunderson, Chief, Office of Air Force History between 1972 and 1974. Mr. Max Rosenberg, Deputy Chief Historian, prepared the plan for writing the book and helped shepherd the manuscript through several stages of writing and production. Mr. Rosenberg and Dr. Stanley L. Falk, Chief Historian of the Air Force, also reviewed drafts of the book and suggested revisions which substantially improved it. Mr. Carl Berger, Chief, Histories Division, served as overall editor.

Acknowledgements also are due to Gerard E. Hasselwander, Historical Research Branch, Albert F. Simpson Historical Research Center, Maxwell AFB, Ala., who compiled the list of key Air Force civilian and military personnel for the war period, and to Lt. Col. Raymond E. Fredette (USAF, ret), who wrote the accounts of the Air Force Medal of Honor recipients. Mr. David Schoem and Mrs. Gail Guido, Chief and Archivist, respectively, in the Support Division, Office of Air Force History, provided general administrative and research assistance while Mr. William Mattson, Mrs. Eleanor C. Patterson, Mrs. Elizabeth B. Schwartzmann, and Mrs. Selma Shear typed the several drafts.

Mr. Lawrence J. Paszek, Chief Editorial Branch Office of Air Force History, prepared the manuscript for publication. He and Mr. Deane J. Allen of the Editorial Branch collected and selected most of the illustrations. Their sources included the photographic collections of the Air Force, Army, Navy, and Marine Corps, as well as those of other government agencies. Mrs. Frances Lewis and Mrs. Mabel B. Sneed, 1361st Photographic Squadron, Aerospace Audio-Visual Service, provided substantial research assistance in this effort. Mr. Andrew Poggen-pohl, Art Editor, *National Geographic Magazine*, kindly supplied a number of color and black-and-white photographs. Several other private sources also loaned illustrations from their collections. Acknowledgements will be found in a separate section in the back matter.

This casebound book containing battle area maps and over 600 photographs was designed by Dudley Kruhm, Typography and Design Division, Government Printing Office.

The paintings are reproductions of the originals in the official Air Force Art Collection, administered by the Office of Information.

Contents

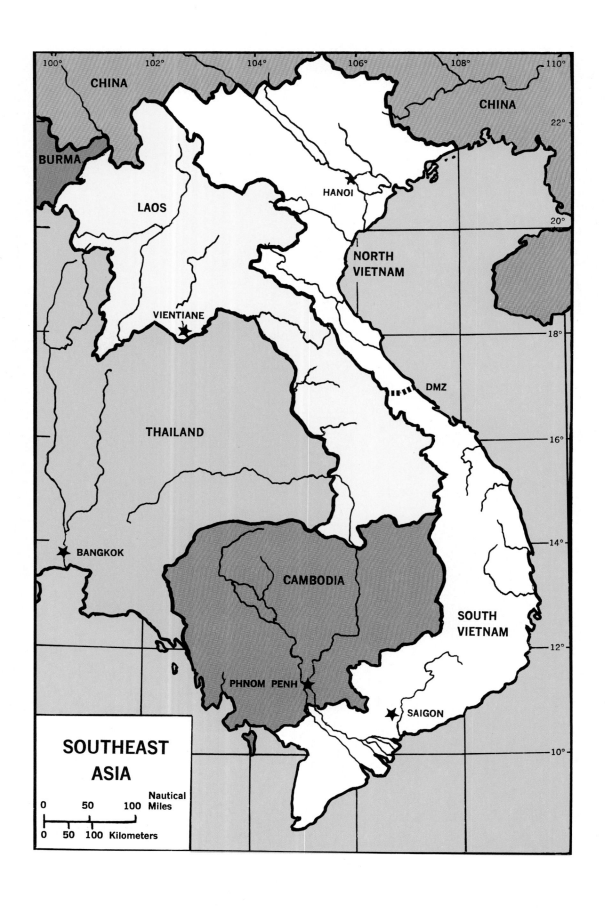

SOUTHEAST
ASIA

Chapter I

Introduction

U.S. Army Air Forces' fighters and bombers flew their first combat missions in Southeast Asia during World War II. From bases in India, China, and the Philippines, they went into action against Japanese land, sea, and air targets throughout the area, including those in enemy-occupied French Indochina. Among targets attacked by AAF planes in 1942-1944 were Haiphong harbor, Hanoi's Gia Lam airfield, and Japanese shipping in the Gulf of Tonkin. Beginning in June 1944 B-29 crews joined the air campaign. Flying from Indian bases, they bombed Japanese ammunition and supply dumps, oil storage facilities, naval installations, and other targets at Saigon, Phnom Penh, Bangkok, Rangoon, and Singapore. The Superforts also mined nearby Cap St. Jacques (Vung Tau), and Cam Ranh Bay. In the spring and summer of 1945, Philippine-based fighters and bombers swept the coastal railroad, hitting targets at Phan Rang, Nha Trang, Tuy Hoa, and Tourane (Da Nang). On 15 August 1945, following the atomic bomb attacks on Hiroshima and Nagasaki, Japan surrendered.

Sixteen years later Air Force crews returned to several of the places bombed during World War II—to Thailand and the territory of the beleaguered Republic of Vietnam (South Vietnam). The latter for several years had been subjected to guerrilla attacks supported by its northern neighbor, the Democratic Republic of Vietnam (North Vietnam).From bases in Thailand and South Vietnam, Air Force pilots during the early 1960's began flying the first of thousands of combat missions over the Republic of Vietnam and southern Laos, the latter tne location of the famous Ho Chi Minh trail. In time this new war spilled over into North Vietnam and Cambodia. For some of the participating airmen, Southeast Asia became the scene of the third war they had fought in less than a quarter of a century.

However, for most members of the U.S. Air Force who served 1-year tours of duty (many of them had multiple tours) in the area, the war against the Viet Cong and North Vietnamese was their first experience in combat. Along with air veterans of World War II and Korea, they were ordered into combat by three Presidents of the United States. The first of these chief executives—John F. Kennedy—had concluded that the United States should provide additional military assistance to South Vietnam and the Royal Laotian Government (RLG) to prevent their takeover by Communist forces. His successors, Lyndon B. Johnson and Richard M. Nixon, also reaffirmed their support for the preservation of non-Communist governments in the area. Initially backed wholeheartedly by Congress and the American people, their decisions ultimately resulted in the longest, most controversial, and financially most costly war in the nation's history.

Origins of the War

The conflict in Southeast Asia had origins in the Vietnamese nationalist movement going back to the end of World War I, aimed at ending French colonial rule. The government of France, however, resisted all Vietnamese efforts to achieve their independence. Following Nazi Germany's conquest of France in 1940, Japan moved in on Indochina intending to incorporate that territory into its empire. But after the defeat of Germany in 1945, the French determined to reassert their colonial rule. However, President Franklin D. Roosevelt in 1943 had urged the freeing of all colonial peoples, including those of Indochina, in the postwar period.

During the last months of the war, U.S. agents had been parachuted into the hills of Annam where they joined up with insurgent forces led by Ho Chi Minh. These local forces, known as the Viet Minh, included both Communist and non-Communist elements, all united in their desire for independence. The Americans brought with them a small supply of rifles, mortars, machineguns, grenades, and bazookas and began training Ho's troops to use them against Japanese occupation troops. On 15 August 1945, following Japan's surrender, President Harry S. Truman issued General Order No. 1 governing procedures for disarming Japanese forces in the Far East. In the case of Indochina, he designated the 16th parallel as the line north of which Chinese Nationalist troops would disarm the Japanese. South of that line British forces were to accept the Japanese surrender.

On 9 September 1945, when advance elements of about 200,000 Chinese troops arrived in Hanoi, they found that Ho Chi Minh's forces had already taken control of the northern region, replaced all French street signs with Vietnamese ones, and issued a Declaration of Independence on 2 September establishing the Democratic Republic of Vietnam. On 12 September British Commonwealth forces landed at Tan Son Nhut airfield outside Saigon accompanied by a detachment of 150 French troops. Three weeks earlier British authorities in London had determined to restore France's administration of Indochina. By 23 September the French, with the help of the British, reassumed control of Saigon. The French subsequently began negotiations with the Chinese to permit French military forces to move into the northern part of Vietnam. An agreement was reached and, in March 1946, a French military force arrived at Haiphong to relieve the Chinese Army of its responsibilities under General Order No. 1. The French commander, Gen. Jacques Leclerc, began negotiations with Ho and, on 6 March, an accord was reached. Under its provisions, the French agreed to recognize the Democratic Republic of Vietnam "as a free state, having its Government, its Parliament, its army, and its finances, and forming a part of the Indochinese Federation and the French Union."

Further negotiations spelling out details of Vietnamese independence got under way in the spring of 1946 at Dalat, at a time when Vietnamese guerrilla warfare was under way in southern Vietnam (Cochinchina). But the discussions foundered on the issue of Vietnamese autonomy, whereupon the French announced the establishment of an "independent" Cochinchina within the French Union. This act only exacerbated the situation and stimulated guerrilla warfare in the south. Another attempt to reach an agreement came during the summer of 1946, when Ho and a Viet Minh delegation travelled to France for 2 more months of discussion of the issue. Once again, the talks failed over the issue of Vietnamese independence. The Viet Minh delegation returned home and, shortly after, forces commanded by Gen. Vo Nguyen Giap launched a series of attacks on French posts and truck convoys, inflicting heavy casualties and provoking general hostilities.

While these events were unfolding in Southeast Asia, Washington's attention was focused on a divided Europe whose eastern half was firmly under Soviet control. An additional cause for worry was the substantial political support the Communist parties of France and Italy began winning during the early postwar years.

American officials felt it was essential to restore France so as to enable her to reassume her historic role in western Europe. Support of French policy in Indochina followed. Thus, the United States accepted the French proposal to give limited autonomy to the Associated States of Vietnam, Laos, and Cambodia. A number of Vietnamese—such as Emperor Bao Dai—went along with the French and he emerged as head of the new State of Vietnam (which incorporated Cochinchina). The United States recognized the Bao Dai government on 3 February 1950.

Meanwhile, the guerrilla war had spread and France found it necessary to send more military resources to Indochina. Exacerbating the French situation was the arrival of Mao Tse-tung's victorious troops on the northern border of Vietnam in December 1949. Ho's Viet Minh immediately recognized the new Chinese Communist government, and was recognized in turn by Peking, Moscow, and the satellite regimes of Eastern Europe. On 16 February 1950 France formally requested American military and economic assistance in prosecuting the Indochina war.

At this point the Truman administration undertook an evaluation of the situation in Southeast Asia. It concluded that "the threat of Communist aggression in Indochina is only one phase of anticipated Communist plans to seize all of Southeast Asia." In National Security Council Memorandum 64, dated 27 February 1950, it further stated that "all practicable measures [should] be taken to prevent further Communist expansion in Southeast Asia...The neighboring countries of Thailand and Burma could be expected to fall under Communist domination if Indochina were controlled by a Communist-dominated government. The balance of Southeast Asia would then be in grave hazard." Subsequently, on 1 May 1950, President Truman approved an initial allotment of $10 million for French Indochina.

The U.S. Air Force in Indochina

Starting in the summer of 1950 and during the next two decades, U.S. Air Force personnel—military advisors, maintenance and supply experts, combat crews, etc.—were ordered into French Indochina and later to its successor states, South Vietnam, Laos, and Cambodia in support of national policy. Besides serving as members of the Military Assistance Advisory Group (MAAG) in Saigon beginning in July 1950, USAF personnel during the early 1950's were sent to Indochina on temporary duty (TDY) for specific purposes. For example, in January 1953 a Philippine-based Air Force aircraft maintenance and supply detachment was sent to Nha Trang airfield to help the French to maintain C-47 transports lent to them for use against the Viet Minh. The detachment completed its work and withdrew in August 1953.

In February 1954, several months prior to the crisis surrounding the battle of Dien Bien Phu, several hundred USAF mechanics were again sent to Indochina to help keep other U.S.-loan aircraft in flying condition. In the early spring of 1954, at the request of the French the Air Force helped fly in troop reinforcements from North Africa and France to bolster the deteriorating military situation at Dien Bien Phu. Just prior to the climax of the battle in May, President Dwight D. Eisenhower and his advisers mulled over U.S. intervention in the form of a possible Air Force and U.S. Navy tactical strike, to include the use of B-29 bombers, to relieve the enemy's pressure on the French garrison. In this regard, Brig. Gen. Joseph D. Caldara, commander of the Far East Air Forces Bomber Command in Japan, in April 1954 reconnoitered the Dien Bien Phu

(1-2) The U.S. government loaned France a number of Air Force transports to bolster French Air Force airlift operations against Viet Minh forces. (3, 5) In the 1960's, Air Force C-123's, converted into spray aircraft, were employed to defoliate jungle vegetation which provided cover for guerrillas who ambushed military and civilian traffic in South Vietnam. (4) An Air Force Forward Air Controller discusses a mission with his Vietnamese counterpart. (6) President Eisenhower (l.) and Secretary of State Dulles (r.) confer in the White House with President Ngo Dinh Diem of the Republic of Vietnam, 8 May 1957. (7) Viet Minh prisoners captured by the French unload military supplies from a USAF C-54.

1

3

4

5

6

7

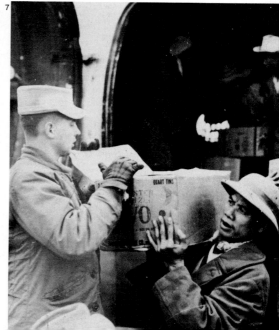

battlefield in a B-17 and concluded that a B-29 strike would be successful.

However, in Washington key members of the Congress balked at U.S. military intervention unless the British agreed to participate. When Prime Minister Winston Churchill refused to go along, the President dropped the idea of an air strike. On 7 May 1954 the French were overwhelmed by Viet Minh troops under General Giap, his victory in effect marking the end of nearly a century of French rule in Indochina. The very next day, at a previously scheduled international conference in Geneva, Switzerland, representatives of the major powers and of the Indochinese people met to discuss a cease fire agreement, which was subsequently approved on 20-21 July 1954.

The conferees recognized the independence of Vietnam, Cambodia, and Laos. They agreed that Vietnam would be temporarily divided at the 17th parallel pending nationwide elections to be held in July 1956 to unify the country. Under terms of separate agreements signed by the French and the Viet Minh, France agreed to withdraw her forces and presence over a period of several years. The Geneva Protocols prohibited the reinforcement of local military forces or reequipping them with improved armaments beyond what was in the country in mid-1954. The Protocols did not require the U.S. Military Assistance Advisory Group—then at an authorized strength of 342 men—to withdraw from South Vietnam. The Geneva agreement also established an International Control Commission (ICC) to supervise the various agreements.

At the 17th parallel, a demilitarized zone (DMZ) was created between the two Vietnams with people on both sides being allowed to resettle wherever they wished. Some 900,000 Vietnamese in the northern region chose to go south, over 300,000 of them being evacuate by U.S. Navy vessels.

More than 100,000 Viet Minh soldiers and civilians in the south went north, where some formed the military cadres that led the subsequent armed struggle in the south. Meanwhile, in Hanoi, Ho Chi Minh on 11 October 1954 once more proclaimed the establishment of the Democratic Republic of Vietnam. In Saigon the State of Vietnam, originally sponsored by the French, emerged under a new leader, Premier and later President Ngo Dinh Diem. He proclaimed his state a Republic and was immediately recognized by President Eisenhower.

In September 1954 the United States also sponsored creation of an eight-nation Southeast Asia Treaty Organization (SEATO), which threw a mantle of protection over Laos, Cambodia, and "the free territory under the jurisdiction of the State of Vietnam. . ." The Senate ratified the SEATO treaty on 1 February 1955. Meanwhile, the United States transferred its economic and military assistance from France to the new Saigon government and to Laos and Cambodia. President Eisenhower, who accepted the "domino theory" as expressed in NSC 64—i.e., that all of Southeast Asia would fall under Communist rule if Ho Chi Minh's government controlled all of Vietnam—decided to assist Saigon to expand its armed forces.

Thus, he approved Diem's plans to build an Army of the Republic of Vietnam (ARVN), consisting of 4 conventional infantry divisions, 6 light divisions, an airborne brigade-size combat team, 13 territorial regiments, support troops, and limited air and naval forces. The small Vietnamese Air Force (VNAF) was authorized 4,140 men and was equipped with obsolete, non-jet aircraft. It consisted of an F8F fighter squadron, two C-47 squadrons, two L-19 (liaison) squadrons, and an H-19 helicopter unit. The MAAG took over training responsibility of most South Vietnamese forces after France relinquished command authority on

This Soviet Ilyushin transport was photographed dropping supplies to leftist rebels in Laos. President Kennedy told a Washington press conference the Russians had flown more than 1,000 sorties on behalf of the Pathet Lao.

12 February 1955. The French, however, continued to train the VNAF until May 1957.

In 1956, the year when national elections were to be held to unify the country, South Vietnam—which had not been a party to the French-Viet-Minh military agreement or the Geneva Accords and had strongly protested the election provision—decided to ignore the entire matter. Diem argued that the northerners would not be able to vote freely under Ho's one-party rule and that the bloc vote of the North would overwhelm those cast in the South. The fact was, however, that although a Communist, Ho Chi Minh was—as President Eisenhower once remarked—a legendary hero to the Vietnamese people and would probably have won any nationwide election. In any event, the election was not held and for several years the two Vietnams went their separate ways. But in May 1959 the Central Committee of the North Vietnamese Lao Dong (workers, i.e., Communist) Party—having firmly established control over the countryside by suppressing peasant resistance —called for reunifying the country through armed struggle.

Shortly thereafter, a North Vietnamese Army (NVA) transportation group began work on the Ho Chi Minh trail, the infiltration route through Laos to the South. The first of an initial 4,500-man military cadre—most ethnic southerners who had received training and indoctrination in the north—arrived in South Vietnam. These hardcore Viet Cong cadres were funnelled into Communist jungle base areas in Tay Ninh province on the Cambodian border (later designated by American officials as War Zone C), an area northwest of Saigon (War Zone D), and in the dense U Minh forest area of the Ca Mau peninsula.

Meanwhile, Viet Cong terrorism had steadily increased between mid-1957 and mid-1959, and several MAAG personnel fell victim. Thus, on 8 July 1959 a U.S. Army major and master sergeant were killed in a Viet Cong attack on Bien Hoa. Two months later, several Viet Cong companies ambushed a South Vietnamese army force searching for guerrillas in the marshy Plain of Reeds southwest of Saigon. According to the Viet Cong, this incident marked the official start of the armed struggle. Reacting to it, American officials in October 1959 recommended an increase of the strength of the MAAG from 342 men to 685 so as to provide for U.S. Army Special Forces teams to train ARVN rangers for border patrols. Despite Communist protests to the ICC, Washington on 5 May approved the recommendation. The Special Forces teams arrived in South Vietnam by the end of October.

The Eisenhower administration's primary interest at this time was to improve South Vietnam's counterinsurgency efforts. Not until several months later did it give serious attention to the Vietnamese Air Force, after its commander, Col. Nguyen Xuan Vinh, grounded all of his old F8F fighters because they were unsafe for flight. The United States responded in September 1960 by shipping the first of 25 U.S. Navy AD-6 aircraft to Vietnam to replace the F8F's. Later, Washington also agreed to provide the VNAF 11 H-34 helicopters. The first four arrived in Vietnam in December 1960, followed by the others over the subsequent 3 months. However, logistical actions to support the AD-6's and H-34's lagged and many of the aircraft soon were out of commission for lack of parts.

Meanwhile, MAAG and Pacific Command (PACOM) officials drew up a counterinsurgency plan which called for providing substantial U.S. aid to the South Vietnamese in dealing with insurgency. The draft plan, completed by the Commander in Chief, Pacific (CINCPAC) in April 1960, was approved by the Joint Chiefs of Staff (JCS). The latter proposed that South

USAF technicians served on temporary duty in Indochina to assist the French Air Force to maintain C-47 aircraft transferred to France.

9

Vietnam unify its military command, enlarge the army, and augment slightly (by 499 men) the Vietnamese Air Force.

Kennedy Administration Policies

Two weeks before John F. Kennedy was inaugurated as President in January 1961, Soviet Premier Nikita Khrushchev made a speech in Moscow to the Communist Party Congress which had a decisive influence on the new chief executive's view of events in Southeast Asia. Describing various kinds of wars which might occur in the future, Khrushchev announced that the Soviet Union would "wholeheartedly" support wars of national liberation, examples of which were, he said, "the armed struggle waged by the people of Vietnam and the present war of the Algerian people. . . ." Impressed by Khrushchev's speech, President Kennedy indorsed the counterinsurgency plan in principle and ordered his key assistants to undertake a major study of doctrine and force requirements to support it. Almost concurrently, Hanoi announced the establishment within South Vietnam of the National Front for the Liberation of Vietnam (NLF).

Kennedy had scarcely settled in office when he was faced with a series of crises centering on Southeast Asia, including a deteriorating situation in Laos, where the government was threatened by Communist Pathet Lao forces. In a press conference statement on 23 March 1961, the President told the American people that:

> Soviet planes, I regret to say, have been conspicuous in a large-scale airlift into the battle area—over. . . 1,000 sorties since last December 13th, plus a whole supporting set of combat specialists, mainly from Communist North Viet-Nam, and heavier weapons have been provided from outside, all with the clear object of destroying by military action the agreed neutrality of Laos. . .We strongly and unreservedly support the goal of a neutral and independent Laos, tied to no outside power or group of powers. . .

Within South Vietnam, similar forces continued to threaten the Diem government. Whereupon, in May 1961 Mr. Kennedy dispatched Vice President Lyndon B. Johnson to South Vietnam to consult with Diem. Subsequently, President Kennedy agreed to increase U.S. military assistance to South Vietnam. It included, in the case of the Air Force, the dispatch of a mobile control and reporting post (CRP) from the United States to Tan Son Nhut Air Base (AB) outside Sai-

Ho Chi Minh visited Moscow on the 44th anniversary of the birth of the Soviet state, 7 November 1961. Among the Communist leaders present were (l. to r.) Blas Roca of Cuba; Ho; Soviet Premier Nikita Khrushchev; Janos Kadar of Hungary; Soviet President Leonid Brezhnev; Deputy Premier Frel Koslov; Presidium member Mikhail Suslov; and First Deputy Premier Anastas Mikoyan.

10

gon. A detachment of the 507th Tactical Control Group departed Shaw AFB, S.C., on 26 September 1961. By 5 October the control and reporting post was operational and began providing radar control and warning in the Saigon area while also serving as a facility in which to train VNAF radar technicians.

In 1961, the President also approved "in principle" a 30,000-man increase in South Vietnam's armed forces. The Vietnamese Air Force was authorized its second fighter squadron, a third liaison squadron, and a photo reconnaissance unit. Secretary of Defense Robert S. McNamara directed that the Vietnamese be provided armed T-28 trainer aircraft for the fighter squadron. The U.S. ambassador in Saigon, Frederick E. Nolting, Jr., rejected a separate Air Force proposal to equip the VNAF reconnaissance unit with four RT/T-33 jets, citing the prohibition on jet aircraft in the Geneva Protocols. The third liaison squadron was equipped with L-19's, transferred from the VNAF training center at Nha Trang.

President Kennedy also approved the establishment of a U.S. South Vietnamese combat development and test center in Vietnam, under the direction of the Defense Department's Advanced Research Projects Agency, for the purpose of learning and improving counterinsurgency techniques and tactics. Among the ideas listed for examination was the use of aerial-delivered defoliants to reduce jungle cover along major highways, where Viet Cong units frequently ambushed government troops. That such a project was needed became apparent to two U.S. Congressmen who visited South Vietnam in late 1961 for a first-hand look at the war. Rep. William E. Minshall later reported that 15 miles outside of Saigon the situation remained "very tenuous. . .very strained. The roads are being cut every night. There are road blocks set up every night and you can hear mortar fire every night."

Gen. Curtis E. LeMay, Air Force Chief of Staff, responded to the President's interest in having the armed forces prepared to fight guerrilla wars by establishing the 4400th Combat Crew Training Squadron (Jungle Jim) at Eglin AFB, Fla, on 14 April 1961. It quickly attracted highly motivated airmen who were rapidly qualified to conduct sub rosa air commando operations. On 11 October the President authorized deployment of a Jungle Jim detachment to South Vietnam for training purposes. After Saigon approved, Detachment 2A, 4400th Combat Crew Training Squadron—designated Farm Gate—departed the United States for Bien Hoa, South Vietnam. Farm Gate included 151 officers and men and 8 T-28's, 4 SC-47's and 4 RB-26's. The T-28's and SC-47's arrived at Bien Hoa on 4 November 1961; the RB-26's reached Vietnam some time after 18 December 1961. All aircraft carried Vietnamese Air Force markings.

Meanwhile, in the fall of 1961, Communist Pathet Lao forces accelerated their operations against the Royal Government of Laos. At the same time several Viet Cong units of up to 1,500 men began cutting strategic highways in the vicinity of Saigon and other urban areas. This notable rise of insurgent activities led President Diem to proclaim a state of emergency. Surprised by this outburst of Communist activities, USAF advisors asked for the deployment of a detachment of four RF-101's to Tan Son Nhut to conduct reconnaissance missions over Vietnam and Laos. An invitation from the South Vietnamese for the U.S. Air Force to take part in an air show in October 1961 provided the occasion to send these jets into the area. Between 20 October and 21 November, these aircraft flew 67 sorties. Early in November, four RF-101's of the 45th Tactical Reconnaissance Squadron based in Japan were deployed to Don Muang Airport, Thailand, to augment and then replace the Tan Son Nhut-based detachment. By the end of 1961, the 45th had flown some 130 missions.

President Kennedy—concerned about a lack of confidence in Saigon resulting from the recent Viet Cong successes—on 13 November 1961 approved recommendations made by Gen. Maxwell D. Taylor and Dr. Walt W. Rostow, a national security advisor, both recently returned from a visit to South Vietnam. To increase Vietnamese military mobility, the President authorized deployment of three U.S. Army H-21 helicopter companies (40

aircraft), a USAF squadron of 16 C-123 assault transport planes (code name Mule Train), and the loan to the VNAF of 30 T-28 aircraft. On 30 November the President permitted an aerial spray flight of six C-123's (Ranch Hand)—which had arrived at Clark AB in the Philippines— to continue on to Vietnam to undertake "carefully controlled" defoliation operations. Most of the USAF units were in place in South Vietnam in early 1962. They came under the command of Brig. Gen. Rollen H. Anthis, who landed at Tan Son Nhut on 20 November to assume command of four numbered detachments, three located in South

USAF spray missions to defoliate jungle vegetation, to eliminate ambush sites, generated much controversy during the war.

(Above) Dr. James W. Brown (2nd from left), a civilian expert assigned to the Pentagon, directed the initial defoliation tests in South Vietnam.

Forward Air Controller (FAC) in a L-19 and two VNAF AD-6's flew overhead. The operation resulted in 2 Viet Cong killed, 1 wounded, and 46 suspects captured. The Viet Cong radio transmitter went off the air and was not located.

The U.S. military units dispatched to South Vietnam—initially viewed by President Kennedy as serving in a combat "training" role—were authorized to "fire back if fired upon." A major prohibition on their operations was to avoid injuring or killing noncombatants. As a consequence, although Air Force reconnaissance planes discovered many Viet Cong targets and President Diem urged vigorous air action against them, USAF pilots did not attack because of concern over possible harm to Vietnamese civilians. In December 1961 Secretary McNamara authorized, and the JCS directed Gen. Emmett O'Donnell, Commander in Chief, Pacific Air Forces (CINCPACAF), to deploy a tactical air control system (TACS) to South Vietnam to provide "cooperative" use of VNAF and USAF strike, reconnaissance, and transport capabilities.

On 26 December 1961 Washington issued a new directive prohibiting Farm Gate aircraft from engaging in combat operations over South Vietnam except when a Vietnamese crewman was aboard or when the VNAF lacked the ability to perform certain missions. In the months and years that followed, those simple rules of engagement grew into many pages of detailed operating instructions telling Air Force pilots what they could or could not do in combat. The President and his chief advisors through much of the war retained tight controls over aerial operations in Southeast Asia. Their reasons were clear—to avoid the military intervention of Communist China, as had occurred during the Korean War, or that of the Soviet Union.

Vietnam, and one in Thailand. His initial organization was designated as 2nd ADVON.

During the waning days of 1961, the first combined U.S.-South Vietnamese air mobile operation was launched against the Viet Cong's War Zone D headquarters northeast of Saigon. Its purpose was to locate and capture a clandestine Viet Cong radio transmitter. Two newly arrived U.S. Army helicopter companies lifted 360 Vietnamese airborne troops to five landing zones in the area on 23 December. Additional troops were brought in on the 27th. During the critical phases of these helicopter lifts, a Vietnamese

Chapter II. Air Operations In South Vietnam

1962 - 1964

In January 1962 the Farm Gate detachment began training 25 VNAF pilots to fly T-28's of the newly organized 2d Fighter Squadron. It set up several classes for the Vietnamese and taught them methods of day and night bombing, rocketry, and gunnery. Other USAF personnel taught Vietnamese ground crews T-28 maintenance and supply procedures. By March 1962 all 25 pilots had been checked out in formation flying, tactics, and instruments, and shortly after, the squadron was declared operational. The Americans found that the VNAF airmen were excellent pilots, although few had night flying experience. One reason for this was that some of the U.S. aircraft provided under the Military Assistance Program —particularly the 1st VNAF Fighter Squadron's obsolete AD-6's—lacked landing lights or serviceable artificial horizon instruments.

Because the Viet Cong became active mostly after dark, the Americans emphasized the importance of night operations. Thus, shortly after their arrival in South Vietnam, the Farm Gate crews began experimenting with aerial flares, dropped from an SC-47, to light up a target for night strikes by the Vietnamese Air Force. The technique worked well and was quickly adopted by VNAF airmen, who began flying their own flare missions on 5 February 1962. The success of the flare-and-strike technique—the Viet Cong would break off their attacks when the flares ignited—led Secretary McNamara to direct that Vietnamese

villages be equipped with radios to facilitate calls for air support. By June 1962 more than 520 radios had been distributed.

In the early weeks of 1962 USAF crews also began test defoliation flights along the highway between Bien Hoa and Vung Tau in an effort to destroy the heavy jungle vegetation, perfect cover for enemy troops. These operations stirred the Viet Cong into denunciations of the United States for resorting to "chemical warfare." As it turned out, the initial defoliation spray was dispensed too thinly and the vegetation was unaffected. On 2 February, during a training mission, a C-123 crashed, killing the crew of three. It was the first Air Force plane lost in South Vietnam.

Nine days later a second USAF aircraft—an SC-47—also crashed while flying a psychological warfare leaflet dispensing mission near Dalat. Six Air Force personnel, two U.S. Army men, and one Vietnamese airman died. In subsequently criticizing the operation, Secretary McNamara reemphasized that U.S. forces were supposed to be training the Vietnamese and not engaging in combat activities.

Early in 1962 the Air Force also began to assist the Vietnamese in setting up a Tactical Air Control System (TACS). It initially relied upon USAF radars at Tan Son Nhut and Da Nang and a Vietnamese-operated radar at Pleiku. This radar network, which provided limited aircraft control and warning coverage over all of South Vietnam, soon began picking up tracks of numerous unidentified aircraft. Some of these later proved to be U.S. Army helicopters or light planes, which had arrived in South Vietnam beginning in late 1961. Ironically, the TACS was first tested operationally on 27 February when two disaffected VNAF pilots strafed and bombed the presidential palace in Saigon. One plane was shot down and the other escaped to Cambodia.

The system was next exercised during the night of 19 and 20 March 1962 when unidentified low-flying aircraft were detected over the Central Highlands. Concerned about them, Diem requested—and Ambassador Nolting quickly arranged—the deployment of USAF jet interceptors from Clark to Tan Son Nhut. On 22 March four F-102's began flying missions over South Vietnam. After flying 21 sorties, they were relieved a week later by U.S. Navy interceptors on a rotational basis. USAF and Navy crews failed to find any enemy aircraft.

Subsequently, the Tactical Air Control System was refined and expanded to provide the communication network which enabled the Seventh Air Force commander to exercise centralized control over his forces and to monitor the air/ground situation. Within this system, the Tactical Air Control Center (TACC) at Tan Son Nhut allowed the air commander to plan and coordinate the diverse operations of his tactical forces within the four nations of Indochina. A number of Control and Reporting Centers came directly under the Center and supervised activities of subordinate radar elements known as Control and Reporting Posts.

While work on the Tactical Air Control System proceeded, USAF advisors were encouraging VNAF airmen to attack Viet Cong jungle sanctuaries in an effort to keep the insurgents off balance. In this regard, in 1962 Adm. Harry D. Felt, Commander in Chief, Pacific, proposed that Saigon's ground forces undertake offensive operations to root out the enemy from those areas and pacify the countryside. A pacification program was subsequently drawn up, based on a proposal made by Robert G.K. Thompson, head of the British Advisory Mission in Saigon (1961-1965). Drawing upon Britain's experiences with Chinese terrorists in Malaya in 1948-1959, Thompson recommended the South Vietnamese undertake a strategic hamlet program. The idea was to build fortified hamlets in relatively safe "white" areas. From there ARVN troops would move farther and farther into Viet Cong "red" areas—"like a spreading oil spot"—thus presumably driving the insurgents out of the country entirely.

On 16 March 1962, in a much publicized start of the strategic hamlet program, the ARVN 5th Division launched Operation Sunrise. It began with a motorized deployment of ARVN troops to the southern fringes of the Viet Cong's Zone D sanctuary in Binh Duong province. Once there, the soldiers moved out to uproot Vietnamese peasants—believed to be supplying the insurgents with food—to relocate elsewhere in fortified hamlets they were compelled to build. Following the success of this initial operation, President Diem ordered a rapid expansion of the strategic hamlet program.

Meanwhile, U.S. Army advisors were working to develop ARVN airborne helicopter assault tactics, using equipment of two U.S. Army companies which had arrived in Vietnam in late 1961. Almost at once a problem arose over fixed-wing/air-ground coordination. According to directives issued by the newly organized U.S. Military Assistance Command, Vietnam (USMACV),* all helicopter operations into areas where enemy opposi-

---

*Established on 8 February 1962 with Gen. Paul D. Harkins, U.S. Army, as commander.

tion was expected were required to have fixed-wing tactical air cover. U.S. Army corps advisors who controlled helicopter usage, however, tended to ignore the requirement.

In April 1962, during a visit to South Vietnam, General LeMay learned that Army advisors were not calling for fixed-wing air support, that only about 10 percent of ARVN heliborne operations were accompanied by VNAF aircraft, and that the Air Support Operations Center and Joint Operations Center at Tan Son Nhut frequently were not informed about such operations. Concerned about this situation, LeMay subsequently obtained permission to assign air liaison officers (ALO's) to all ARVN corps and division headquarters and USAF forward air controllers to augment VNAF liaison squadrons. Moreover, soon after the Viet Cong succeeded in shooting down four Army H-21 helicopters, Admiral Felt directed General Harkins to make maximum use of the fixed-wing aircraft during offensive operations. This produced an immediate increase in the number of ARVN calls for fighter cover. For example, whereas during the first 5 months of 1962 only 81 fighter flights supported helicopter assault operations, during July alone there were 139 sorties. Between 1 May and 12 August 1962, approximately 40 percent of all ARVN operations employed fixed-wing air support.

Meanwhile, the Viet Cong continued to exploit the jungle environment with great skill to interdict South Vietnamese road and rail traffic. On 16 June two enemy battalions ambushed an ARVN convoy south of Ben Cat, killing 23 Vietnamese soldiers and 2 U.S. Army advisors. Following this incident and a rash of lesser ones, General Anthis recommended—and General Harkins approved—the mandatory use of air cover over all Vietnamese road and train convoys. The Vietnamese Joint General Staff issued the necessary directive. There followed a complete turnaround in the number of enemy ambushes. During the first 8 months of 1962, the Viet Cong ambushed convoys on 462 occasions; thereafter, for more than a year, no air-escorted convoy was hit.

On 23 July Secretary McNamara—mindful of President Kennedy's policy that the major task of U.S. advisors was to prepare Republic of Vietnam Armed Forces (RVNAF) for combat—ordered an increase in the training of their troops and delivery of additional equipment so as to phase out U.S. combat, advisory, and logistic support activities. At the same time, he honored General Harkins' request for two more U.S. Army helicopter companies to support the ARVN's expanding ground operations. Harkins and McNamara initially delayed acting on a request from General Anthis to augment Farm Gate with 5 T-28's, 10 B-26's, and 2 C-47's to enable him to meet the support requirements. The delay resulted from the fact that the request had not been presented to the JCS and was contrary to the President's policy. It was not until November 1962 that CINCPAC recommended the measure to the Joint Chiefs, who spent another month studying the proposal before recommending it to the Defense Secretary. Not until the proposal was cleared by the State Department 2 weeks later did Mc-Namara recommend the President's approval. Another 11 days elapsed before the White House gave the "go-ahead."

Aerial reconnaissance was another area where the Air Force could not keep pace with expanding combat operations (see also Chapter XII). In 1962 the Vietnamese Air Force possessed two camera-equipped C-45's to conduct photo reconnaissance flights; at the same time, its visual reconnaissance activities had been reduced following transfer of L-19 pilots to fighter cockpits. The few RF-101's at Don Muang were heavily involved in meeting intelligence requirements in both Vietnam and Laos. All combat film was processed in Saigon or at an Air Force laboratory at Don Muang. However, the time between receipt of a request for aerial photos and their delivery proved much too lengthy in a situation involving fast-moving, elusive guerrilla troops who could hide in jungle growth.

To correct this situation Harkins proposed—and Admiral Felt authorized—equipping the VNAF with a tactical reconnaissance squadron composed of 4 RT 33's, 3 RC-47's, 18 RT-28's and several field processing centers. McNamara eliminated the RT-33 jet aircraft and approved the squadron. In September the VNAF activated the 716th Reconnaissance Squadron at Tan Son Nhut with two RC-45's while awaiting delivery of the other equipment. Meanwhile, Farm Gate crews obtained two RB-26's to meet the growing needs for reconnaissance photography.

In early 1962 the Joint Operations Center Airlift Branch—manned by Air Force personnel—prepared daily schedules for the C-123's. Inadequate aerial port and mission control facilities caused serious inefficiencies, however. To overcome these problems, MACV in September organized a theater-level managerial apparatus known as the Southeast Asia Airlift System (SEAAS). It consisted of C-123 units, aerial ports, and countrywide control detachments, which operated in support of MACV J-4 workload allocations. Meanwhile, a second C-123 squadron arrived in South Vietnam to beef up the airlift system. In April 1962, to stretch the scant aircrew resources of the VNAF, 30 USAF pilots (who became known as the Dirty Thirty) were detailed to serve with the Vietnamese C-47 squadrons, allowing transfer of some Vietnamese pilots to T-28 units (see also Chapter IX).

Meanwhile, after several U.S. Army light transport aircraft were lost to enemy fire in Vietnam, General Harkins recommended deployment of the Army's HU-1A (Huey) Helicopter gunships to provide local fire support for air mobile operations. The Joint Chiefs of Staff recommended and Secretary McNamara approved the additional deployment in order to test under field conditions the concept of armed helicopters. In September, 15 Huey gunships arrived in South Vietnam. They were joined later by six OV-1 Mohawk turboprop observation aircraft, equipped with .50 caliber machineguns as well as cameras.

The National Campaign Plan

During the late summer and fall of 1962, General Harkins' staff drafted a National Campaign Plan (NCP) designed to defeat the Viet Cong. Under this plan the Vietnamese armed forces would be reorganized preparatory to launching a three-phased military operation. Initially, their mission was to drive the enemy back into his base sanctuaries inside South Vietnam. This done, the Vietnamese would launch a general offensive or "explosion" of all their forces in all corners of the country to destroy the enemy. Finally, it would be followed by a consolidation phase during which Saigon's authority would be extended throughout the Republic. Harkins proposed the general ARVN offensive begin in early 1963, after the Buddhist Tet holiday; he thought it could produce a military victory by year's end.

On 8 October 1962 he briefed Secretary McNamara on the plan and secured his approval to submit it to the South Vietnamese. President Diem endorsed the concept and on 26 November issued orders to reorganize the Vietnamese armed forces. Vietnamese Army, Navy, Air Force and Special Forces commands were subsequently activated as major operational components serving under a

Joint General Staff (JGS). Beyond the Capital Military District, the country was divided into four corps tactical zones (CTZ's). A new Joint Operations Center, set up to serve the Vietnamese General Staff, impacted upon the existing VNAF-USAF Joint Operations Center. The latter, twice redesignated, eventually emerged as the Air Operations Center (AOC).

Meanwhile, Admiral Felt and General Anthis alerted Harkins to the fact that there was a serious shortage of fixed-wing aircraft to support the nationwide offensive and reminded him of long-pending Air Force requests to strengthen Farm Gate units. Whereupon, on 7 November 1962, Harkins authorized an increase of 5 T-28's, 10 B-26's, and 2 C-47's. There was a delay in receiving approval from Washington, and it was not until 31 December 1962 that President Kennedy authorized the increase in the number of USAF aircraft in South Vietnam.

Although the additional aircraft arrived at South Vietnam in January 1963, General Anthis was worried about the national campaign plan. He thought it would place demands upon the Vietnamese Air Force far beyond its capability, especially since its scheduled expansion and training would be taking place during the "explosion" phase of the plan. Citing the sizable gap between expected requirements and available air assets, he asked for the interim deployment of one USAF T-28 squadron, one B-26 squadron, two RF-101 reconnaissance aircraft (bringing the total to six), and two RB-26's for local photographic services at Da Nang and Pleiku. General Harkins' headquarters, then completing detailed studies on several parts of the three-pronged NCP, did not immediately respond.

A highly relevant aspect of the campaign involved the movement of essential supplies to support it. MACV proposed using U.S. Navy ships to deliver supplies to several other major port centers in South Vietnam. From there USAF C-123's would airlift the cargo to airfields in the four corps tactical zones, from which U.S. Army aircraft would deliver the war materiel to frontline units. To support this plan, Harkins requested deployment of two more C-123 squadrons and one CV-2 Caribou unit to join one recently deployed to the theater.

While the buildup of offensive forces got underway, the South Vietnamese launched a series of ground-air operations in support of the strategic hamlet program. In October U.S. Army Huey gunships began working with the ARVN 21st Division in the Ca Mau peninsula. Elsewhere, northeast of Saigon, C-123's and C-47's on 20 November dropped 500 ARVN paratroopers into the eastern fringes of the Viet Cong's Zone D sanctuary. From this base of operations, Vietnamese rangers on 19 December launched a nighttime drive through the jungle accompanied by B-26's and T-28's overhead. U.S. Army advisors reported general-purpose and napalm bombs dropped by these aircraft had penetrated the jungle cover with good effects.

Elsewhere, an ARVN heliborne operation was launched just before Christmas Day 1962 near Tuy Hoa in the II Corps Tactical Zone. Twenty-nine U.S. Army H-21's were committed to the operation without fixed-wing air support. The first three helicopters safely landed the Vietnamese troops, but six others were suddenly hit by hidden Viet Cong automatic weapons, which inflicted a number of casualties. A U.S. Army company commander told the famous war correspondent, Richard Tregaskis, the casualties were caused by the fact that "there had been no softening-up" attack at the landing zone (LZ) before the helicopters went in.

No such error was made on the morning of 2 January 1963 when the

JGS committed the entire VNAF-USAF force at Bien Hoa to Operation Burning Arrow, a maximum hour-long air strike against pinpoint enemy targets in the Tay Ninh area. The preliminary fixed-wing bombardment apparently surprised the enemy and was followed by air drops and a landing of helicopters carrying paratroopers and rangers who seized their objectives against very light resistance. Subsequent intelligence received from Communist safe havens in Cambodia revealed that a number of NLF leaders had been killed and wounded.

Unfortunately, within hours of this success the ARVN 7th Division suffered a major defeat in an operation to seize a Viet Cong radio transmitter near the village of Ap Bac, approximately 15 miles northwest of My Tho. The division commander believed a Viet Cong company was encamped at Ap Bac. His plan called for heliborne troops to land in an arc north and west of Ap Bac and then sweep south to meet an armored M-113 amphibious vehicle company moving to the north.

Although informed that no tactical air support was available (all strike aircraft having been committed to the Tay Ninh operation), U.S. Army officials agreed to use Huey gunships for cover, escort, and fire support. Unknown to the division commander and his senior U.S. Army advisor, Lt. Col. John P. Vann, a well-armed Viet Cong battalion—equipped with several heavy machine guns and automatic rifles—was dug in under tree lines adjacent to the planned helicopter landing zones. As the heliborne force went in, it came under heavy fire which the Huey gunships were unable to suppress. Five helicopters were destroyed and nine others damaged.

At mid-morning, the Air Operations Center received emergency calls for help and diverted two AD-6's to the scene. Unfortunately, friendly artillery firing through the air space forced the AD-6's to hold up their attack against plainly visible enemy positions. A B-26 replacing them arrived after the artillery stopped firing and dropped napalm; two additional AD-6's and six T-28's also provided air support. Later, another B-26 and two AD-6's were dispatched. The B-26, although striking with accuracy, was finally forced away by artillery fire. To add to the general confusion, Vietnamese FAC's were unable to direct air strikes with any accuracy. The enemy's fire continued to range freely over the rice paddies, inflicting telling losses on crews of the armored personnel carriers. In the late afternoon, six C-123's arrived overhead with three companies of ARVN paratroop reinforcements but the IV Corps commander, Brig. Gen. Huyn Van Cao, ordered them dropped west of Ap Bac even though the Viet Cong were withdrawing to the east. During the night the enemy escaped, while confused ARVN troops engaged each other in firefights.

Friendly casualties at Ap Bac included 65 Vietnamese troops and 3 U.S. advisors killed and 100 Vietnamese and 6 U.S. advisors wounded. According to the Viet Cong, this victory was a major turning point in their war effort. It rejuvenated their flagging morale and taught them tactics which were described in a new slogan, "wipe-out-enemy-posts-and-annihilate-enemy-reinforcements." Highly critical American press coverage of the battle for Ap Bac left President Diem festering with bitterness.

During a visit to Saigon several days later, Admiral Felt strongly criticized MACV for having allowed the Ap Bac operation to proceed without fixed-wing air support. He asked the Vietnamese JGS to require the mandatory employment of tactical air units in all future heliborne operations. Subsequently, when briefed on the extent of air cover required to support the National Campaign Plan, Felt bluntly labeled the plan infeasible and called for its revision. He urged sup-

Battle of AP Bac
Jan 1963

port of General Anthis' earlier request for two liaison squadrons but only one of two C-123 squadrons, and also acknowledged the Air Force's need for two additional RF-101's and two RB-26's. He also recommended to Washington that Farm Gate strength be increased to permit the Air Force to fly more sorties with existing aircraft. Shortly afterwards, the Air Force was directed to double Farm Gate's strength. Admiral Felt also indorsed Harkins' request to bring in a second Caribou squadron, plus 8 U-1A liaison aircraft, and 10 UH-1B's for use by U.S. Army senior corps advisors.

In Washington, however, senior officials still hoped to limit U.S. military involvement. On 25 March 1962 McNamara decided to send the C-123 squadron recommended by Felt but only one USAF liaison squadron and one U.S. Army O-1A squadron. He directed that they be operated no more than 1 year, after which they were to be turned over to the Vietnamese. Subsequently, the Air Force deployed an additional C-123 squadron to Da Nang, where it arrived on 17 April. The Army Caribou company reached Vung Tau in July. O-1 assets of another

Army company were divided among U.S. Army senior corps advisors. On 8 July 1963 the Air Force activated the 19th Tactical Air Support Squadron at Bien Hoa; it became fully operational in mid-September.

Meanwhile, General Anthis had readied an air strike team of B-26's at Pleiku and a similar T-28 strike unit at Soc Trang to support the impending ARVN ground operations in the II and IV Corps areas. The Pleiku airstrip had been upgraded but the improved 3,200-foot Soc Trang runway could accommodate only the T-28's. Even these planes had difficulty landing at Soc Trang at night or when rain slicked the short runway. Under these conditions, the T-28's could take off but were unable to land safely and normally would head for Tan Son Nhut. In addition to the Farm Gate units, the VNAF maintained an A-1H detachment at Pleiku and also operated eight T-28's at Da Nang in support of I Corps operations.

On 22 February 1963 the Vietnamese JGS issued a general offensive plan, closely patterned after MACV's suggested national campaign plan. It called for corps commanders to begin initial operations against the Viet Cong by mid-March 1963, to be followed by a general offensive on a date to be announced by the Joint General Staff. The freedom accorded the corps commanders, however, resulted mostly in uncoordinated operations. For example, air liaison officers in I Corps reported that the ARVN 1st and 2d Divisions in the north—content to control the coastal plains—followed a live-and-let-live policy with the enemy forces in the mountains to the west. The corps commander kept tight control on air strikes in his area, requiring prior authorization from himself or his chief of staff. Unfortunately, there were times when the operations center received requests for emergency air support but the two officers could not be located.

(1) A1C Norman L. Morgan inspects AC-47 miniguns. (2) The first AC-47 gunship and its crew. (3) Gunship interior. (4) F-100 releases its ordnance on a bombing mission over South Vietnam. (5) An Air Force bomber unloads a napalm bomb on enemy forces dug in along a river bank in South Vietnam. (6) Maj. Robert P. Knopf, a gunship commander, relaxes between missions. (7) Gunship at Nha Trang Air Base, South Vietnam. (8) SSgt Allen D. Niehaus loads ammunition into a minigun. (9) USAF O-1E pilots on a FAC mission. (10) Side-firing miniguns.

1

3

4

7

5

8

9

6

10

In the II Corps area, the ARVN 22d Division—which had deprived the Viet Cong of food sources by resettling many of the Montagnard tribesmen—policed the Central Highlands. Elsewhere, along the coast the 9th Division undertook clear-and-hold operations in Binh Dinh and Phu Yen provinces. The 25th, which became operational in January 1963, undertook to pacify the guerrilla-ridden coastal province of Quang Ngai. Both the 9th and 25th asked for deployment of air strike teams at Qui Nhon and Quang Ngai City, but the limited resources made this impossible. Instead, VNAF T-28's and FAC's were sent to nearby airfields whenever ground operations were planned.

Unfortunately, even when given advance notice of up to 48 hours, Nha Trang-based T-28's were seldom able to react on time. During a month-long campaign launched by some 10,000 Vietnamese Army and Marine troops on 24 April 1963 against the Do-Xa mountain redoubt, the VNAF moved a forward echelon of the Air Operations Center to Plateau Gi and launched a heavy 3-day preliminary bombardment of enemy strongpoints. The combined ground-air assaults enabled Vietnamese troops to overrun the Do-Xa area. Elsewhere, Viet Cong troops, taking advantage of the 25th Division's preoccupation at Do-Xa, attacked Quang Ngai hamlets. However, provincial defense units inflicted heavy casualties on them and drove them off.

In II Corps, pacification appeared to be a complete success, with the Communists clearly thrown on the defensive by mid-year. At this point, General Harkins recommended—and the JGS approved—redeploying the ARVN 9th Division southward to the Mekong Delta, where the enemy had maintained a strong presence for many years. However, the Viet Cong's decline in II Corps proved transitory. During the last half of 1963, South Vietnamese military effectiveness declined—apparently due to the government's disarray during the Buddhist crisis (see discussion below)—the Viet Cong returned to their Do-Xa mountain stronghold.

In the III and IV Corps, the Communists continued to dominate large parts of the countryside despite ARVN efforts. Factors inhibiting successful air operations there included inadequate air-ground communications and a shortage of VNAF forward air controllers. In Tay Ninh province bordering Cambodia, the ARVN 5th Division came to rely more and more on U.S. Army helicopter gunships to provide local air support, primarily because it could not get in touch with the air operations center. When fixed-wing air support was finally provided, ARVN forces were able to penetrate into Zone D and the enemy's headquarters plus several camps along the Ma Da river. This success, however, also proved to be transitory. The Viet Cong later returned to their burned-out Zone D headquarters, dug deeper into the earth, and built stronger log-covered bunkers which enabled them to survive all but direct air strikes.

In the IV Corps area, the battered ARVN 7th Division—still recovering from its Ap Bac defeat—showed little initiative against the enemy, even though it had good intelligence on Viet Cong activity. Captured documents disclosed that the enemy was moving rice from the Delta through the 7th Division's area to feed his troops in Zones C and D. To stop these shipments, Col. Winston P. Anderson, the 2d Air Division's Director of Operations, in March 1963 obtained MACV and JGS authorization to undertake quick reaction air surveillance and strikes in the 7th Division area, using ARVN personnel as forward air guides to mark targets. However, VNAF officials refused to accept targets marked by ARVN troops, rather than by forward air controllers.

In the lower regions of the Delta, the ARVN 21st Division frequently called upon five USAF T-28's at Soc Trang to provide air cover and support for helicopter operations, often launched on the spur of the moment against relatively well armed Viet Cong. However, both T-28's and B-26's were too vulnerable to enemy ground fire. In February 1963, after two B-26's were shot down, Lt. Col. Miles M. Doyle, the Farm Gate detachment commander, requested additional aircraft for his unit. But General Anthis did not have the aircraft to give him. Indeed, in March 1963 the Air Force was able to honor only about 60 percent of the requests from Delta-based units for immediate air support.

Effects of the 1963 Buddhist Troubles

During the spring of 1963 there was a notable cooling of American-South Vietnamese relations against the background of growing Buddhist opposition to President Diem. The problem surfaced in May 1963 when the Buddhists—disaffected by Diem's policies—organized street demonstrations in the ancient capital of Hue. When civil guard troops fired upon them, a riot ensued. During the next 2 months the unrest spread to Saigon, which witnessed the self-immolation of a Buddhist priest in the heart of the capital. This incident shook the government—as well as television audiences around the world—and brought down upon Diem's head a torrent of international criticism. As the political situation deteriorated, so did the morale of the Vietnamese armed forces and their effectiveness in the field.

While the Buddhist crisis continued to dominate the headlines, the Viet Cong increased their attacks against the strategic hamlets during June and July 1963. Their tactics were shrewd and effective. If a probing showed

Viet Cong troops cross an improvised foot bridge in South Vietnam.

South Vietnamese defenses were "soft"—as in the Ban Me Thuot area—the Viet Cong launched sudden night attacks which were successful. Where hamlets were well-defended, as in I Corps in Quang Ngai province, the enemy sent in infiltration teams to urge the people to join "the struggle of the Buddhists." The effects of the crisis were soon reflected in the decline of VNAF-USAF tactical sorties during the last half of 1963.

Thus, VNAF flights fell from a high of 1,013 sorties flown in May to 736 in September and 831 in October. As for the Farm Gate detachment—succeeded in the summer of 1963 by the 1st Air Commando Squadron—it had planned to double its combat sorties. However, its intentions were thwarted by aircraft losses to enemy fire and declining aircraft serviceability. The latter situation was highlighted on 16 August when a wing broke off a B-26 and its crew died in the crash. By 11 October the squadron was down to 9 T-28's and 12 B-26's, with the latter under flight restrictions to avoid undue wing stress.

After mid-1963, calls by embattled Vietnamese outposts for air support increased noticeably. In June the Air Force flew 70 flare and 40 strike sorties, in July 75/52, and in August 79/62. C-47 pilots were swamped with many other unanswered calls for help. In September the 2d Air Division placed some C-123's on flare duty and managed to provide 172 flare/132 strike sorties. During this period no outpost or hamlet assisted by a flare-and-strike team was ever overrun; others went under because of lack of such support or because their calls for help were never received by the Air Operations Center.

During the period May through August 1963, the VNAF-USAF force was unable to fill 534 preplanned air support requests from III Corps alone—167 for lack of aircraft and 244 for lack of VNAF forward air controllers. It was not suprising that III

25

Corps ARVN commanders gave up and turned to the more readily available U.S. Army gunships.

The gravest situation was in the southernmost regions of the Delta, where during the late summer of 1963 the Viet Cong launched open field warfare with well-armed, highly motivated battalion-sized forces. On the night of 10 September enemy mortar squads laid down a barrage on the Soc Trang airstrip while other troops attacked two district towns some 70 miles to the southwest. During the Soc Trang attack, four American pilots managed to get airborne in two T-28's and helped beat off the enemy. These USAF airmen later received commendations for their initiative and a reprimand for engaging in combat without the required VNAF crewmen aboard. After 4 days of continuous fighting, heliborne Vietnamese marines defeated the enemy around the two district towns, helped by paratroopers dropped from C-47 and C-123 aircraft. The towns, however, were reduced to rubble. During the fight a Viet Cong .50-caliber machinegun downed an Air Force T-28.

On 19 October the ARVN 21st Division was ambushed near Loc Ninh in Chuong Thien province. Responding to this emergency, the Air Operations Center committed two A-1H's, one B-26, and five T-28's—the only aircraft available--to cover Army helicopters sent to the scene. All aircraft expended their munitions by mid-morning in a futile attempt to silence enemy guns, which downed one helicopter. Other aircraft from Bien Hoa and several T-28's managed 31 more sorties before the day's end. The Viet Cong, however, held their positions, withdrawing after dark. Friendly losses were 41 personnel killed and 84 wounded ((including 12 Americans). In addition to the downed helicopter, enemy fire damaged two B-26's and six T-28's. The Viet Cong hailed Loc Ninh as another victory equal to that at Ap Bac 10

1

2

months before.

In late September Secretary McNamara and General Taylor, Chairman of the JCS, visited South Vietnam. McNamara urged Diem to deploy additional troops to the Delta and to slow construction of strategic hamlets until existing ones could be protected. While in Saigon he also reviewed the Southeast Asia airlift system which-- under the management of Col. Thomas B. Kennedy, a veteran airlift commander--had met all requirements with capacity to spare. Since logistic requirements had never reached MACV's estimate of 34,000 tons a month to support the general offensive, McNamara ordered the return to

(1) An A-1E *Skyraider* attacks enemy supply areas.
(2) An A-1E assigned to the 602nd Air Commando Squadron.

(1) B-57 Canberra tactical bombers on a mission over the Mekong Delta. (2) The last VNAF graduating class trained to fly the A-1H by USAF crewmen.

tember 1963 the President commented publicly that the Saigon government had "gotten out of touch with the people" but that there was still time for it to regain their support through policy and personnel changes. By this time, however, dissident Vietnamese officers under the leadership of Gen. Duong Van Minh had begun to plan a military coup to overthrow Diem.

Departure of the ARVN 9th Division to the Delta and the relocation of the IV Corps Tactical Zone south of the Mekong, effective 1 November, insured the success of the coup. These actions upset the delicate balance of military forces maintaining Diem in power. On 1 November 1963 the coup leaders launched their revolt. To forestall intervention by the Vietnamese Air Force, they seized its commander. His deputy sided with the rebels and sent four A-1H's and two T-28's against the presidential compound in Saigon. A move by loyal Diem troops to Saigon was deterred by the threat of air attack. On 2 November Diem and his brother Nhu surrendered to the rebels and were killed. The same day a Military Revolutionary Council of ARVN generals and colonels led by General Minh formally took over the government and began the wholesale removal of Diemist officials. This action, together with their lack of administrative experience, soon produced governmental paralysis.

Reacting to Diem's overthrow and the governmental disarray, the enemy launched numerous attacks throughout South Vietnam. During this emergency USAF and VNAF pilots flew 284 flare and 298 strike sorties during November in defense of threatened hamlets and outposts. However, the demoralized ARVN ground forces were no match for the enemy and, before month's end, Viet Cong forces had captured enough weapons to arm five 300-man battalions. Thus, in I Corps, the ARVN 21st Division was

the United States of one Army CV-2 Caribou company by December as part of a planned 1,000-man U.S. force reduction. He also called for an accelerated buildup of the South Vietnamese armed forces to allow the early withdrawal of the remaining 15,640 American military men in the country.

Back in Washington, McNamara and Taylor reported to President Kennedy that Diem's repressive measures against the Buddhists would likely affect the Allied military effort. The new U.S. Ambassador to Saigon, Henry Cabot Lodge—he replaced Nolting on 22 August—concluded that Diem and his brother, Ngo Dinh Nhu, head of the secret police, were hopelessly alienated from the people. On 2 Sep-

ambushed in An Xuyen province on 24 November as it mounted a heliborne attack against a Viet Cong battalion at Chu Lai. The hidden enemy force, equipped with five 7.9-mm machine guns and a twin .50 caliber weapon, shot down 1 helicopter and 1 T-28 and damaged 10 helicopters, 2 VNAF A-1H's, and 1 T-28.

In III Corps, the failure of an ARVN 5th Division officer to use fixed-wing air support apparently contributed to another major defeat on 31 December. The unit involved, the 32d Ranger Battalion, was surrounded west of Ben Cat. The Division's G-3—instead of asking a VNAF forward air controller and two A-1H's orbiting overhead with full loads of 100-pound bombs to provide assistance--called for and used three flights of Huey gunships which proved ineffective. The rangers took heavy casualties in a battle which might have produced an ARVN victory but instead ended 1963—the year of the general offensive—with another disheartening defeat.

Earlier, President Kennedy--in his last public statement on Vietnam before his assassination—on 14 November reiterated America's pledge to continue to assist the South Vietnamese to maintain their independence. His successor, Lyndon B. Johnson, reaffirmed that commitment. On 21 February 1964, in one of his first public comments on the war, President Johnson warned Hanoi to end its support of the insurgent forces in South Vietnam and Laos. Although he appointed a committee of State and Defense Department representatives to study ways to increase pressure on North Vietnam, he reiterated the past policy that the South Vietnamese and Laotian people were primarily responsible for their own defense. Thus, on 3 December 1963 the first 1,000 American military men departed South Vietnam in accordance with McNamara's previous announcements. Among them were members of the famed Air

Force "Dirty Thirty" C-47 pilots and the U.S. Army's lst Aviation Company.

Efforts to Revitalize Military Operations

When General Minh's junta assumed power in November 1963, it announced plans to improve the effectiveness of the armed forces by placing them directly under the four corps commanders. The latter were made responsible for carrying the war to the enemy. Subsequently, the ARVN on 18 January 1964 launched the largest helicopter operation ever undertaken in South Vietnam up to that time. It involved 115 helicopters which airlifted 1,100 troops into Zone D. The operation went smoothly but unfortunately not a single Viet Cong could be found in the area.

Unsuccessful operations such as these, combined with continuing political instability, sparked yet another coup on 30 January. Maj. Gen Nguyen Khanh, commander of I Corps, flew to Saigon, ousted General Minh's council, and stated his intention to increase operations against the enemy. On 22 February, he issued his "Chien Thang National Pacification Plan," a modification of Thompson's "spreading oil stain" proposal. It called for launching a series of clear-and-hold operations in relatively secure areas. From there the Viet Cong would be rolled back while simultaneously a "new life development program" would get under way to raise the people's standard of living. Khanh gave the four corps commanders complete responsibility for the clear-and-hold operations and follow-up actions in their respective areas. General Harkins thought the plan had a good chance to succeed, providing Khanh's fragile government stayed in power.

On 31 January, Maj. Gen. Joseph H. Moore arrived in Saigon to assume command of the 2d Air Division from

General Anthis. In reviewing Khanh's plan, General Moore was alarmed by a provision in it which called for assigning VNAF units to the corps commanders. However, the new VNAF commander, Nguyen Cao Ky, quickly assured Moore he would not allow his air force to be parceled out. Ky interpreted the plan's wording to require assignment of VNAF units to corps tactical zones, not to individual corps commanders. Subsequently, he organized separate VNAF wing headquarters at Da Nang and Pleiku under the command of two knowledgeable air officers. They became the principal VNAF advisors to the I and II Corps commanders. He also proposed to set up similar wing headquarters for the III and IV Corps in 1965.

In keeping with Washington's policy of expanding VNAF air capabilities so that U.S. units and equipment could be withdrawn, MACV and 2nd Air Division in early 1964 undertook major reviews of the military situation. Although their findings were not encouraging, they prepared plans for the withdrawal of the Air Force's 19th Tactical Air Support Squadron in June 1964, followed in 1965 by the 1st Air Commando Squadron. To make up for this loss, several VNAF squadrons were to be equipped with A-1's, T-28's, and C-47's. Meanwhile, the 2d Air Division's aircraft were taking a beating from the enemy and age. In February two T-28's were lost to machinegun fire and, on the 11th, all B-26's were grounded after a wing failed during a combat flight.

On 17 February 1964, during a MACV meeting, Harkins' new deputy, Gen. William C. Westmoreland (he arrived in Saigon on 27 January), urged something be done to restore the Air Force's "Sunday punch." In Hawaii, Gen. Jacob E. Smart, who succeeded General O'Donnell on 1 August 1963 as Commander in Chief, Pacific Air Forces, reasoned that the Geneva prohibition against introducing jets into Vietnam was no longer pertinent. He recommended deployment to South Vietnam of one of two B-57 light jet bomber squadrons. Secretary McNamara, however, rejected the proposal on the grounds that it not only would violate the Geneva agreement but was contrary to Washington's policy of preparing the Vietnamese to fight their own war. He did, however, agree to further strengthen Saigon's air force and authorized equipping a new VNAF squadron with A-1H's and to replace the 1st Air Commando Squadron's T-28 and B-26 two-seat aircraft with 25 A-1E attack bombers.

These decisions, unfortunately, came too late for two T-28 Air Force pilots and their Vietnamese crewmen. On 24 March 1964 one plane--piloted by Capt. Edwin G. Shank, Jr.--crashed after its wing sheared off during a bomb run, killing both men. On 9 April a second T-28, piloted by Capt. Robert Brumett, went into a dive and failed to come out. Other pilots watched with horror as the wings fell off and the plane plowed into a rice paddy. A few days before this second crash, General Moore had noted that with the loss of B-26 aircraft and suspected weakness in the T-28's, "the 2d Air Division is practically flat out of business." However, by borrowing nine surplus T-28B's from the VNAF, the 1st Air Commando Squadron managed to stay operational but pilot morale sagged.

Meanwhile, the Viet Cong were expanding their military operations, apparently in connection with a diplomatic offensive by Hanoi to neutralize all of Indochina. They began on the Ca Mau peninsula, where the insurgents boasted they could take any district town at any time. They proved their prowess on 12 April 1964 with a dawn attack on the district capital of Kien Long. VNAF A-1H's performed valiantly under flare lights, destroying a Viet Cong 105-mm howitzer and, after

(1) USAF strike aircraft of the 3d Tactical Fighter Wing provided close air support to the U.S. Army's 11th Armored Cavalry which attacked enemy positions northwest of Saigon. (2) Rebellious VNAF pilots, flying AD-6 fighter bombers, attacked President Diem's palace, May 1962. He was unharmed. (3) C-123. (4) Capt. Thomas A. Dwelle, USAF, poses in front of his A-1E at Bien Hoa AB, South Vietnam. (5) A Vietnamese government observation post, 1963. (6) An A-1H Skyraider attacks enemy forces. (7) Capt. Phan Lang Sue, commander, VNAF 516th Fighter Squadron lands at Nha Trang after completing a mission.

1

2

3

4

6

5

7

daybreak, providing relays of close air support strikes. One fighter took out an enemy machinegun set up less than 100 meters from ARVN troops. Despite the valiant air-ground defense of Kien Long, the enemy succeeded in overrunning the city, killing more than 300 ARVN troops. Some 200 civilians also were left dead or wounded. This defeat was followed by widespread terrorist attacks throughout the country. One daring Viet Cong operation took place on 2 May 1964, when an underwater demolition team sank the USS *Card,* which had been unloading helicopters at the Saigon waterfront.

Secretary McNamara, concluding that more aerial firepower was needed, authorized the Air Force to equip a second USAF air commando squadron with A-1E's. Nevertheless, during his next visit to Saigon in May 1964, he reiterated the administration's policy that all U.S. airmen should be out of combat within a matter of months. In addition, he decided that Air Force pilots could no longer fly combat missions, even with Vietnamese observers aboard. They were told to limit their activities to providing bona fide training only. To balance the loss of USAF strike support, he further directed that four VNAF squadrons be outfitted with A-1H's as soon as possible and he authorized VNAF expansion by another two squadrons, which were to take over from the two USAF air units scheduled for withdrawal.

Meanwhile, on 12 March General Harkins submitted a plan to the Pentagon to reorganize the command structure in Vietnam to eliminate overlapping responsibilities between the U.S. Military Assistance Advisory Group (established 12 February 1954) and the U.S. Military Assistance Command, Vietnam (established 8 February 1962). His goal was to eliminate the advisory group as an intervening command so as to be able to respond more directly to Saigon's military requirements. The JCS approved Har-

kins' proposal in April 1964 and it became effective on 15 May. Although Air Force officials felt that USAF doctrines and organizational views were being ignored, the 2d Air Division did gain some strength and stature under the reorganization. The Air Force Advisory Group, formerly a part of the MAAG, was reassigned to the Division, thus bringing all USAF activities in Vietnam under one agency. MACV, which had "coordinating authority" for the Air Force reconnaissance effort over Laos, subdelegated it to the 2d Air Division.

Subsequently, changes were made in the top level commanders. On 20 June General Westmoreland succeeded Harkins as Commander, MACV. On 1 July, Adm. Ulysses S. Grant Sharp replaced Admiral Felt as CINCPAC and Gen. Hunter Harris succeeded General Smart as CINCPACAF. Also, on 1 July, General Taylor was designated the U.S. Ambassador to Saigon, succeeding Henry Cabot Lodge.

Continuing Military Reversals

After Hanoi's diplomatic efforts to convene an international conference to neutralize all of Indochina had failed—President Johnson termed it "only another name for a Communist takeover"—the Viet Cong turned July 1964 into the bloodiest month to date. On the 6th, enemy troops struck the Nam Dong Special Forces camp in I Corps, killing 55 ARVN troops, 2 U.S. rangers, and an Australian advisor. Although a flare plane illuminated the area, no VNAF strike aircraft were available to respond to calls for help. Fifteen days later the Viet Cong ambushed 400 ARVN troops in Chuong Thien province in the Delta. After the battle only 82 able-bodied survivors could be found. Nearly an hour elapsed before a VNAF forward air

An A-1E at Qui Nhon, May 1965.

controller arrived over the battle site. Strike aircraft from Bien Hoa did not arrive for 1½ hours.

With the Chuong Thien disaster in mind, Westmoreland asked General Moore and Brig. Gen. Delk M. Oden, commander of the U.S. Army Support Command, Vietnam, to prepare an agreement to govern coordination of all aviation activity in South Vietnam. They subsequently proposed to collocate MACV's Army Air Operations Section with the Joint USAF-VNAF Air Operations Center at Tan Son Nhut and to collocate air support centers in the corps areas. Henceforth, senior U.S. Army advisors would conduct preplanning conferences on at least a daily basis with their Air Force counterparts to insure full utilization of fixed-wing strike aircraft. The new arrangement became effective in August 1964.

Moore also was authorized to establish a VNAF air request net manned by Vietnamese personnel so as to enable ARVN commanders to flash calls for air assistance directly to an air support center. Intermediate ARVN headquarters, monitoring the requests, could cancel them only if there were more urgent ones. The VNAF net was installed in the four corps areas by the end of 1964. Although ARVN commanders were unhappy with the arrangement, the Vietnamese high command on 1 March 1965 directed that the VNAF net would serve as the primary system for obtaining emergency air support.

The first direct clash between North Vietnamese and American forces occurred on 2 August 1964 when enemy torpedo boats attacked the *Maddox* while it was on patrol in the Gulf of Tonkin. The attack was apparently in retaliation for U.S. sponsored South Vietnamese raids along the North Vietnamese coast. Two nights later, the *Maddox* and a second destroyer, the USS *C. Turner Joy*, reported additional enemy attacks against them. Whereupon, President Johnson ordered a retaliatory strike against North Vietnamese coastal torpedo bases and an oil storage depot on 5 August. The President then requested and Congress on 7 August adopted the Gulf of Tonkin resolution. It authorized Mr. Johnson to use all measures—including the commitment of the armed forces—to assist South Vietnam

33

to defend its independence and territory. During this crisis two B-57 squadrons were dispatched from Clark AB in the Philippines to Bien Hoa. In addition, USAF F-100 and F-102 squadrons were sent to Da Nang and still other fighters moved into Thailand.

A white paper subsequently issued by Hanoi admitted the North Vietnamese patrol boats had fired upon the *Maddox* on 2 August because of its support of South Vietnamese naval incursions. It denied, however, that NVA boats were in the area where the second attack reportedly occurred. In any event, Hanoi signalled its determination to fight by redeploying 30 MIG fighters from a South China base to Phuc Yen airfield on 7 August. Several weeks later, the 325th Division of the North Vietnamese Army headed down the Ho Chi Minh trail towards South Vietnam. During this period, Viet Cong regiments in Zones C and D--augmented by guerrillas brought up from the Delta--were formed into the 9th Viet Cong Division. This unit in early autumn began to move to the coastal regions of Phuoc Tuy province, where it was outfitted with Soviet and Chinese weapons apparently brought in by sea.

Meanwhile, Ambassador Taylor sought new ways to shore up the South Vietnamese. On 18 August, he recommended to Washington that further military steps be taken "to gain time for the Khanh government to develop a certain stability." One of his proposed actions called for "a carefully orchestrated bombing attack" against North Vietnam, aimed primarily at infiltration and other military targets. While these recommendations were being reviewed in Washington, dissident ARVN troops from IV Corps--led by Brig. Gen. Lam Van Phat—in

September moved against Khanh but withdrew from Saigon after General Ky sent his VNAF units over the city. The political crisis was temporarily resolved on 26 October following installation of a provisional civilian government headed by Tran Van Huong, Saigon's former mayor. However, Premier Huong found himself unable to bring order to the administration.

Against this background of continuing governmental instability, the Viet Cong seized additional portions of the South Vietnamese countryside and launched a series of attacks aimed specifically against the Americans. On the night of 1 November 1964, Viet Cong squads easily approached within 400 yards of Bien Hoa's perimeter and shelled the crowded airfield with 81mm mortars. Four Americans were killed and 72 others wounded. Losses included 5 B-57's destroyed and 15 damaged as well as 4 VNAF A-1's destroyed or damaged. At this point, Ambassador Taylor concluded that while a viable Saigon government could not be created through military actions alone, a campaign to reduce or halt the continuing flow of reinforcements to the Viet Cong from the north might resolve some of South Vietnam's problems. He suggested that air operations beyond the borders of the country could contribute to that objective.

In late November, Taylor was recalled to Washington for critical weeklong discussions with the President and his key Defense and State Department advisors on future courses of action. They agreed the political chaos in South Vietnam had to be arrested and further coups avoided. They also agreed that a graduated military response against North Vietnamese lines of communication(LOC's) would help Saigon's morale and the effectiveness of ARVN operations. Whereupon, on 2 December 1964 President Johnson approved a program of controlled air strikes against

enemy LOC's in Laos to "signal" his determination to counter Hanoi's increasing military activities and to strengthen the governments of South Vietnam and Laos. On his return to Saigon, Taylor passed word of these decisions and of U.S. reaffirmation of support of Premier Huong to the South Vietnamese. On 20 December, however, General Khanh's Armed Forces Council withdrew its support of Huong and the governmental crisis remained unresolved.

Meanwhile, good flying weather in December 1964 allowed VNAF and USAF airmen to score heavily against Viet Cong units. On 9-10 December VNAF crews helped in the successful ARVN defense of Tam Ky in Quang Tin province and An Lao in Binh Dinh province, both in I Corps. In the IV Corps area, VNAF A-1H and USAF A-1E Skyraiders inflicted more than 400 casualties and were credited with averting destruction of a regional force company surrounded near Long My after a convoy was ambushed. Altogether, the air forces claimed an estimated 2,500 Viet Cong troops killed during the November-December period--more than 60 percent of all reported enemy deaths.

Despite these successes, South Vietnam came increasingly under enemy attack. On Christmas Eve, the Viet Cong exploded a powerful charge in the Brink Hotel bachelor officers quarters in downtown Saigon, killing 2 and wounding 71 Americans. On 27 December, the Viet Cong's 9th Division attacked Binh Gia village in Phuoc Tuy province, southeast of Saigon, setting off a 6-day battle during which the 33d Ranger and 4th Marine Battalions were virtually destroyed. ARVN armored and mechanized forces sent to their aid also took heavy casualties. The battle of Binh Gia, the Viet Cong later boasted, marked the end of insurgency phase of its campaign and the start of conventional field operations.

Chapter III

The In-Country Air War

1965—1972

As 1965 opened, there was a desperate feeling among American officials in Washington and Saigon that something had to be done to raise South Vietnamese morale and reverse the depressing political and military situation. In early January, General Khanh agreed to continue supporting Premier Huong, but at month's end he ousted Huong from office. South Vietnam's governmental turmoil did not end for another 6 months. During that period the military installed and removed a second civilian premier and, finally, ousted Khanh himself, who then went into exile. On 21 June, the Armed Forces Council installed Maj. Gen. Nguyen Van Thieu as the new chief of state and Air Marshal Ky as prime minister.

While the South Vietnamese were still struggling to organize a viable government, the Viet Cong launched a series of destructive attacks on allied facilities. Thus, in the early morning of 7 February 1965, enemy mortar and demolition teams struck with 81-mm mortars against the U.S. advisory compound and airstrip at the ARVN II Corps headquarters in the Pleiku area, killing 8 Americans and wounding more than 100. Five U.S. helicopters were destroyed and other aircraft damaged. An hour later the Viet Cong attacked and set fire to aviation storage tanks at Tuy Hoa airfield. Fortunately, there were no casualties.

These events triggered a meeting in Washington of the National Security Council and President Johnson's decision to order immediate retaliatory air raids against barracks and staging areas in the southern reaches of North Vietnam. That same afternoon, although the target areas were covered by clouds, 49 aircraft from naval carriers struck North Vietnamese Army barracks at Dong Hoi. The USAF-VNAF portion of the retaliatory response was held up because of adverse weather. However, the next afternoon—accompanied by 20 F-100's flying flak suppression sorties—28 VNAF A-1's hit barracks at Chap Le. The President, emphasizing that these air strikes (Operation Flaming Dart) were reprisals for the earlier attacks, reiterated that the United States sought no wider war.

The enemy replied on 8 February when the Viet Cong struck Soc Trang airfield without inflicting casualties or damage. Two days later, however, they blew up a U.S. Army enlisted men's barracks at Qui Nhon, killing 23 Americans, 7 Vietnamese, and wounding many others. The Allies responded immediately, launching Air Force, Navy, and VNAF planes against NVA barracks at Chanh Hoa and Vit Thu Lu. Despite these strikes, the enemy was undeterred and announced he would continue to attack U.S. military installations throughout South Vietnam. The reprisal raids, however, did temporarily lift the sagging morale of the South Vietnamese.

In addition to mounting attacks against the Americans, Viet Cong troops managed to achieve impressive gains in the II Corps area. Whereupon, on 19 February General Westmore-

-10 Bronco.

(1) Secretary McNamara (l.) and Gen. Earle G. Wheeler, Chairman, of the Joint Chiefs of Staff, visit Saigon on 25 November 1965, where they conferred with Lt. Gen. Nguyen Huu Co and Ambassador Henry Cabot Lodge. (2) Gen. Curtis E. LeMay, Air Force Chief of Staff (l.) consults with Gen. Paul D. Harkins, Commander, U.S. Military Assistance Command, Vietnam, in April 1962. (3) Gen. William H. Blanchard, Air Force Vice Chief of Staff (1.), Secretary of the Air Force Eugene M. Zuckert, and Gen. John P. McConnell, Air Force Chief of Staff.

1

3

(1) Prime Minister Nguyen Cao Ky (l.) confers with Lt. Gen. Joseph H. Moore, Commander, 2d Air Division. (2) Gen. John D. Ryan, Commander in Chief, Pacific Air Forces visits with Binh Thuy AB in Vietnam, September 1967, and greets Maj. Clifford R. Crooker, an 0-2A FAC pilot. (3) Gen. George S. Brown, Commander, 7th Air Force, accompanies Secretary of the Air Force Robert C. Seamans on a tour of USAF activities in South Vietnam. (4) Gen. John D. Lavelle, Commander, 7th Air Force greets Gen. Creighton W. Abrams, Commander, U.S. Military Assistance Command, Vietnam.

land—invoking authority given him 3 weeks earlier to use jet aircraft under emergency conditions—sent 24 Air Force B-57's against the Viet Cong 9th Division's base camp deep in the jungles of Phuoc Long province along the Cambodian border. Two days later an Army special forces team and a Civilian Irregular Defense Group (CIDG) company were caught in a Communist ambush at the Mang Yang pass on Route 19. Supported by F-100 and B-57 strikes, which prevented the enemy from overrunning Allied forces, U.S. helicopters moved in and successfully evacuated 220 men who might otherwise have been lost.

The events of February 1965 marked a turning point in the history of the war, although the military situation in Vietnam remained discouraging. In Washington, officials no longer talked about withdrawing American military advisors. Instead, they now recommended deployment of additional U.S. forces to Southeast Asia, proposals which the President generally approved. While a campaign of air strikes against North Vietnam was being readied and launched, Washington also lifted major restrictions on air strikes within South Vietnam. On 6 March, Westmoreland received authorization to use U.S. aircraft whenever the VNAF could not respond on a timely basis. The former requirement that USAF planes carry Vietnamese crew members was dropped.

On 8 March the 9th Marine Expeditionary Brigade landed at Da Nang to secure American installations there. On 5 May the Army's 173d Airborne Brigade arrived at Bien Hoa to defend the military complex there. By the end of May 50,000 American troops were in South Vietnam, 10,000 of them Air Force, and more were to come. On 25 July the President, deciding that an even larger force commitment was necessary to save South Vietnam, authorized an additional troop buildup to 125,000 men.

As the American ground forces increased, so did U.S. air power. In February 1965, the Strategic Air Command deployed two B-52 squadrons to Andersen Air Force Base, Guam, for possible use over South Vietnam. In April the Air Force activated four 0-1 squadrons in South Vietnam. The first U.S. Marine F-4B's arrived at Da Nang on 12 April and immediately began flying close air support missions. A number of Air Force tactical fighter and bomber squadrons also deployed to Vietnam on temporary duty assignments, which were later made permanent. In October 1965 the first of five F-100 squadrons moved to Bien Hoa and Da Nang. They were followed in November by F-4C Phantoms of the 12th Tactical Fighter Wing, which were based at Cam Ranh Bay, and experimental AC-47 gunships at Tan Son Nhut. By year's end, the Air Force had more than 500 aircraft and 21,000 men at eight major bases in South Vietnam.

Other SEATO nations also sent military, medical, or civic action units to South Vietnam. They included a 1,557-man Australian ground-air task force, a New Zealand howitzer battery, a Philippine civic action group, and the Queen's Cobra Regiment from Thailand. The largest third-country contribution came from the Republic of Korea which was not a SEATO member. It initially dispatched one infantry division and a marine brigade totalling 20,600 men by the end of 1965. Later, Korea sent a second infantry division to Vietnam.

Viet Cong/NVA strength also continued to grow and enabled the enemy to retain the initiative and ability to interdict almost any line of communications within South Vietnam they chose. For example, Communist forces during 1965 almost totally isolated the Central Highlands of South Vietnam. To help counter enemy activity, President Johnson on 1 April authorized Westmoreland to employ

Gen. Hunter Harris, Commander in Chief, PACAF, stops at Pleiku AB during an inspection of USAF units.

American troops not only to defend American bases but also to join with the South Vietnamese in taking the fight to the enemy. On the 18th, the giant Air Force B-52's were brought into play for the first time. Flying from Andersen AFB, they struck a suspected Communist troop base area in Binh Duong province north of Saigon. Although the initial attack was unsuccessful—ground patrols could find little damage before the enemy drove them out of the area—the operation marked the beginning of extensive B-52 operations throughout Southeast Asia (see also Chapter VIII).

Aware of the military weakness of South Vietnam, General Westmoreland decided the first phase of Allied operations should consist of a holding action in areas already under Saigon's control. Beyond those areas, he proposed a series of "spoiling attacks" against enemy positions to keep the Communists off balance while the Allied force buildup continued. That is, the emphasis was to be on "search and destroy" operations rather than to seize and hold new territory. Under this strategy, air power was called upon to support all major ground unit actions while also assisting small special forces reconnaissance teams and outposts collecting intelligence of Viet Cong/NVA activity along South Vietnam's Cambodian and Laotian borders.

The deployment of USAF, Navy, and Marine units to Southeast Asia during the first half of 1965 represented the greatest gathering of American airpower in one locality since the Korean War. More than 142,000 USAF combat sorties of all types were flown and in excess of 56,000 tons of munitions dropped on enemy targets. The joint USAF-VNAF effort alone accounted for an estimated 15,000 enemy dead and thousands of other casualties during the period.

The first major combat action involving American troops came in August 1965 in I Corps. During Operation Starlight, elements of the 3d Marine Division detected and pinned down the 2d Viet Cong Regiment, which found itself trapped along the coastal lowlands of Quang Ngai province, 15 miles from Chu Lai. With their backs to the sea, the enemy fought a bitter 2-day battle during which they suffered more than 700 casualties. Pilots of the 3d Marine Air Wing effectively shut off escape attempts by the Viet Cong.

In the Central Highlands in II Corps, the North Vietnamese launched a large-scale attack against the Plei Me Special Forces camp in October. An enemy regiment of an estimated 2,200 troops began its assault on 18 October and tried vainly during the next 10 days to overrun it in the face of intensive USAF air strikes. On several occasions the ferocity of their attack carried enemy troops to within 20 yards of the stronghold, only to be beaten back. In support of the camp, Air Force pilots flew 696 sorties and dropped more than 1,500,000 pounds of bombs on the attackers.

An even bloodier operation soon followed. Two NVA regiments were found in the Plei Me area, which set in motion a month-long American and ARVN search and destroy sweep which killed an estimated 1,800 enemy troops. This offensive was supported by 384 tactical air strikes, 96 B-52 sorties, and numerous night flare missions. The Communist troops fought hard, giving ground only grudgingly. However, the pounding from the air took a heavy toll, enemy resistance finally broke, and the survivors fled across the South Vietnamese border into Cambodia. But the allied side was not always successful. In November 1965 a South Vietnamese regiment, which had defeated the Viet Cong 281st Regiment, was overrun by the 272d Viet Cong Regiment, suffered heavy casualties and was put out of action. Its Vietnamese commander

Gen. Vo Nguyen Giap, North Vietnamese Defense Minister.

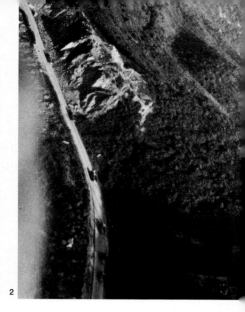

1

2

(1) 2d Lt. Edward Ridgley, CO, 3d Battalion, 9th Infantry Division, calls in an air strike. (2) An allied truck convoy heading for Khe Sanh. (3) Elements of the U.S. Army's 1st Infantry Division arrive at Vung Tau Bay on 13 July 1965 as part of the buildup of U.S. Forces in Vietnam. (4) ARVN troops march to helicopter prior to launching an operation against enemy forces in Can Tho, February 1966. (5) Australian airmen arrive in South Vietnam, August 1964. (6) Troops of the Korean Tiger Division prepare to board a C-130 at Qui Nhon AB for airlift to Phan Rang AB, May 1966. (7) An airman inspects aircraft ordnance prior to a mission. (8) Resupply drop at Ben Het, South Vietnam.

3

4

5

6

7

8

was killed in the battle.

During 1966 American troop strength continued to grow, reaching a total of 385,000. The allies also were bolstered by arrival of a second Korean infantry division and additional Australian and New Zealand forces. Other air equipment arriving in South Vietnam included an F-5 fighter squadron, two F-4 squadrons, and additional AC-47 gunships.

On 24 January 1966 fierce fighting broke out during search and destroy operations in I Corps involving some 20,000 1st Air Cavalry Division troops in Binh Dinh province and the U.S. Marines in the adjacent Quang Ngai province. Their objective was the 19th and 98th North Vietnamese Regiments and the 1st and 2d Viet Cong Regiments. The operations were highlighted by excellent cooperation among Air Force, Navy, Marine, and VNAF air crews who provided round-the-clock support. AC-47 gunships were especially effective at night in inflicting heavy casualties on the enemy. When the operations ended 6 weeks later, the Air Force had flown more than 1,100 combat support missions.

The only significant enemy success during the year occurred in March in the A Shau Valley when a Special Forces camp was overrun. Located astride a section of the Ho Chi Minh trail, two miles from the Laotian border and 60 miles southwest of Da Nang, the camp was defended by 219 Vietnamese irregulars and 149 Chinese Nung mercenaries, assisted by 17 American Special Forces advisors. Before dawn on 9 March an estimated 2,000 North Vietnamese regulars opened an attack on the outpost. Poor weather limited the number of sorties that could be flown the first day to 29. A CH-3C rescue helicopter managed to land and evacuate 26 wounded defenders that day. An AC-47 gunship reached the scene but was shot down; three of its six-man crew were rescued by helicopter, two were

killed, and one was missing in action.

On 10 March the NVA launched repeated assaults against the camp under cover of a thick overcast which hid the tops of the surrounding hills and mountains. Almost miraculously an A-1E pilot made his way into the valley through an opening in the cloud cover. Other aircraft followed him down and flew 210 strikes that temporarily slowed the enemy attack. According to one American survivor of the battle, tactical aircrews tried to hold off the enemy by flying strikes under such dangerous conditions that they "had no business being there." General Westmoreland later called the air support there one of the most courageous displays of airmanship in the history of aviation. The camp commander, Capt. Tennis Carter, USA, estimated the A-1E pilots of the 1st Air Commando Squadron killed 500 enemy troops outside the camp walls.

During the day's action, Maj. Bernard C. Fisher became the Air Force's first Medal of Honor recipient in Southeast Asia, when he made a daring rescue of a downed fellow pilot, Maj. D. Wayne Myers. Myers' badly damaged A-1E had crash-landed on the camp's chewed up airstrip. Major Fisher made a quick decision to try to rescue Myers. Covered by his two wingmen, Fisher managed to land his A-1 on the debris-strewn runway, taxied its full length, spotted Myers at the edge of the strip, wheeled around, picked him up, and then took off through a rain of enemy fire.

On the evening of 10 March, the camp was abandoned. Strike aircraft forced the enemy back while rescue helicopters went in and picked up the survivors. Of the 17 Americans, 5 were killed and the other 12 wounded. Only 172 of the camp's 368 Vietnamese and Nung defenders survived to be evacuated. The North Vietnamese suffered an estimated 800 deaths, most of them attributed to air strikes. As the last hel-

New Zealand artillery unit arrives in South Vietnam.

icopter departed, the enemy moved in and subsequently began developing the camp as a major logistic base with connecting roads to the Ho Chi Minh trail. Two years would elapse before any allied troops returned to retake the A Shau valley.

In mid-1966 General Westmoreland prepared to begin Phase II operations —a series of offensive actions aimed at blunting enemy advances into the highlands and neutralizing NVA/Viet Cong food and manpower resources in coastal regions. Planned to run through 1967, this phase emphasized Special Forces operations and employment of his fast growing USAF strength, now directed by his new Deputy for Air, Lt. Gen. William W. Momyer* (who also wore a second hat as commander of the Seventh Air Force, which replaced the 2d Air Division on 1 April). Long range ground reconnaissance patrols, working out of fortified base camps, infiltrated into enemy areas seeking weak spots and potential targets. In turn these base camps became the enemy's priority target.

On 2 June 1966 U.S. Army and ARVN elements moved against a North Vietnamese regiment at Tou Monong in the highlands of Kontum province. A vicious battle ensued which lasted 19 days and resulted in more than 500 enemy dead and decimation of the NVA regiment. Air units played a major role during the battle. At times, the opposing forces were so close that strike pilots were forced to try pinpoint bombing well inside the usual strike limitations. In one instance, a company commander called for and received air strikes on his own positions, which were being overrun. The strikes stopped the attack long enough for the Americans to establish a new defense perimeter.

A milestone of significance to General Westmoreland's operations was

Royal Australian Air Force helicopter gunship goes into action against enemy troops.

*He succeeded General Moore on 1 July 1966.

17 June 1966, when the B-52's completed their first year of action over Southeast Asia. Westmoreland later wrote: "The B-52's were so valuable that I personally dealt with requests [for B-52 strikes] from field commanders, reviewed the targets, and normally allocated the available bomber resources on a daily basis." The MACV commander also "continued to urge that action be taken to substantially increase B-52 sorties."

About this time, two actions were taken to enhance B-52 flexibility of operation. The first of these involved introduction of the Combat Skyspot bombing system, whereby ground radar control units directed the big bombers over an enemy target and indicated the exact moment of bomb release. The system reduced planning time and provided a flexibility of operations which allowed diversion of the B-52's to targets of opportunity. The second innovation was establishment of a six-aircraft force of B-52's which was kept on continuous alert on Guam and which could be launched quickly whenever a battlefield situation required their assistance.

Another highlight of 1966 operations was the defeat of the Viet Cong 9th Division, which had an almost unbroken string of victories to its credit. In June and July, the 1st U.S. Infantry Division and the ARVN 5th Division—supported by tactical air units—launched attacks on the 9th, then massing for an attempt to seize the provincial capital of An Loc. In a series of five engagements, they soundly whipped the enemy division, forcing it to withdraw to sanctuaries deep in War Zone C, northwest of Saigon. It left behind more than 850 dead.

Subsequently, the 9th Division was outfitted with fresh troops and new equipment. In October—bolstered by the NVA 101st North Vietnamese Regiment—the 9th returned to action, this time in an operation aimed at a Special Forces camp at Suoi Da. It pur-

sued a classic strategy—initiate an attack with a minimal force, trigger a rescue mission by relieving troops who would then be decimated by the main enemy force through ambushes and counterattacks. Initially, the scenario unfolded as planned. Four companies of U.S. mobile strike forces were heliborne into landing zones south and east of Suoi Da, where they were immediately attacked by the enemy. One company was overrun and the others had to withdraw or be evacuated by helicopter.

Responding to this pressure, Westmoreland committed some 22,000 troops from the U.S. 1st, 4th, and 25th Divisions, and the 173d Airborne Brigade. This triggered a raging 9-day battle with the enemy stubbornly holding his ground. Tactical air strikes came in so continuously that aircraft frequently were stacked 1,000 feet above each other waiting to drop their

bombs. Their pressure, plus the heavy pounding by the B-52's, finally broke the enemy's resistance. More than 2,500 tactical sorties were flown in support of the American troops, including 487 immediate requests for close air support. The B-52's flew 225 sorties. In addition to this strike support, 3,300 tactical airlift sorties delivered 8,900 tons of cargo to the ground forces and transported more than 11,400 men into and out of the battle zone.

By early November 1966, the battle was over. Allied forces had killed more than 1,100 enemy troops and wounded hundreds more and seized enormous quantities of weapons, ammunition, and supplies, including 2,000 tons of rice. The 9th Viet Cong Division was so badly whipped that it was unable to return to combat until the spring of 1967.

Taking stock at year's end, U.S.

A CH-3E helicopter airlifts troops on a mission against enemy forces, June 1968.

46

An Air Force cameraman photographs a machine gunner strafing an enemy position.

officials estimated that North Vietnam —in order to make up for the huge Viet Cong losses—had been forced to commit more than 58,000 NVA regulars and take over a greater share of the fighting, especially in the two northern corps areas. They estimated this boosted total enemy forces to 282,000—110,000 being North Vietnamese, 112,000 guerrilla troops, 40,000 political cadre, and 20,000 support personnel. That enemy morale was low was testified to by captured soldiers who complained about the allied heavy bombardment (especially those by the B-52's) and their personal hardships—inadequate food and supplies and long separations from home and family.

The increasing effectiveness of air power in 1966 was in large measure the result of improved tactics and weapons. Airborne forward air controllers developed an effective system of visual reconnaissance. Assigned to specific geographic areas, they were able to identify changes in the landscape below which might indicate the enemy presence. Night reconnaissance operations were enhanced by several research and development programs and by refinement of existing instrumentation. A particularly useful device was the starlight scope, developed by the Army, which amplified starlight and moonlight so that its operator could see movement on the ground quite clearly at night. Infrared viewers also facilitated night aerial reconnaissance operations. Munitions introduced into the inventory included cluster bombs, each containing several hundred bomblets, and a delayed-action bomb capable of penetrating heavy tree cover and then exploding on the ground. Another tactic of importance was the routine employment of USAF fixed-wing gunships for night

47

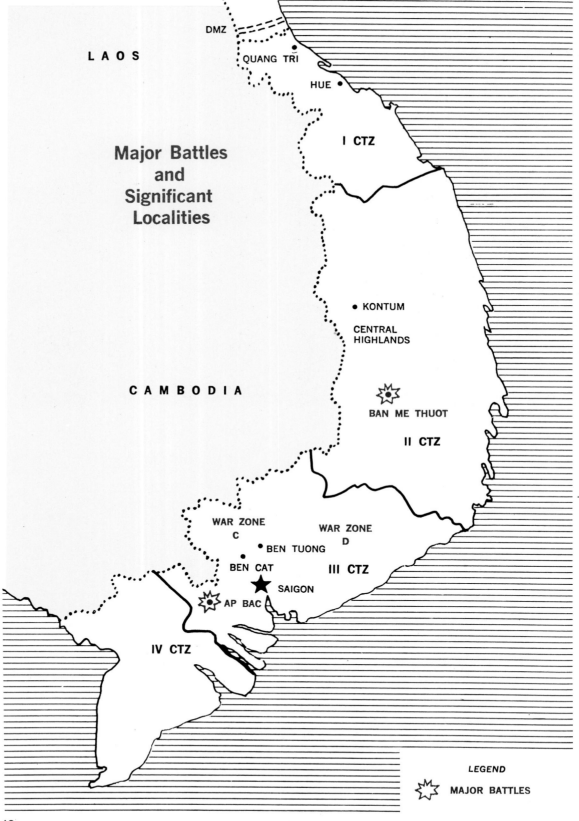

Major Battles
and
Significant
Localities

LAOS

DMZ

QUANG TRI

HUE

I CTZ

KONTUM

CENTRAL
HIGHLANDS

CAMBODIA

BAN ME THUOT

II CTZ

WAR ZONE
C

WAR ZONE
D

BEN TUONG

BEN CAT

III CTZ

SAIGON

AP BAC

IV CTZ

LEGEND

MAJOR BATTLES

hamlet defense. Their ability to remain aloft for many hours and to respond quickly to calls for close air support proved indispensable to hundreds of besieged posts, villages, and hamlets.

The Combined Campaign Plan

During 1967, as the buildup of U.S. forces in Vietnam continued, American strength in the war zone rose from 385,000 to 486,000 personnel and enabled the allies to continue to pursue the enemy. In accordance with a joint Vietnamese-American "Combined Campaign Plan," ARVN troops were given the mission of pacifying the countryside while U.S. and allied forces conducted combat operations against NVA and Viet Cong units.

A move to root out Communist forces in the Central Highland provinces of Pleiku and Kontum got under way on 1 January and continued periodically throughout the year. During the first 95-day phase, designated Operation Sam Houston, elements of the 4th and 25th Infantry Divisions concentrated on destroying the NVA's 1st Division operating from bases inside Cambodia. This was followed in April with the 6-month-long Operation Francis Marion. Finally, in November, there occurred the Battle of Dak To in Kontum province, supported by massive tactical and B-52 strikes—more than 2,000 in number. At times, the battle was fought so closely that napalm and cluster bomb units fell within 22 and 27 yards of friendly positions while larger 750-pounders were dropped within 77 yards. The Communists broke off the fight after losing more than 1,600 dead and sustaining many more wounded. MACV attributed more than 70 percent of the enemy casualties to air strikes.

In the III Corps area, U.S. and Vietnamese troops on 8 January 1967 launched another sweep into the "Iron Triangle." This 60-square-mile jungle area contained the suspected location of the Viet Cong's 4th Military Region headquarters, which directed operations in the Saigon area. A 3-week offensive, it involved troops of the 1st and 25th Infantry Divisions, the 173d Airborne Brigade, and the 11th Armored Cavalry Regiment, plus ARVN forces. They succeeded in overrunning a vast "underground city," destroyed the enemy headquarters, and seized enough rice to feed 13,000 men for a year. They also seized almost a half-million pages of enemy documents and captured 213 enemy personnel. According to the U.S. Army ground commander on the scene, the air strikes—1,113 tactical and 102 B-52 sorties—were responsible for the majority of the 720 enemy dead.

The Iron Triangle offensive had barely ended when General Westmoreland initiated the largest operation of the year in the same corps area. It involved 22 U.S. and four ARVN battalions which were set into motion on 22 February against reoccupied enemy bases in War Zone C. It also saw the first American parachute assault of the war aimed at intercepting any enemy troops attempting to flee into Cambodia. Initially, the enemy sought to avoid combat but later began to challenge the American forces, paying heavily for it. According to their own captured casualty lists, the enemy sustained 2,728 deaths and several thousand wounded. The allied troops also captured 600 crew-served weapons, 800 tons of rice, and vast amounts of ammunition, medical supplies, and field equipment.

The Air Force flew more than 5,000 tactical strike sorties and 125 B-52 sorties during the 83-day operation. In all, USAF crews dropped 12,000 tons of munitions, much of it in a softening-up zone just ahead of advancing troops. USAF crews also airlifted 11,307 tons of supplies in 2,057 sorties. Both officers and men of the

Army's 1st Infantry Division praised the air support in the following words: "We find the enemy, we fix the enemy, air destroys the enemy." High-ranking Viet Cong defectors later reported that the Allied operation was a major disaster for their side. Loss of the base camps in War Zone C led to large-scale deterioration of their forces throughout the III Corps area and a revamping of their operational tactics. Enemy main force units were forced to pull back into Cambodian sanctuaries, taking with them hospitals, supply depots, and training centers.

Military experts from China, Cuba, and North Korea reportedly visited South Vietnam in the spring of 1967 during Operation Junction City and apparently concluded that time was no longer on Hanoi's side. Communist forces had not won a single major battle in almost 2 years. U.S. firepower, especially tactical air, had decimated their main force strength. Desertion was rampant and the Viet Cong infrastructure was being destroyed.

It was against this background that General Giap and other North Vietnamese officials flew to Moscow in March 1967 seeking additional military and economic aid. The Soviets subsequently announced they would send Hanoi "even more planes, high-altitude missiles, artillery and infantry weapons, together with factories, means of transportation, petroleum products, iron and steel and nonferrous metal equipment, food, and fertilizer." Indeed, the number of Soviet vessels reaching North Vietnamese ports rose from 122 in 1966 to 185 in 1967. In September Giap claimed in articles published in his armed forces newspaper, *Quang Doi Nhan Dan*, that the allied pacification program had failed. He forecast very heavy fighting ahead and a Communist victory. He did so in the context of a strategy which he claimed had drawn allied troops to remote areas, thus enabling Communist guerrilla forces to achieve victory in the heavily populated zones of South Vietnam.

But Giap's statements were an attempt at deception. Instead of relying on the badly battered Viet Cong forces, beginning in the spring and summer of 1967 he deployed 37 NVA battalions into the area just north of

Viet Cong guerrillas fire bolt action rifles against low-flying allied aircraft.

Fire support in defense of an outpost near the Cambodian border.

the DMZ preparatory to launching a full-scale invasion of South Vietnam. The allies detected the threat and hastened completion of a line of fortified bases just south of the DMZ. On 6 April Giap made his first move, launching attacks against Quang Tri City and the neighboring towns of Lang Vei and Hai Lang. The North Vietnamese also opened up intense and continuous barrages of mortar and artillery fire against the allied bases near the DMZ. Shortly after, NVA troops began moving into position around Khe Sanh. On 16 May MACV called in tactical air power to silence enemy artillery in the area. Within 2 days, 30 sites were put out of action. General Westmoreland also deployed Army troops to the northern province of I Corps to support the Marines.

In a further effort to halt enemy shelling of the Marine border base at Con Thien, an air plan was devised and refined under the direction of General Momyer—its goal was the destruction of the Communist positions to the north. Designated Operation Neutralize, it began on 12 September 1967 and employed Air Force,

Navy, and Marine strike aircraft plus off-shore naval guns and Marine heavy artillery. During the 49-day operation, FAC pilots played a key role, flying dangerously close to enemy positions north of the DMZ and pinpointing them for strike aircraft. B-52's saturated NVA troop sites. Special long-range ground reconnaissance patrols were used whenever possible to enter target areas to assess bomb damage and locate additional targets. By the time the operation ended, more than 3,100 tactical and 820 B-52 sorties had been flown. Of these, 916 were under Combat Skyspot control because of inclement weather. The shelling of Con Thien dwindled away after Operation Neutralize succeeded in destroying 146 enemy gun, mortar, and rocket positions, and damaging 83 others.

These American offensive actions succeeded in blunting North Vietnamese efforts to prevent the Allied construction of the line of bases south of the DMZ and capped the failure of General Giap's Phase I strategy. His setpiece battles did not drain off American strength from populated areas, as hoped. Indeed, U.S. air pow-

51

er was more than adequate to defeat the enemy whenever and wherever he massed. The NVA next turned its attention further south to areas closer to its Cambodian sanctuaries, where it could more easily move out and harass Allied positions in South Vietnam. On 27 November the enemy hit at the village of Song Be in Phuoc Long province and two days later at Loc Ninh near the Cambodian border in neighboring Binh Long province. In both instances, they were soundly beaten.

During a visit to Washington in November 1967, General Westmoreland reported directly to the President and the American people. In an address to the National Press Club, he expressed confidence that the tide was turning and that the allies were winning the war. The enemy, he said, was staking his hopes on a tactical victory to influence American public opinion and force the United States to throw in the towel. By the end of 1967, the enemy had not achieved that goal but evidence was piling up of a noticeable buildup of his forces in their Cambodian and Laotian sanctuaries for yet another try.

The 1968 Tet Offensive

At the beginning of 1968, more than 486,000 Americans—56,000 of them U.S. Air Force personnel—were in South Vietnam. During this climactic year, the Air Force flew 840,117 combat sorties in support of allied ground forces. A new forward air controller aircraft, the OV-10A, made its appearance and night operations were enhanced by introduction of low-light-level television equipment and a laser guided bomb. The year also saw General Giap order implementation of Phases II and III of his offensive plan within 10 days of each other. One of his targets was the Marine base at Khe Sanh, selected—according to some ad-

ministration officials—as the place where Gia hoped to emulate his great Viet Minh victory over the French achieved 14 years earlier at Dien Bien Phu. Located on a plateau in the northwestern corner of I Corps and commanding the approaches to Dong Ha and Quang Tri City from the west, Khe Sanh was an important strategic post. By capturing it, the North Vietnamese would have an almost unobstructed invasion route in the northernmost provinces, from where they could outflank American positions south of the DMZ. Anticipating such an attack, General Westmoreland decided—and the members of the JCS agreed—to defend the base.

On 21 January 1968 the North Vietnamese unleashed a heavy mortar, artillery, and rocket attack on the Marine base and began assaulting outlying defenses west of it. This attack triggered Operation Niagara, an air campaign in defense of Khe Sanh. That day, nearly 600 tactical sorties (including 49 by the B-52's) were launched against enemy positions. Before the campaign ended 2½ months later, control of all tactical air units—Air Force, Navy, and Marine—had been centralized under General Momyer as the Single Manager for Air, effective 8 March. In the case of I Corps, Momyer made use of the Marines' direct air support center at Da Nang, enlarged it, and assigned non-Marines there. To coordinate tactical air operations, Seventh Air force deployed a C-130E Airborne Battlefield Command and Control Center to the northern corps.

The extensive use of air power at Khe Sanh paid off. More than 24,000 tactical and 2,700 B-52 sorties dropped 110,000 tons of ordnance. The heavy air attacks—averaging 300 tactical sorties a day with a three-ship B-52 cell arriving overhead every 90 or so minutes during the height of the battle—destroyed enemy bunkers and supplies, exploded his ammunition dumps in the area, and caved in his

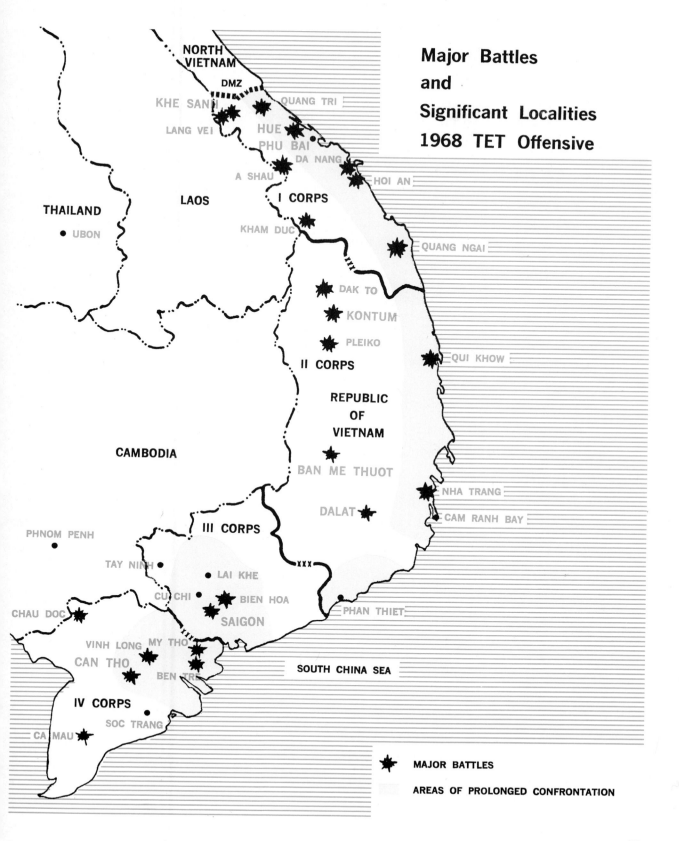

Major Battles
and
Significant Localities
1968 TET Offensive

NORTH VIETNAM

DMZ

KHE SANH

LANG VEI

QUANG TRI

HUE

PHU BAI

DA NANG

A SHAU

HOI AN

LAOS

I CORPS

KHAM DUC

QUANG NGAI

THAILAND

UBON

DAK TO

KONTUM

PLEIKO

II CORPS

QUI KHOW

REPUBLIC
OF
VIETNAM

CAMBODIA

BAN ME THUOT

DALAT

NHA TRANG

CAM RANH BAY

PHNOM PENH

III CORPS

TAY NINH

LAI KHE

CU CHI

BIEN HOA

SAIGON

PHAN THIET

CHAU DOC

VINH LONG

MY THO

CAN THO

BEN TRE

SOUTH CHINA SEA

IV CORPS

CA MAU

SOC TRANG

MAJOR BATTLES

AREAS OF PROLONGED CONFRONTATION

53

1

ON MARCH 12, 1966 AIRMOBILE MAJOR WAYNE ?OM
WAS FORCED DOWN ON THE AIRFIELD AT ASHAU NEAR
CAMBODIAN BORDER. THE AIRFIELD WAS UNDER
V.C. ATTACK. MOMENTS LATER MAJOR BERNARD FI
LANDED HIS A1E SKYRAIDER IN THE FACE OF SOME
V.C. TROOPS AND EFFECTED THIS INCREDIBLE RE?
S SKYRAIDERS SHOT UP FROM THE
FIELD WAS BURNING AND THEIR GASWAS IN
A DRY PAIL AT THE ENEMY GROUND TROOPS AND

3

4

(1) An EB-66 leads a flight of eight F-4 Phantoms on a bombing mission through a low overcast. (2) This painting depicts the daring rescue by Maj. Bernard C. Fisher of a downed USAF pilot, Maj. D. Wayne Myers, at a Special Forces camp in the A Shau valley, 2 miles from the Laotian border, in March 1966. For his feat, Major Fisher became the first Air Force Medal of Honor winner in Vietnam. (3) An F-100 Super Sabre fires rockets at enemy troops in South Vietnam. (4) An A-1E Skyraider attacks a Viet Cong target with a phosphorus bomb. (5) An A-1E attacks Viet Cong forces with 500-lb bombs.

5

tunnels near the Khe Sanh perimeter. At night, AC-47 gunships kept up a constant chatter of fire against enemy troops. Because of poor weather, about 62 percent of all strikes were directed to their targets by Combat Skyspot.

Nine days after the siege of Khe Sanh began, NVA and Viet Cong troops launched the Tet Offensive of 1968. In simultaneous attacks throughout South Vietnam, they struck at 36 of 44 provincial capitals, five of six autonomous cities, 23 airfields, and numerous district capitals and hamlets. Saigon and the old imperial capital of Hue were among the prime targets. This nationwide enemy offensive apparently had as its ultimate goal the disintegration of the South Vietnamese armed forces, to be followed—as Communist dogma had it—by the people rallying to the NLF. But that did not happen.

The initial fury of the attack did enable the enemy to seize at least temporary control of 10 provincial capitals, and he succeeded in penetrating Saigon, Quang Tri City, Da Nang, Nha Trang, and Kontum City. However, except for Hue, which took the allies several weeks of rugged fighting to clear, the enemy was ousted in two or three days. Most of 23 airfields attacked by the enemy were soon back in full operation.

Despite the heavy demands placed upon it to help defend Khe Sanh, the Seventh Air Force was still able to provide enough firepower to be a major factor in the defeat of the enemy offensive. Within Saigon and Hue, the Air Force launched carefully controlled strikes against enemy lodgments. Outside the cities USAF crews launched heavy attacks against Communist forces. Forward air controllers remained aloft around the clock directing strikes at enemy storage areas, troop areas, and providing close air support for allied units in contact with Viet Cong and NVA forces. At Hue,

only a trickle of essential supplies reached the besieged NVA troops. B-52's continued saturation raids on suspected enemy areas.

By late February it was evident that the Tet offensive had failed, and Hanoi's dream of a collapse of the South Vietnamese government and armed forces was chimerical. Instead, Viet Cong/NVA troops had suffered heavy losses—an estimated 45,000 men (8,000 of them in and around Hue alone). Unfortunately there also was a heavy civilian toll. More than 14,000 died, some of them (as in Hue) victims of NVA execution squads. Another 24,000 were wounded and 627,000 left homeless.

The extent and nature of the 1968 Communist Tet offensive proved to be a political disaster to the Johnson administration. The American people —who had only recently been assured the allies were winning the war—were shocked by the enemy's ability to strike throughout South Vietnam, even to the gates of the U.S. Embassy in Saigon. News accounts and particularly television films showing the devastation wrought by the enemy seriously hurt the administration. While additional U.S. troops were dispatched to bolster Westmoreland's forces, Washington attempted to speed up the previously planned third phase of American strategy, that is, to turn over most of the responsibility for the war to the South Vietnamese.

As domestic criticism of the administration reached a crescendo against the background of an earlier embarrassing incident—North Korea's seizure of the USS *Pueblo* on 24 January 1968 in the Sea of Japan—President Johnson on 31 March ordered a halt to all bombings north of the 20th parallel. He hoped this action would induce Hanoi to begin peace negotiations. At the same time the President announced he would not run for a second full term of office. Hanoi's leaders agreed to meet in Paris to begin the discussions, but they also continued to pour troops into South Vietnam at the rate of about 22,000 per month.

By mid-April intelligence revealed another enemy buildup in progress around Hue. Accordingly, on 19 April the allies mounted Operation Delaware/Lam Son 216, aimed at destroying the NVA logistic base in the A Shau Valley and denying the enemy an essential source of supply and a line of communication for further operations against Hue. A Viet Cong colonel, defecting to the South the same day, disclosed plans for a terrorist attack against Saigon beginning 4 May. It proved the start of another nationwide wave of assaults against 109 military installations and cities, including 21 airfields. Once again, U.S. air power played a major role battering the weary enemy.

Although visibly weakened, the Communists continued to probe allied defenses. They established a stronghold at Cap Mui Lay on the coast just south of the Demilitarized Zone, and harassed nearby U.S. Marine positions with mortar and artillery fire. On 1 July a week-long well-coordinated bombardment by air, Marine artillery, and naval guns was begun against enemy positions. Almost 1,800 tactical and 210 B-52 missions saturated the area and destroyed some 2,000 Communist gun positions and structures. Shortly thereafter, alerted that 11 NVA regiments were massing for another assault on Saigon, Gen. Creighton W. Abrams (he succeeded Westmoreland on 11 June 1968) launched a large number of "spoiling operations" and air strikes. Electronic sensors, monitored by reconnaissance aircraft, girded the city to alert the allies to the expected attack. When finally launched in mid-August, the enemy assault proved quite ineffective and was easily repelled.

Three weeks earlier, on 23 July 1968, Maj. Gen. Robert F. Worley, Vice Commander of the Seventh Air Force, was killed when an RF-4C jet he was piloting northwest of Da Nang was hit by ground fire and crashed. The second pilot in the plane ejected safely, however, and was rescued. General Worley became the second Air Force general killed while on an operational mission. The first, Maj. Gen. William J. Crumm, commander of SAC's 3d Air Division, died in a mid-air collision of two B-52's on 6 July 1967 (see Chapter VIII).

As part of Hanoi's continuing effort to influence American public opinion and the peace talks (which began in Paris in May but quickly bogged down), General Giap on 23 August sent 4,000 NVA 1st Army Division regulars against the Duc Lap Special Forces camp, located some 3 miles from the Cambodian border and 15 miles from Ban Me Thuot. The 2,500 South Vietnamese, Montagnards, and Americans defending the camp were taken by surprise and the perimeter breached. However, 30 minutes after the first call for help went out, U.S. Army helicopter gunships arrived in the area, followed 15 minutes later by AC-47 gunships. Placing the attackers under heavy fire, the AC-47's remained overhead spotting and "hosing down" enemy units as they appeared. Their effectiveness drew high praise from the defenders. In all, more than 100 gunship and 392 tactical air sorties were flown in support of Duc Lap. The senior Army advisor on the scene, Col Rex R. Sage, later credited USAF tactical air and gunships with having saved the camp from being overrun.

In October 1968, finally recognizing that it could not occupy and control the South Vietnamese countryside, Hanoi began withdrawing 30,000 to 40,000 troops. On 31 October, after receiving assurances from the North Vietnamese that "serious" talks to end the war would get under way in Paris, President Johnson ordered a halt of all bombings north of the DMZ effec-

2

(1) U.S. Army 7th Infantry trooper carries an M-60 machine gun past rubble of a residential section of Cholon, Saigon, following the 1968 enemy Tet offensive, January-February 1968. (2) Hue city officials help prepare victims of the Communist Tet Offensive for burial. (3) A Skyraider approaches Qui Nhon. (4) Smoke and dust obscure part of the Marine base at Khe Sanh, during North Vietnam's unsuccessful attempt to seize it in the 1968 Tet offensive. (5) Rocket attack on Duc To, 15 November 1967. (6) Weapons and ammunition seized from the enemy following the battle of Bong Son. (7) Vietnamese marines assemble Chinese-made 240-mm rockets, captured during an allied sweep northwest of Saigon, 1969. (8) A South Vietnamese outpost constructed in a tree-top served as a vantage point for ARVN rangers near Trunglap.

1

3

4

7

5

8

6

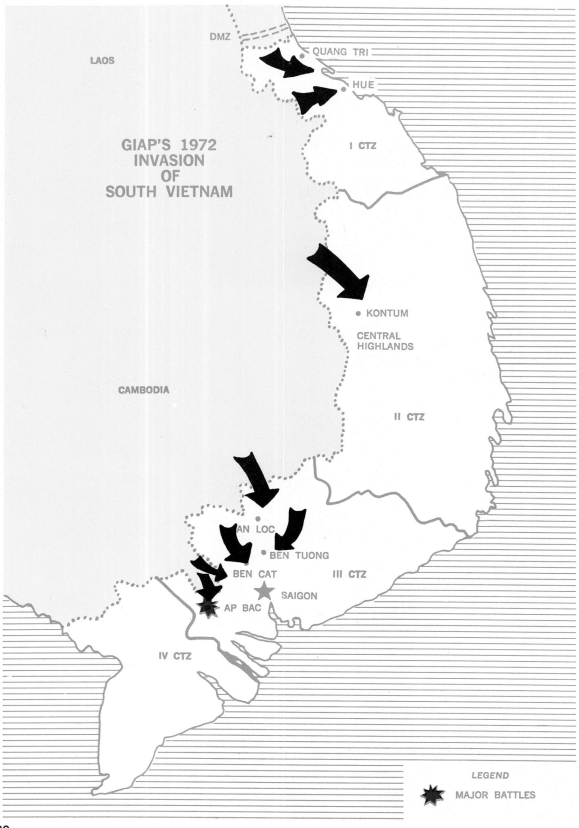

GIAP'S 1972
INVASION
OF
SOUTH VIETNAM

LAOS

DMZ

QUANG TRI

HUE

I CTZ

KONTUM

CENTRAL
HIGHLANDS

CAMBODIA

II CTZ

AN LOC

BEN TUONG

BEN CAT

III CTZ

SAIGON

AP BAC

IV CTZ

LEGEND

MAJOR BATTLES

60

tive 0800 Washington time on 1 November. Beforehand, the U.S. delegation in Paris explained to Hanoi's representatives that the United States would end "all bombardments and all acts involving the use of force" *but* that U.S. air reconnaissance would continue. The Americans repeatedly used the above phrase in their talks with the Communists, arguing that reconnaissance was "not an act involving the use of force." The North Vietnamese accepted the phrase and used it in their statement to the international press after the cessation of the bombings.

Vietnamization and Withdrawal

A few days later Richard M. Nixon defeated Hubert H. Humphrey in the 1968 presidential elections. During the campaign Nixon had pledged to bring American troops home while winning an honorable peace. An obvious aspect of this policy was to speed "Vietnamization" of the war effort. In March 1969 Secretary of Defense Melvin R. Laird visited South Vietnam to discuss an accelerated buildup of the Vietnamese armed forces (see Chapter XX). Thereafter, President Nixon met with President Thieu and gained his approval for the buildup. On 8 June Mr. Nixon then announced his plan to withdraw U.S. combat troops. The first of these Americans departed Vietnam in July. By year's end 69,000 had been withdrawn.

Meanwhile, the Air Force not only continued to assist allied operations in South Vietnam against enemy forces in the border regions but soon emerged as the primary military arm to support the policies of Vietnamization and withdrawal. Thus, a multi-battalion helicopter-airborne Marine assault during May-June in the A Shau Valley was preceded by 94 preplanned sorties and 28 immediate sorties which

B-52 Pilot

prepared the landing zone and provided air cover. The Commanding General, III Marine Amphibious Force, was unstinting in his praise of the USAF fighter pilots, air liaison officers, forward air controllers, and other participants. The Air Force also continued to support U.S. Army fire support bases, many of them situated in exposed positions. On 7 June, the enemy tried to overrun one of the bases astride a major enemy line of communication into Tay Ninh province. Responding to a call for help, USAF fighters struck the Communist force with bombs and napalm while gunships supported the action with flares and minigun fire. A subsequent sweep of the area revealed 323 enemy troops killed, all attributed to air power. Friendly casualties totaled seven wounded.

During the same period—between 8 May and 2 July 1969—the enemy launched an intensive attack on the Ben Het Civilian Irregular Defense Group camp. FAC's flew 571 sorties and AC-47's and AC-119's more than 100. Tactical air swarmed overhead in 1,828 sorties and SAC bombers, 804 sorties. Nearly 20,000 tons of bombs assailed the enemy day and night, in all kinds of weather, and finally forced the enemy to retreat.

In August 1969 the Air Force conducted "spoiling operations" in an effort to keep Communist troops off balance. Thus, when intelligence disclosed an enemy troop buildup in Bing Long province near An Loc and Loc Ninh—close to the Cambodian border in III Corps—B-52's struck numerous times and inflicted extensive damage on the enemy force. During the last months of the year, B-52 Stratoforts helped ARVN troops counter a major enemy threat in the Bu Prang and Duc Lap areas of Quang Duc province. In November the B-52's hit 57 enemy targets and struck 24 more during the first half of December. During the next 5 weeks the heavy bombers unloaded more than 30 mil-

1

2

3

4

(1) Damage caused at the U.S. Embassy, Saigon, during the 1968 Tet Offensive. (2) Vietnamese Sgt Con Nha Tan and USAF Technical Sgt Richard H. Nelson, a weapons maintenance advisor, load flares aboard a C-47. (3) Damage caused by a rocket attack at Qui Nhon, 18 May 1965. (4) A civilian dashes water on the smoldering remains of his home following a Viet Cong rocket attack, Aug. 1968. (5) Maj. Bernard C. Fisher, Juna, Idaho (l.) and Maj. D. Wayne Myers, Newport, Wash., following the March 1966 rescue of the latter at an airstrip in the A Shau valley. (6) U.S. and Vietnamese A-1E pilots discuss a mission against the enemy, 1965. (7) A VNAF A-1H pulls away after unloading his ordnance on an enemy target.

5

6

7

lion pounds of bombs against enemy troop concentrations, staging areas, and fortifications. Indeed, in 1969 General Abrams came to depend more and more on USAF air power to keep the enemy from massing while U.S. forces withdrew and the Vietnamese armed forces buildup went forward.

In 1970, when the first USAF elements also began to leave Southeast Asia, the VNAF grew to 9 tactical wings and some 40,000 personnel and greatly expanded its training program. Its inventory of nearly 700 aircraft included A-1's, A-37's, F-5's, AC-47's, O-1's, and C-119's. Despite the enemy's reduced activity in South Vietnam, a noticeable buildup was detected in the "Fishhook" area of Cambodia, immediately across the border from Tay Ninh province. In response, the President authorized a major incursion into the enemy's Cambodian sanctuary by allied troops, supported by extensive American and Vietnamese tactical air units (see Chapter VII). However, both the U.S. and Vietnamese Air Forces also continued flying strike missions inside South Vietnam. By the end of 1970 the Air Force had flown 48,064 attack sorties, while the VNAF flew another 28,249—almost 40 percent of the total sorties over Vietnam.

Even as the U.S. withdrawal continued into 1971, the allies laid plans to send an ARVN invasion force into the southern panhandle of Laos to seize Tchepone on the Ho Chi Minh trail, destroy enemy forces, and interdict NVA traffic into South Vietnam and Cambodia. Crossing into Laos on 30 January 1971, the South Vietnamese were supported by a large tactical air fleet. The NVA reacted strongly, sending in large numbers of tanks, artillery, and AA weapons to fight the South Vietnamese. Elements of ARVN forces managed to reach the Tchepone area with the help of massive USAF B-52 and tactical air strikes. Casualties were heavy on both sides. The North

Vietnamese lost about 13,000 men and an estimated 20,000 tons of munitions. The South Vietnamese, having suffered 5,000 dead, retreated from Laos without achieving the initial objectives of the incursion.

By December 1971 the Air Force had reduced its inventory of fighter and strike aircraft in South Vietnam to 277 (from a high in June 1968 of 737). The number of personnel in-country also declined dramatically—from the 1968 peak of 54,434 to 28,791 at the end of 1971. By then the Vietnamese Air Force was responsible for about 70 percent of all air combat operations. The enemy—temporarily put on the defensive by the moves into Cambodia in 1970 and Laos in 1971—began deploying new NVA forces southward in preparation for another major offensive. They deposited a huge amount of supplies in their old sanctuary areas near the Central Highlands. U.S. intelligence detected the enemy buildup but NVA plans for the impending operation were unknown. In an effort to meet the threat, in mid-February 1972 hundreds of sorties were flown against NVA targets just north of the DMZ.

Some 6 weeks later—on 30 March 1972—the North Vietnamese launched a large, three-pronged invasion of South Vietnam, spearheaded by tanks and mobile armor units. One NVA force swept south across the DMZ, its goal apparently the conquest of the northern provinces and the seizure of Hue. The initial NVA surge led to the seizure of Quang Tri City. A second NVA force drove from Laos into the Central Highlands, and a third effort involved a drive from Cambodia into Binh Long and Tay Ninh provinces, northwest of Saigon.

Fierce fighting ensued on all three fronts, with tactical aircraft and B-52's launching repeated strikes against the advancing NVA armored units. The enemy's greatest success was in the northern provinces, but perhaps the

Soviet tanks.

64

most critical and potentially most disastrous battle occurred at An Loc. There, the badly outnumbered and outgunned South Vietnamese stood their ground within the besieged city and survived the heaviest enemy attacks of the entire war. They and the city were saved in large measure by air power, much of it supplied by the Vietnamese Air Force. More than 10,000 tactical and 254 B-52 strikes were flown in support of ARVN forces. Air Force gunships once again proved invaluable at night turning back attacking NVA troops. When the battle for An Loc was over near the end of June, the enemy force there had lost all of its tanks and artillery.

In the Central Highlands, the fight started out well for the Communists. Employing Soviet-built T-54 tanks and heavy armor, the North Vietnamese quickly seized control of much of Kontum province. The Air Force responded to this crisis by redeploying additional strike aircraft to South Vietnam and by considerably increasing fighter strength in Thailand. This bolstered force helped decimate enemy units, with AC-119 and AC-130 gunships being especially effective in the open highland country. By 1 June the North Vietnamese began withdrawing from some of their advance positions.

By the summer of 1972 the battles of An Loc and the highland regions were largely over, and attention turned to the northern provinces where the NVA had seized considerable amounts of South Vietnamese territory. Heavy air strikes had helped stop the enemy advance and destroyed much of his armored forces. But when the fighting wound down, the North Vietnamese were in control of much of the countryside below the DMZ plus a strip of South Vietnam's territory running along the Laotian and Cambodian borders. The major population centers, however, remained under the South Vietnamese. Still, North Vietnam retained substantial lodgements

Demolished VNAF C-47 following an April 1966 enemy mortar attack on Tan Son Nhut.

within the Republic of Vietnam, which posed a continuing threat to the Saigon government.

From the U.S. point of view, perhaps the most heartening aspect of the enemy offensive—which cost North Vietnam an estimated 120,000 casualties and heavy equipment losses—was the performance of the Vietnamese Air Force. VNAF pilots—many of them with 4,000 hours of combat flying under their belts—demonstrated great skill and initiative in attacking the NVA. During 1972, they flew 40,000 strike sorties in support of ARVN ground forces, most of whose troops held on and fought valiantly.Some units did panic and abandoned Quang Tri City during the early phases of the Communist offensive, but the ARVN subsequently recaptured it.

Against the background of the massive NVA invasion of South Vietnam in the spring of 1972, President Nixon ordered renewed bombing of North Vietnam by both tactical aircraft and B-52's. On 8 May he also authorized the mining of the harbors and river inlets of North Vietnam to prevent the rapid delivery of replacement arms, munitions, and other war essentials from the Soviet Union and Communist China (see Chapter IV). This latest interdiction campaign against North Vietnam continued throughout the summer and early fall of 1972.

In October Dr. Henry Kissinger, the President's Special Assistant for National Security Affairs, returned from the Paris negotiations to inform the nation that "peace is at hand," and the bombing of North Vietnam was halted. Unfortunately, at the last moment the enemy balked over some of the ceasefire provisions, that is, Hanoi insisted that the United States install a coalition government in Saigon. A 2-month deadlock ensued, which led the President to order new and more drastic measures to end the war. On 18 December 1972, on his orders, the heaviest air attacks of the war were

1

GIẤY THÔNG-HÀNH

SAFE-CONDUCT PASS TO BE HONORED BY ALL VIETNAMESE GOVERNMENT AGENCIES AND ALLIED FORCES

이 안전보장패쓰는 월남정부와 모든 연합군에 의해 인정된 것입니다.

รัฐบาลเวียดนามและหน่วยพันธมิตร ยินดีให้เกียรติแก่ผู้ถือบัตรผ่านปลอดภัยนี้.

(Front)

2

3

SAFE-CONDUCT PASS TO BE HONORED BY ALL VIETNAMESE GOVERNMENT AGENCIES AND ALLIED FORCES

MANG TẤM GIẤY THÔNG HÀNH
nầy về cộng tác với Chánh Phủ
Quốc Gia các bạn sẽ được :

● Đón tiếp tử tế
● Bảo đảm an ninh
● Đải ngộ tương xứng

Nguyễn Cao Kỳ

TẤM GIẤY THÔNG HÀNH NẦY CÓ GIÁ TRỊ VỚI TẤT CẢ CƠ-QUAN
QUÂN CHÍNH VIỆT-NAM CỘNG-HÒA VÀ LỰC-LƯỢNG ĐỒNG-MINH.

2

(Back)

4

(1&2) Propaganda leaflet operations. (3&4) An enemy soldier holds a surrender leaflet. (5) A Vietnamese officer speaks to villagers of Ap Trung, northwest of My Tho. (6) South Vietnamese psychological warfare team hands out leaflets to villagers. (7) A Viet Cong surrenders to government troops after picking up a propaganda leaflet. (8) Airmen loading a leaflet bomb.

5

6

7

8

launched against military targets within Hanoi and Haiphong; on 29 December, the North Vietnamese agreed to proceed with the negotiations. A nine-point agreement was finally worked out and formally signed on 27 January 1973.

Under the agreement, U.S. forces would withdraw from South Vietnam and all prisoners of war would be returned within 60 days. The United States tacitly recognized that the North Vietnamese were in strength within the territory of South Vietnam. Indeed, for the first time, North Vietnam acknowledged that it had 100,000 troops in the northern and western parts of the Republic of Vietnam. Exactly on schedule, on 28 March 1973, the last American military personnel departed South Vietnam, and MACV headquarters was inactivated. Thus, after more than a dozen years, an active American military role in South Vietnam came to an end.

Chapter IV. The Air War Against North Vietnam

As noted in Chapter II, the United States launched its first air strikes against North Vietnam in August 1964 in response to the attack on the Navy destroyer, *USS Maddox.* Navy carrier planes hit four North Vietnamese coastal torpedo bases and an oil storage facility. On 2 December, the President said he favored a limited air campaign against Communist lines of communication used to support the insurgency in South Vietnam. The second air strike against North Vietnam, nicknamed "Flaming Dart I," was launched by the Navy on 7 February 1965 after enemy mortar and demolition teams attacked U.S. and South Vietnamese military facilities near Pleiku. The following day, as part of this riposte, VNAF A-1's—accompanied by 20 F-100's flying flak suppression sorties and 28 VNAF A-1H's, commanded by Lt. Col. Andrew Chapman of the 3d Tactical Group 2d Air Division—dropped general purpose bombs on the Chap Le barracks. Several of the 20 accompanying USAF F-100's attacked enemy antiaircraft artillery (AAA) sites. Three RF-101's provided photographic coverage. On 11 February, a third air strike ("Flaming Dart II") was conducted by Navy, USAF, and VNAF aircraft against NVA barracks at Chanh Hoa and Vit Thu Lu. It was in response to another enemy attack, this time against U.S. facilities at Qui Nhon which killed more than 20 Americans.

A 19-day pause followed the second Flaming Dart strikes. When air attacks against the North resumed on 2 March 1965, they carried the appellation "Rolling Thunder." On that date, General Moore dispatched 25 F-105's and 20 B-57's—accompanied by KC-135 refueling tankers and other supporting aircraft—which hit an NVA ammunition depot at Xom Bong about 35 miles above the DMZ, causing heavy damage.

The Rolling Thunder campaign was substantially different from those of World War I and II, resembling rather the geographically limited air war over Korea. That is to say, President Johnson—determined to avoid a larger conflict with China and the Soviet Union—imposed stringent controls on air operations. The strikes had a threefold purpose: to raise the morale of the South Vietnamese, impose a penalty on Hanoi for supporting aggression in the South, and reduce infiltration of men and supplies into the South. The air campaign also was based on the hope that the gradual destruction of North Vietnam's military bases and constant attacks on its lines of communications (LOC's) would bring its leaders to the negotiating table.

The restrictions imposed upon the Air Force made execution of Rolling Thunder strikes very complex. Coordination of USAF and VNAF air operations devolved upon General Moore and his successors. Besides being responsible to Washington authorities and the commanders of the two unified commands—Admiral Sharp and General Westmoreland—the 2d Air Division commander also was required to work closely with the U.S. ambassadors in Saigon, Vientiane, and Bangkok. In undertaking air strikes, political considerations were usually paramount. For example, squadrons based in Thailand could attack targets in North Vietnam and Laos but not in South Vietnam. In June 1965 General Moore was assigned the additional job of serving as MACV Deputy Commander for Air Operations, but it did not greatly increase his authority or alter his responsibilities for three separate but related areas of operations—South Vietnam, North Vietnam, and Laos.

The President retained such firm control of the air campaign against the North that no important target or new target areas could be hit without his approval. His decisions were relayed through Secretary McNamara to the Joint Chiefs, who then issued strike directives to CINCPAC. The latter, in turn, apportioned fixed targets and armed reconnaissance routes among the U.S. Air Force, U.S. Navy, and the Vietnamese Air Force, with USAF crews normally providing air cover for the VNAF, which later withdrew from northern operations to concentrate on supporting ARVN forces within South Vietnam. In conducting operations over the North, the American crews were enjoined to minimize civilian casualties as much as possible. This policy—and the overall target restraints imposed by the White House and Pentagon officials—helped avoid in North Vietnam the heavy civilian losses that characterized bombings on both sides in World War II.

The initial air strikes were limited primarily to enemy radar and bridges between the 17th and 19th parallels. Later, the airmen were allowed to hit a number of other military targets below the 20th parallel. The first target hit above the 20th parallel, the Quang Soui barracks, was attacked on 22 May 1965 by Air Force F-105's and the first above Hanoi in late June. After mid-1965, the airmen were authorized to attack important bridges and segments of the northwest and northeast rail lines between Hanoi and the Chinese border. For an extended period, Washington exempted from attack

sanctuary areas around Hanoi and Haiphong, a buffer zone near China, surface-to-air missile (SAM) sites, and MIG bases located within the Hanoi-Haiphong areas. After the first few sporadic strikes, Rolling Thunder pilots on 19 March began flying strike sorties against individual targets and target areas on a weekly basis. Beginning on 9 July 1965, targets were programmed on a biweekly basis; after 1965 new targets were selected periodically.

The first Air Force tactical strikes were by aircraft already in South Vietnam and Thailand. As additional air units arrived, those assigned missions against targets in North Vietnam and Laos—and a portion of the B-52 fleet—were sent to six large airfields, some newly built, in Thailand. USAF strength in Thailand grew from about 1,000 personnel and 83 aircraft in early 1965 to a peak of 35,000 personnel and 600 aircraft in 1968. U.S. Navy aircraft and South Vietnam-based Marine aircraft also flew many missions over North Vietnam and Laos.

The principal Air Force tactical strike aircraft during Rolling Thunder operations was the F-105 Thunderchief. Mass-produced after the Korean War, it served throughout the war in Southeast Asia. A newer fighter, the twin-seat F-4 Phantom II manned by an aircraft commander and a weapons system officer,* initially was used in a combat air patrol (CAP) role. Committed to battle gradually, it flew its first strike mission at the end of May 1965 and its first armed reconnaissance mission in August. A third Air Force fighter, the twin-seat, swept-wing F-111A, reached Thailand in March 1968, underwent combat evaluation that year, and was withdrawn. Subsequently, in the latter stages of the war, this sophisticated night and all-weather aircraft returned to South-

*The latter was originally a trained pilot, but later USAF employed navigators.

east Asia and flew regular combat missions.

A number of older, lower-performance and more vulnerable aircraft were used briefly or sparingly over the North. The F-100 Super Sabre and the F-104 Starfighter saw action chiefly in a support role above the DMZ. Some Starfighters flew strike missions and the B-57 Canberra light bomber was employed largely in night operations. Eventually, all were withdrawn from northern missions, with the F-100 being used primarily for close air support in South Vietnam.

The B-52 Stratofortresses made their debut over North Vietnam in April 1966 with a strike near Mu Gia pass. During the next 6 1/2 years, these heavy bombers were employed against enemy targets in North Vietnam's panhandle, staying far away from the dangerous SA-2 missile sites located mostly in the Hanoi-Haiphong area. Based initially on Guam and later in Thailand, the B-52's were primarily employed to interdict North Vietnamese lines of communication leading to the DMZ and the Ho Chi Minh trail in Laos. On these missions, they normally dropped 25 to 30 tons of ordnance. Gen. John P. McConnell, LeMay's successor as Air Force Chief of Staff, remarked on the irony of the use of these strategic bombers to hit tactical targets. But it was only one of several improvisations introduced by the Air Force in waging the unorthodox air war.

The role played by SAC's KC-135 air refueling tankers proved vital to the execution of Rolling Thunder (see Chapter XI). Prior to 1965 they had been used primarily to refuel B-52's but they also had provided mid-air refueling service to tactical aircraft deploying from one part of the world to another. Gen. William W. Momyer, commander of the Seventh Air Force (1966-1968), observed that few airmen "foresaw that air refueling would become a basic part of the scheme of

F-105's in Thailand.

employment of fighter forces over North Vietnam." Since much of the USAF tactical air fleet was based some 350 nautical miles from their targets in the North, refueling was essential if the F-105's and F-4's were to deliver substantial ordnance loads on their targets. The KC-135's also enabled many fuel-short or damaged aircraft to return safely to their bases.

Among the problems facing U.S. airmen flying over North Vietnam were the heavy forests, the jungle terrain, and the annual northeast monsoon which was most severe from mid-October to mid-March. All affected operations over the North. They also placed a premium on the ability of reconnaissance aircraft to locate enemy targets and assess bomb damage. To obtain this information, the Air Force employed a number of manned and unmanned aircraft. Perhaps the most famous was the U-2, which first attracted worldwide attention in May 1960, when Soviet missilemen shot one down over central Russia while it was on a high-altitude reconnaissance mission. Later, in the fall of 1962, a SAC U-2 detected the first Soviet strategic missiles deployed in Cuba. In Southeast Asia, the U-2 flew reconnaissance missions over North Vietnam beginning in 1965 (see also Chapter XII).

Throughout the war zone, the Air Force also operated other reconnaissance aircraft, including the RB-57, the workhorse RF-101, the RF-4C, and drones. Some of these aircraft, equipped with infrared and side-looking radar, helped advance the technology of reconnaissance during the war. In 1965, SAC's Ryan 147D (and other model) drones made their initial flights over North Vietnam. Dropped from DC-130 transports, they were able to obtain photo intelligence over the Hanoi area. As North Vietnam began developing a modern air defense system, the Air Force also began using aircraft capable of obtaining

FRESCO (MIG-17)

FISHBED (MIG-21)

4

5

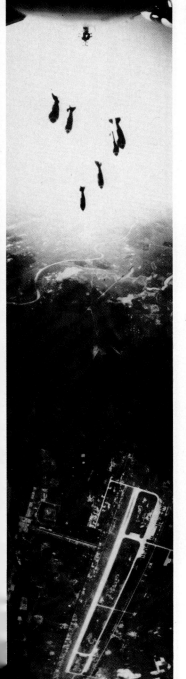

6

KIEN AN A/F

7

(1) F-105's in Thailand. (2&3) An Air Force reconnaissance photo of Phuc Yen airfield near Hanoi shows MIG-17's and MIG-21's in revetments. (4) An F-4 Phantom. (5) President Johnson in October 1967 personally approved this first strike against enemy MIG's at Phuc Yen. (6) Kien Am airfield with MIG's in revetments. (7) Gia Lam airfield near Hanoi. It was off limits from attack throughout most of the War. L. to r.: AN-2 Colt, MIG-21, and MIG-17.

target data via various electronic methods.

Rolling Thunder, 1965-1968

From the first handful of strikes over the North in early 1965, Air Force and Navy attack sorties rose from 1,500 in April to a peak of about 4,000 in September. In October, with the onset of the northeast monsoon, they declined steeply. While the weather was good, U.S. pilots destroyed or damaged a variety of military targets: bridges, vehicles, rolling stock, barracks areas, supply and ammunition depots, ferries, watercraft, and antiaircraft artillery and radar sites. They bombed railroad tracks and roads to prevent the movement of men and supplies. The results of the air strikes could not be accurately assessed and became the subject of considerable debate. But they reduced or delayed the enemy's operations and infiltration into the South. They led the North Vietnamese to adopt the practice of travelling under cover of night and bad weather —taking full advantage of forested or jungle terrain. They also diverted considerable manpower and materiel to repair their roads, rail lines, and bridges and increased their antiaircraft defenses.

Because of the limitations imposed on air operations, war materiel from the Soviet Union, China, and other Communist countries flowed in easily through Haiphong and other North Vietnamese ports and over rail lines from Kunming and Nanning, China— all of which helped Hanoi to make up for its losses and which facilitated a rapid air defense buildup. During 1965, for example, North Vietnam's AAA inventory expanded from an estimated 1,000 guns to 2,000 pieces and about 400 antiaircraft sites by year's end. These consisted primarily of 37- and 57-mm guns but included a few 85-mm and 100-mm weapons as well.

Smaller but deadly automatic weapons—which inflicted much of the losses and damage to U.S. aircraft—also proliferated.

The Soviet surface-to-air missiles were first detected by a SAC U-2 aircraft on 5 April 1965. By year's end, USAF and Navy reconnaissance had pinpointed 56 SAM sites. The North Vietnamese, who took great pains to conceal them, readily abandoned sites to build new ones. By building a large number of sites, some of them equipped with dummy missiles to deceive USAF crews, they were able to use a "launch and move" tactic. They employed a similar tactic with their AAA guns. Another key element of Hanoi's air defenses was the North Vietnamese Air Force (NVAF), which was equipped with 50 to 60 MIG-15's and MIG-17's plus a few IL-28 bombers. Although the MIG's began challenging U.S. strike aircraft at an early date, they did not become a serious threat until 1966-1967. The sum of the enemy's array of AAA guns, automatic weapons, SAM's, and the MIG force— backed up by an expanding defense radar complex—enabled Hanoi to build one of the most formidable air defense systems ever devised.

On 23 July 1965, after several months of USAF operations against North Vietnamese targets, the first F-4C was downed by an SA-2 missile. Four days later, with Washington's approval, Air Force Thunderchiefs mounted the first strike of the war against the SAM's. In August, a Navy aircraft was downed by a SAM, which led to a series of special U.S. "Iron Hand" missions aimed at North Vietnam's rapidly expanding SA-2 sites. At first, most of them were in the Hanoi-Haiphong sanctuary area and thus could not be attacked, but others were emplaced along major rail and road junctions, bridges, and cities north and south of the North Vietnamese capital. In known SAM areas, Air Force pilots would drop to lower altitudes to

Crews flying strike missions over North Vietnam were continually hampered by heavy flak over the target areas.

74

avoid the SA-2's but this tactic made them more vulnerable to conventional AAA and especially to smaller automatic weapons. By mid-1965, the latter were credited with shooting down most of the approximately 50 Air Force and Navy aircraft lost over North Vietnam.

An electronic war subsequently ensued between U.S. tactical aircraft and the enemy's complex of radar-controlled AAA guns and SAM's and other defense radars. The Air Force employed specially equipped aircraft to counter SAM radars. Initially, fighter pilots relied on the electronically equipped EB-66's and "Wild Weasel" F-100's and F-105's to neutralize or warn them of radar emissions from enemy "Fan Song" equipment which signalled that they were being tracked or that a SAM firing was imminent. These countermeasures plus the SA-2's generally poor guidance system kept losses low. Thus, of the approximately 180 SAM's launched in 1965, only 11 succeeded in downing an aircraft, 5 of which were Air Force. Nonetheless, the inhibiting and harassing effects of the SAM's had considerable impact on air operations. After 1966, the fighters carried electronic countermeasure pods of their own. A number of EB-66's and Wild Weasel aircraft continued to be used, however.

The North Vietnamese Air Force, flying from airfields which Washington officials decided should not be hit because of their location in the heavily populated Hanoi-Haiphong area, was not a major threat to USAF pilots during 1965. Although North Vietnamese pilots shot down two F-105's in a surprise attack in April, throughout the year the American airmen clearly held the upper hand in aerial fighting. In June Navy pilots downed two enemy aircraft. On 10 July the Air Force scored its initial kills, when Captains Thomas S. Roberts and Ronald C. Anderson in one F-4 and Captains

Kenneth E. Holcombe and Arthur C. Clark in another were credited with the shoot-down of two MIG-17's.

Early in the year, several Air Force EC-121's were deployed over the Gulf of Tonkin to maintain a "MIG watch" over Southeast Asia. Flying missions off the coast of North Vietnam, these aircraft not only were able to alert U.S. fighter and support aircraft of approaching MIG's, but also served as airborne radar and communication platforms. They also warned American pilots who flew too near the Chinese border and they assisted air-sea searches for downed air crews. Later, the EC-121's equipment was employed in an integrated fashion with the Navy's seabased radars, enabling U.S. pilots to obtain a variety of additional timely information about the enemy's and their own air operations over the North.

The political restraints placed by the President on air operations over North Vietnam denied U.S. pilots certain advantages of surprise. Another problem was the relatively small geographical area overflown by Rolling Thunder crews. It forced pilots to use specific air corridors going into (ingressing) and departing (egressing) a target, a task made all the more difficult by the need to avoid civilian casualties as much as possible. A third operational factor was the weather cycle in North Vietnam, which generally allowed optimum operations in late mornings or afternoons when clouds and fog were minimal or absent. All of these factors contributed to stereotyped American air tactics which the enemy quickly became aware of and which enabled him to deploy his AAA defenses to great advantage. Also, the relatively short duty tours created much turmoil in air operations. Experienced airmen were constantly departing and less experienced replacements arriving, which diluted both planning and flying expertise in the theater.

Shrike and Standard Arm missiles on an F-105.

(1&2) Maj. Donald J. Kutyna flew missions over North Vietnam in an F-105 which he named the *Polish Glider* (3) F-111's and F-4's at Takhli AB, Thailand. (4) F-105 (color painting). (5) An F-105 unloads 750-lb bombs on North Vietnam's Hoa Lac airfield. (6) USAF strike aircraft destroy a North Vietnamese oil storage facility near Hanoi. (7) Captured enemy 37-mm AAA gun. (8) F-4E Phantoms arrive at Korat AB, Thailand, November 1968. (9) An EB-66 controls a flight of F-105's on a mission over North Vietnam's panhandle. July 1966. (10) Air Force bombers destroyed more than 30 enemy supply trucks in North Vietnam.

5

6

HA NOI 3.7 NM

7

8

9

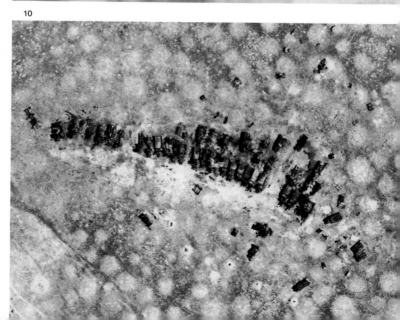

10

Rolling Thunder Route Packages in North Vietnam

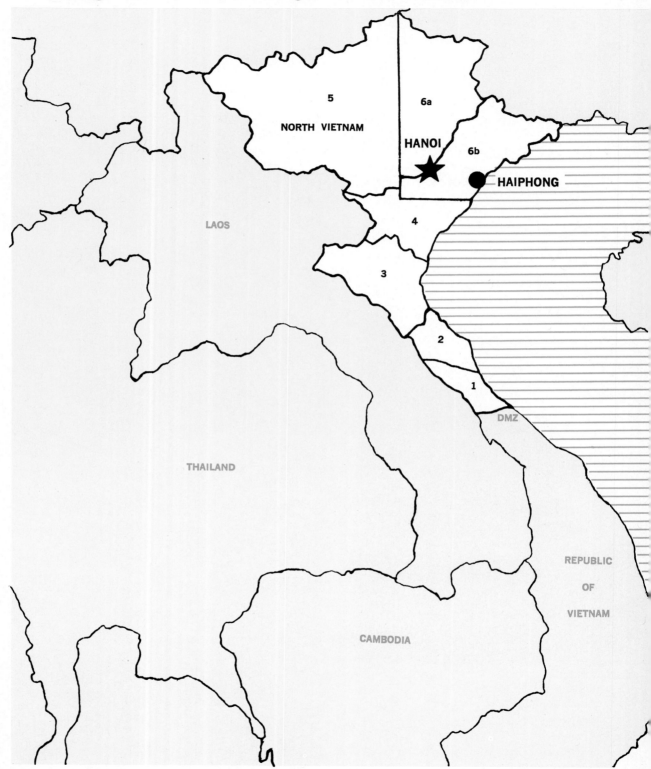

To reduce mission interference between land-based Air Force and Navy carrier aircraft operating over North Vietnam, in December 1965—after consulting with Air Force and Navy officials—Admiral Sharp divided the bombing area into six major "route packages." Generally, the longer-range USAF fighters attacked the inland route package targets; the shorter-range Navy aircraft concentrated on those near the coast. In April 1966, General Westmoreland assumed responsibility for armed reconnaissance and intelligence analysis of the "extended battlefield" area of Route Package I above the DMZ as it affected allied operations in South Vietnam. CINCPAC continued to control air operations in the other route packages.

The Bombing Pauses

During the first 2 years of operations over the North, President Johson periodically ordered bombing pauses in an effort to bring Hanoi's leaders around to discuss a political settlement of the war. The first bombing pause of about 6 day's duration was ordered in mid-May. The second one began on Christmas Eve 1965 and continued until 30 January 1966. In both instances, North Vietnam did not respond to U.S. action and, indeed, used the bombing respites to rebuild its strength and speed the infiltration of men and supplies southward. USAF reconnaissance also disclosed major North Vietnamese efforts to repair damaged roads and bridges and to install more air defense weapons. President Johnson also approved briefer bombing standdowns, to permit celebration of the annual Vietnamese new year ("Tet"), Buddha's birthday, Christmas, and New Year's Day.

When U.S. diplomatic efforts to get the North Vietnamese to the conference table got nowhere, the President in the late spring of 1966 approved a series of heavier air strikes against North Vietnam. Added to the approved target list were POL storage facilities at Haiphong, Hanoi, Nguyen Ke, Bac Gian, Do Son, and Duong Nham. Others included a power plant and cement factory in Hanoi, an important road-and-rail and road bridge on the northwest line, and an early warning and ground control intercept radar facility at Kep. The first major POL strike was conducted on 29 June 1966 when Air Force F-105's hit a 32-tank farm less than 4 miles from Hanoi. About 95 percent of the target area was destroyed. Navy aircraft struck another important POL facility near Haiphong.

Beginning on 9 July 1966, as part of an expanded Rolling Thunder program, U.S. aircraft bombed additional POL facilities, flew extended armed reconnaissance missions throughout the North (except for most of the Hanoi-Haiphong sanctuary area), and began heavier bombing of the northeast and northwest rail lines in Route Packages V and VI. Admiral Sharp assigned interdiction of the railroads to the Air Force. Additional pressure against the enemy was brought to bear on 20 July when the Air Force and Marines launched a new campaign (Tally Ho) against infiltration routes and targets between the DMZ and the area 30 miles northward in Route Package I. The U.S. air offensive expanded in the ensuing weeks, peaking at about 12,000 sorties in September.

By that time, Rolling Thunder had taken a heavy toll of enemy equipment, destroying or damaging several thousand trucks and watercraft, hundreds of railway cars and bridges, many ammunition and storage supply areas, and two-thirds of the enemy's POL storage capacity. Many sorties were flown against AAA, SA-2, and other air defense facilities, thousands of cuts were made in enemy road and rail networks. To counter this air campaign, Hanoi was forced to divert an

1   2

ORGANIZATION, 7TH AIR FORCE AND 7/13TH AIR FORCE

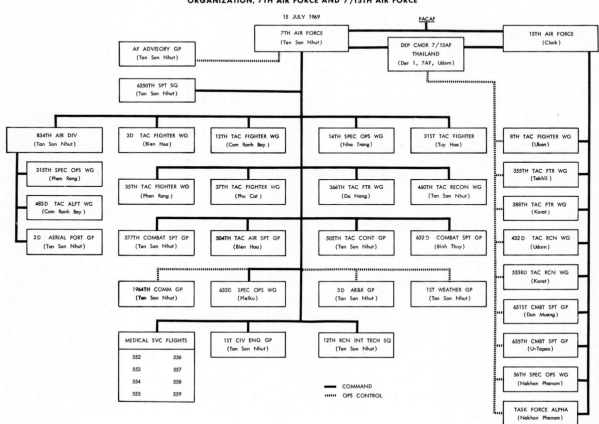

15 JULY 1969

PACAF

7TH AIR FORCE
(Tan Son Nhut)

DEP CMDR 7/13AF
THAILAND
(Det 1, 7AF, Udorn)

13TH AIR FORCE
(Clark)

AF ADVISORY GP
(Tan Son Nhut)

6250TH SPT SQ
(Tan Son Nhut)

834TH AIR DIV
(Tan Son Nhut)

315TH SPEC OPS WG
(Phan Rang)

483D TAC ALFT WG
(Com Ranh Bay)

2D AERIAL PORT GP
(Tan Son Nhut)

3D TAC FIGHTER WG
(Bien Hoa)

12TH TAC FIGHTER WG
(Cam Ranh Bay)

14TH SPEC OPS WG
(Nha Trang)

31ST TAC FIGHTER
(Tuy Hoa)

8TH TAC FIGHTER WG
(Ubon)

35TH TAC FIGHTER WG
(Phan Rang)

37TH TAC FIGHTER WG
(Phu Cat)

366TH TAC FTR WG
(Da Nang)

460TH TAC RECON WG
(Tan Son Nhut)

355TH TAC FTR WG
(Takhli)

388TH TAC FTR WG
(Korat)

377TH COMBAT SPT GP
(Tan Son Nhut)

504TH TAC AIR SPT GP
(Bien Hoa)

505TH TAC CONT GP
(Tan Son Nhut)

632D COMBAT SPT GP
(Binh Thuy)

432D TAC RCN WG
(Udorn)

553RD TAC RCN WG
(Korat)

1964TH COMM GP
(Tan Son Nhut)

633D SPEC OPS WG
(Pleiku)

3D AR&R GP

1ST WEATHER GP
(Tan Son Nhut)

631ST CMBT SPT GP
(Don Muang)

635TH CMBT SPT GP
(U-Tapao)

MEDICAL SVC FLIGHTS

552	556
553	557
554	558
555	559

1ST CIV ENG GP
(Tan Son Nhut)

12TH RCN INT TECH SQ
(Tan Son Nhut)

56TH SPEC OPS WG
(Nakhon Phanom)

TASK FORCE ALPHA
(Nakhon Phanom)

━━━ COMMAND
▪▪▪▪ OPS CONTROL

3

(1) Sgt Leonard B. Williams (left) works on F-100 converters at Phan Rang AB, South Vietnam. Sgt Philip J. Smith adjusts the drag chute cable (2) Col. Robin Olds, Commander, 8th Tactical Fighter Wing, is carried off by his men after completing his 100th mission over North Vietnam (3) B-52's drop bombs on a Viet Cong stronghold (4) F-4 Phantoms destroy 6 of 11 spans of the Lang Giai bridge in North Vietnam, 25 May 1972.

4

estimated 200,000 to 300,000 full and part-time workers to repair roads, railway lines, bridges, and other facilities, and to man its air defenses.

Although infiltration southward could not be stopped, U.S. commanders in South Vietnam credited the bombing with reducing the number of enemy battalion-sized attacks. A new Rolling Thunder program, dated 12 November, added more targets including the Van Vien vehicle depot and the Yen Vien railroad yards, both within the environs of Hanoi. These targets, struck by Air Force and Navy pilots in December 1966, produced collateral damage and civilian deaths which led to a political and diplomatic furor. By the end of 1966, U.S. tactical aircraft had flown about 106,500 attack sorties and B-52's another 280 over North Vietnam, dropping at least 165,000 tons of bombs.

The North Vietnamese accepted the tremendous losses and fought back. By dispersing and concealing much of their POL supply, they were able to reduce the full impact of the air attacks. Bad flying weather and extensive use of manpower enabled the North Vietnamese to keep open portions of the northern rail lines so that some supplies continued to flow in from China. More importantly, Haiphong and other ports—still off-limits to U.S. aircraft—daily unloaded thousands of tons of war materiel. Despite the air attacks, AAA and especially small automatic weapons took a rising toll of American aircraft, downing a total of 455 by the end of 1966 and damaging many more. The number of SAM sites rose to about 150 during the year, but improved flying tactics—plus the installation of electronic countermeasure (ECM) equipment on U.S. aircraft—reduced the effectiveness of the missiles.

Until September 1966 the North Vietnamese Air Force made only sporadic attempts to interfere with Rolling Thunder operations. But on 3 September NVN pilots went on the offensive. Equipped with MIG-21's carrying infrared-homing air-to-air missiles, they operated freely from five bases—Phuc Yen, Kep, Gia Lam, Kien An, and Hoa Loc—in the Hanoi area which could not be attacked. Confronted by daily MIG-21 challenges, General Momyer temporarily diverted Air Force F-4C's from their primary strike mission to exclusive aerial combat against the MIG's.

A favorite MIG tactic was to pop up suddenly and try to force the heavily laden F-105's to jettison their bombs before reaching their targets. To offset this, Sidewinder-equipped Phantoms flew at lower altitudes to enable their pilots to spot the MIG's earlier and then used their higher acceleration and speed in hit and run tactics. They avoided turning fights because the MIG's had great maneuverability. The EC-121's helped materially by alerting the F4's to the presence of the enemy aircraft. During 1966, U.S. fighters shot down 23 MIG's, 17 of them credited to USAF crews, as against a loss of 9 aircraft, 5 of them Air Force.

Early in 1967, Washington officials approved new Rolling Thunder targets closer to Hanoi. To protect vital industrial and LOC facilities, North Vietnamese pilots—operating with nearly 100 MIG's—were thrown into the air battle. To dampen their ardor, General Momyer and his staff devised a ruse nicknamed Operation Bolo. The details were worked out and executed by Col. Robin Olds, Commander of the 8th Tactical Fighter Wing. Baited by what appeared to be a normal Rolling Thunder strike by F-105's, the NVAF on 2 January suddenly found itself engaging F-4's in the largest aerial battle of the war to that time. Colonel Olds and his pilots shot down 7 MIG's in 12 minutes without losing an aircraft. Olds personally downed two of them. On 6 January 1967 the North Vietnamese lost two more MIG's.

Destroyed bridge in Laos, 1965.

Stunned by the losses, the NVAF stood down to regroup and retrain.

The American air offensive continued into March and April. On 10-11 March, F-105's and F-4C's hit the sprawling Thai Nguyen iron and steel plant about 30 miles from Hanoi. Air Force and Navy follow-up strikes also hit portions of the plant. The attacks disrupted but did not completely halt pig iron or steel production. Also, for the first time, Air Force jets struck the *Canal Des Rapides* railway and highway bridge, 4 miles north of Hanoi. Enemy pilots did not attempt to challenge American aircraft again until the spring of 1967, which saw 50 engagements fought in April and 72 in May, the largest 1-month total of the war. During the fierce May battles Air Force crews destroyed 20 MIG's—7 of them on the 13th and 6 on the 20th.

A revised Rolling Thunder target list issued on 20 July permitted air attacks on 16 additional fixed targets and 23 road, rail, and waterway segments inside the restricted Hanoi-Haiphong area. Bridges, bypasses, rail yards, and military storage areas were bombed in an effort to slow or halt traffic between the two cities and to points north and south. On 2 August 1967 Hanoi's famous Paul Doumer railway and highway bridge was hit for the first time. The center span was knocked down and two other spans were damaged. Struck again on 25 October, another span went down and finally, on 19 December, the rebuilt center span was dropped again.

Despite these successes, the North Vietnamese during the year managed to inflict a steady toll on the Air Force and Navy, and their MIG's were unusually aggressive. The increasing losses led Washington to approve—for the first time—the destruction of most of the MIG bases. Beginning in April 1967, Air Force and Navy pilots repeatedly bombed Kep, Hoa Lac, and Kien An airfields, destroying several MIG's on the ground in the process.

An Air Force reconnaissance photograph of damage at Phuc Yen.

Many of the MIG's flew to nearby Chinese bases. On 16 August 1967, General Momyer told a Senate committee that ". . . we have driven the MIG's out of the sky for all practical purposes. . . ." However, the enemy aircraft returned with improved tactics, and the Johnson administration authorized an attack on Phuc Yen, their principal base.

By early 1968 neither U.S. air superiority, Rolling Thunder, nor air-ground operations within South Vietnam deterred Hanoi's leaders from continuing their efforts to destroy the Saigon government. Although suffering heavy manpower and materiel losses, the North Vietnamese were able to continue the conflict with the help of communist regimes in Moscow and Peking. Washington's military restraints— aimed at avoiding a wider war—permitted foreign military assistance to flow unhampered through the seaports of North Vietnam. In addition, the enemy had almost unrestricted use of Cambodian territory adjacent to South Vietnam for stockpiling supplies (much of it flowing in from Cambodia's major seaport at Kom Pong Som) and for resting and regrouping their troops.

In taking advantage of the opportunities provided by American restraint, the Communists conceived a plan for a major offensive against the Republic of Vietnam in hopes of achieving a dramatic victory—such as they had won over the French at Dien Bien Phu in 1954—which would persuade Washington and Saigon to acknowledge their defeat. Whereupon, in late January 1968 they laid siege to the Marine base at Khe Sanh and then, at month's end, they launched the famous Tet offensive throughout South Vietnam. At Khe Sanh, the allies threw the enemy back with heavy losses. Elsewhere, after initial but brief gains, the enemy's nationwide offensive slowly sputtered out and was

BRIDGE INTERDICTION
NORTH VIETNAM

RAILROAD BRIDGE
PHU DIEN CHAU
18-58-20N 105-34-55E

HIGHWAY BRIDGE NORTHWEST
BAI DUC THON
18-04-05N 105-49-30E

PRE-STRIKE

PHU DIEN CHAU 1.6 NM

4 APRIL 1965

PRE-STRIKE

BAI DUC THON 0.8 NM

8 APRIL 1965

POST-STRIKE

17 APRIL 1965

DESTROYED SPAN

DAMAGED SPAN

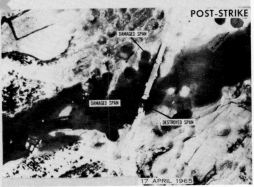

POST-STRIKE

DAMAGED SPAN

DAMAGED SPAN

DESTROYED SPAN

17 APRIL 1965

1

2

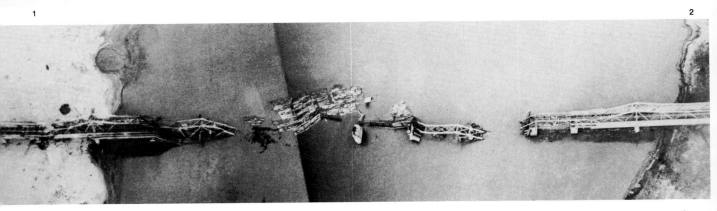

3

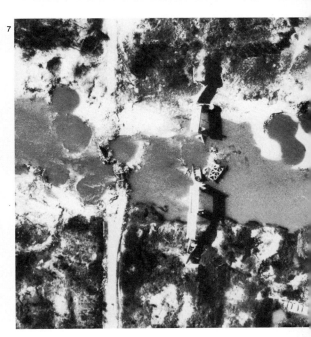

(2&3) USAF F-105's destroyed the Doumer Bridge on 18 December 1967. After the North Vietnamese rebuilt it, U.S. bombers destroyed it again in 1972. (4) RF-101 Voodoo pilot photographs a railroad bridge 135 miles south of Hanoi, April 1965. (5) An RF-101 casts a shadow over a missing span of the My Duc highway bridge in North Vietnam, 22 April 1965. (6) North Vietnamese highway bridge, destroyed by F-105's. (7) Destroyed highway and railroad bridge about 5 miles north-northwest of Dong Hoi, North Vietnam. (8) Destroyed bridge between Yen Bai and Bao Ha, North Vietnam, 22 May 1972.

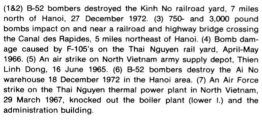

1

2

3

(1&2) B-52 bombers destroyed the Kinh No railroad yard, 7 miles north of Hanoi, 27 December 1972. (3) 750- and 3,000 pound bombs impact on and near a railroad and highway bridge crossing the Canal des Rapides, 5 miles northeast of Hanoi. (4) Bomb damage caused by F-105's on the Thai Nguyen rail yard, April-May 1966. (5) An air strike on North Vietnam army supply depot, Thien Linh Dong, 16 June 1965. (6) B-52 bombers destroy the Ai No warehouse 18 December 1972 in the Hanoi area. (7) An Air Force strike on the Thai Nguyen thermal power plant in North Vietnam, 29 March 1967, knocked out the boiler plant (lower l.) and the administration building.

4

THIEN LINH DONG ARMY SUPPLY DEPOT

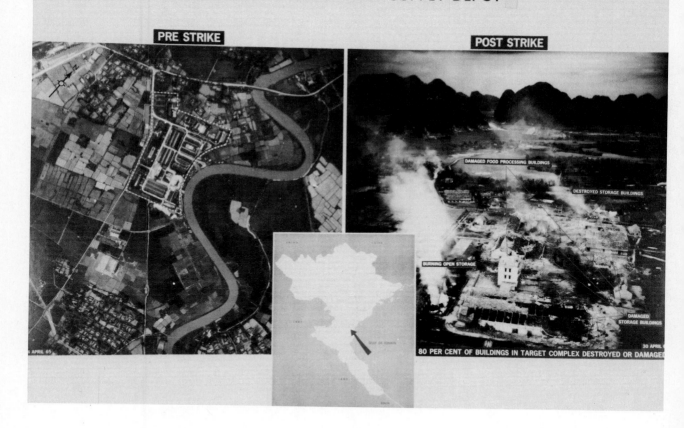

PRE STRIKE

POST STRIKE

DAMAGED FOOD PROCESSING BUILDINGS

DESTROYED STORAGE BUILDINGS

BURNING OPEN STORAGE

DAMAGED STORAGE BUILDINGS

80 PER CENT OF BUILDINGS IN TARGET COMPLEX DESTROYED OR DAMAGED

5

6   7

CHINA

BAC CAN BRIDGE

YEN BAI

LANG CHI

KEP

UONG BI
THERMAL
POWER PLANT

HANOI ★

DONG EM

HAIPHONG

PHU LY

N. VIETNAM

NINH
BINH
BRIDGE

LAOS

GULF OF TONKIN

THANH HOA

SURFACE-TO-AIR MISSILE ENVELOPE
1966

slowed, halted, and reversed. But if the North Vietnamese military campaign did not succeed, it did lead to a change in American war policies. As noted in Chapter III, President Johnson on 31 March ordered a halt to the bombing of North Vietnam north of the 20th parallel, then north of the 19th parallel. As a *quid pro quo,* the Hanoi regime agreed to meet with U.S. delegates in Paris to discuss an end to the conflict. In the meantime, the Air Force and other services virtually doubled their air strikes in the area

below the 19th parallel, interdicting enemy troop and supply movements across the DMZ into South Vietnam. They also stepped up raids against enemy positions in southern Laos.

In Paris, after many meetings and months of deadlock between the two sides on how to bring the war to an end, American and North Vietnamese representatives agreed on a certain "essential understanding" enabling President Johnson on 31 October 1968 to end all air, naval, and artillery bombardment of North Vietnam as of

A sequence of frames showing the destruction of a USAF RF-4C reconnaissance plane by an SA-2 missile, 12 August 1967. The 2-man crew, Lt. Col. Edwin L. Atterberry and Maj. Thomas V. Parrott successfully ejected and were captured and interned. Colonel Atterberry died in captivity.

A North Vietnamese SAM missile.

0800 hours Washington time, 1 November. The understanding, as Mr. Johnson expressed it, was that the other side intended "to join us in deescalating the war and moving seriously towards peace."

Ninety minutes before the President's order was issued, Maj. Frank C. Lenahan of the 8th Tactical Fighter Wing made the last target run in an F-4D against a target near Dong Hoi. Thus, 3 years and 9 months after it began, Rolling Thunder operations came to an end. The Air Force and the other services had flown approximately 304,000 tactical and 2,380 B-52 sorties and dropped 643,000 tons of bombs on North Vietnam's war-making industry, transportation net, and air defense complex. Notwithstanding the variety of constraints imposed on air power, the post-1965 aerial assault on North Vietnam helped to reduce the movement of manpower and supplies going southward and contributed to the 1968 diplomatic efforts to lower the tempo of combat.

Except for Air Force and Navy reconnaissance missions, which were permitted in a separate understanding between the Americans and North Vietnamese in Paris, all air operations over the North ceased. Later—after President Nixon assumed office—U.S. retaliatory air strikes were launched against enemy air defense units which began firing at U.S. reconnaissance aircraft in violation of the above "un-

derstanding." In February 1970, after the North Vietnamese again fired upon U.S. reconnaissance aircraft, the President authorized certain "protective reaction" strikes against NVA anti-aircraft and SAM sites and also enemy airfields. When U.S. aircraft continued to receive ground fire, the President ordered "reinforced protective reaction" strikes on the enemy's air defense system.

The first of these latter missions were flown during the first 4 days in May 1970. Nearly 500 Air Force and Navy aircraft hit missile and AAA sites and NVA logistic facilities near Barthelemy pass, Ban Karai pass, and a sector north of the DMZ. During the next 6 months interim smaller strikes were flown. On 21 November the Air Force launched two major operations over the North. The first involved a joint Air Force and Army commando attempt to rescue American prisoners of war (POW's) believed confined at the Son Tay prison compound, about 20 miles northwest of Hanoi. Planned by Air Force Brig. Gen. Leroy J. Manor and Army Col. Arthur D. Simons, the volunteer commando force flew 400 miles from bases in Thailand to Son Tay in HH-53 helicopters, with A-1E Skyraiders and specially equipped C-130E's providing support. As it landed, Air Force and Navy aircraft launched heavy diversionary strikes in the area to distract the North Vietnamese. Members of the commando force

3

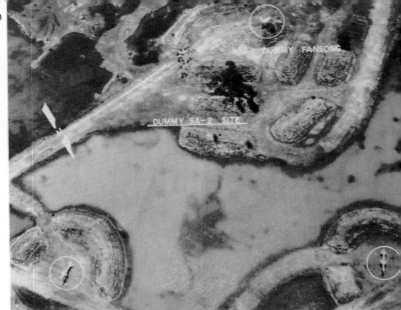

(1) Enemy mobile AAA units near Haiphong. (2) An alert sends North Vietnamese pilots scrambling for their MIG aircraft. (3) A dummy SA-2 site in North Vietnam. (4) Soviet ships delivered not only thousands of trucks to the North Vietnamese but also tanks, rockets, and other implements of war. (5) North Vietnamese 37-mm gunners fire at U.S. jets, August 1965. (8) An SA-2 site in the Hanoi area.

2

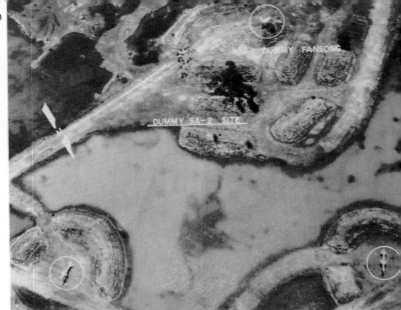

4

USSR MER SHIP VITIM
ENROUTE TO HAIPHONG
10 JAN 69

DECK CARGO 51 ZIL-151 TRUCKS

5

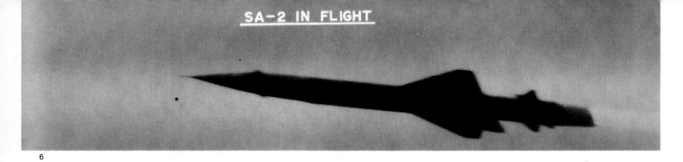

SA-2 IN FLIGHT

6

7

SHADOW OF SA-2 DETONATION

8

20X

FAN SONG RAD

SA 2 MARK II

BAMBOO MATTING

quickly discovered, to their dismay, that the prison compound contained no prisoners. During the 28 minutes the rescuers were on the ground, they killed about 25 North Vietnamese defenders. The only American casualty was an enlisted man who suffered a broken ankle. One helicopter was destroyed on landing.

About 6 hours later, the second operation of the day was launched after an RF-4 aircraft was lost. An armada of 200 Air Force and Navy strike aircraft —supported by 50 other planes— launched a major retaliatory strike in the vicinity of the Mu Gia and Ban Karai passes and the DMZ. Their targets included SA-2 missile sites, enemy trucks, and supply and transportation facilities. All aircraft returned safely to their bases.

During the 2 years after Rolling Thunder operations ended on 1 November 1968, the United States had flown more than 60 separate strike missions in retaliation to ground fire. When the North Vietnamese continued to fire at U.S. reconnaissance aircraft, Washington officials authorized stepped up "reinforced protective reaction" strikes. In February 1971, the Air Force launched Operation Louisville Slugger. Flying 67 sorties, USAF crews destroyed 5 SAM sites, 15 SAM missile transporters, and 15 vehicles in the Ban Karai pass area. On 21-22 March, the Air Force teamed up with the Navy in Operation Fracture Cross Alpha during which they flew 234 strike and 20 armed reconnaissance sorties against enemy SAM sites. In August 1971, in an effort to curb enemy road construction across the DMZ into Military Region I* in South Vietnam, Air Force jets flew 473 sorties, seeding the road with munitions and sensors. On 21 September, flying in poor weather, 196 U.S. tactical aircraft hit three POL storage areas

south of Dong Hoi, destroying about 350,000 gallons of fuel. It was the first all-instrument air strike, employing exclusively the long-range electronic navigation (LORAN) position fixing bomb system.

These intermittent protective reaction strikes—launched mostly in the southern panhandle of North Vietnam —did not affect Hanoi's efforts to rebuild and reconstitute its air force. By late 1971, it had an inventory of about 250 MIG's, 90 of them MIG-21's, and once more it prepared to challenge American operations over the North and, to a limited extent, over Laos. By this time the North Vietnamese Air Force was operating out of 10 MIG-capable bases, 3 of them located in the panhandle area. USAF and Navy pilots, who over the years had achieved roughly a 2 1/2 to 1 victory ratio over MIG fighters in aerial battles, saw the odds drop. However, this was attributed to the U.S. rules of engagement, which again exempted MIG air bases and to the geographical and electronic advantages possessed by the defenders rather than to the superiority of enemy pilots.

To counter the enemy air threat, EC-121 aircraft—which had redeployed from Southeast Asia after Rolling Thunder operations ended in 1968—were returned to the theater to resume their "MIG watch." Once again, as in 1967 when the NVAF last posed a serious threat to air operations over the North, USAF commanders urged that MIG air bases be attacked. Washington officials agreed, and on 7-8 November USAF and Navy pilots bombed airfields at Dong Hoi, Vinh, and Quan Lang. After neutralizing these air bases, U.S. pilots on 26-30 December launched the heaviest

Capt. Lawrence H. Pettit, 55th Tactical Fighter Squadron, discusses his MIG kill with his crew chief, Sgt Horace G. McGruder.

---

*The four corps tactical zones were redesignated Military Regions in July 1970.

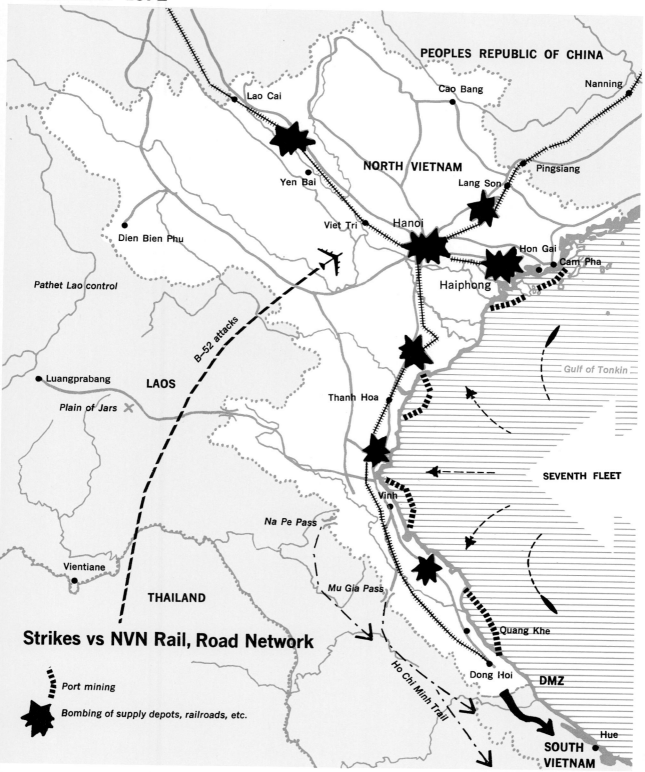

USAF Linebacker II Offensive Against North Vietnam December 1972

PEOPLES REPUBLIC OF CHINA

Nanning

Cao Bang

Lao Cai

NORTH VIETNAM

Pingsiang

Yen Bai

Lang Son

Dien Bien Phu

Viet Tri

Hanoi

Hon Gai

Cam Pha

Pathet Lao control

Haiphong

Gulf of Tonkin

Luangprabang

LAOS

Plain of Jars ✕

Thanh Hoa

SEVENTH FLEET

B-52 attacks

Vientiane

Na Pe Pass

Vinh

THAILAND

Mu Gia Pass

Strikes vs NVN Rail, Road Network

Quang Khe

Ho Chi Minh Trail

Port mining

Dong Hoi

DMZ

Bombing of supply depots, railroads, etc.

Hue

SOUTH VIETNAM

93

air strikes since 1968—1,025 sorties—against a variety of military targets south of the 20th parallel.

The Communist Spring Offensive, 1972

Still hoping to end the war through negotiations, the Nixon administration kept a tight rein on its principal bargaining card—air power. Hanoi, however, was thinking in terms of another military offensive. By late 1971 evidence began to accumulate that Hanoi was planning a large-scale invasion of South Vietnam. Gen. John D. Lavelle,* who in August 1971 succeeded Gen. Lucius D. Clay, Jr., as Seventh Air Force commander, requested the recall of certain USAF units to the theater. By the spring of 1972, North Vietnam had assembled a force of about 200,000 men for a push into the South.

The invasion began on 29-30 March 1972, with some enemy forces rolling directly across the DMZ into Military Region I while others penetrated into Military Region II from Laos. All were supported by considerable numbers of tanks and other armored vehicles. The South Vietnamese army, although greatly improved since 1968, was still plagued by poor leadership and morale and was forced to retreat. U.S. air power—plus the strengthened Vietnamese Air Force—was thrown into the battle. Air Force F-105's, F-4's, A-7's, AC-130's and B-52's were joined by Navy and Marine aircraft in pounding the enemy daily between the 20th parallel in the North and the battle lines inside South Vietnam. Bolstered by aircraft reinforcements from the United States and elsewhere, attack sorties over the extended battlefield averaged 15,000 per month, almost two-thirds of the peak monthly rate in 1968.

---

* General Lavelle was recalled from his post in March 1972, charged with having authorized certain "protective reaction" strikes beyond those permitted by the rules of engagement. He was succeeded as Seventh Air Force commander by Gen. John W. Vogt.

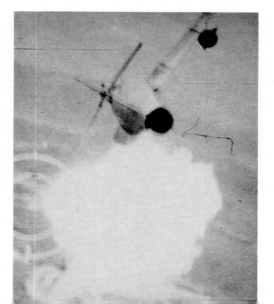

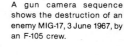

A gun camera sequence shows the destruction of an enemy MIG-17, 3 June 1967, by an F-105 crew.

With Hanoi's forces ensconced inside South Vietnam and determined, despite heavy casualties, to maintain their positions below the DMZ, President Nixon on 8 May suspended the peace talks in Paris and authorized the launching of Operation Linebacker. For the first time, the United States imposed a naval blockade and mined the waters of Haiphong and other North Vietnamese ports. Simultaneously, the President authorized a renewal of air strikes throughout North Vietnam above the 20th parallel. Old and new targets were struck, including the rebuilt Paul Doumer bridge in Hanoi, bridges along the northwest and northeast rail lines from China, fuel dumps, warehouses, marshalling yards, rolling stock, vehicles, power plants, and a POL pipeline running from China. All recently emplaced SA-2 missile sites in or near the DMZ were destroyed as were many SA-2 and AAA sites further north.

To degrade or neutralize North Vietnam's rebuilt or new bristling air defenses, the Air Force made full use of its electronic technology. It employed EB-66's, Wild Weasel F-105's, and EC-135's to augment electronic countermeasure equipment used by most fighter aircraft. It also employed a profusion of laser and optically-guided bombs, which had been developed in the late 1960's. Mostly 2,000 pounders, the guided bombs enabled fighter crews to strike targets with great accuracy. Thus, the spans of the strongly defended Than Hoa bridge—which had withstood U.S. bombs for years and had cost the Air Force and Navy a number of downed aircraft—were dropped in one strike by an F-4 with guided bombs.

By June 1972 North Vietnam's offensive had stalled outside of Hue and elsewhere as South Vietnamese ground forces began to fight back. On 29 June, President Nixon reported that with the mining of the harbors and bombing of military targets in the North—particularly the railroads and oil supplies—the situation "has been completely turned around.... The South Vietnamese are now on the offensive." He reiterated his proposal of 8 May for an international ceasefire and the return of American prisoners of war, warning that the United States intended to bargain from strength. The peace talks resumed in Paris on 13 July. In the ensuing weeks, Saigon's forces, heavily supported by U.S. and VNAF air strikes, continued their offensive against the 200,000 enemy troops who had seized control of large portions of the South Vietnamese countryside.

Meanwhile, North Vietnamese pilots were reacting aggressively in the Hanoi-Haiphong area in an effort to drive American pilots out of the skies over their heartland. The renewed American-North Vietnamese air battles shortly produced several Air Force aces. On 28 August 1972, Capt. Richard S. Ritchie, flying an F-4D Phantom II, participated in his fifth shootdown and became the nation's second ace. (The U.S. Navy produced the first.) His weapons system officer, Capt. Charles DeBellevue, who had flown with Ritchie in three previous "kills," became an ace on 9 September when he destroyed his fifth and sixth MIG's, becoming the first weapon systems officer to achieve this status. Capt. Jeffrey S. Feinstein, also an F-4 weapons system officer, became an ace on 13 October when he helped bag his fifth MIG. These were the only Air Force aces of the war. A Navy pilot and a WSO likewise became aces.

The 11-Day Air Campaign

On 23 October 1972, when it seemed that the Paris talks were leading to an agreement to end the war, the United States again halted air operations above the 20th parallel. Soon after, however, the negotiations

95

(1) Six F-4C crews pose before their planes in April 1966, following destruction of six MIG aircraft over North Vietnam. (2) The first MIG downed during the war was credited to Capts. Kenneth E. Holcombe and Arthur C. Clark, 10 July 1965. Flight commander Maj. Richard Hall gets a ride on the shoulders of the other flight members: (l. to r.) Capt. Ronald C. Anderson, Kenneth E. Holcombe, Capt. Harold Anderson, Capt. Arthur C. Clark, and Capt. Wilbure Anderson. (3) After their 3 June 1967 shootdowns of MIG-17's Capt. Larry D. Wiggins and Maj. Arthur L. Kuster review the tactics they used. (4) Col. Robin Olds, commander of the 8th Tactical Fighter Wing, and other airmen pose on the occasionof the unit's 15th air victory over enemy MIG's. (5) Capt. Jeffery S. Feinstein, a weapons system officer was credited with five aerial victories over enemy MIG's.

2

4

3

5

1

4

2

(1) 1st. Lt. Clifton P. Dunnegan, of the 8th Tactical Fighter Wing, shot down 1 of 7 enemy MIG's destroyed over North Vietnam on 2 January 1967. (2) Capt. Charles B. De Bellevue, credited with six aerial victories, poses with Col. Scott G. Smith and Capt. Richard S. Ritchie, who became the first USAF ace in Southeast Asia. (3) The five general officers shown below are World War II aces with five or more enemy aircraft "kills" to their credits, for a total of 41½ victories-directed USAF operations in Southeast Asia during 1966-1967. They are: Lt. Gen. (later General) William W. Momyer (center, front), 7th Air Force commander. The others are (l. to r.). Maj. Gen Gordon M. Graham, vice commander; Brig. Gen. Franklin A. Nichols, chief of staff; Brig. Gen. Donavon F. Smith, chief of the Air Force Advisory Group in Vietnam; and Brig. Gen. William D. Dunham, deputy chief of staff for operations. (4) Maj. Robert G. Dilger, F-4C commander (r.) and his pilot, 1st. Lt. Mack Thies (center) report to their CO, Lt. Col. Hoyt S. Vandenberg, Jr., how they destroyed a MIG-17 during a dogfight over North Vietnam, 1 May 1967.

3

stalled amid indications that Hanoi might renew its offensive in South Vietnam. Whereupon, President Nixon ordered a resumption of air strikes above the 20th parallel. There followed a final 11-day bombing campaign, nicknamed Operation Linebacker II, which resulted in one of the heaviest aerial assaults of the war. The Air Force dispatched F-105's, F-4's, F-111's, and—for the first time, B-52's—over the heavily defended enemy capital and the adjacent Haiphong port. The tactical aircraft flew more than 1,000 sorties, the B-52's about 740, most of them against targets previously on the restricted list. They included rail yards, power plants, communication facilities, air defense radars, Haiphong's docks and shipping facilities, POL stores, and ammunition supply areas. They repeatedly bombed the principal NVAF MIG bases and transportation facilities.

The North Vietnamese responded by launching most of their inventory of about 1,000 SAM's and opening up a heavy barrage of AAA fire against the attackers, but USAF electronic countermeasures helped keep losses to a minimum. Of 26 aircraft lost, 15 were B-52's which were downed by SAM's. Three others were badly damaged. However, by 28 December the enemy defenses had been all but obliterated and during the last 2 days of the campaign, the B-52's flew over Hanoi and Haiphong without suffering any damage.

Deprived of most of their air bases, North Vietnamese pilots were able to launch only 32 aircraft of which 8 were shot down, 2 by B-52 tail gunners. Hanoi claimed the strikes on Hanoi-Haiphong produced substantial collateral damage and more than 1,000 fatalities. Considering the size of the air assault, the bombing was well controlled and not indiscriminate. Impacting fragments from enemy SAM's contributed to the destruction.

(Above) B-52 unloads its bombs.

(1) Weather observer SSgt Ronald L. Galy and equipment repairman Sgt George F. Hammett, Jr., inflate a weather balloon in South Vietnam. (2) Maj. John A. Lasley and Sgt Hammett prepare to operate a theodolite. (3) SSgt William E. Collins, chief observer of the weather detachment at Phu Cat AB, South Vietnam. (4) TSgt William S. Grady checks weather observation charts and satellite photographs.

On 30 December 1972, President Nixon announced in Washington that negotiations between Dr. Henry A. Kissinger and North Vietnam's representative, Le Duc Tho, would resume in Paris on 8 January. While the diplomats talked, American air attacks were restricted to areas below the 20th parallel. Air Force, Navy, and Marine fighters flew about 20 sorties per day with B-52's adding 36 to the daily total. On 15 January the United States announced an end to all mining, bombing, shelling, and other offensive actions against North Vietnam. On 23 January, the Paris negotiators signed a nine-point cease-fire agreement effective 28 January, Saigon time.

Thus, air power had played a significant role in preventing the complete takeover of South Vietnam by the northerners and in extracting an agreement to end the war. Between 1968 and 1972, more than 51,000 tactical and 9,800 B-52 sorties were flown against the North, most during the two Linebacker campaigns. The tactical aircraft dropped about 124,000 tons of bombs and the B-52's about 109,000 tons, with their "Sunday punch" missions of late December 1972 being perhaps the most noteworthy. An even heavier rain of bombs pounded enemy forces in South Vietnam's Military Regions I and II.

In addition to the cease-fire, the 23 January 1973 agreement provided for the return of all American and allied POW's within 60 days, establishment of a commission to supervise truce and territorial disputes, the right of the South Vietnamese people to determine their own future peacefully, a promise of U.S. economic aid for the Indochina states, and an affirmation of the neutrality of Laos and Cambodia. The United States tacitly recognized the presence of about 100,000 North Vietnamese troops still entrenched in South Vietnam.

Chapter V

Interdiction in the Laotian Panhandle

On 3 April 1965 an Air Force C-130—equipped with flares and accompanied by two B-57's—flew a night mission over routes 12, 23, and 121 in the southern panhandle of Laos. The crews of the three aircraft searched for Communist vehicles and other enemy targets moving down the Ho Chi Minh trail toward South Vietnam and Cambodia. The mission marked the beginning of Operation Steel Tiger, a limited U.S. air campaign against enemy troop and supply movements within the panhandle of southern Laos. It had been preceded by Operation Barrel Roll, another limited interdiction effort aimed principally against Communist Pathet Lao and North Vietnamese troops which began in December 1964 (see Chapter VI). Both were supported by U.S. reconnaissance missions inaugurated in May 1964 to obtain target information.

The Ho Chi Minh trail, consisting of numerous winding roads and pathways, had served for many years as an infiltration route between the northern and southern sectors of Vietnam. During World War II and after, Vietnamese insurgents used it to fight the Japanese and later the French. After Hanoi launched a guerrilla war against the Saigon government, the trail was used by South Vietnamese "returnees" and indigenous North Vietnamese personnel sent to South Vietnam to aid the Viet Cong effort at unseating President Diem and gaining control of the country. By 1964, the trail had developed into a system of many dry-season truck roads and smaller paths for bicycles and human portage. By early 1965 the trail had become the principal artery by which Communist personnel and

supplies reached the northern sectors of South Vietnam.

The first Steel Tiger strikes—initiated a month after the start of Rolling Thunder attacks against North Vietnam—were directed against enemy personnel and supplies moving into South Vietnam through the DMZ or into the Laotian panhandle. Steel Tiger's mission was one of complementing Rolling Thunder. In both campaigns, political considerations were dominant and affected the tempo of the air strikes, which were generally limited in scope.

In undertaking these operations, Washington's primary concern was to avoid involving Communist China and the Soviet Union in the war, while maintaining the "neutral" status of Laotian Prime Minister Souvanna Phouma's government in Vientiane. This had been guaranteed in the 23 July 1962 Declaration on the Neutrality of Laos, signed by the Peoples Republic of China, the Soviet Union, the United States, France, Great Britain, and other nations. Thus, U.S. officials desired to avoid a large-scale air or ground campaign in Laos by any of the big powers which might undermine Souvanna Phouma's fragile regime. Another constraint on USAF operations in Laos was the Vientiane government's desire not to subject its people or troops to the hazards of unrestricted aerial warfare. Accordingly, the number of U.S. strike sorties, the areas where they could be flown, and the use of ordnance initially were severely restricted.

Because of this, command and control arrangements for Steel Tiger (and other air operations over Laos) were

flare is readied for drop uring a night mission

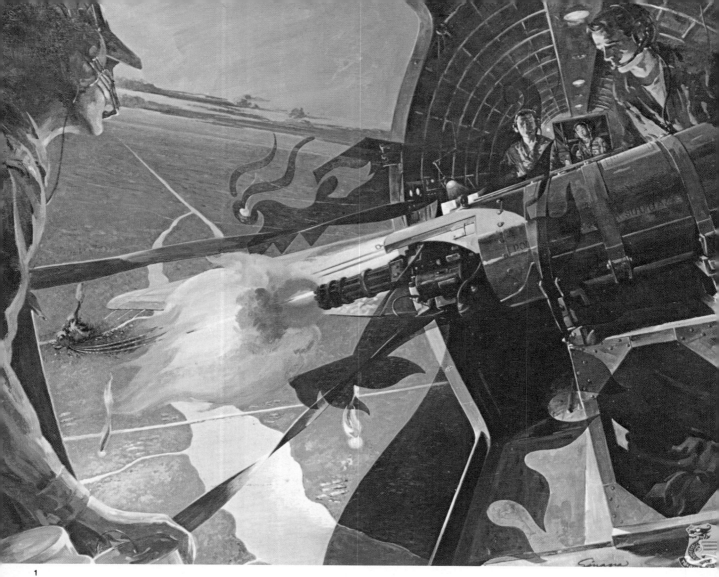

1

(1) A gunship in action (2) Interior of an AC-119 gunship (3) Aerial mines are dropped to interdict an enemy ferry and ford near Tchepone, Laos, 1968 (4) AC-119 gunship over Tan Son Nhut, 1969

2

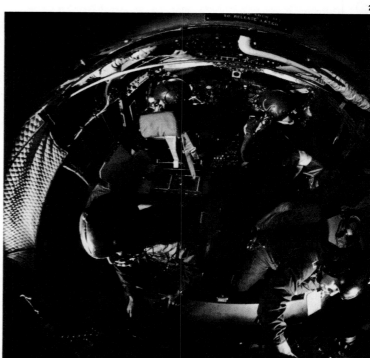

28 NOV 68

FERRY AND FORD

highly complex. The JCS relayed high-level Washington target authorizations to USAF and Navy commanders through CINCPAC in Honolulu and MACV in Saigon. Because USAF planes flying over Laos were based in South Vietnam and Thailand, the U.S. ambassadors in Saigon, Bangkok, and Vientiane also played important roles in controlling air operations. The position of the American ambassador in Vientiane was, however, unique. In the absence of a formal U.S. military command in Laos (such as MACV in South Vietnam), he became the principal American military as well as political authority there. On air operational matters, he normally exercised his authority through the office of the Air Force Attache.

In Saigon, General Moore's 2d Air Division, a MACV component, coordinated Air Force and other U.S. service air units employed in Steel Tiger. To meet political requirements arising from the use of Thai-based Air Force aircraft operating over Laos, General Moore had a Deputy Air Commander located at Udorn RTAFB. In April 1966, when the division was replaced by the Seventh Air Force, he became Deputy Commander, 7th AF/13th AF, reporting to the Seventh on operational matters and to the Thirteenth on administration and logistic matters.

At the start of Steel Tiger operations, the Air Force relied chiefly on the RF-101 and RB-57 for target detection and bomb damage assessment. For air strikes, it employed the F-100, the F-105, and the B-57 bomber—the last normally in conjunction with a C-130 Hercules flareship for night armed reconnaissance. As in the case of operations over northern Laos and North Vietnam, SAC KC-135 tankers were indispensable for refueling aircraft heading to or from targets or target areas. Air Force and Navy strikes initially concentrated on cutting roads and bombing traffic "choke points", particularly along routes leading from the Mu Gia and Nape passes, two principal entry points from North Vietnam into Laos. They also struck trucks, bridges, and troop and storage areas. The Air Force averaged 9 to 10 sorties per day, the Navy a slightly higher number.

Soon after Steel Tiger operations were launched in April 1965, the annual May to October southwest monsoon began sweeping over Laos, sharply curtailing Air Force and Navy operations. Enemy personnel, on the other hand, adept at using jungle growth to conceal their troop and supply movements southward, continued their logistic activities. If the monsoon rains washed out roads and trails, they used watercraft on swollen streams and rivers to transport their men and supplies.

Introduction of New Tactics

By mid-1965, despite the poor weather, Air Force and Navy pilots were flying more than 1,000 Steel Tiger sorties per month. To improve their operations against targets of opportunity, the Air Force placed several F-105's on "strip alert" at a Thai air base. The use of the Thunderchiefs on strip alert (nicknamed "Whiplash") became an enduring Steel Tiger tactic against fleeting targets. Another measure undertaken was to send South Vietnamese ground reconnaissance teams—trained and led by U.S. Army personnel — into the border areas of the Laotian panhandle to locate and determine the extent of enemy traffic along the trail. The first team was flown in and removed by helicopter in October 1965. Other ground reconnaissance teams followed and soon began contributing to Steel Tiger operations by directing strikes on enemy positions, truck parks, and POL, supply, and ammunition stores normally concealed by the jungle growth or bad weather.

As the southwest monsoon subsided in late 1965, the Communists stepped up their infiltration, exceeding earlier U.S. estimates that they would send 4,500 men and 300 tons of supplies monthly into Vietnam. As a result, American and Lao authorities agreed to concentrate more air power on a segment of the Ho Chi Minh trail most contiguous to South Vietnam and used extensively by the infiltrators. Air Force Col. John F. Groom drew up the operational, command, communications, and support requirements for the new air program. Nicknamed Tiger Hound, it began in December 1965. Tiger Hound required more resources than the Air Force had employed in Laos up to that time. An airborne battlefield command and control system was established, involving initially C-47's which were later replaced by C-130's, for overall control of air operations within the strike area. Air Force O-1's and A-1E's, along with Royal Laotian Air Force (RLAF) T-28's, served as FAC's. RF-101's and the newly-arrived RF-4C aircraft, which were equipped with the latest infrared and side-looking radars, also were employed for target detection. UC-123 spray aircraft defoliated jungle growth along roads and trails to improve visibility. The principal strike aircraft were B-57's, F-100's, F-105's, and AC-47 gunships. Substantial Marine, Navy, and Army air joined in the operation. The Army provided additional O-1's for FAC missions while its OV-1 Mohawks, which were equipped with infrared and side-looking radar, were used mostly at night and often flew with Air Force C-130 flareships.

To facilitate the search for and destruction of targets, Tiger Hound rules of engagement were somewhat less stringent than elsewhere in Laos. By the end of December, the Air Force had logged 384 strike sorties in Tiger Hound, 51 of them at night; the other services flew an additional 425 sorties. The chief targets were trucks, storage and bivouac areas, bridges, buildings, and enemy antiaircraft sites. A substantial number concentrated on cutting roads and creating traffic choke points. On 11 December, B-52's struck the Mu Gia pass area, marking their first use in Laos.

In January 1966, the Air Force launched another air program in Laos called Cricket. It involved the use of O-1 and A-1E aircraft, based at Nakhon Phanom RTAFB near the Laotian border, to fly visual reconnaissance or to serve as FAC's in the northern Steel Tiger and southern Barrel Roll sectors. In the Barrel Roll area, the mission was primarily to support friendly ground units; in Steel Tiger, it was armed reconnaissance. Air Force aircraft ranged outward about 300 nautical miles from Nakhon Phanom, concentrating on roads to the south of Mu Gia pass—Routes 12, 23, and 911. RLAF observers flew with some U.S. FAC's to validate targets before allowing the F-100's, F-105's, and AC-47's to strike. The FAC pilots worked with both ground air liaison officers and road reconnaissance teams inside Laos who helped pinpoint targets. Although Cricket was a relatively minor operation, it proved quite effective in destroying or · damaging enemy trucks and supplies.

In early 1966 Tiger Hound operations gathered momentum with each passing month. In March, for example, tactical air strikes destroyed an estimated 210 trucks and damaged about 278 more. SAC B-52's flew more than 400 sorties in the first half of the year, conducting saturation strikes on roads to block enemy traffic and to hit troop encampments, supply dumps, and truck parks. By May, Tiger Hound attacks had destroyed or damaged an estimated 3,000 structures, 1,400 trucks, scores of bridges, and more than 200 automatic weapon and antiaircraft positions.

Recognizing the need for aircraft with a long loitering capability to help

1

2

4

3

5

8

6

(1) View of an AC-119K 20-mm cannon. (2) AC-119K gunship.
(3) An AC-47 fires its miniguns. (4) Loading 20-mm ammunition
on a gunship. (5-6) 15,000-lb bomb used to create jungle landing
zones. (7) An AC-130 gunship at Nha Trang AB. (8) Servicing a
20-mm cannon.

7

locate and attack an enemy concealed by jungle or weather, the Air Force deployed eight slow, nonjet A-26's (of World War II vintage which were re-equipped) to Nakhon Phanom in June 1966. Used in both a hunter and killer role against trucks, these aircraft replaced the older-model AC-47 gunships (which were later succeeded by improved AC-119 and AC-130 gunships). Also in June, the Air Force installed an MSQ-77 Skyspot radar at the base. Its 200-mile range permitted more accurate bombing day or night and in poor weather. The enemy reacted to the increased tempo of air operations by deploying more AAA weapons which took a steady toll of the attacking aircraft.

By May 1966 they had downed 22 U.S. aircraft in the Steel Tiger/Tiger Hound areas. With the onset of the annual southwest monsoons in the spring, air effectiveness again diminished as did the pace of infiltration. To maintain their supply flow southward, the Communists shifted to roads in North Vietnam (route package 1) above the DMZ.

In October 1966, when drier weather returned, the enemy resumed large-scale supply movements and Steel Tiger and Tiger Hound operations intensified once more. From January through April 1967, the dry months of the year in the Laotian panhandle, American pilots flew 2,900 to 3,400 strike sorties per month. In February, in undertaking one of the largest sustained air assaults in Laos, they flew 500 sorties against enemy concentrations opposite Kontum province in South Vietnam, thereby aiding considerably Allied operations against the Communists in that threatened province.

Subsequently, air operational rules were changed following the division of the Steel Tiger/Tiger Hound areas into four zones. In zone one, closest to South Vietnam, pilots had relative freedom to strike targets of opportuni-ty. However, there were progressively more stringent strike rules governing the three zones westward. In those areas targets could not be hit unless authorized by Laotian officers, low-flying U.S. FAC's, or by the office of the American ambassador in Vientiane. In bad weather, all missions had to be under Skyspot radar control.

To maintain an umbrella of air power over the Ho Chi Minh trail, USAF commanders tried new tactics and introduced more specially-equipped aircraft. They also inaugurated the practice of having FAC pilots fly over "target boxes" in the same geographical area on a daily basis. This enabled them to become familiar with the terrain, aided in the detection of the enemy's presence, and simplified the command and control of strike aircraft. The use of additional ground reconnaissance teams led to the discovery of numerous concealed targets or target areas for air strikes. SAC B-52 bombers stepped up their operations, flying 1,718 sorties in the Laotian panhandle in 1967, nearly triple the 617 sorties flown in 1966. The Royal Laotian Air Force flew more T-28 FAC and strike missions, although its main effort continued to be in the Barrel Roll area of northern Laos.

The Air Force's most effective "truck killers" were the AC-119 and AC-130 gunships, the B-57, a few C-123's equipped with special detection devices and BLU bomblet cannisters, and the A-26. Carrying flares and detection devices, these aircraft flew mostly at night when Communist truck travel was heaviest. They also could serve as FAC's, calling in "fast movers" such as F-4C Phantoms for additional strikes. Other aircraft with a FAC capability included Air Force A-1E's, Navy P-1's. and RLAF T-28's. In 1967 O-2's began replacing O-1's and in 1968 the Air Force introduced the larger OV-10 Forward Air Control aircraft. The nighttime detection capability of a few tactical aircraft was enhanced by equipping them with the Starlight Scope, originally developed by the Army for its M-16 rifle. During the last 2 months of 1967 an important advance was made in the Allies' ability to detect enemy movements through the Laotian panhandle. This was a rudimentary, air-supported electronic anti-infiltration system, which consisted of "strings" of seismic and acoustic sensors dropped from aircraft in designated jungle areas. These devices, planted along a number of infiltration roads and trails, almost at once began picking up the sounds and movements of enemy vehicular traffic and personnel movements. The information was transmitted to a high-flying EC-121 which, in turn, retransmitted it to an Air Force infiltration surveillance center at Nakhon Phanom. There data were collated with other intelligence information.

The anti-infiltration detection system had a succession of nicknames, with Igloo White being best known and used the longest. It was another technological innovation for locating an enemy shielded by terrain or bad weather. A unit organized under the command of Air Force Brig. Gen. William P. McBride, named Task Force Alpha, built and operated the infiltration surveillance center. To dispense the sensors, the Air Force relied upon a small number of A-1E's, CH-3 helicopters, and also some F-4D's. Navy OP-2E aircraft also were employed to dispense the sensors. In January-February 1968, after the Communists laid siege to the Marine base at Khe Sanh, General Westmoreland diverted Task Force Alpha resources to its defense. Dropped in the vicinity of the base, the sensors in one instance were able to detect North Vietnamese troop movements and preparations for a large-scale ground assault against the Marine positions. Thus alerted, the threat was thwarted and beaten back by heavy air strikes and Marine artillery fire.

Commando Hunt Operations

As was noted in Chapter III, the Tet offensive and siege of Khe Sanh triggered changes in U.S. policy in Southeast Asia. On 31 March 1968, President Johnson ordered an end to all bombing of North Vietnam above the 19th parallel to facilitate peace negotiations, hopefully paving the way for withdrawal of American troops from the theater while simultaneously strengthening Saigon's military forces. While U.S. air power hit hard at enemy infiltration through the DMZ, the annual southwest monsoon once again reduced Communist traffic in the Laos panhandle and air action against it.

In November 1968, on the basis of an "understanding" reached with Hanoi, the President ended all attacks upon North Vietnam. The enemy threat to South Vietnam, however, remained undiminished. Abatement of the rainy season in Laos, which coincided with the end of all bombing of the North, found infiltration down the Ho Chi Minh trail heavier than ever. To reduce it, the Air Force, Navy, and Marines launched a new air campaign nicknamed Commando Hunt. Its major objectives were to destroy as many supplies as possible being moved down the trail, to tie down enemy manpower, and to further test the effectiveness of the sensor system. Initial operations were confined roughly to a 1,700 square-mile sector of Laos contiguous to South Vietnam. The Air Force employed an array of FAC, strike, and reconnaissance aircraft, B-52's, C-130 airborne battlefield command and control centers, and AC-47 and AC-130 gunships. The gunships proved especially valuable in interdicting enemy truck traffic. In 1969, AC-119 gunships—some manned by Air Force reservists mobilized by President Johnson in May 1968—also flew missions against the trail.

Initially, about 40 percent of all sorties attempted to block narrow road passes, 35 percent hit truck parks and storage areas, 15 percent truck traffic, and 10 percent enemy AAA positions. By the end of April, after 6 months of these operations, U.S. analysts believed that the Commando Hunt operations had destroyed or damaged enough vehicles and supplies to force the Communists to rely more heavily on water routes including the Cambodian port of Kompong Som (apparently with the acquiescence of Cambodian officials). As the pace of the aerial assault quickened, the number of tactical sorties rose from about 4,700 in October 1968, to 12,800 in November, and 15,100 in December. B-52 sorties jumped from 273 in October to more than 600 for each of the last 2 months of the year. During 1968 SAC bombers logged 3,377 sorties over the Laotian panhandle, nearly double the total for 1967. Somewhat greater operational flexibility allowed air commanders in early 1969 facilitated the upward sortie trend. Notwithstanding their rising materiel losses, the Communists doggedly continued to send a substantial flow of supplies through Laos into South Vietnam.

Commando Hunt II, begun in May 1969, coincided with the beginning of the annual southwest monsoon and the usual reduction of enemy movements and U.S. operations over southern Laos. American pilots nonetheless continued to harass or hamper the efforts of the Communists to repair roads and trails washed out by floods. Within North Vietnam, the enemy assembled more manpower, trucks, and watercraft and stockpiled supplies near the Laos border to prepare for the next infiltration surge through Laos after the monsoon abated. They also built a POL pipeline into the southern Laotian panhandle and augmented considerably their antiaircraft defenses. This activity was facilitated greatly, of course, by the end of the bombing of the North and the continued, unrestricted flow of trucks,

(1) A Chinese built truck, captured in Laos, 1971. (2) U.S. Army helicopters supported Lam Son 719 in early 1971. (4) Captured Soviet PT-76 amphibious tank. (5) A North Vietnamese antiaircraft gun captured in Laos by Saigon's troops in 1971. (6) Gunship fires on enemy truck traffic in Laos.

ENEMY TRUCKS 22 MILES NORTH OF MU GIA PASS

guns, equipment, and supplies from China or through Haiphong and other seaports. Gen. George S. Brown, Seventh Air Force commander (August 1968 to September 1970), observed that the enemy had a "free ride" to the borders of Laos and South Vietnam.

Commando Hunt III, launched as the dry season began in November 1969, again witnessed more intense air operations against an expanded flow of enemy troops and supplies southward. The use of many seismic and acoustic sensors, unaffected by darkness and weather, provided considerable data on NVA movements and resulted frequently in more timely air strikes. The AC-119 and AC-130 gunships, and C-123's equipped with bomblet cannisters continued to be the best truck killers. Of the total number of trucks claimed destroyed or damaged between late 1969 and early 1970 (one estimate ranged upwards to 10,000 trucks), the gunships and C-123's were credited with about 48 percent, although they flew a relatively small number of total Commando Hunt sorties. Some analysts believed that no more than 33 percent of the supplies that entered the Ho Chi Minh trail reached South Vietnam while the rest were destroyed, damaged, or consumed en route.

During Commando Hunt III, the tempo of air operations declined gradually. Washington authorities, confident that American objectives in Southeast Asia were being achieved, imposed budgetary limits on the overall U.S. war effort which led to some reduction in Air Force and Navy sortie ceilings. Sortie requirements were reduced beginning 26 February 1970 when enemy traffic in southern Laos suddenly dropped to half of the volume observed in the preceding weeks. Meanwhile, there were requests to use air assets elsewhere. In February 1970, for example, numerous tactical and B-52 missions—the latter for the first time—were diverted to the Barrel Roll

ROUTE 12

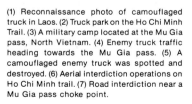

(1) Reconnaissance photo of camouflaged truck in Laos. (2) Truck park on the Ho Chi Minh Trail. (3) A military camp located at the Mu Gia pass, North Vietnam. (4) Enemy truck traffic heading towards the Mu Gia pass. (5) A camouflaged enemy truck was spotted and destroyed. (6) Aerial interdiction operations on Ho Chi Minh trail. (7) Road interdiction near a Mu Gia pass choke point.

112

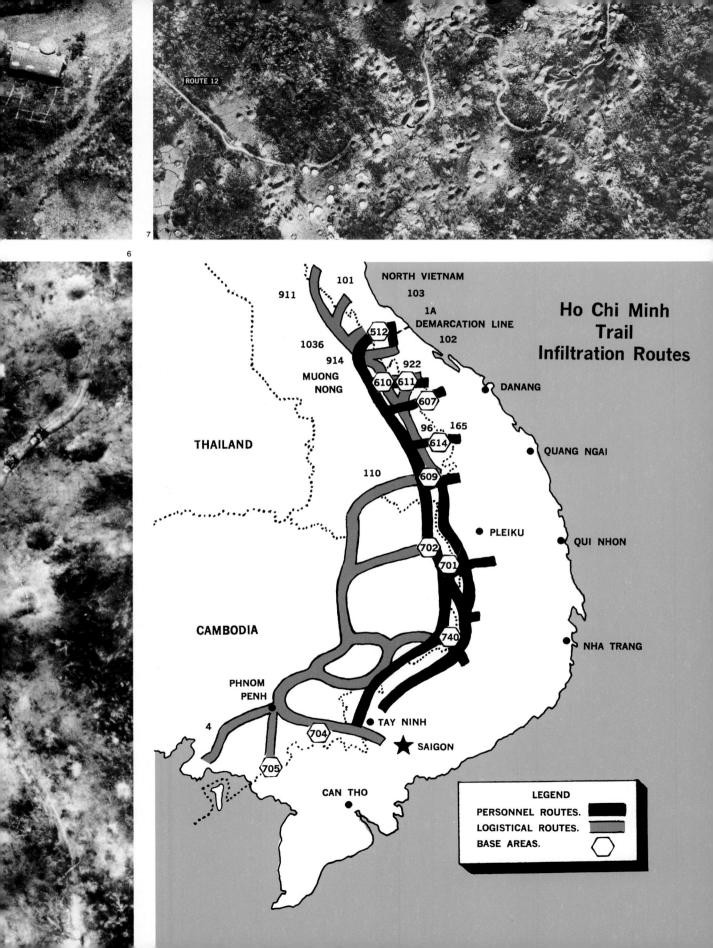

ROUTE 12

7

6

Ho Chi Minh Trail Infiltration Routes

NORTH VIETNAM

101
911
103
1A
DEMARCATION LINE
512
102
1036
914
922
MUONG
NONG
610 611
DANANG
607
96 165
614
QUANG NGAI
110
609
PLEIKU
702
QUI NHON
701
THAILAND
CAMBODIA
740
NHA TRANG
PHNOM
PENH
4
TAY NINH
704
★ SAIGON
705
CAN THO

LEGEND

PERSONNEL ROUTES.	
LOGISTICAL ROUTES.	
BASE AREAS.	

sector of northern Laos to counter stepped up Pathet Lao-North Vietnamese activity there. Other diversions occurred in April and May 1970, when U.S. and South Vietnamese troops invaded the "Parrot's Beak" and "Fishhook" regions of Cambodia to attack Communist base areas and supply concentrations. In fact, air requirements in Cambodia, South Vietnam, and northern Laos for the time being took precedence over those in southern Laos.

Lam Son 719

Late in 1970, attention again was directed to an upsurge of Communist movements in the Laos panhandle. There was evidence of considerable stockpiling around Tchepone, a supply hub on the upper end of the Ho Chi Minh trail, not far from the DMZ. The enemy seemed to be preparing for a major ground offensive into South Vietnam's two northernmost provinces, Quang Tri and Thau Thien.

As the enemy buildup grew, U.S. and South Vietnamese authorities decided to conduct a military thrust across a portion of the Ho Chi Minh trail toward Tchepone with the objective of thwarting the NVA attack and cutting a segment of the infiltration route. As in the earlier invasion of Cambodia, the incursion into Laos promised to "buy time" to insure success of Vietnamization and the withdrawal of U.S. and Allied troops from South Vietnam. Because Congress had prohibited the use of American ground forces in Laos, only South Vietnamese troops were committed to the invasion, supported primarily by U.S. air power. Nicknamed Lam Son 719, the operation was conducted between January and April 1971. Air assets earmarked earlier for Commando Hunt V (October 1970 to April 1971) were diverted to Lam Son 719.

The first phase of the joint South Vietnamese-American undertaking began on 30 October when U.S. ground troops in Quang Tri province cleared an area near the Laotian border in order to establish logistical bases at Khe Sanh and the Vandegrift (Marine) camp. Construction of a new assault air strip and stockpiling of fuel and supplies followed. Air Force C-123 and C-130 transports played a major preparatory role, flying about 1,900 sorties to airlift 12,846 personnel, mostly South Vietnamese troops, and 19,900 tons of cargo to the jump-off areas.

The invasion was launched on 8 February 1971. South Vietnamese troops—drawn from a ranger, airborne, and ARVN infantry division and including some mechanized elements —fought for the first time without accompanying U.S. advisors. Initially, a mechanized unit rolled across the border to establish and secure land lines, while other ARVN troops were airlifted by helicopter to the A Luoi area, south of Route 9 leading to Tchepone. In support of the Vietnamese, the Air Force operated a tactical air control system from the forward direct air support center (DASC) set up and collocated with the U.S. XXIV Corps forward command post at Quang Tri. It also provided most of the O-2 and OV-10 FAC aircraft.

English-speaking Vietnamese flew with the Air Force FAC pilots and aboard C-130 aerial command posts to bridge language difficulties between Vietnamese commanders and ground personnel. Other participating USAF aircraft included F-100's, F-4C's, AC-119's, AC-130's, and B-52's—all for direct support or interdiction purposes. Also supporting the operation were RF-4C's for reconnaissance, A-1E's for air cover rescue missions, and KC-135's for air refueling. C-130, C-123, and C-7 transports airlifted more than 30,000 tons during the invasion. U.S. Marine and Navy aircraft provided considerable tactical support and the Army employed helicopter gunships and hundreds of other helicopters for troop and supply airlift. The VNAF also provided combat and airlift support.

By the end of the first day, 6,200 South Vietnamese troops were in Laos, most of them airlifted to predetermined locations. They built fire bases, conducted patrols, and uncovered numerous supply and ammunition caches. The bodies of many NVA troops were found, killed by air strikes. By 12 February about 10,000 South Vietnamese were in Laos and shortly after their strength peaked at about 17,000. Enemy resistance initially was light to moderate. Meanwhile, U.S. aircraft continued to strike heavily at NVA positions and their LOC's. At night Air Force FAC's, flareships, and gunships provided cover for friendly troops; on 14 February the B-52's launched their first close air support strike. By the 23d, the B-52's had flown 399 sorties, which helped clear the path for the advancing Vietnamese and to prepare helicopter landing zones. Air Force C-130's joined in, unloading 15,000-pound bombs on suspected enemy concentrations and using them to create instant helicopter landing areas.

On 25 February 1971, the North Vietnamese launched a counter offensive. They first attacked the forward support base at A Luoi and expanded their operations in the ensuing 5 days. The size and intensity of their response proved greater than anticipated. Some 24,000 NVA combat troops —supported by about 11,000 support personnel—reached the vicinity of the forward elements of the South Vietnamese force moving westward. The NVA troops were equipped with about 120 tanks, considerable artillery, and a profusion of antiaircraft automatic weapons. The AA guns soon began taking a heavy toll of low-flying U.S. Army helicopters.

With the help of fixed-wing air power, the South Vietnamese briefly contained the enemy assaults and, on 3 March, they resumed their westward drive. On the 7th three battalions reached the area around the logistic hub of Tchepone, the principal objective, where they were joined by two other battalions. Enemy resistance, at first relatively light, grew stiffer between 3-10 March as NVA reinforcements arrived in the Tchepone area. Other NVA attacks of growing strength began to hit the ARVN troops and fire-bases stretching from South Vietnam's border to Tchepone. A number of enemy ambushes inflicted heavy casualties on the invaders.

Faced with mounting personnel and equipment losses, Lt. Gen. Hoang Xuan Lam, the commander of the invasion forces, decided to cut short the operation and ordered a withdrawal. In the hasty retreat that followed, with many personnel being evacuated by helicopter, the South Vietnamese abandoned large quantities of armor, tanks, trucks, and other military hardware. Intense enemy ground fire made helicopter missions extremely dangerous and scores were shot down or seriously damaged, leading to panic among many ARVN troops. However, under massive tactical and B-52 air cover, virtually all South Vietnamese troops were extricated by 24 March. A number of ground reconnaissance units fought a rearguard action as Lam Son 719 officially ended on 6 April.

The cost was high to both sides. The North Vietnamese suffered an estimated 14,500 personnel killed, about 4,800 by air strikes, and unknown numbers of wounded. Aircraft were credited with destroying the greatest part of about 20,000 tons of food and ammunition and 156,000 gallons of fuel. About 1,530 trucks were destroyed and 480 damaged and a NVA tank regiment—with about 74 tanks destroyed and another 24 damaged—was virtually wiped out. The enemy also lost an estimated 6,000 weapons. The South

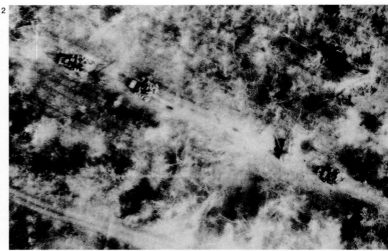

Vietnamese suffered 1,519 killed, 5,423 wounded, and 651 missing in action. ARVN equipment destroyed or captured included about 75 tanks, many armored personnel carriers, 198 crew-served weapons, and about 3,000 individual weapons.

American air support had been massive. More than 8,000 tactical air sorties were flown and some 20,000 tons of ordnance dropped. The B-52's flew 1,358 sorties in direct support of the South Vietnamese troops. U.S. Army helicopters flew thousands of sorties in airlifting troops into and out of Laos, resupplying units, and evacuating casualties. Considering the magnitude of the air effort and the North Vietnamese response to it, aircraft losses were relatively small. The Air Force lost six aircraft, the Navy one. U.S. Army helicopters suffered the heaviest attrition. At least 107 were destroyed and upwards of 600 damaged, many so badly that they would not fly again. American casualties totalled 176 killed, 1,042 wounded, and 42 missing in action. One lesson of Lam Son 719 was that neither the invasion nor the withdrawal would have been possible without the extensive use of air power.

Following the operation, both sides were forced to reconstitute and re-

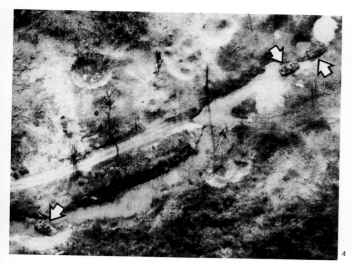

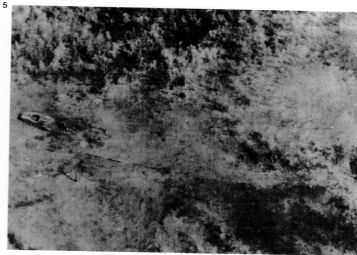

4

(1) U.S. fighter bombers destroy enemy truck in Laos. (2) Four enemy trucks damaged by U.S. aircraft in vicinity of the Mu Gia pass. (3) Air Force fighter-bombers attacked enemy petroleum drum cache on the Ho Chi Minh trail. (4) Three Soviet PT-76 tanks damaged by Air Force fighter bombers. (5) Enemy tanks destroyed in Laos.

equip many of their units. Having suffered by far the largest number of casualties, the North Vietnamese had to replace and retrain many personnel. They also had to repair roads, trails, bridges, and restock stores of food, POL, and ammunition in the battle area. As a consequence, Hanoi's plans for a new major offensive against South Vietnam suffered a temporary setback and bought additional time for Washington and Saigon to advance the on-going Vietnamization program.

Additional Commando Hunt Campaigns

During the annual May to October monsoon in 1971, when Commando Hunt operations diminished, the North Vietnamese maintained an above normal level of activity in southern Laos. They added about 140 miles of new roads to the Ho Chi Minh trail which, by October, brought the total to 2,170 miles—including single lanes, multiple parallel routes, by-passes, and spur roads. They also expanded their air defenses. By late 1971, about 344 antiaircraft guns and thousands of smaller automatic weapons defended vital points along the trail. A number of SA-2 missile sites on the North Vietnamese border and in Laos posed a

new threat, as did rebuilt air bases in southern North Vietnam. The latter enabled MIG pilots to challenge or harass Commando Hunt aircraft. As more North Vietnamese troops arrived, American officials estimated enemy strength in Laos—south and north—at about 96,000. In Cambodia there were about 63,000 North Vietnamese and in South Vietnam about 200,000.

Thus, with the onset of the dry season in late 1971, the Communist threat again was formidable. To counter it, the Air Force launched Commando Hunt VII, extending it beyond the Steel Tiger area of southern Laos. However, there were fewer U.S. aircraft available for Laos because of competing requirements in Cambodia, and North Vietnam where "protective reaction" strikes were under way, and because of U.S. budget cutbacks and the consequent withdrawal of U.S. air and ground units. To compensate for fewer U.S. aircraft, USAF officials called for greater participation in Commando Hunt VII by the indigenous air forces of Laos, Cambodia, and South Vietnam, more flexible employment of U.S. tactical and B-52 aircraft, and the use of the newest technological advances for interdiction.

By 1971, U.S. research and develop-

117

ment activities had wrought many changes in interdiction techniques and ordnance. OV-10 FAC aircraft were now able to direct laser-guided bombs dropped by fighter aircraft flying day or night missions, and also were more effective in assisting air rescue operations. The target-detection and truck-killing capability of the B-57G and the AC-119 and AC-130 gunships had been upgraded. The AC-130 was equipped with a variety of target acquisition devices, including low-light-level television, illuminators, beacon-tracking radar, and infrared sensors. LORAN-equipped F-4's could lead other aircraft not so equipped to targets at night or in bad weather. The Task Force Alpha infiltration center at Nakhon Phanom assumed a more direct operational role while continuing to collect, analyze, and disseminate sensor-gathered data on enemy movements. And pilots had available more deadly types of cluster bombs, more accurate laser-guided bombs, and improved aircraft guns.

Commando Hunt VII operations in the Steel Tiger area of Laos were conducted in three phases. Beginning with Phase I on 1 November 1971, strike aircraft concentrated on hitting several entry points from North Vietnam into Laos, principally the Mu Gia, Ban Karai, and Ban Raving passes and the western end of the DMZ at the 17th parallel. During Phase II, as the North Vietnamese moved supplies further southward along roads and trails in the Laotian panhandle, strike aircraft shifted attacks to those routes in order to create "blocking belts" at key transportation points or areas. These were formed first by cutting a road with laser-guided bombs and then seeding the road area with air-dropped land mines. When ground sensors detected the enemy clearing minefields or bypassing the belt area, aircraft were quickly dispatched to the scene. During Phase III operations in early 1972, U.S. tactical and B-52 aircraft

HIGHWAY BRIDGE, ROUTE 9
TCHEPONE AREA, LAOS
16-42N 106-13E

ROUTE 9
TCHEPONE 1.4 NM
BY-PASS ROAD
STAIRWAY
SE BANG HIENG (RIVER)

This bridge in the Tchepone areas of Laos, destroyed in early 1964, was rebuilt by enemy forces and later downed again.

shifted their attacks to seven principal exit points from Laos into South Vietnam and Cambodia.

Commando Hunt VII operations were completed at the end of March 1972. By then, U.S. tactical aircraft had flown about 31,500 sorties in the Laotian panhandle, with the Air Force flying more than half of this total. As previously, the B-52's participated, flying 3,176 strikes. About 70 percent of the tactical missions were directed against interdiction points, trucks, and storage areas. Many of the strikes triggered explosions and secondary fires, and analysts estimated that the enemy lost many of his trucks and a substantial part of about 31,000 tons of supplies moving through southern Laos during the 5-month campaign. Despite intense enemy AAA fire in some areas, the United States lost only 13 aircraft in the Steel Tiger sector during Commando Hunt VII.

118

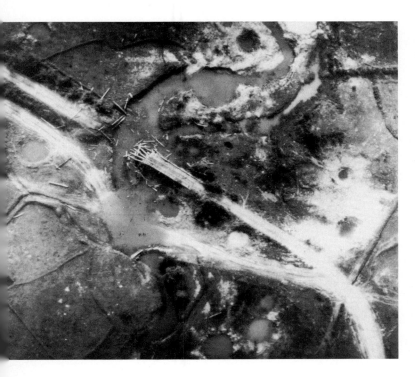

AF aircraft interdicted this
'ge in Laos in 1969.

Air Power Shifts Again

While absorbing its losses in Laos, the Hanoi regime remained free from air attacks north of the DMZ, except for occasional protective reaction air strikes, to build up its troop strength and supplies. In April 1972, as the northeast monsoon began to abate, the North Vietnamese launched their "spring offensive," sending about 100,000 men into northern South Vietnam. The United States responded forcefully, with President Nixon ordering mining harbors of the North for the first time, renewed regular strikes above the DMZ, and a buildup of U.S. units to provide air support to South Vietnamese forces. Augmented by 50 more B-52's, American air units again pounded the enemy. By July, the NVA offensive had been contained, but the North Vietnamese had succeeded in seizing large portions of South Vietnamese territory in the northern and western portions of the Republic of

Vietnam. As a result of Hanoi's spring invasion of South Vietnam, air strikes in Laos dropped to the lowest level since 1965. In September the tempo increased with B-52's concentrating on the Steel Tiger area and tactical aircraft hitting enemy troops in the northern part of the country. In October, as the southwest monsoon declined, the North Vietnamese for the first time in several years did not step up drastically their infiltration activity in southern Laos. The Air Force, in turn, did not launch another Commando Hunt campaign. It continued, however, to fly air strikes against segments of the Ho Chi Minh trail, employing for the first time the A-7D Corsair II for close air support of friendly Lao units and the swept-wing F-111 for armed reconnaissance. Both aircraft possessed sophisticated radar equipment for poor weather operations.

These air missions continued at a low but steady pace until 18 December 1972, when Linebacker II operations were launched against the North Vietnamese capital area, including the port of Haiphong. The 11-day Linebacker II campaign was followed on 23 January 1973 by the signing of an accord, effective on the 28th, Saigon time, between the United States and North Vietnam providing for the release of all American and allied prisoners of war in exchange for a U.S. withdrawal of all combat forces from South Vietnam. However, tactical and B-52 sorties continued to be flown in the Laotian panhandle until 21 February 1973, when the rival Laotian factions reached a ceasefire agreement. The bombing, halted the next day, was renewed on 23 February at the request of the Vientiane government because of ceasefire violations. The B-52's returned to action in April, again in connection with a breakdown in the ceasefire. With the completion of these strikes against targets on the Plain of Jars, all American air operations in Laos ceased.

Chapter VI

Air Operations over Northern Laos

After nearly 9 years of operations over northern Laos, the Air Force on 17 April 1973 flew its last combat sortie in support of the Royal Laotian Government (RLG). Unlike the Steel Tiger interdiction strikes against North Vietnamese traffic on the Ho Chi Minh trail in the Laotian panhandle discussed above, the northern operations, known as Barrel Roll, primarily supported friendly government ground forces—the Royal Laotian Army and Neutralist troops but especially the army of Maj. Gen. Vang Pao, consisting of about 5,000 CIA-trained Meo tribesmen, a mountain people living within Laos. Operating mostly as irregulars, the Meos did much of the fighting, helping to defend an area which included the capital at Vientiane and the politically important Plain of Jars. Northeast of the plain were Sam Neua province, the Pathet Lao capital of the same name, and major east-west roads leading to and from North Vietnam.

Air Force operations over northern Laos had their origins in the failure of the Geneva Accords of 23 July 1962. Signed by the United States, the Soviet Union, the two Vietnams, and eight other countries, the agreement recognized Laos as a neutral, independent country to be ruled by a tripartite government divided among Rightists, Neutralists, and the Pathet Lao. Foreign military personnel—other than accredited military attaches—were prohibited from being stationed in Laos. Thus, the 750-man U.S. Military Assistance Advisory Group—which had been in Laos for about 2 years before the accords were

signed—had to leave, its departure being monitored by the International Control Commission. But on the other side, North Vietnamese forces lingered on in Pathet Lao territory and prevented the ICC from inspections by obstructive tactics which were abetted by the Communist member of the Commission.

When efforts by Prime Minister Souvanna Phouma to form a tripartite coalition government proved unsuccessful, he requested American economic and military aid, including supplies, spare parts, and aircraft for the Royal Laotian Air Force. T-28 fighter-bombers were subsequently delivered to the RLAF, replacing worn-out T-6's. To manage the increased materiel flow, the United States maintained in its embassy in Laos a small contingent of civilians (most of them retired military men). In the spring of 1964, after Pathet Lao and NVA forces launched attacks against Neutralist forces on the Plain of Jars, government troops evacuated the area. This prompted the Neutralist general, Kong Le, to warn RLG officials that without immediate air support all would be lost to the Communists.

Thereafter, with Washington's approval, Leonard Unger, the U.S. ambassador in Vientiane, released the fuzes for the bombs previously delivered and allowed the Laotian Air Force to attack with live ordnance. He also proposed, and Souvanna Phouma approved the use of low-level reconnaissance sorties in early June 1964. Souvanna authorized the use of tactical fighters to accompany the unarmed

121

jets after one of the reconnaissance aircraft was lost on 6 June. Following the second loss of a Yankee Team aircraft, President Johnson ordered a retaliatory strike by eight F-100's on 9 June against a Communist AAA installation at Xieng Khouang on the Plain of Jars.

Three months earlier, in response to Souvanna Phouma's request for help to the RLAF, the Air Force deployed Detachment 6, 1st Air Commando Wing, to Udorn, Thailand. Two of its major jobs were to establish a T-28 flight checkout system for Laotian pilots and to assist with aircraft maintenance. Forty-one airmen, along with four aircraft, opened for business at Udorn in April 1964. Subsequently, as support of friendly ground operations increased, Air Force personnel were assigned to work as ground controllers or forward air guides in Laos, since few Laotians could speak English and none were familiar with procedures for directing air strikes against enemy positions. In early 1965, Detachment 6 began training English-speaking Lao and Meo personnel to direct air strikes from the ground. As these personnel became proficient, USAF airmen withdrew from this role.

When Barrel Roll operations got under way in December 1964, the U.S. ambassador in Vientiane as head of the "country team"—that is, all Americans officially assigned to the embassy—assumed responsibility for the direction, coordination, and supervision of U.S. military activities—almost entirely air—in support of the government. The Air Force attache and a small contingent of military and CIA personnel assisted him.

Although Unger and his successors—Ambassadors William H. Sullivan and G. McMurtrie Godley—did not concern themselves with details of operations (the number or types of planes employed), they validated all targets and none could be bombed without their permission. Strikes were limited to specific areas and conduct-ed under strict rules of engagement.

As the tempo of operations increased, the Air Force in November 1965 established Headquarters 2d Air Division/Thirteenth Air Force at Udorn, some 45 miles from Vientiane to serve as a focal point for Laotian air support requests. The commander, a major general, as the senior Air Force representative in Thailand, had multiple responsibilities: he reported to the American ambassadors in Thailand and Laos on military matters in their respective areas; to the Commander, Thirteenth Air Force for administrative and logistic matters involving USAF units in Thailand; and to the Commander, Second Air Division in Saigon for the combat operations of those units. Thus, the Second Air Division actually issued the directives (the daily "frag" orders) for Barrel Roll missions in the Laotian panhandle. The Udorn headquarters in April 1966 was redesignated as 7th/13th Air Force following establishment of Seventh Air Force at Tan Son Nhut AB, South Vietnam.

The Effects of Weather

As elsewhere in Southeast Asia, the seasonal weather was a major factor in the ground struggle between government forces and the Pathet Lao/NVA in northern Laos. Enemy troops normally became active during the dry season between October and April. In the 6 months of the wet season that followed, the weaker government forces became active. Thus, with the onset of the dry season in the fall of 1965, enemy troops launched their largest offensive up to that time in an attempt to eliminate all government outposts on the Plain of Jars and establish secure lines of communication. The expanded fighting brought a sizable increase in the embassy workload and led the Secretary of Defense to increase the attaché staff to 117 military and 5 civilian personnel—42 of them from the Air Force.

The number of Air Force personnel continued to increase during the next several years until it totaled 125 in 1969. They helped establish Air Operations Centers within the five military regions of Laos, which were jointly manned by Laotian and USAF airmen to manage air support requests. In addition, the Air Force assigned forward air controllers to Royal Laotian Army units and Vang Pao's Meo forces as a means of overcoming the language barrier between them and the strike aircraft crews. Operating under the designation of Raven, these FAC's flew O-1's, U-17's, and T-28's on 6-month tours of duty. And, as necessary, the Air Force deployed a C-47 airborne battlefield command and control center to the area.

Despite the American air assistance, enemy forces overran a number of government posts in Sam Neua province in early 1966, including the key airfield at Na Khang—known as Lima Site 36 (LS-36)—which fell on 17 February. On 20 March a two-battalion enemy force seized a Neutralist stronghold and induced defection of its troops. To ease the pressure on friendly forces, USAF pilots flew 32 strike sorties daily, some with aircraft diverted from North Vietnam and the Ho Chi Minh trail.

The air strikes gradually took a heavy toll of enemy resources, destroying large quantities of supplies patiently built up over the previous year and slowing down his offensive. This success enabled Vang Pao's irregulars to take the offensive with the start of the wet season and recover a number of government posts, including Lima Site 36. By August 1966, the irregulars had reached Nam Bac, only 45 miles from the North Vietnamese border and a major point on the historic invasion corridor from the north. In effect, the Communist Pathet Lao dry season offensive of 1965-1966 had been a failure.

North Vietnam reacted to this turn of events by dispatching 14,000 first-line troops to northern Laos, bringing the total Communist strength to about 50,000 men for the start of the next dry season offensive. As the weather improved during the fall of 1966, enemy forces moved against government-controlled Lima Sites in northern Laos. By early January 1967 they had advanced to Na Khan where the Meo, supported by Thai T-28 pilots (trained by USAF instructors), drove them back. When the enemy tried to overrun LS-52, located some 20 miles from the Pathet Lao capital at Sam Neua, allied air power again saved the day. Frustrated by these setbacks, the Communists on 2 February mortared the Luang Prabang airfield, destroying eight aircraft and badly damaging three others as well as the air operations center. The attack was unprecedented, since both sides had always considered the royal capital immune.

The airfield attack had a major impact on the opposing forces. The government troops became demoralized while the enemy appeared to gain a new momentum. On 4 April, he again struck at LS-52, attacking from three sides. Adverse weather deprived the government troops of their air support and they quickly fled, only to fall into an ambush, and were severely mauled by the North Vietnamese. For the next 2 months, operations were at a low level. Then, on 16 July, the enemy again struck the airfield at Luang Prabang, destroying 10 or 11 T-28's along with a major portion of the government's ammunition supply. The raid left the RLAF with only 38 T-28's. Pending delivery of additional aircraft, Seventh Air Force in July diverted sorties from Rolling Thunder to take up the slack.

After slowly rebuilding his forces, Vang Pao on 2 August 1967 attacked and captured Muong Ngan, depriving the enemy of the year's rice harvest in that area. Both sides then built up

1

2

3

4

5 6

7

(1) Munitions storage area at Vietiane, Laos, 1970. (2) 20,000 Laotian refugees were evacuated from Saravane in 2½ days by three American C-46 transports. (3) A De Havilland transport delivered supplies to remote Laotian bases. (4) An Air Force F-111 takes off from a U.S. base. (5-6) Damage caused by an enemy rocket attack which destroyed six aircraft and damaged three others at the Vientiane airport on 2 February 1967. (7) Royal Laotian forces captured this Soviet-built PT-76 tank on the Plain of Jars.

their forces in the Nam Bac valley in anticipation of the dry season offensive. The government tried to move first, but weather and inadequate logistic support produced costly delays. Then, in early September, the T-28's inadvertently bombed their own troops, who promptly fled. Subsequent air strikes were poorly coordinated and controlled and by mid-October the situation at Nam Bac was critical. A relief operation proved far too complicated to succeed, although Vang Pao's guerrilla force gradually fought its way toward Nam Bac. Finally, during the night of 14-15 January—with Vang Pao's force only 12 kilometers away—the Royal Laotian garrison abandoned the town and fled into the jungle. Of the 4,000-man garrison, only 1,400 were eventually accounted for. They left behind seven 105-mm howitzers, thirty-six 60-mm mortars, forty-two 57-mm recoilless rifles, and more than 1 million pounds of ammunition.

The Loss of Lima Site 85

Following this success, the enemy turned his attention to Lima Site 85, isolated on a 5,200-foot mountain 25 miles west of Sam Neua and 160 miles west of Hanoi, deep within Pathet Lao territory. Accessible from only one side of the mountain, LS-85 was near a 700-foot dirt landing strip which had been scratched out in a narrow valley several hundred feet below. In 1966 the Air Force installed a tactical air navigation system there, primarily for the direction of aircraft headed for North Vietnam and northern Laos. Late in 1967 the Air Force replaced the original facility with an all-weather navigation system, operated and maintained by 19 USAF personnel.

The increased activity on the mountain's heights aroused North Vietnamese suspicions and, on 12 January 1968—in one of the bizarre air actions of the war—Soviet-manufactured, single engine NVAF Colt aircraft (AN-2's) attacked the site, the crews firing machineguns out the windows. At this point an American helicopter with security forces aboard returned fire and shot down one Colt. A second NVAF plane crashed while attacking the site, and a third Colt was chased toward North Vietnam by the U.S. helicopter. The third aircraft was forced to crash land some 18 miles north of the site in Laos. Whereupon, the North Vietnamese sent units to seize LS-85. By 10 March they had captured the landing strip and then advanced up a supposedly invulnerable side to the top of the mountain, where they defeated in hand-to-hand combat some 100 Meo guarding the site. Once there, they methodically destroyed the radar equipment. Of the 19 Air Force personnel operating the equipment, 12 managed to escape and were rescued by helicopters, 4 bodies were seen in the ruins of the facility, and 3 remained unaccounted for.

Following the loss of Lima Site 85, the enemy launched a drive against Vang Pao's troops. Friendly outposts fell one by one while most Air Force and RLAF planes remained grounded by weather. By early May the Communists had massed five battalions at Na Khang, which was defended by some 1,500 men. At this point the weather improved, enabling Allied airmen to fly several hundred sorties which blunted the enemy thrust. In June Vang Pao went over to the offensive and drove the enemy back towards Sam Neua. Before the summer was over, his forces and other friendly troops—supported by some 700 Air Force sorties—had recaptured most of the posts and territory previously lost to the enemy.

At the beginning of the 1968 dry season, when the enemy normally launched his offensive, Vang Pao decided to seize the initiative by heading straight for Lima Site 85. In December, as his troops reached the mountain site, they received heavy mortar fire from the enemy. Whereupon, Air Force FAC's directed numerous strikes against the Communist positions. Seventh Air Force allocated 250 sorties for the operation, 50 being flown daily for 5 days. After the enemy guns fell silent, the Meo recaptured the airstrip. It proved a transitory success; on Christmas Day three fresh Communist battalions from Sam Neua counterattacked and drove the Meo from the area. Lima Site 85 remained in enemy hands.

NVA troops also moved to regain control of Route 7 and the Plain of Jars. By late February they were threatening Lima Site 36, the scene of repeated fighting and the location of the only tactical air control system in northeast Laos. An all-out air effort was launched to save the site. However, so many aircraft were diverted to the scene that the FAC's found it necessary to return some to their original targets because they could not properly handle them. Unfortunately, the enemy troops had dispersed in small groups and the FAC's—assuming they were hidden in the jungle—directed most of the ordnance there. An AC-47 gunship also went to the support of the badly battered government troops. On 1 March, however, after all their officers had been killed, the Laotian troops abandoned LS-36 and withdrew under cover of USAF aircraft.

Following their capture of the site, the Communists turned their attention to Vang Pao's headquarters at Long Tieng (Lima Site 20A). As a countermove, Vang Pao proposed a three-pronged preemptive attack with air cover to seize the main towns on the Plain of Jars (including the provincial capital of Xieng Khouang), interdict Route 7 east and west of Ban Ban, and capture Tha Thom south of the plain. However, his American advisors urged a less ambitious offensive, which he

accepted and which began on 23 March 1969. It involved a two-pronged attack with air support along the plain's western rim with separate advances to the enemy's rear. In advance of the attack, on 17 March, Seventh Air Force and RLAF units launched the first of a series of attacks against enemy targets. During the first 4 days, 261 Air Force and 43 RLAF sorties struck more than 600 enemy structures, including bunkers and trenches. Of 345 targets in the Xieng Khouang area, 192 were knocked out.

By the time these air operations ended on 7 April, the Allied air forces had flown 730 sorties. They were credited with causing hundreds of secondary explosions and fires but, more importantly, they enabled Vang Pao's troops to walk virtually unopposed into Xieng Khouang in late April, a feat thought impossible at the start of the campaign. There they found large caches of supplies, including trucks, jeeps, 37-mm guns, and armored personnel carriers.

Following the capture of Xieng Khouang, the Meo leader launched diversionary attacks on Routes 61 and 7 to force the enemy to withdraw from Routes 4 and 5 south and east of Muong Soui, the old Neutralist headquarters and gateway from the Plain of Jars to the major north-south road between the two Laotian capital cities of Vientiane and Luang Prabang. The Air Attaché in Vientiane requested an augmentation of 50 sorties a day for 5 days in addition to the 70 regular Barrel Roll sorties to support the operation. Unfortunately, bad weather interfered with bombing some 150 targets, and Vang Pao's troops met stiff resistance from enemy units sent from Sam Neua.

At the same time, NVA troops opened their offensive against Muong Soui. About 4,000 Neutralist troops backed by a 300-man Thai artillery unit, defended the town. Both sides

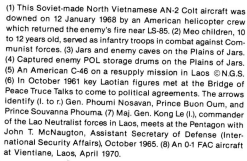

(1) This Soviet-made North Vietnamese AN-2 Colt aircraft was downed on 12 January 1968 by an American helicopter crew which returned the enemy's fire near LS-85. (2) Meo children, 10 to 12 years old, served as infantry troops in combat against Communist forces. (3) Jars and enemy caves on the Plains of Jars. (4) Captured enemy POL storage drums on the Plains of Jars. (5) An American C-46 on a resupply mission in Laos © N.G.S. (6) In October 1961 key Laotian figures met at the Bridge of Peace Truce Talks to come to political agreements. The arrows identify (l. to r.) Gen. Phoumi Nosavan, Prince Buon Oum, and Prince Souvanna Phouma (7) Maj. Gen. Kong Le (l.), commander of the Lao Neutralist forces in Laos, meets at the Pentagon with John T. McNaugton, Assistant Secretary of Defense (International Security Affairs), October 1965. (8) An 0-1 FAC aircraft at Vientiane, Laos, April 1970.

realized that its capture would be a serious blow to Souvanna Phouma's government. Although the Neutralist force outnumbered the NVA troops by three to one, the latter had been ordered to take Muong Soui at all costs. At first light on 24 June 1969, as the NVA launched a tank-led attack, Raven FAC's directed air strikes which destroyed three and damaged a fourth tank. But the NVA pressed on and captured three 155-mm and five 105-mm guns, plus portions of the nearby dirt strip (Lima Site 108). The fighting then died down and remained sporadic for 3 days. By this time the Neutralist troops—traditionally poor fighters to begin with—were in complete disarray and an evacuation was ordered. Sixteen American helicopters covered by support aircraft managed to extract the Thais and Neutralists, including 200 families of the latter. Air strikes destroyed stores and equipment left behind, including nineteen 105-mm guns, 84 trucks and 1 helicopter previously shot down.

The loss of Muong Soui was a heavy blow to the Royal Government. Despite the general gloom, Vang Pao decided to go over to the offensive in an effort to retake the town. On 1 July 1969 the Air Force flew 50 strikes against Communist forces in Muong Soui, destroying 30 bunkers and producing 18 secondary explosions. Helped by their "flying artillery," the Meo met little resistance until they neared the town, when Vang Pao's plans went awry. Some 1,000 Neutralist troops committed to the operation did not move as planned and adverse weather hampered vitally needed air operations. On 8 July only six sorties could be flown; on the 12th, there were none. Without air support, the government advance slowed to a virtual standstill. On 12 July the enemy launched a counteroffensive which overran the government forces, inflicting heavy casualties and ending the operation.

A Major Government Victory

Vang Pao next proposed an operation which one embassy official called the "first major victory in the history of the Royal Government." His plan called for RLG troops to reestablish the government's presence on the southern fringes of the Plain of Jars, while his Meo guerrillas—operating from several Lima Sites (LS-2, LS-6, LS-32, and LS-201) in enemy-held territory—disrupted supply lines to the rear, particularly on Route 7. Poor weather again restricted air support. Thus, although Seventh Air Force scheduled 200 Barrel Roll sorties a day, less than half were executed. The weather improved somewhat in mid-August, and both the Meo and Royal Army forces were able to chalk up some good progress. The latter cleared an area along both the southeastern and southwestern edges of the plain. Vang Pao's guerrillas, supported by heavy air strikes, gathered momentum far beyond what was originally expected, cleared sizable areas around the Lima sites, and cut enemy lines of communication, particularly on Route 7. The jubilant general pressed his advantage, assisted by some 200 Barrel Roll sorties daily.

Aerial reconnaissance soon disclosed that Allied air operations had deprived the enemy of fuel and ammunition and caused him to abandon his tanks and trucks in major portions of the Plain of Jars. Government troops moved in quickly and on 12 September reoccupied Xieng Khouang, meeting no opposition. They captured enormous caches of supplies, including more than 3 million rounds of ammunition, 150,000 gallons of gasoline, 12 tanks, 30 trucks, and 13 jeeps. On 28 September government forces retook Muong Soui, again without opposition.

But with the start of the 1969-1970 dry season, the enemy once again became active, particularly along

Route 7 and the northern portions of the Plain of Jars, where battalion and company-sized engagements increased. Air sorties in the region declined as the Air Force shifted its attention to the Ho Chi Minh trail. Taking advantage of the air lull, fresh NVA troops moved back into northern Laos, and their construction crews set about repairing roads leading southward. By December, a vigorous North Vietnamese offensive was well under way. On the other hand, the Meo—untrained in conventional warfare—were weary. Indeed, after more than 8 years of fighting, they had suffered so many casualties that 10 and 12 year old boys formed a substantial portion of their force.

The results of the expanding fighting were predictable. On 12 January 1970, NVA forces captured Phou Nok Kok, the northeast entry point to the Plain of Jars on Route 7. In February Xieng Khouang and its airstrip fell as the youthful Meo panicked and fled at the sight of the advancing tanks. The town's garrison of 1,500 men also walked away.

At this point, the United States resorted to the B-52, using it for the first time to attack enemy positions in northern Laos. CINCPAC had earlier proposed such an operation when Communist forces had threatened the royal capital. But it was not until 7 months later that Washington authorities approved the use of the B-52's to support the Laotian government. The first raid took place on 17-18 February 1970. In 36 sorties, the B-52's dropped 1,078 tons of munitions on NVA and Pathet Lao positions on the Plain of Jars, causing many secondary explosions and inflicting numerous casualties. Thereafter, until 1973, the Stratofortresses flew several thousand sorties against enemy targets in northern Laos.

With the momentum gained from the easy capture of Xieng Khouang, the NVA moved on Muong Soui. On 24

February, at the first sign of the approaching enemy, the town's 120-man defending force fled. Thus, almost overnight the government position on the plain had collapsed and the positions of the two sides were back to that of a year earlier. At this point, Vang Pao's immediate concern was to secure his main headquarters at Long Tieng (LS-20A). He deployed his troops along a string of hilltop sites, forming them into a crescent-shaped line around the southwest corner of the plain. USAF crews supported him with numerous interdiction strikes along Route 7 in an attempt to hinder enemy supply movements. Additionally, after sunset each day, other aircraft seeded the road with antipersonnel mines to delay repair of the bombed roadbed. AC-47, AC-119, and AC-130 gunships flew nightly, attacking truck traffic. Despite these efforts, the enemy managed to circle undetected to the rear of Vang Pao's troops and, on 17 March 1970 appeared around Sam Thong and Long Tieng. Early on the 18th, the Communist troops were spotted only 2 miles from the camp, and the airstrip at Sam Thong came under heavy attack. Despite poor weather, Seventh Air Force dispatched strike aircraft but thick haze and smoke interfered with the pilots' ability to locate communist positions.

Just when things appeared darkest, Thai reinforcements arrived and positioned themselves on the south ridge. Other government reinforcements were airlifted in on the 19th, increasing friendly forces to about 2,000 men. The enemy, who had occupied portions of the skyline ridge overlooking the airstrip, began firing into the valley. RLAF T-28 strikes on their position initially had little effect. USAF A-1's and T-28's during the next 2 days joined in the attacks on the NVA troops.

On 24 March, with the weather clearing, USAF and RLAF sorties plus ground artillery pounded the enemy

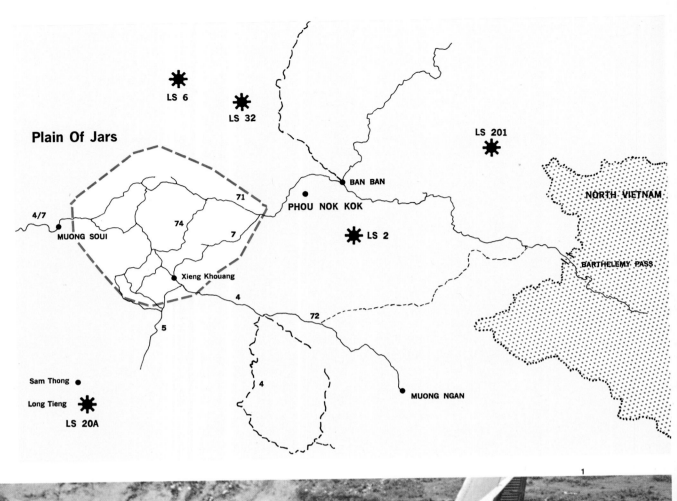

Plain Of Jars

LS 6

LS 32

LS 201

NORTH VIETNAM

4/7

74

71

7

BAN BAN

PHOU NOK KOK

LS 2

MUONG SOUI

BARTHELEMY PASS

Xieng Khouang

4

5

72

4

Sam Thong

Long Tieng

MUONG NGAN

LS 20A

1

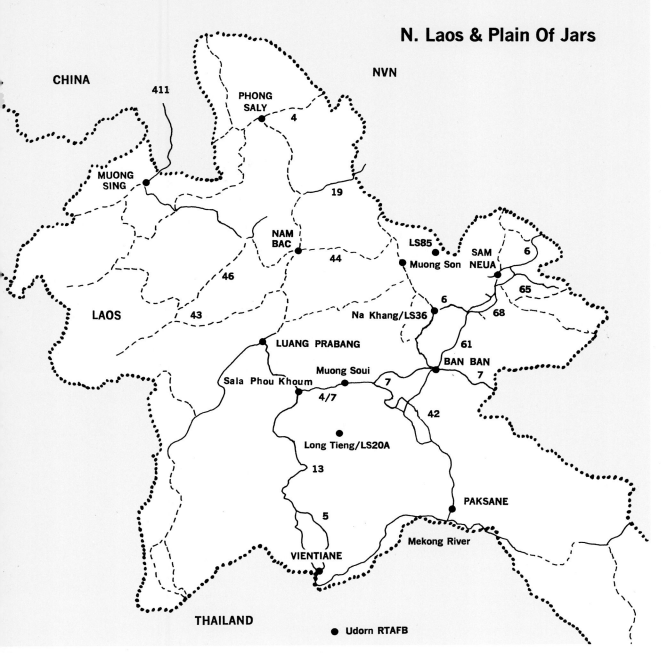

N. Laos & Plain Of Jars

CHINA

NVN

411

PHONG
SALY

4

MUONG
SING

19

NAM
BAC

LS85

SAM
NEUA

6

Muong Son

44

46

6

65

LAOS

43

Na Khang/LS36

68

LUANG PRABANG

61

BAN BAN

7

Muong Soui

7

Sala Phou Khoum

4/7

42

Long Tieng/LS20A

13

PAKSANE

5

Mekong River

VIENTIANE

THAILAND

● Udorn RTAFB

2

(1) Off-loading supplies from Lima Site 32 in Laos. (2) A 155-mm howitzer at Lima Site 15 at Ban Na, Laos.

133

1

2

on the ridgeline. During the afternoon the Meo moved out to clear the NVA from the ridge, succeeded, and then beat off an enemy counterattack. The next day, as more Royal Army reinforcements arrived, the RLAF flew 43 sorties even though the weather again deteriorated. On 26 March, after Seventh Air Force launched 185 sorties, the NVA departed the area, with Vang Pao's troops following cautiously behind. Long Tieng had been saved.

During the next 2 years the struggle between government and Communist forces continued to swing back and forth with the monsoon seasons, but the enemy clearly was on the ascendancy. Thus, by March 1971—a year after Long Tieng had survived the enemy's 1970 offense—Communist troops returned to the skyline ridge and seized new positions, although this time they did not try to capture Vang Pao's headquarters. The Meo leader's subsequent wet season offensive, launched in April, initially was successful in driving NVA forces from the Long Tieng

area. However, by late August the offensive had stalled.

The government had managed to hang on to certain positions on the northern portion of the Plain of Jars, but by year's end they had been virtually eliminated by five NVA regiments, which were equipped with 130-mm guns. These units then moved out against Long Tieng once more. To try to stop the enemy's advance, the Royal Government in January 1972 brought in reinforcements and launched some 1,500 strike sorties. The Seventh Air Force flew almost as many. Despite these attacks, the enemy by mid-March were back in the vicinity of Long Tieng and began employing their 130-mm guns to batter government positions. The guns, difficult to spot from the air, were even more difficult to hit. Several were finally destroyed by USAF laser-guided bombs, but the enemy replaced them and continued long distance shelling. At the start of the wet season in mid-April, the Communists again withdrew from the Long Tieng area but this time

(1) LS-161 area of Laos. (2) Gen Vang Pao, commander of Meo forces. (3) An American C-46 lands at a Laotian base. © N.G.S. (4) The Command Post Center at Vientiane, Laos, coordinated air operations against Pathet Lao and North Vietnamese forces. (5) T-28 aircraft at Vientiane, Laos, 1970.

134

no further than a day's march.

In August, after recovering from this latest siege, the government undertook a new offensive, but it was poorly coordinated and ran into stiff enemy resistance. By November 1972 the Communists were a scant 16 miles from Long Tieng, the best position they had ever had prior to launching their annual dry season offensive. To ease the threat, the Air Force launched a heavy B-52 and F-111 air attack against enemy troop and artillery positions, which also came under fire from other USAF aircraft. This intensive air campaign completely overwhelmed the North Vietnamese and Pathet Lao, who broke off the siege.

Meanwhile, peace talks between the contending Lao factions had gotten under way. On 10 November 1972 Premier Souvanna Phouma received the ranking member of the Pathet Lao delegation, Phoumi Vongvichit, in Vientiane. Anticipating an in-place ceasefire in the near future, the Communist forces undertook to eliminate the last government enclaves in the northern portions of the Plain of Jars, rather than try another offensive against Long Tieng. By year's end, some of these posts had managed to hold out with the help of aerial resupply and tactical strikes.

On 21 February 1973, less than a month after North Vietnam and the United States signed a ceasefire agreement, the Laotians followed suit. U.S. bombing operations were promptly halted, only to be renewed on 23 February at the request of the Vientiane government after Communist ceasefire violations. On that date, the B-52's launched a heavy attack against enemy positions near Paksong on the Bolovens Plateau. A second enemy ceasefire infringement brought the Stratofortresses back in April with a final strike south of the Plain of Jars. When the dust settled, some 9 years of USAF operations over Laos came to an end.

Chapter VII

Air War in Cambodia

One of the issues that troubled American military leaders was the Presidential prohibition against allied operations into North Vietnamese and Viet Cong sanctuaries in Cambodia and Laos. As early as January 1964, General Taylor, then Chairman of the Joint Chiefs of Staff, noted to Secretary McNamara that the war was being fought entirely on Communist terms. The enemy, he said

> ...has determined the locale, the timing and the tactics of the battle while our own actions are essentially reactive. One reason for this is the fact that we have obliged ourselves to labor under self-imposed restrictions with respect to impending external aid to the Viet Cong. These restrictions include keeping the war within the boundaries of South Vietnam.

But in January 1965 President Johnson hoped to avoid a major expansion of the war. However, aware that a serious problem existed, he approved a series of small, covert cross-border military operations. Initiated on 1 February, they involved small-scale American and Vietnamese hit-and-run raids against enemy lines of communication in southern North Vietnam and the Laotian panhandle. These initial cross-border operations proved so successful that Secretary McNamara on 16 March recommended their continuance on a larger scale. He reiterated, however, that the existing "in-country" war strategy was "generally sound and adequate." But there were contrary views. For example, the Director of Central Intelligence, John A. McCone, argued that the allied program would never be completely satisfactory "so long as it permits the Viet Cong a sanctuary in Cambodia and Laos and a continuing uninterrupted and unmolested source of support and reinforcement from North Vietnam through Laos."

Periodically, the Joint Chiefs of Staff would suggest specific measures to take the initiative from the enemy. Thus, in August 1964 they proposed breaking up Viet Cong sanctuaries in the Cambodia-South Vietnam border area "through the conduct of 'hot pursuit' operations...as required." The President rejected the recommendation at that time and again in 1965 and 1966. In early 1966 Premier Ky pressed U.S. officials for action against the Cambodian sanctuaries. The administration, however, continued to forbid such operations except for self-defense in emergency situations, such as "shooting across the border." In September 1966 General Westmoreland became increasingly concerned about the threat of large enemy forces in Laos, Cambodia, and North Vietnam. His staff studied possible courses of action to counter them, but there was no change in the President's policy prohibiting border crossings.

In March 1967 South Vietnam's leaders met with President Johnson on Guam and again expressed their frustration over the enemy sanctuaries. The President replied that he was just as concerned as they were but did not pursue the issue further. Five months later, Admiral Sharp raised the subject while appearing before a Senate Special Investigating Subcommittee examining restrictions imposed on the air war against North Vietnam. Sharp complained that the allies were limited to essentially "defense" actions, but the enemy attacked "from sanctuaries across the DMZ, from Laos, and from Cambodia, and moves his forces at will across these borders." Political restraints, the admiral noted, had ruled out ground operations to deprive the enemy of those sanctuaries.

t. Laird Johnson, 8th ical Fighter Wing, cks his F-4 ordnance r to flying the unit's last bat mission in Southeast

1

2 3

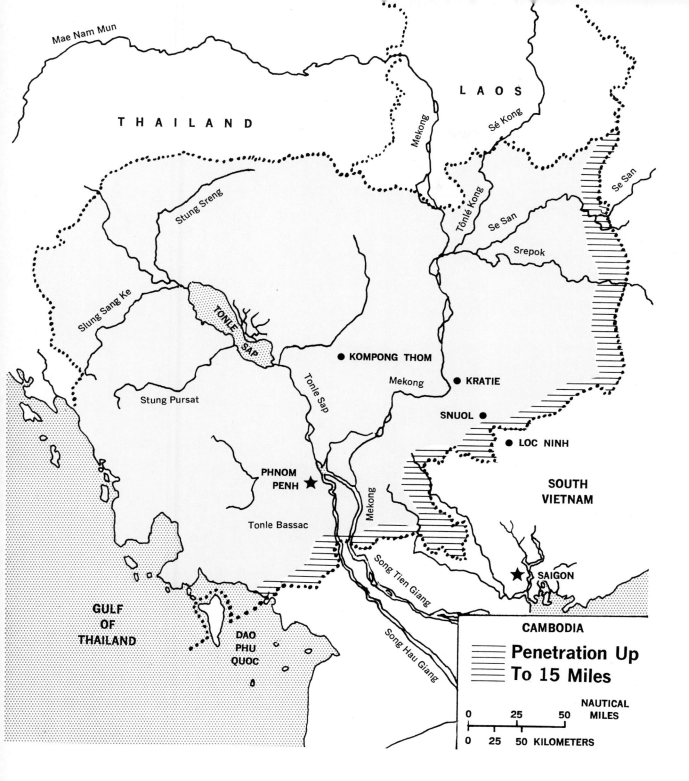

THAILAND

Mae Nam Mun

LAOS

Mekong

Sé Kong

Stung Sreng

Tônlé Kong

Se San

Se San

Srepok

Slung Sang Ke

TONLE SAP

Stung Pursat

● KOMPONG THOM

Mekong

● KRATIE

Tonle Sap

SNUOL ●

● LOC NINH

PHNOM
PENH ★

SOUTH
VIETNAM

Tonle Bassac

Mekong

★ SAIGON

Song Tien Giang

CAMBODIA

GULF
OF
THAILAND

DAO
PHU
QUOC

Song Hau Giang

Penetration Up
To 15 Miles

NAUTICAL
MILES

0   25   50

0   25   50 KILOMETERS

(1) Allied forces seized enemy rice supplies. (2) A cache of enemy rifles and
other weapons in Cambodia. (3) An Air-Force F-4 of the 366th Tactical Fighter
Wing, Da Nang AB, sweeps through smoke of a previous strike to lay its ordnance on an enemy bunker complex in the Fish Hook area of Cambodia.

139

Some 4 months later a prestigious voice was heard on the subject. From his retirement home at Gettysburg, Pa., former President Eisenhower on 24 November 1967 publicly advocated "hot pursuit, even in the air," into Cambodia and Laos "to remove a thorn in our sides." Apparently as a direct result of Eisenhower's remarks —endorsed by Gen. Omar N. Bradley, a former chairman of the JCS—the Department of State on 4 December dispatched a diplomatic note to Cambodia complaining about the use of its territory by the Communists. "The root cause of incidents affecting Cambodia territory," the department said, "is the Viet Cong and North Vietnamese presence in the frontier region and their use of Cambodian territory in violation of the neutrality of Cambodia."

Cambodia's leader, Prince Norodom Sihanouk, on 24 December officially denied that "foreign armed forces" were implanted on Cambodian soil. However, in an interview appearing in the *Washington Post* on 29 December, Sihanouk conceded that "small units" of Communist forces had entered Cambodia "under pressure from American forces." He went on to suggest that "if limited combat breaks out between American and Vietnam [Communist] forces" in uninhabited areas of Cambodia, "it goes without saying that we would not interfere militarily." The Cambodian chief suggested that President Johnson send an emissary, preferably Sen. Mike Mansfield, to Phnom Penh to discuss possible U.S. military actions against Communist forces inside his country.

On 1 January 1968, responding to a press conference query, President Johnson said that he had read the account "with a great deal of interest —and I might say pleasure," and that Sihanouk's remarks were being studied. Three days later the White House announced the U.S. ambassador to

India, Chester A. Bowles, would soon meet with Sihanouk. Secretary of State Dean Rusk, asked whether Sihanouk's message indicated the door was open for "hot pursuit into his territory," responded that it was a "hypothetical question." He said that if the Cambodian government could assure its own neutrality and territorial integrity with the aid of the International Control Commission, then the question would not arise.

On 8 January the first of several meetings between Ambassador Bowles and Prince Sihanouk took place in Phnom Penh. The envoy also met with the Cambodian prime minister and other government officials. During subsequent discussions with Sihanouk, the ambassador assured him that the United States had no desire to conduct military operations inside his country. Sihanouk accepted these assurances and later told Bowles that "he would not object to the United States engaging in 'hot pursuit' in unpopulated areas of Cambodia." He added that he could not say this publicly or officially.

What President Johnson thought of Bowles' report and what operations he planned to authorize is not known. Whatever these plans, they were aborted at the end of January when Communist forces—operating out of Cambodia, Laos, and North Vietnam— launched their famous Tet offensive throughout South Vietnam. In the early weeks of fighting, NVA and Viet Cong troops temporarily occupied dozens of South Vietnamese cities and towns, including portions of the ancient capital of Hue. As noted in Chapter II, the 1968 Tet offensive killed and injured thousands of people and wreaked enormous physical damage in South Vietnam. Among its victims, politically, was President Johnson. On 31 March he announced that he would not seek re-election and invited Hanoi to negotiate a settlement of the war. As an inducement, he ordered a halt to bombing of most of North Vietnam. In May 1968 the negotiations got under way in Paris, but quickly bogged down. On 31 October, in a final effort to obtain a settlement before he left office, Mr. Johnson ordered a total ban on air, naval, and artillery bombardment of North Vietnam. But he also warned Hanoi that the end of U.S. operations above the DMZ "must not risk the lives of our men and that the United States would react in such a situation."

President Nixon Orders the Bombing of Cambodia

The North Vietnamese claimed credit for the "overthrow" of the Johnson administration by the U.S. electorate. They also apparently decided to keep up the pressure on the new President, Richard M. Nixon. Thus, the new chief executive had scarcely assumed office in January 1969 when the enemy launched another, if smaller, nationwide offensive on 23 February, shelling Saigon, scores of other cities and towns, and numerous military bases. Not surprisingly, the President concluded that North Vietnam had no intention of going along with the understanding which ended the bombing of North Vietnam. He had before him at this time an 11 February 1969 request from General Abrams, Westmoreland's successor as MACV commander, for authority to bomb enemy bases in Cambodia using B-52's. Whereupon, Mr. Nixon authorized the use of the big bombers against the enemy's rear bases in Cambodia and directed that the bombing be kept secret.

Thus, on 18 March 1969—operating under cover of special security and reporting procedures—the B-52 campaign was launched against NVA/Viet Cong sanctuaries inside Cambodia. To insure secrecy—required to protect Prince Sihanouk's position (in July 1969 he agreed to restore diplomatic relations with the United States,

broken off since 1965)—the Defense Department announced these B-52 strikes as being against targets in South Vietnam. The sorties, all of which were flown at night, were directed by ground control radar units. During pre-mission briefings, pilots and navigators of the aircraft were told to react to all directions for bomb release from the ground control personnel. In all, between 18 March 1969 and 26 May 1970, the B-52's flew 4,308 sorties and dropped 120,578 tons of munitions on enemy base camps and headquarters in Cambodia.

Four months after the bombing began, the Cambodian parliament in August 1969 elected a new government headed by Lt. Gen. Lon Nol, the Army Chief of Staff. During the next several months, he and Prince Sihanouk tried unsuccessfully to secure international assistance in removing the North Vietnamese and Viet Cong troops from Cambodian soil. In March 1970, while Prince Sihanouk was visiting Europe, the Cambodian government boldly demanded withdrawal of all North Vietnamese. Shortly after, on the 18th, Lon Nol announced the overthrow of Prince Sihanouk and the establishment of the Khmer Republic. Sihanouk subsequently formed a government-in-exile in Peking. The Lon Nol government soon found itself threatened by an estimated 40,000 North Vietnamese and Viet Cong troops and appealed for arms assistance. By 20 April 1970 enemy forces had taken control of large areas of the country and had cut roads within 15 miles of Phnom Penh. This apparent threat triggered an American/ South Vietnamese invasion of Cambodia to root out and destroy the NVA/Viet Cong forces. From the U.S. viewpoint, the operation was long overdue and essential to safeguard the withdrawal of the bulk of American forces from South Vietnam under President Nixon's Vietnamization policy.

The operation began on 24 April when USAF and VNAF tactical aircraft launched strikes against enemy targets in Cambodia. On 29 April and 1 May, 48,000 South Vietnamese and 42,000 American troops drove across the border. Initially, the tactical air strikes, like the operations of the ground troops they were supporting, were limited to areas within 18 miles of the South Vietnamese-Cambodian border. On 14 May, however, a special tactical air strike was launched against a major truck park and storage area in Cambodia beyond the 18-mile zone, along the Xe Kong river near the Laotian border. In addition to the numerous tactical sorties, there were hundreds of B-52 strikes against the enemy.

By 29 June all American and most South Vietnamese troops had withdrawn from Cambodia. In just 60 days the allied ground forces had penetrated up to 20 miles beyond the border and overrun an area totally dominated by the North Vietnamese Army and the Viet Cong. During the operation, the allies killed more than 11,300 troops and captured 2,300 prisoners. They also captured 22,892 individual weapons; more than 15 million rounds of ammunition; 143,000 rockets, mortars, and recoilless rifle rounds; over 199,000 antiaircraft rounds; 5,500 mines, 62,000 grenades, and 83,000 pounds of explosives. They also seized more than 430 vehicles and destroyed 11,600 bunkers and other military structures.

On 30 June 1970, the day after the allied withdrawal, Air Force tactical aircraft began flying air strikes against enemy forces west of the Mekong River, which were menacing the town of Kompong Thom. When attempts by Lon Nol's troops to advance overland to the town failed despite air support, USAF crews turned their attention to roads leading from enemy-occupied Laos toward Kompong Thom. This interdiction attempt failed, however, because the flat terrain permitted the enemy to bypass cratered segments of the highway. Aerial efforts to defend Kompong Thom finally bore fruit when 182 fighter-bomber and 37 gunship strikes between 31 July and 9 August 1970 forced the enemy to fall back. Similar aerial support—60 tactical and 15 gunship sorties—enabled Lon Nol's troops to recapture Skoun, an important highway junction west of the Mekong.

To improve communications between air and ground forces in Cambodia, the Air Force initially assigned an airborne radio relay station (a modified transport) to the combat zone. Later, an elaborately equipped airborne battlefield command and control center was positioned over Cambodia to direct close air support strikes. Problems of language, however, interfered with operations. Some Cambodian officers understood English, but few Americans could speak the local languages. Since the nearest thing to a common tongue was French, a carryover from colonial days, the Air Force used French-speaking volunteers to fly with FAC's and serve as interpreters. The Cambodians also made an effort to find and assign English-speaking officers as forward air guides with infantry units, thereby permitting direct communication between Cambodian ground commanders and Air Force forward air controllers.

By early November 1970 Communist forces had seized perhaps one-half of Cambodia's territory, including several uninhabited regions, despite the tremendous air support provided the Cambodian Army. When the latter proved unable to keep the highway open between the capital and Kompong Som, the nation's major seaport, allied attention turned to the use of river transport to deliver supplies to Phnom Penh. Delivery of supplies via the Mekong River from Vietnam to Cambodia became essential because of costs and the limited capacity of airlift. Whereupon, Communist forces began interdicting river traffic along a stretch of the Mekong, about 70 miles in length, where it cuts through an area of open flatlands. By January 1971 the enemy had achieved sufficient control of the region to strike almost at will against river traffic, firing from ambush with rocket launchers and recoilless rifles. To ensure the capital's survival, the allies instituted a convoy system, with as many as 46 ships and small craft of the South Vietnamese Navy escorting 10 or more merchantmen and tankers at a time.

USAF planes and Army helicopters assisted Cambodian and South Vietnamese airmen in providing air cover for the convoys. Later, U.S. Navy planes and helicopters also escorted the convoys. Because so many villages dotted the Mekong's banks, a forward air controller had to be present during such air escort operations. During an ambush, the FAC solicited strike clearance from officers familiar with the area so as not to endanger noncombatants. Only after the FAC received strike authorization could the aerial escorts expend their munitions. Similarly, when friendly troops were involved in clearing operations along river banks, tight control over allied aircraft strikes was necessary.

During the summer of 1971 U.S. air units supported Cambodian operations to reopen the Phnom Penh-Kompong Som highway and the road to Kompong Thom. The latter drive occurred in September and was judged a success. The most important USAF action was taken against an enemy force deployed in a rubber plantation near Chamkar Andong. The aerial attack forced the enemy to abandon his entrenchments there. A napalm strike upon the village of Kompong Thmar routed the defenders and destroyed their munitions stockpile. On the other hand, the enemy got close enough to

Phnom Penh to bombard the airport with artillery shells and rockets, causing extensive damage to Cambodian Air Force planes. Communist rockets also hit an oil depot near the capital in September, destroying about 40 percent of Cambodia's fuel storage capacity and millions of gallons of petroleum. The United States replaced the loss with increased POL shipments.

During 1971 the Lon Nol government continued to require the military assistance of South Vietnam and U.S. air power. On several occasions, Saigon forces ventured across the border to attack NVA bases and supply dumps. During one such operation in June, the NVA badly mauled an ARVN task force which fell back in confusion. Because of poor flying weather, the troops initially lacked air support. As the skies cleared, hundreds of sorties were launched against the North Vietnamese. In September and October, ARVN troops were more successful. After stopping an enemy attack upon their positions along the Cambodian border, ARVN troops on 20 September went over to the offensive and reopened the highway between Tay Ninh, South Vietnam, and Krek, Cambodia. While the Vietnamese did the fighting, 1,500 U.S. troops moved behind them in a supporting position inside South Vietnam. Enemy targets in the Tay Ninh-Krek area took a battering from the air, with B-52's dropping 1,000 tons of bombs on the first day of the operation. As the sweep was ending, however, an American fighter-bomber accidentally attacked a South Vietnamese unit, killing 18 and wounding 7.

In Peking, where he was living in exile, Prince Sihanouk claimed that Lon Nol clung to power "only through the intervention of the U.S. Air Force." While somewhat exaggerated, the fact was that air power had influenced those battles in which trained and motivated Cambodian troops had

Among the Soviet and Chinese manufactured weapons seized during the allied incursion into Cambodia were 22,800 individual weapons, more than 15 million rounds of ammunition, and 143,000 rockets, mortars and recoilless rifle rounds.

proved successful. On the other hand, allied air power could not save ill-trained, poorly led units from defeat. As the Cambodians suffered repeated setbacks, their reliance on South Vietnamese ground forces increased. Early in 1972, ARVN troops were withdrawn in anticipation of an enemy attack on the South Vietnamese capital. When it failed to materialize, the troops were sent back to Cambodia where they launched several operations into enemy-held territory.

One of these ARVN incursions in March 1972 proved especially successful. The South Vietnamese, supported by B-52 strikes, seized enough rice from the enemy to feed 10,000 men for 3 months. Also, one B-52 raid caused spectacular damage; the advancing infantry found the bombs had made a direct hit, shattering bunkers of reinforced concrete, killing the occupants, and destroying supplies stored inside. Nevertheless, the enemy still remained in control of large portions of Cambodia east of the Mekong, but still proved incapable of capturing the capital and ousting Lon Nol. U.S. aircrews continued to fly missions against them, even after the ceasefire in South Vietnam became effective in January 1973.

By this time a major portion of the enemy forces threatening the capital were local insurgents of the Khmer

Rouge. When they launched an assault on Phnom Penh early in 1973, Cambodia's government quickly requested American help and a massive bombardment got under way. By May an armada of USAF aircraft—including B-52's, F-111's, A-7's, and AC-130's —were launching repeated strikes against enemy targets on the outskirts of the capital. At times, crowds gathered on the west bank of the Mekong to watch them hit Khmer Rouge forces on the opposite shore. Eighty percent of these strikes were against local insurgents and apparently thwarted their plan to capture the capital in the summer of 1973. At one point, when it appeared the enemy might block river traffic again, the Air Force launched

(1) Cambodian troops were trained by the South Vietnamese at the Lam Son Training Center. (2) U.S. Army engineers examine supply crates left behind by fleeing enemy troops. (3) In March 1970, the Cambodian Defense Minister Lt. Gen. Lon Nol, seized control of the government and announced the overthrow of Prince Sihanouk, then visiting in Europe. (4) Lon Nol visited Cambodian troops in September 1970.

(1) Cambodian troops trained in Vietnam prepare to board U.S. Air Force C-123K at Nha Trang for the flight back to Cambodia. (2) Sihanouk visited Communist China in October 1965. Shown (l. to r.): Chairman Mao Tse-Tung, Peng Chen, Sihanouk, and China's Chief of State, Liu Shao-chi. (3) Prince Sihanouk met with North Vietnamese Premier Pham Van Dong in Peking in November 1971.

an emergency C-130 airlift from U-Tapao to Phnom Penh's airport. It delivered munitions, rice, military equipment, and occasionally POL. This C-130 resupply effort was temporarily halted, however, when the river convoys succeeded in forcing their way to the capital with the help of aerial escort.

Congressional Criticism

The continuing bombing of Cambodia in the spring and summer of 1973 stirred renewed Congressional criticism at home of the war. Members of the House of Representatives tacked on amendments to several administration bills prohibiting the use of appropriated funds for bomb-

ing Cambodian targets. On 27 June the President vetoed one such bill and the House sustained the veto. Later, President Nixon informed Congress that he would not oppose legislation calling for a halt in the bombing within 45 days (on 15 August 1973) instead of requiring an immediate bombing halt. Congress accepted this compromise and on 1 July passed Public Law 93-52 cutting off all funds "to finance directly or indirectly combat activities by United States military forces in or over or from off the shores of South Vietnam, Laos or Cambodia." Mr. Nixon signed the bill into law on 1 July.

As the deadline drew near, the Air Force became involved in two tragic accidents. On 6 August a B-52 mistakenly dropped 20 tons of bombs on the friendly town of Neak Luong, 38 miles southeast of Phnom Penh. The raid killed or wounded more than 400 people. Two days later, American bombs hit a village on an island in the Mekong, just 3 miles from Neak Luong, causing at least 16 casualties. The last U.S. air strike in Cambodia occurred on the morning of 15 August 1973, when an A-7 Corsair, piloted by Capt. Lonnie O. Ratley, returned to its home base in Thailand, marking an end to the nation's longest war. USAF C-130's, however, continued to deliver needed supplies to the Cambodians after that date.

147

Chapter VIII

B-52 Arc Light Operations

Of all the Air Force weapons employed during the war in southeast Asia, none had a more devastating effect on the enemy than the B-52 Stratofortress. Originally built in the 1950's as the nation's long range, deep penetration nuclear bomber, the B-52 demonstrated awesome conventional power against Communist forces and military facilities in the two Vietnams, Laos, and Cambodia. In the early 1960's, as U.S. involvement in Southeast Asia grew, the Air Force modified some of the big bombers for conventional warfare by installing external racks capable of carrying 24 bombs and increasing the internal load from 9 to 27 bombs. Thus, *in toto*, the modified B-52 could carry 51 of the 500-pound or 750-pound bombs. As a final touch, the bomber's white and highly visible nuclear blast reflective underside was repainted black to make it undetectable by the naked eye at high altitude.

The Air Force flew its first B-52 strike against the Communists on 18 June 1965. The aircraft participating in this initial Arc Light strike—elements of the 2d and 320th Bombardment Wings—had deployed to Andersen AFB, Guam, from the United States on 17 February. The target was a suspected Viet Cong base north of Saigon in Binh Duong province containing sizable forces spread out over a large area. Earlier strikes at this type of target using tactical aircraft in saturation pattern bombing had proved unproductive. Thus the reason for the switch to the B-52.

There were several unfortunate aspects to this first B-52 mission. Two

flight of B-52 bombers as en from the cockpit of other Stratofortress.

of the huge bombers collided during the course of aerial refueling and both plunged in flames into the Pacific. Eight of 12 crewmen died. The results of this mission proved difficult to come by and were fragmentary at best. Three Special Forces teams sent into the jungle area could find little target damage before enemy snipers drove them out of the area. Shortly after the strike, numerous newspaper editorials severely criticized government officials for the operation's insignificant results and the apparent incongruity of "...swatting flies with sledgehammers." General Westmoreland, however, was well-satisfied, pointing out that the bombs had been on target and the strike "very disruptive" to the Viet Cong.

Secretary of Defense McNamara, speaking before a Senate subcommittee on the subject, provided the rationale behind the decision to use B-52's over area targets:

> We are faced with very, very heavy jungle in certain portions of South Vietnam, jungle so heavy that it is impossible to find an aiming point in it. We know some of these jungles are used by the Vietcong for base camps and for storage areas. . . .You can imagine that without an ability to find an aiming point there, there is only one way of bombing it and that is with a random pattern. . . .With the force we had (B-52's) trained as it was in pattern bombing. . .the military commanders felt—and I believe this was a proper use of the weapons— that these strikes would destroy certain of the Viet Cong base areas, and, as a matter of fact, they did. . . .There is no other feasible way of doing it. We propose to continue.

During the first few months of

149

operations, SAC responded to strike requests received from MACV, which had to be approved by CINCPAC and the JCS. Once the MACV staff learned how to use the big bomber effectively and results of the first few missions revealed extremely accurate bombing, Westmoreland became convinced of the B-52's worth and noted that it was "here to stay." Washington authorities still had reservations and placed severe controls on B-52 employment. One such control called for approval in Washington, sometimes at the White House level, of all proposed targets. In time, as Arc Light operations expanded, approval authority was delegated below the Washington level, but the White House, Office of the Secretary of Defense, and the JCS continued to receive information copies of all requests. There were other Arc Light restrictions which remained in effect throughout the war. These were primarily measures to safeguard noncombatants and religious shrines in target areas.

Supporting the Ground Forces

In November 1965, the B-52's directly supported American ground forces for the first time. The 1st Air Cavalry Division—after repelling an attack in the area of the Special Forces camp at Plei Me in the Central Highlands—pursued the retreating Viet Cong in a mop-up operation near Pleiku. On the 14th the division drove the harried enemy into the la Drang Valley. There, near the Cambodian border along the foothills of the Chu Phong mountains, the American troops uncovered a secret base area containing two regular NVA regiments and additional Viet Cong units. The enemy attempted to overwhelm their pursuers with repeated counterattacks. As fierce ground fighting continued, on 16 November a hurriedly dispatched force of 18 B-52's poured 344 tons of bombs on enemy positions along the

southeast slopes of the mountains. Successive Arc Light strikes, together with tactical aircraft sorties (almost 400 sorties combined) and artillery fire helped turn the enemy back. In all, the B-52's flew 96 sorties and dropped 1,795 tons of bombs in support of the 1st Cavalry.

In December, the B-52's were called in again, on this occasion in support of Third Marine Amphibious Force (III MAF) operations (Harvest Moon) in the northern portion of South Vietnam. The Marines had joined ARVN troops about 20 miles south of Da Nang to repel an advancing enemy force. When Lt. Gen. Lewis W. Walt, III MAF commander, asked for air support, Westmoreland noted the availability of B-52's. Walt then proposed their use against a large scale enemy build-up of supplies and reinforcements in a rear area. On 12 December the Marine general observed the first B-52 strike from a helicopter 1,000 feet aloft in the vicinity of the target area. Walt subsequently wired SAC's commander: "We are more than impressed with the results; we are delighted. The timing was precise, the bombing accurate, and the overall effort awesome to behold."

On 13 and 14 December the B-52's delivered additional strikes which were just as impressive. General Walt subsequently remarked that the big bombers had provided "not quite close air support but just next to it." Marine reconnaissance patrols combed the area after the first strike and discovered between 50 and 60 enemy dead. The bombing also uncovered a storage area consisting of a series of caves and bunkers.

In October 1965 the Air Force began further modification of the B-52—to increase internal loading from 27 to 84 of the 500- or 750-pound bombs. The modified Stratoforts went operational in March 1966 and were involved in the first Arc Light mission across the DMZ into North Vietnam. On 11 April and again on the 26th, they struck the Mu Gia pass, the mountainous funnel through which NVA men and materiel passed on the way to the northern reaches of the Ho Chi Minh trail. During the first strike, the largest single Arc Light attack to date and the largest bombing operation since World War II, the B-52's dropped some 600 tons of bombs.

Concurrently with deployment of the modified B-52, the Air Force installed Combat Skyspot, a ground-directed bombing system, in South Vietnam. The system employed existing SAC mobile ground radar guidance units and permitted MACV's targeting section considerably more latitude because selection of targets would no longer depend on a nearby, prominent geographical feature; they had only to be within range of Combat Skyspot equipment. Using the radar, a controller would direct the bombers along a designated route to a bomb drop point, providing enroute corrected headings and speed as needed. Then, at the proper moment, the pilot received a signal to release his bombs. Combat Skyspot not only provided flexibility in targeting, but its accuracy soon surpassed that of the previously used radar synchronous bombing. In time, practically all combat areas of Southeast Asia were within range of one or more of the growing number of Combat Skyspot facilities in the countryside. Six SAC personnel—members of the 1st Combat Evaluation Group— lost their lives during the construction phase, when they were ambushed and killed near Dong Ha Air Base while conducting a site location survey.

In April 1966, Operation Birmingham, a combined U.S. 1st Infantry and 25th ARVN Division search and destroy effort into War Zone C in Tay Ninh province near the Cambodian border, got under way, the first anti-Communist operation there since 1962. However, for months before the operation, B-52's repeatedly bombed the area and were directly responsible for increasing numbers of Viet Cong troops defecting. In support of Birmingham, the B-52's flew 162 sorties and dropped 3,118 tons of ordnance, including 220 tons of anti-personnel munitions. The first two strikes alone destroyed 14 Viet Cong base camps, 435 buildings and huts, 1,267 tons of rice, and other materiel. The following 10 strikes between 30 April and 9 May constituted the heaviest B-52 support to a ground operation to that time.

Some 6 months later, War Zone C again became the scene of another major search and destroy operation (Attleboro) which drew B-52 support. Beginning 8 November, the B-52's in 200 sorties dropped more than 4,000 tons of ordnance during the next 17 days. Evaluation of the bombing results proved difficult, although MACV reported numerous hits on the Communist headquarters and the death of at least one top leader.

Ammunition stores and deeply dug enemy trenches and tunnels were primary B-52 targets in support of Operation Cedar Falls, conducted during 8-26 January 1967. Cedar Falls involved a concentrated ground assault upon an enemy stronghold covering 25 square miles of the Iron Triangle, 20 miles northwest of Saigon. Fifteen B-52 strikes hit a tunnel system that, at places, was 12 to 20 feet beneath the earth's surface. Many of the tunnels were destroyed and there were numerous secondary explosions of enemy ammunition stores. Cedar Falls resulted in 720 enemy killed, the majority of them by Seventh Air Force and B-52 air strikes. In this operation, the heavy bombers demonstrated that the enemy could no longer regard any fortified area as a sanctuary safe from attack.

In February the Army launched Operation Junction City against the 9th Viet Cong Division ensconced in a War Zone C base area held since the war with France. Lasting from 22 Feb-

1

2

3

EXPLOSIVES A

4

5

6

7

(1) A maintenance man checks out a B-52 tail gun prior to a mission. (2) Preparing a B-52 for a mission. (3) B-52's dropped various bombs, including 750- and 1,000-pounders. (4) SAC maintenance men worked around the clock to get B-52's back into the air during the December 1972 "Linebacker" strikes of Hanoi. (5) B-52's in revetments at the U-Tapao Royal Thai Airfield. (6) Three B-52's taxi out preparatory to taking off on a mission. (7) A B-52 lifts off at U-Tapao. (8) Camouflaged B-52D.

8

1
2

3

5

(1) Loading bombs on a B-52 wing. (2) Loading bombs on B-52 internal racks. (3) Liftoff from a SAC base. (4) Fisheye lens view of a B-52. (5) B-52 target area in Vietnam. (6) Refueling enroute to the target. (7) B-52's destroyed a rail yard 7 miles north of Hanoi, December 1972.

4

6   7

ruary through 14 May 1967, the operation employed together for the first time all different types of combat forces—some 35,000 men under the control of the U.S. Army's II Field Force. Arc Light support totalled 126 sorties and 4,723 tons of bombs dropped. When the operation was over, 2,700 enemy dead were found and numerous defensive positions uncovered.

In April 1967 the Air Force obtained a second B-52 base at U-Tapao, Thailand, from which to conduct operations. There were two important reasons for striking from U-Tapao. The Thai base was only 2 to 5 hours distant from the targets, whereas the Guam-based bombers required 12 hours flying time and at least one aerial refueling from KC-135A tankers. The other factor was the ever-increasing rate of flights, which made concomitant demands on base facilities for parking, maintenance, supply, and other such requirements.

That summer, for the second time since the start of Arc Light operations, a mid-air collision caused fatalities. In this instance, on 7 July Maj. Gen. William J. Crumm, commander of all B-52 forces in the Pacific, was among the six crewmen who were lost.

On 1 September 1967, the enemy opened an intensive bombardment of Con Thien, a Marine base located just south of the DMZ. It appeared at first that the steady barrage of rocket, mortar, and artillery fire was preparatory to a major ground offensive across the DMZ. Later, Westmoreland characterized the attack as an enemy effort to repeat its spectacular 1954 win at Dien Bien Phu. It was thwarted, however, by Operation Neutralize, which integrated B-52 and tactical aircraft, field artillery, and naval firepower on the North Vietnamese positions. Fully 90 percent of B-52 sorties during September were against the enemy in the Con Thien area. A prime B-52 target was enemy gun positions 6 miles north of Con Thien which were bombed around the clock for days at a time. On 4 October, Westmoreland reported that U.S. forces had inflicted "a Dien Bien Phu in reverse." The enemy lost an estimated 3,000 men killed or wounded, about 10 percent of NVA forces in the DMZ, before breaking off the battle.

During November 1967 a major fight occurred in and around the Special Forces camp at Dak To, when elements of the 4th U.S. Infantry Division clashed with the 1st NVA Division. The Air Force directed 228 B-52 sorties against 32 targets in the area. During the same month, 36 sorties were flown in close support of U.S. Army and ARVN troops engaged in repelling a Viet Cong attack near Loc Ninh in III Corps.

The first quarter of 1968 saw Arc Light missions directed primarily on targets around the Marine base of Khe Sanh in the northwest corner of South Vietnam. Here for nearly 3 months three Marine regiments and their Vietnamese Ranger allies were surrounded by two or more NVA divisions with some 20,000 to 30,000 men and became the focal point of worldwide interest. When it became clear that the enemy was about to move in force against the Marine base, General Westmoreland on 14 January put Operation Niagara into effect—a joint air campaign dedicated to maintaining the American position at Khe Sanh. As part of Niagara, B-52's flew 461 missions, 2,707 sorties, and dropped 75,-631 tons of ordnance between 14 January and 31 March.

The B-52 targets initially consisted of enemy staging, assembly, and storage areas and gun positions around the outpost. Bombs were released to fall no closer than 3,300 yards of friendly positions. When air observers detected extensive enemy bunker complexes within the buffer zone, however, B-52's were ordered to bomb within one-sixth of a mile of the base perimeter. The first such strike occurred on 26 February under the anxious eyes of the Marine commander at Khe Sanh, concerned about the effects of close-in bombing on his own bunkers and trenches. The accuracy of the first ground radar-directed strikes dispelled those anxieties. Only enemy fortifications and positions were destroyed.

Succeeding close-in strikes devastated enemy positions along the camp perimeter, resulted in numerous secondary explosions, and lifted the spirits of the Marines. Altogether, over a period of a little more than a month, B-52's flew 101 close-in missions totalling 589 sorties. Accurate and complete bomb damage assessment was difficult—initially because of adverse weather including low-lying fog, but later because the ground became so thoroughly pockmarked with overlapping B-52 bomb craters that it was impossible to determine which strikes were responsible for a specific crater.

A major contribution to Arc Light's success at Khe Sanh was adoption of the Bugle Note scheduling technique devised by SAC's 3d Air Division, director of B-52 operations in Southeast Asia. By fully utilizing the ground radar bombing system and obtaining maximum performance from aircrews, bomb loaders, and maintenance crews, the division was able to keep aloft an unbroken stream of six aircraft that struck Khe Sanh targets every 3 hours. Bugle Note also allowed MACV to change targets as late as 2 hours prior to target time. The system proved so successful that it was soon used on a regular daily basis.

The additional sorties that General Westmoreland required not only for Khe Sanh but elsewhere during the simultaneous Tet offensive were provided by B-52's newly deployed to the western Pacific in response to North Korea's seizure of the USS *Pueblo* in January. That B-52 force, stationed at Kadena AB, Okinawa, subsequently joined in the combat operations over Vietnam.

From a rate of approximately 300 sorties each month late in 1965, the B-52 effort had gradually increased to a rate of 800 sorties during 1967, and for the first 2 weeks in February 1968 had risen to the 1,200-sortie level. On 15 February, at Westmoreland's request, Washington officials authorized an increase to 1,800 sorties monthly and the use of the Kadena-based B-52 force Although viewed at first as temporary, this new sortie rate remained in effect until 1969 when Defense Department economies forced a cutback to 1,600.

In early April 1968, during Operation Pegasus, the 1st Cavalry Division (Mobile) spearheaded a breakthrough of enemy positions on Route 9 and relieved the Marine base. The siege of Khe Sanh was over. Several months after the battle, General Westmoreland observed:

> The thing that broke their back basically was the fire of the B-52's. Now yes, we did have additional fire power. We were putting in around 100 TAC air sorties a day. We had sixteen 175-mm guns of the U.S. Army that were moved within range of Khe Sanh base and they fired a number of rounds each day and they did an excellent job but the big gun, the heavyweight of fire power, was the tremendous tonnage of bombs dropped by our B-52's. Without question the amount of fire power put on that piece of real estate exceeded anything that had ever been seen before in history by any foe and the enemy was hurt, his back was broken by air power.

MACV's analysis of the battle credited the B-52 with preventing any large massing of enemy troops required to overrun the base. In one instance, a prisoner of war reported, 75 percent of an 1,800-man regiment had been killed by a single Arc Light strike. The bombers also succeeded in tearing up the enemy's logistic lines to the battlefield and causing immense materiel losses.

Later in April the U.S. Army launched an offensive—Operation Delaware—against enemy bases in the A Shau valley near the Laotian border, directly west of Da Nang. Arc Light aircraft struck 123 targets with 726 sorties. During the remainder of 1968, B-52's supported a variety of troop operations and interdiction efforts. Highlights of the summer bombing period were strikes against NVA troop and supply targets 15 miles north of the DMZ on 14 July (the deepest B-52 penetration north to date) and, 4 days later, the first B-52 strike against North Vietnamese surface-to-air missile sites.

In March 1969, as Operation Menu, B-52's were directed against Communist sanctuaries in Cambodia (see Chapter VII). Between 18 March, when the first B-52 strike was launched against the sanctuaries, and 15 August 1973, when all bombing was halted, B-52 crews flew 16,527 sorties and dropped 383,851 tons of munitions on Viet Cong/NVA and Khmer Rouge targets. Similarly unannounced bombings (Operation Good Look) against enemy targets occurred in northern Laos in 1970, after NVA forces massed for a major attack against government outposts in and around the Plain of Jars. Between February and May, 149 sorties were flown against enemy troops, preventing a major defeat of Laotian government forces. During 1970-1973 more than 2,500 sorties struck enemy targets in northern Laos. The Strategic Air Command flew its last Good Look sortie on 17 April 1973.

In South Vietnam, the remote Special Forces camp at Ben Het in the western sector of II Corps, came under enemy siege in May 1969 and was the scene of heavy fighting for the next 2 months. Before the siege was lifted, B-52's had flown 804 sorties against 140 targets in that area. The bombers struck almost daily, with many of the targets being changed at the last

moment because of the enemy's frequent moves. A SAC officer with the advanced echelon reported:"From 21 to 27 June, we had 98 sorties around Ben Het. Every target box, except one, was changed. Some were changed, two, three, and four times... Most were in close support." By 2 July Ben Het defenders felt certain the enemy had departed. Air power, with its big gun, the B-52, was credited with keeping the enemy force at bay and preventing a major assault.

On 1 May 1970, shortly before American and ARVN forces invaded the Parrot's Beak and Fishhook areas of Cambodia, B-52's flew six "softening-up" missions in front of the advancing troops. During the 2-month period that the ground forces remained in Cambodia, Arc Light sorties totalled 763, of which 653 supported six ground operations. Authorities had not restricted the B-52's to the 18-mile penetration limit set for U.S. ground forces, and the bombers often ranged beyond the line, hitting target areas suspected of containing the long sought Communist headquarters of the Central Office of South Vietnam (COSVN).

The Laotian Incursion

The Cambodian incursion was followed in early 1971 by a second cross-border operation into the Laotian panhandle. Initiated in February, it was undertaken by South Vietnamese forces only (see Chapter V). Designated Lam Son 719, the operation was aimed at disrupting the southward movement of troops and materiel on the Ho Chi Minh trail. From 8 February, when ARVN forces crossed into Laos, until 24 March, the final day of the operation, B-52's flew 1,358 sorties and dropped more than 32,000 tons of bombs. Many of the strikes were used to carve out landing zones for helicopters supporting the ground advance toward Tchepone. The Laotian incursion also marked a return to close-in bombing, sometimes less than 1,000 feet from friendly positions. On 21 February, in one of the most productive strikes of the war, Arc Light crews were credited with killing 698 enemy troops. The North Vietnamese that day had unwisely massed for an assault on an ARVN-held hill, presenting a perfect target for the B-52's.

Earlier, on 12 February, the ARVN command reported B-52 strikes had hit the headquarters of the NVA 308th Division, killing 35. Arc Light damage reports throughout the operation were meager, but two strike areas searched on 25 February uncovered 142 dead, plus 4 tons of mortars and ammunition destroyed. At times, units of the ARVN 1st Infantry Division employed a daring tactic calculated to keep enemy troops in a designated B-52 target area. After locating the enemy and forwarding the target coordinates, ARVN units would engage the enemy in a firefight, then break off and withdraw just before the planned Arc Light strike. On 27 February, for example, the 1st Battalion, 3d Infantry Regiment counted 29 enemy soldiers killed during such an action. Speaking of the B-52's, Brig. Gen. Phan Van Phu, commander of the 1st Infantry Division, said:

> The enemy tries to get very close to us, hoping we will get hit by one of our own bombs. We let them come close, then pull back just before the air strikes, closing again when the bombers are finished. If you want to kill people you must use maximum air. During the heavy fighting around Fire Support Base Lo Lo early in the week, I called for B-52 strikes within 300 yards of my unit. Many of the nearly 1,700 enemy soldiers reported killed in that fighting died in those strikes.

Early in 1972, MACV intelligence sources obtained strong indications of a forthcoming NVA offensive. Unusually large southbound troop and logistic movements were detected along the Ho Chi Minh trail. Part of

MACV's strategy to counter the build-up was to hit the new targets with B-52's "as hard as possible" before the enemy initiated the assault phase of operations. The Secretary of Defense authorized the Air Force to increase the monthly sortie rate, set at 1,000 since July 1971, to 1,200 as of 8 February. On the same day, 29 B-52's deployed from the United States to Guam to permit sortie expansion to 1,500 per month. In April and May, three other deployments brought the number of B-52's available for SEA duty to 200 and some 3,150 sorties each month (as compared to the pre-1972 force of 42 bombers and 1,000 sorties). The last augmentation marked the first entry of the B-52G into Arc Light operations. The newer G's were not modified to carry the larger payload, but their longer flying range reduced aerial refueling requirements.

When Hanoi finally unleashed its 1972 offensive late in March, it consisted of a three-prong NVA thrust toward Quang Tri City, Kontum, and An Loc (see Chapter III). On 30 March, three enemy divisions moved across the DMZ and in the first week scored a series of stunning victories, dislodging ARVN troops from 14 positions before they regrouped on the outskirts of Quang Tri City.

During that hectic week, the B-52's flew 132 sorties in an attempt to stem the onslaught. B-52 support strikes against enemy units and materiel moving through the DMZ continued through all of April. One B-52 was hit by a SAM on 9 April but managed to land at Da Nang. A counteroffensive launched by the ARVN in mid-April was unsuccessful and Quang Tri City fell on 1 May. In bombing enemy positions east of the city, three Arc Light strikes were credited with 300 enemy killed. After capturing the city, the NVA regrouped and moved southward toward Hue where ARVN forces had hastily erected a defense line. An ARVN operation, launched on the

161

1

2

3

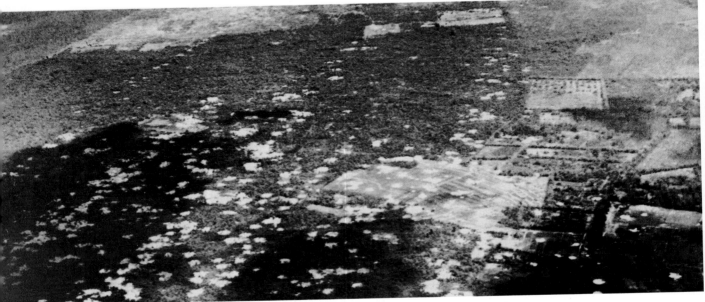

4

5

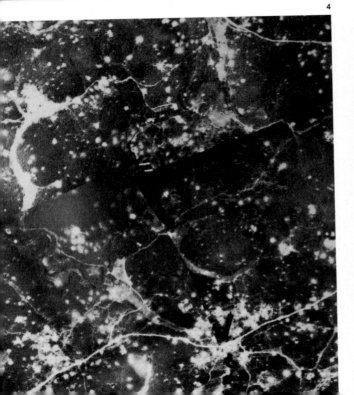

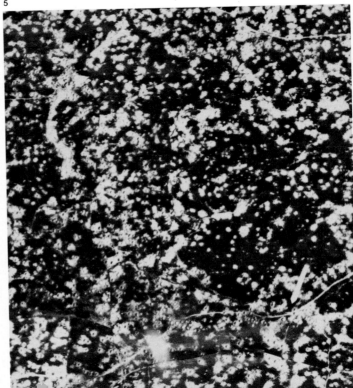

6

8

(1-2) Preparing to load bombs prior to a mission. (3) Carpet bombing in support of Operation Junction City, March 1967. (4-5) Before and after. The photo on the left shows an area of the DMZ prior to intense air strikes. The second photo shows extensive cratering caused from B-52 bomber and tactical airstrikes. (6) Bombs away. (7) Highlands surrounding the A Shau Valley of South Vietnam show craters produced by B-52 strikes. Truck parks on either side of the road were destroyed. (8) Carpet bombing in support of Operation Junction City in March 1967.

7

heels of a B-52 strike, led to a continuing engagement with the 29th NVA Regiment and the recapture of Fire Support Base Bastogne on 15 May. In later action around the fire support base, a B-52 was credited with 60 enemy fatalities and permitted the capture of large quantities of weapons and ammunition. By 28 June, the enemy in Quang Tri province had been forced onto the defensive and B-52's continued to batter the retreating enemy.

Elsewhere, at Kontum, the NVA achieved an early success. The invaders overran Rocket Ridge, a strategic high point south of Dak To, and cut Route 14, Kontum's lifeline to the south. Throughout this period, B-52's hit suspected enemy troop positions and logistic lines. By 16 May the NVA had gathered in force before Kontum and begun assaults on the ARVN defensive positions. Close-in B-52 strikes were used to counter the advance. One Arc Light strike on 18 May decimated the 48th Regiment, 320th NVA Division, killing 180 (their bodies were later found in a single mass grave). The heaviest fighting, on 23-24 May, had full Arc Light support. On 25 May the enemy was thrown back from Kontum, and by 6 June he was in full retreat. Between 30 March and 30 June, there were 2,262 sorties against 795 targets in Military Region II, virtually all of them in direct support of the ARVN's successful defense of Kontum.

The third prong of the enemy offensive, in Military Region III, first concentrated on Loc Ninh. Troops crossed over from Cambodia on 5 April and took the city the next day. The enemy then moved toward An Loc, the provincial capital, some 12 miles to the south and succeeded in cutting its main supply route. Arc Light struck repeatedly at enemy positions near Loc Ninh and along the road to An Loc. Between 6-28 April, 117 targets—most near the fighting at An Loc—received B-52 treatment.

1

2

3

Thirty percent of the sorties were of the close-in type. On one occasion, the B-52's hit an enemy force moving through the target area, destroying 3 or 4 tanks and killing approximately 100 soldiers.

Between 29 April and 16 May, the period of the heaviest fighting, a stalemate ensued with intense artillery exchanges. On the night of 12-13 May, the enemy took advantage of bad flying weather to launch a major tank-supported attack. It soon stalled, however, after B-52's destroyed the tanks and blew up an ammunition dump. The bombers also aided ARVN relief units making their way toward the beleaguered troops in An Loc, but their progress was slow. Heavy fighting continued until 23 June, when the relief column finally broke through. The B-52 again played a major role, as two raids spaced 15 minutes apart caught the NVA blocking force by surprise, destroyed it, and opened the way into the city. By 26 June, major enemy forces had withdrawn from An Loc and only small pockets of resistance remained.

B-52's Over Hanoi

While the fighting raged in South Vietnam, the B-52's also struck deep into North Vietnam. In the first strike on 9 April 1972, 12 B-52's bombed underground POL storage tanks and a railroad yard at Vinh. Although many buildings in the POL area were destroyed, none of the underground tanks were visibly damaged. The railroad yard, however, was cut in 4 places, and 1 locomotive and 10 cars destroyed. Three days later, 18 B-52's hit the Bai Thuong airfield, peppering the runway and taxiways with craters and destroying one MIG-17 along with one occupied and three unoccupied AAA sites. On 15 April, 17 B-52's struck Haiphong's POL storage area; the North Vietnamese fired 35 SAM's but all missed the bombers. Strike results were good, with 15 surface and two

(1) 750-pound bombs awaiting loading on a B-52. (2) B-52 on a hard stand. (3) A portion of the Kihn No rail yards damaged by B-52 strike. (4) Each B-52 carried a variety of bombs including 750 pounders. (5) Enemy rail siding was put out of service. (6) Rail cars carrying petroleum supplies destroyed by B-52's.

underground tanks destroyed—or about one-third of the facility's capacity. The B-52's also cut rail lines in the area and smashed 30 pieces of rolling stock and 66 structures.

Two strikes, each involving 18 B-52's, were made against targets in the Thanh Hoa area on 21 and 23 April. About 25 SAM's were fired at the attackers on each day and one missile hit its mark. The striken bomber reached Da Nang safely with no crew losses. Cumulative damage included 16 buildings destroyed at the Hamm Rong transshipment point, and 3 large structures completely or partially destroyed in a warehouse area. Rail lines on the western approach to the Thanh Hoa railroad-highway bridge were cut and the thermal power plant damaged.

In October 1972 peace negotiations resumed in Paris, but optimism for an agreement proved short-lived. On 13 December, the North Vietnamese broke off the discussions. In the hope of forcing a settlement, President Nixon ordered heavy air strikes against military targets in the Hanoi and Haiphong area which had not been previously attacked. These Linebacker II operations spanned an 11-day period between 18 and 29 December (with a 24-hour pause in bombing on Christmas day) and included more than 700 B-52 sorties against rail and ship yards, command and control facilities, warehouses and transshipment points, power plants, railway bridges, rolling stock, MIG bases, and air defense sites. The B-52's bombed relentlessly around the clock in the rainy monsoon weather.

The damage inflicted by the Stratoforts was awesome. At the Gia Lam railroad yard and repair facility, four buildings were destroyed and two damaged, railroad tracks received numerous cuts, and direct hits were made on military supplies. Bombing the barracks at Bac Mai airfield resulted in 31 being destroyed, as were large portions of an adjoining military

Start of the Paris peace talks between the United States and the Democratic Republic of Vietnam. Secretary Kissinger is 2d from the right. Directly across the table is the senior North Vietnamese negotiator, Le Duc Tho (2d from left).

storage complex. Nine warehouses at the Yen Vien warehouse center were destroyed and 10 damaged. A B-52 strike against the Yen Vien railroad yard uprooted tracks, switches, and rolling stock, destroyed 2 locomotives and 9 warehouses, and damaged 10 buildings of an adjoining warehouse center. At the Van Dien Army supply depot, 12 warehouses were destroyed and 11 damaged.

The B-52's, along with F-4's and F-111's also hit hard at electrical power production and POL supplies during the "Eleven Day War." Subsequent assessment revealed that 80 percent of North Vietnam's electrical power production and 25 percent of its POL were destroyed. The bombing of a major petroleum storage area in Hanoi caused 30 large secondary explosions and destruction of two buildings. The Haiphong petroleum storage area was hit repeatedly. Secondary fires and explosions destroyed or damaged twenty 50,000-gallon POL tanks and countless 55-gallon drums. Other facilities destroyed and damaged included buildings at the Than Am and Bac Giang petroleum storage areas and four support buildings at the Thai Nguyen thermal power plant.

The results of the short but intense

In the spring of 1969 President Nixon conferred with South Vietnamese President Nguyen Van Thieu at Midway Island. During this meeting Mr. Nixon announced plans to begin the withdrawal of U. S. forces in Southeast Asia.

B-52 campaign were impressive, but not without substantial cost. The air defenses of Hanoi and Haiphong were extensive, highly sophisticated, and were years in the making. The cities were two of the most heavily defended areas in the world. Because all portions of Linebacker II got under way more or less concurrently, the Air Force had no opportunity to send tactical aircraft to wipe out the enemy's air defenses, particularly the greatest threat to the high-flying B-52—the numerous SAM-2 missile sites that encircled both cities. There were about 1,000 SAM's fired during the first few days of the bombing campaign, but their number slackened off noticeably after B-52 and tactical aircraft eliminated many launching sites and the supply of missiles was depleted.

In all, the North Vietnamese shot down 15 B-52's. Of the 92 air crewmen aboard, 33 bailed out and were taken prisoner. Air Force rescue teams recovered another 26. Four crewmen died in a crash landing and 29 were reported missing. In exacting that toll in men and machinery, the North Vietnamese had mounted a defense unparalleled in its ferocity. Finding their normal tracking procedures inade-

quate, they had resorted to salvoing large numbers of missiles in a shotgun pattern into the calculated path of the on-coming aircraft.

By 28 December, American airmen had swept away virtually all of the enemy's defenses, and the B-52's were free to roam the skies of North Vietnam. Most of the SAM sites and their tracking radars had been neutralized and most MIG-21 interceptors were immobilized on their battered airfields. B-52D tail gunners marked up a kill against a MIG-21 on 18 December and again on 24 December. These were the first recorded by B-52's during the 7-1/2 years of Arc Light operations. On 30 December Hanoi agreed to resume the peace talks, which culminated in the 27 January agreement.

It was not until 15 January that the Air Force stopped B-52 missions over North Vietnam, although restricting them to below the 20th parallel. During those 15 days, in 532 sorties, they bombed such logistic targets as truck parks, storage areas, and transshipment points. The final B-52 sorties in South Vietnam occurred on 27 January, the day of the peace agreement. B-52's continued to fly missions over Laos until 17 April and over Cambodia until 15 August 1973, when more than 8 years of Arc Light operations came to an end.

Between June 1965 and August 1973, the Strategic Air Command scheduled 126,663 Stratofortress combat sorties, of which 126,615 were actually launched. The number of aircraft reaching the target area was 125,479 with 124,532 successfully releasing their bombs on the targets. Geographically, 55 percent of the sorties were flown against targets in South Vietnam, 27 percent in Laos, 12 percent in Cambodia, and 6 percent in North Vietnam. Altogether, the Air Force lost 31 B-52's—18 from hostile fire (all over North Vietnam) and 13 from other operational causes.

167

Chapter IX

Tactical Airlift

Major roles of air transport in support of U.S. ground operations were demonstrated during the Second World War. In western Europe and in Burma thousands of twin-engine C-47's—originally procured to parachute assault troops into combat—were far more often used as conventional carriers of men and supplies theaterwide. During the Korean War, the 315th Air Division operated more than 200 Far East Air Forces transports under a centralized theater system. After the Korean armistice, USAF airlift concepts were broadened to encompass another primary role—supporting short-notice transoceanic deployments of U.S.-based tactical air forces. Later, the Kennedy administration's interest in limited war gave impetus to concepts of airmobile tactics in ground warfare. This led the Air Force again to focus its tactical airlift fleet toward the ground battle, meshing its capabilities with the airlift forces of the U.S. Army.

Forces and Organization

The first USAF transports sent to Vietnam were four C-47's, which arrived at Bien Hoa AB on 16 November 1961 as part of the Farm Gate detachment. The C-47 airlifters performed diverse missions—support flights for Farm Gate, airdrops of Vietnamese paratroops, and night flareship operations. Their most demanding task, however, was to resupply U.S. Army Special Forces detachments at remote locations throughout South Vietnam. Such deliveries were often by airdrop, either by parachute or free-fall, the C-47's escorted by fire-suppressing Farm Gate or VNAF strike aircraft. In 1963 the number of C-47's increased to six, but airlift tasks gradually yielded to gunship roles.

The Vietnamese Air Force also used C-47's, organized in a two-squadron group commanded in 1962 by Lt. Col. Nguyen Cao Ky, future VNAF commander who later served as Prime Minister and Vice President of his country. A shortage of VNAF pilots in early 1962 led the Air Force to assign USAF pilots to the two squadrons. Thus, in April, 30 American officers arrived in Saigon to serve as co-pilots with otherwise all-Vietnamese C-47 crews. The "Dirty Thirty" Americans soon appreciated the flying skills of their VNAF counterparts and acquiesced to their own co-pilot roles. Some at first criticized the informality of Vietnamese flying methods, but all came to agree that these were often the surest, given the difficult flying environment. Ky's tactful leadership preserved good relations between the two groups. A second contingent replaced the original Dirty Thirty officers in the spring of 1963. The project ended in December 1963, although the idea was temporarily revived in modified form in 1965. The VNAF airlift squadrons remained healthy, frequently transporting the Vietnamese airborne battalions in their nationwide reserve role.

The larger, twin-engine C-123 Providers gradually took over the role of USAF C-47's in South Vietnam. The Provider had been tagged as "obsolescent" as early as 1956 and in 1961 was scheduled for retirement from the active inventory. Instead, in December 1961 a squadron of 16 C-123's began deploying to Vietnam (Project Mule Train) to provide "tactical airlift support of South Vietnamese armed forces." The first four ships reached Tan Son Nhut on 2 January 1962. A second C-123 squadron entered Vietnam in the spring of 1962, a third in 1963, and a fourth in 1964. All eventually were assigned to the 315th Air

plies dropped from Air rce C-130's drift toward ops in the drop zone in A Shau valley, April 1968

169

Commando Wing. The C-123's thus became until 1965 the principal airlift element in South Vietnam. Their ability to land on short and rough fields proved most valuable, and the four squadrons remained in South Vietnam until 1970. During 1967-1968 the aircraft underwent major modifications —a supplementary jet engine was installed under each nacelle, and improved brakes, flaps, and landing gear were provided—all of which enhanced C-123 payload, climb, and short-field performance.

Dominating airlift operations in Vietnam after early 1965 was the C-130 Hercules. Equipped with four turboprop engines and first flown in 1954, the C-130 was far superior in performance to earlier tactical transports. Its 15-ton payload, for example, was three times that of the C-123. In 1961 three squdrons of C-130A's were stationed in the western Pacific under the 315th Air Division in Japan; a fourth squadron deployed in the spring of 1962. These units assisted in deploying a U.S. ground and air task force to Thailand in May 1962 and regularly airlifted personnel and cargo into South Vietnam from offshore locations before 1965. They occasionally made deliveries between points in South Vietnam, making extra stops while transiting from offshore or deploying to an in-country base for short periods. When President Johnson ordered U.S. ground units into South Vietnam, the C-130's during 8-12 March 1965 deployed a Marine battalion landing team from Okinawa to Da Nang. On 4-7 May 1965 the C-130 fleet carried the Army's 173rd Airborne Brigade from Okinawa to South Vietnam in 140 flights.

C-130 in-country missions from South Vietnamese bases became routine in April 1965. Thereafter, aircraft and crews rotated into South Vietnam on 1- or 2-week cycles from home bases in the Philippines, Taiwan, Okinawa, and Japan. By the end of 1965 the

in-country force had grown to 32 ships, positioned at four bases. Airlift requirements expanded with the scope of ground combat, the C-130 force in South Vietnam reaching 96 ships in February 1968. The rotational scheme was retained—offshore basing exploited existing maintenance facilities, reduced in-country construction and manpower requirements, and reduced exposure to enemy shelling. In an emergency, the in-country force could be quickly augmented.

In the spring of 1965 the offshore C-130 force increased to eight squadrons, including four on temporary duty from TAC. The force grew to 12 permanently assigned squadrons by mid-1966 and reached a peak of 15 (including 3 temporarily deployed TAC) in early 1968. The 315th Air Division also controlled a C-124 squadron based at Tachikawa, employing these four-engine craft for overwater transport and occasional hauls of outsized items within Southeast Asia.

Within Vietnam, the C-123's and C-130's were centrally controlled through the Common Service Airlift System (CSAS) and its Airlift Control Center (ALCC) at Tan Son Nhut. In the spring of 1966 MACV established the Joint Movements Transportation Board and the Traffic Management Agency for theater-level management. The Board reviewed monthly forecasts of airlift requirements and capabilities and made allocations as necessary, while the Agency gave daily attention to priorities and controlled the flow of cargo to aerial ports. For emergency moves, the MACV Command Operations Center could levy special flights, bypassing the transportation agencies. The ALCC scheduled the aircraft flights and controlled the daily missions.

The ALCC functioned countrywide through local airlift control elements, liaison officers, field mission commanders, and mobile combat control teams—all linked by often trouble-some radio and land-line communications. The whole apparatus was placed under the 834th Air Division upon its activation on 15 October 1966. Also assigned to the 834th were the 315th Wing and its C-123 squadrons, along with three in-country aerial port squadrons and numerous subordinate aerial port detachments. Expansion of the aerial port system tended to lag behind workload requirements, a condition intensified by shortages and break-downs in cargo handling equipment.

Also assigned to the 834th Air Division—but employed outside the centralized scheduling system—were six squadrons of C-7A Caribou transports. These twin-engine reciprocating aircraft had been purchased by the U.S. Army in the early 1960's to support its airmobile forces. An Army Caribou company deployed to South Vietnam in the spring of 1962. By 1966 the force had expanded to six companies and operated under the scheduling and mission control of specified Army corps and divisions. In April 1966 the Army and Air Force chiefs of staff agreed to transfer the Caribous to the Air Force. Later that year, USAF air and ground crewmen entered the Army companies as trainees and replacements. On 1 January 1967 the six companies officially became Air Force squadrons, based at three locations and assigned to the 483d Tactical Airlift Wing at Cam Ranh Bay. For the most part, the squadrons continued to operate under Army scheduling. The Air Force acquiesced in this "dedicated user" procedure, although it was a departure from its doctrine of centralized control.

Airlift in the Ground War

Basic to Allied strategy were search-and-destroy operations, penetrating remote regions used by the enemy. Pivotal in these ventures were the fixed-wing transports, which lifted multi-battalion task forces to forward airheads and resupplied them with POL and ammunition. The Army helicopters, which performed local assaults and short-haul distribution of supplies, often refueled and rearmed at the C-130 airhead. Highway lines of communication supplemented air delivery when feasible, but airlift avoided the problem of enemy road ambushes, enabling the Allies to operate—like Communist forces—in a "war without fronts."

Before 1965, during the period of Mule Train C-123 operations, such combat applications of tactical airlift were only glimpsed. Each day several C-123's and VNAF C-47's formed an alert element ready to move Vietnamese paratroops on instant notice. Although the airlift force was rarely exercised in this fashion, it did conduct a series of paratroop assaults, some preplanned and others in response to enemy ground attacks. These operations were uniformly disappointing, due to poor coordination, inaccurate drops, or the troopers' inability to close with the enemy.

By contrast, the C-123's won praise in airlanded troop deployments, hauling multi-battalion Vietnamese forces for reinforcement or offensive purposes. Efforts to mesh the best of C-123 and helicopter assault qualities had gratifying results, as exemplified during Allied operations in the Mekong delta in March 1964, when the Providers delivered fuel and ordnance for Army helicopters at forward dirt strips. More significant than the assault roles, however, was the C-123's vital service in assisting Farm Gate C-47's in resupplying Special Forces camps.

Demands for airlift increased substantially in 1965, after the arrival in South Vietnam of large U.S. Army contingents. Among the first were two paratroop brigades, seen by General Westmoreland as a central reserve force quickly available for offensive or reaction operations. In August 1965

1

2

3

4

5

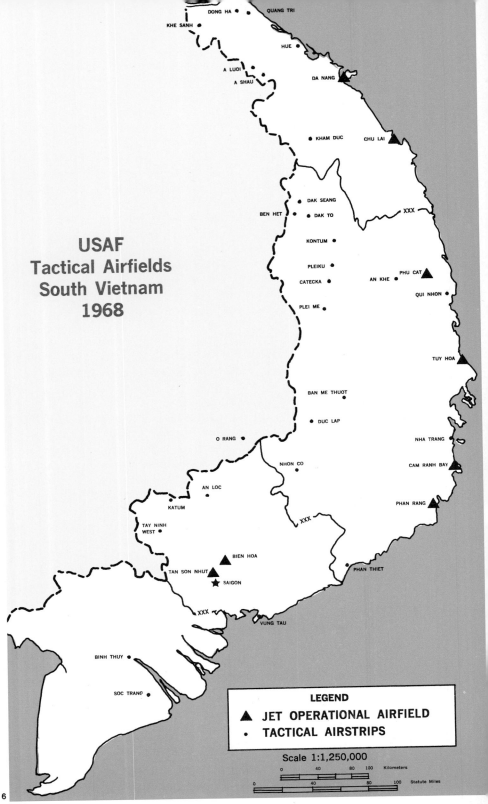

USAF
Tactical Airfields
South Vietnam
1968

KHE SANH
DONG HA
QUANG TRI
HUE
A LUOI
A SHAU
DA NANG

KHAM DUC
CHU LAI

DAK SEANG
BEN HET
DAK TO
XXX
KONTUM
PLEIKU
AN KHE
PHU CAT
CATECKA
QUI NHON
PLEI ME

TUY HOA

BAN ME THUOT
DUC LAP

O RANG
NHA TRANG

NHON CO
CAM RANH BAY

AN LOC
PHAN RANG
KATUM
TAY NINH
WEST
XXX
BIEN HOA
TAN SON NHUT
PHAN THIET
★ SAIGON

XXX
VUNG TAU

BINH THUY

SOC TRANG

LEGEND
▲ JET OPERATIONAL AIRFIELD
• TACTICAL AIRSTRIPS

Scale 1:1,250,000

0   40   80   100   Kilometers

0   40   80   100   Statute Miles

© N.G.S.

6

7

9

(1) 105 Howitzer being loaded on a USAF C-123. (2) Unloading jeep and cargo. (3) Unloading a howitzer. (4) Troops airborne on a mission over South Vietnam. (5) Air Force C-123 lands at the Khe Sanh air strip. (6) USAF Tactical Airfields in South Vietnam. (7) Delivering supplies to an airstrip in South Vietnam. (8-9) Paratroops jump from Air Force C-123 Providers. (10) Unloading Army ordnance.

10

the 173rd Airborne Brigade was airlifted from Bien Hoa to Pleiku in 150 C-130 flights for just this purpose. Then, after returning to its home base, the 173d began a series of sweeps over the Saigon plain, relying on a mix of truck, helicopter, and air transport support. During Operation New Life-65, which began on 21 November 1965, the 173d made a helicopter assault into a dirt airstrip 40 miles east of Bien Hoa. The first C-130 landed within 1 hour, and another 70 C-130 sorties followed during the next 36 hours to deliver both troops and cargo. Overland communications established by the third day enabled the C-130's to reduce their effort to 10 sorties daily.

The key role played by air transport also was seen in the operations of the 1st Brigade, 101st Airborne Division, during the spring and summer of 1966. The brigade made five successive moves, each requiring some 200 C-130 lifts and each operation largely sustained by air resupply. The C-130's first airlifted the brigade from Tuy Hoa to Phan Thiet early in April, next to the highlands airstrip at Nhon Co later that month, then north to Cheo Reo in May, then to Dak To soon after, and finally back to Tuy Hoa in July.

In the fall of 1965, soon after its arrival at An Khe, the 1st Cavalry Division undertook operations requiring a major airlift effort by the Air Force. When strong NVA forces attacked Plei Me camp south of Pleiku, General Westmoreland committed the division. Its assault helicopters consumed large amounts of fuel in the battle area and almost depleted available stocks, despite the efforts of the Army's Caribous and Chinook helicopters to sustain an air line of communications. Faced with this emergency, MACV called for USAF airlift forces. On the morning of 29 October, the C-130's began an extended stream from Saigon, hauling POL and munitions to the main Pleiku field for redistribution by helicopter to the battle area. After

several days, the C-130's landed closer to the battleground on a dirt strip at Catecka Tea Plantation, where the division's helicopters refueled. Over a period of 29 days, the Air Force delivered to the 1st Cavalry Division an average of 186 tons per day, most of it POL. These operations indicated that in the future airmobile forces would require substantial logistical airlift support from the Air Force, probably greater than that required by conventional ground forces.

Airlift support for the conventional units in search-and-destroy operations was exemplified during Operation Birmingham, a 4-week air deployment into Tay Ninh province beginning 24 April 1966. The C-130's flew 56 D-Day sorties into the 4,600-foot dirt strip at Tay Ninh. C-123's lifted other forces to smaller, nearby strips. An around-the-clock resupply airlift into Tay Ninh followed to sustain the two-brigade force. The Air Force averaged 424 tons daily the first week, close to the forecast requirements. A land line of communications, opened on 1 May, reduced the burden on the C-130's which were also supporting the airborne brigade at Nhon Co. Army helicopters carried supplies from Tay Ninh to field units, while Caribous provided courier service between Saigon base camps and the battle scene. During the second week of Birmingham, the runway at Tay Ninh deteriorated from heavy rains, which also halted ground movement. By the time the operation ended on 17 May, the C-130's and C-123's had flown nearly 1,000 sorties and delivered nearly 10,000 tons of cargo for the division.

C-130 parachute capabilities were exercised during Operation Junction City early in 1967. The operation got under way on 22 February with airmobile assults using all available helicopters. Executed simultaneously was the war's only battalion-sized parachute assult by American troops. Thirteen C-130's departed from Bien Hoa on schedule; the troopers of the 173rd Brigade jumped as planned at 0900. All landed in the drop zone at Katum near the Cambodian border. There was negligible opposition, although one C-130 received a single hit. At 0927, 10 C-130's dropped the brigade's equipment, returning at 1300 to make additional cargo drops. Some of these loads landed in swamp areas, complicating retrieval. Five cargo-carrying Hercules sustained hits, none seriously.

On the second day, the Air Force launched 38 C-130 resupply sorties, but bad weather reduced drop accuracy. During the next 5 days, coordination and accuracy improved with daily drops averaging 100 tons. During the final stages of the operation in late March, the C-130's made airdrops to a "floating brigade," using drop zone locations which the ground unit provided by radio. The drops in support of Junction City totalled 1,700 tons. The sustained effort strained the Army's parachute rigging capability, but also eased the workload of the Army's resupply helicopters and provided USAF crews with invaluable experience.

Airlanded operations in support of subsequent Army offensives followed the pattern of the earlier ones. In November 1967, C-130's in some 250 sorties flew the 173d to Dak To. In the 3 weeks of heavy fighting that followed, daily streams of C-130's delivered more than 5,000 tons, landing on a much-patched and busy 4,200-foot asphalt strip. Enemy shelling on the 15th destroyed a 1,300-ton ammunition dump and two parked C-130's. Crewmen courageously taxied a third Hercules from the inferno and received Silver Stars for their deed. Although land deliveries supplemented the air resupply, General Westmoreland later remarked that "along with the gallantry and tenacity of our forces, our tremendously successful air logistic operations was the key to the victory."

Combat operations in the northern portion of South Vietnam created special transportation problems for Allied forces. In 1966 highway communications north of Da Nang were in disrepair and highly insecure, while port facilities and airfields near the DMZ were primitive. In July the Marines deployed their forces immediately below the DMZ, using more than 250 trips by Marine KC-130's—with some aid from USAF aircraft—into the red dirt airstrip at Dong Ha. The allies later surfaced the strip and also opened a second all-weather field at Quang Tri. These projects required large quantities of scarce airstrip matting, as did the Khe Sanh strip improvement to the west. A prolonged C-130 airdrop supported operations and airstrip construction at Khe Sanh during the fall of 1967. The effort required cooperation among Navy suppliers at Da Nang, Army parachute riggers, Air Force crews, and the Marines at Khe Sanh.

The air supply of Khe Sanh during the first 4 months of 1968 represented a remarkable achievement, enabling 6,000 Allied defenders to survive under heavy NVA pressure until reopening of land communications in April. Favored by absolute air supremacy and the proximity of Khe Sanh to Da Nang (30 minutes), the Khe Sanh airlift nevertheless faced major problems stemming from difficult weather and the enemy's imaginative use of firepower. For much of the period, Communist fire forced a halt to C-130 landings and limited severely those by C-123's, thus necessitating reliance on airdrops. The Air Force overcame its hitherto chronic weakness in dropping supplies during poor visibility, by using ground radar to guide the C-130's to precise points over the Khe Sanh runway. The foul weather helped screen the transports from enemy gunners, although it also hindered fire suppression efforts by allied fighters. On most days the ability of Marine retrieval parties to clear loads from the rough drop zone limited the volume of supplies. Late in the siege C-130's began bulk deliveries within the Khe Sanh main perimeter using low-level extraction techniques.

Between 21 January and 8 April, the Air Force delivered 12,400 tons to Khe Sanh. The C-130's accounted for more than 90 percent of the total in 496 drops, 67 extractions, and 273 landings. C-123's made 105 drops and 179 landings; C-7 Caribous made 8 landings. During the early weeks, Marine KC-130's also delivered cargo. Throughout the siege, Marine helicopters resupplied hill positions outside the perimeter. During February alone, they hauled well over 1,000 tons. Supply levels never became dangerously low. Three C-123's and one Marine C-130 were destroyed during the battle.

The 1968 Communist Tet offensive severely challenged the airlift crews. The early attacks at Tan Son Nhut and many of the up-country airstrips temporarily dislocated the airlift system. However, transport crews managed to fly numerous emergency troop and supply missions on behalf of hard-pressed garrisons. By 3 February, the fourth day of the offensive, countrywide airlift sorties regained former levels. Sortie totals increased thereafter as crews flew to the limit of their capacity and as additional planes and crews arrived from offshore. With surface lines of communication disrupted throughout the month, demands for airlift remained high. The most critical area was the northern provinces, where winter monsoon weather and airspace congestion hampered resupply of expanded allied forces. But in all regions, the recovery from the enemy offensive depended upon the air transport system. Missions into Khe Sanh were unaffected by the Tet attacks.

Efforts of airlift crews were extraor-

dinary in two other 1968 operations. The first was Operation Delaware, the air invasion of the A Shau valley in April. Once more the C-130's faced a gauntlet of enemy fire and bad weather, this time without the assistance of ground radar. In daily supply drops to the 1st Cavalry Division at A Luoi, the C-130 crews used their radar and doppler equipment to navigate up the cloud-filled valley, breaking out just before visual release of cargo. During the 9-day period starting 26 April, the C-130's in 165 flights dropped 2,300 tons, nearly all of it ammunition. Drops continued even during one period when the weather was so bad that helicopters could not operate. One C-130 and its crew was lost to enemy fire; four others received major battle damage. The cavalry division commander termed the C-130 effort "one of the most magnificent displays of courage and airmanship that I have ever seen." A rebuilt A Luoi airstrip received its first Caribou on 2 May and its first C-123 and C-130 2 days later. Before rain closed the airstrip on the 11th, USAF transports made 113 landings, more than half by C-130's.

The air evacuation of the allied garrison at the Kham Duc mountain post on 12 May 1968 was equally spectacular. Intermittently through much of the day, Army and Marine helicopters lifted out survivors, while allied air strikes held off the enemy on all sides. During the morning a C-130 landed but received heavy damage, then departed with only three passengers, fuel steaming from shrapnel holes and tires stripped away. A C-123 made a successful morning pickup. In early afternoon, three C-130's attempted pickups. Enemy fire destroyed one after it took off with more than 100 civilian passengers; another, crippled in landing, was abandoned. Only the third made a successful landing and evacuation. Then, late in the afternoon, three C-130's succeeded in bringing out the last of the garrison. Of 1,500 survivors

A C-7 aircraft offloads cargo at isolated camp

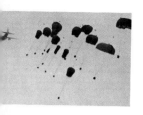

Supplies delivered by parachute

of Kham Duc, the Air Force flew out more than 500, nearly all in the final crucial minutes before the outpost fell.

One final act of valor ensued. Under orders to bring in a three-man USAF control team and unaware that the evacuation was already completed, a final C-130 landed at the now-hostile Kham Duc strip. Radio conversations soon after the Hercules took off made known the blunder. A C-123 made a touch-and-go landing and spotted the three men. A second C-123, piloted by Lt. Col. Joe M. Jackson and Maj. Jesse W. Campbell, landed under heavy fire and successfully removed the team. For his role in the rescue effort Jackson received the Medal of Honor, the only airlifter of the war so honored. Jackson wore the award with dignity in the years that followed, representing the thousands of USAF airlifters who shared pride in his recognition.

The small payload capacity of the C-7 Caribou normally discouraged its use in major tactical operations. On the other hand, excellent maneuverability at low altitude and slow airspeed enabled the Caribou to make accurate drops into small places. Furthermore, its small payloads were appropriate for garrisons lacking heavy recovery equipment; finally, simplicity of construction minimized the C-7's vulnerability to ground fire. Thus, the Caribou was used frequently for emergency drops, of which three were particularly noteworthy—the resupply of Duc Lap in August 1968, Ben Het in the spring of 1969, and Dak Seang a year later. The garrisons at all three survived heavy enemy pressure with the help of air-delivered supplies; hostile fire was severe in each instance, necessitating special tactics. At Duc Lap, the Caribou flew in at tree-top level, popping up to 300 feet at the last moment for the release. At Ben Het, the C-7's made run-ins at intervals of about 20 seconds, in coordination with pre-planned fire suppression from covering fighter aircraft. Similar tactics were less successful at Dak Seang, where three aircraft were lost in the first week of operations. The force then went over to night drops, the drop zone marked by signal fires and airborne flareships. During the battle, the C-7's made 125 drops over Dak Seang, releasing 250 tons; the garrison recovered 94 percent of these supplies.

Airlift efforts during 1969-1971 included massive support of the allied incursions into Cambodia and southern Laos. During 9 weeks commencing on 28 April 1970, aircraft of the 834th Air Division delivered 60,000 tons to more than 20 airfields in South Vietnam immediately adjacent to Cambodia. Ammunition lifts from Bien Hoa for a short period approached 1,000 tons daily. Missions into Cambodia were less extensive, but included more than 150 C-7 flights into the border strip at O Rang and several C-130 ammunition drops to U.S. forces near O Rang. Lam Son 719 was preceded by 250 C-130 flights, hauling a Vietnamese airborne division and other ARVN forces from Saigon to Dong Ha and Quang Tri. Over a 7-week period during the Laotian operation, the C-130's delivered more than 14,000 tons to a reconstructed logistics base at Khe Sanh. During the same period, C-141's of the Military Airlift Command flew some in-country movements to reduce aerial port backlogs.

The major North Vietnamese spring offensive in 1972 led to frequent Air Force supply flights in support of the defenders of Kontum and An Loc, two primary objectives of the enemy. Sustained air resupply into isolated Kontum began in April, with day landings halting on 17 May after enemy shells damaged several C-130's, burned two VNAF C-123's, and destroyed a C-130E. C-130 landings resumed exclusively at night on 18-19

1

2

(1) ARVN paratroopers board a C-130 prior to dropping into a Viet Cong area. (2) Parachute touchdown. (3) An Air Force combat control team watches Vietnamese paratroopers drop into a Viet Cong area. (4) A load master notifies pilot of completion of drop as ammunition pallet loads go out a C-123 rear door. (5) General McConnell (l.) congratulates Sgt Joseph F. Mack after presenting him and Capt. Joseph K. Glenn (center) the Silver Star and Distinguished Flying Cross. The two airmen were cited for heroic action in saving their damaged C-130 in 1967 during the battle of Dak To. (6) A C-123 taxis at an Army Special Forces camp. (7) Parachute drop from a C-123 transport to Marines at Khe Sanh. (8) A C-7 lands at Khe Sanh. (9) An Air Force combat controller team directs C-130 aerial delivery of equipment to troops in Tay Ninh province.

3

7

8

4

5

6

3

(1) A C-130 airdrops 105mm howitzers, prepared for the drop by ARVN troops, 1967. (2) C-123's airlifted U.S. Marines into Calu, South Vietnam, along with 6 tons of equipment. (3) C-130's delivered troops and supplies to a Tay Ninh airstrip during Operation Birmingham, April 1966. (4) A C-130 drops supplies to Marines at Khe Sanh, April 1968.

4

May, with 17 aircraft overcoming extreme hazards to make successful deliveries. Resupply continued nightly under cover of allied gunships, although in one instance a C-130 delayed its departure past dawn and was destroyed by ground fire. On 25 May the enemy seized a part of the runway, closing the field to landings. The supply burden momentarily fell upon VNAF and U.S. Army helicopters, but on the 28th C-130's began drops into one corner of the airfield. Although bundle recovery was difficult and slow, more than 2,000 tons were dropped in 130 sorties before C-130 night landings could be resumed on 8 June.

Aerial resupply to the 20,000 defenders and refugees at An Loc began in April, with deliveries by VNAF and U.S. helicopters and VNAF C-123's approximating 20 tons daily. Loss of a VNAF helicopter and a C-123 to enemy fire caused successive suspensions of these efforts. Air Force C-130's began daylight drops on 18 April. The first four aircraft successfully parachuted supplies but each received battle damage; a fifth ship went down west of the city. To reduce exposure, altitudes were raised above 6,000 feet, dropping with ground radar guidance. "High-altitude, low-opening" parachute techniques proved unsuccessful, however, as numerous chutes failed, in part because of inexperienced Vietnamese packers. The C-130's resumed low-level conventional drops even though all ships continued to receive hits.

On 26 April, after another C-130 was lost, the Air Force switched to night drops. Conducted visually with light signals, these too proved unsatisfactory, as many bundles missed the mark and some fell into enemy hands. The low point occurred the night of 2-3 May, when the C-130's failed to make a single successful delivery. Loss of a third C-130 on the following evening caused the cancellation of further

1

2

(1-3) C-130's delivering supplies to allied troops by airdrop and arresting cable.

182

night missions. High altitude, daylight drops were resumed on 5 May but now with the assistance of American parachute riggers brought in from Okinawa. Half of the parachutes opened properly and only one of the 24 bundles dropped that date fell into enemy hands. On 8 May the An Loc defenders recovered 68 of the 88 tons dropped. The drops became increasingly successful thereafter, the airlifters exclusively resupplying the defenders until the end of the siege on 18 June. In all, C-130's dropped 7,600 tons into the beleaguered city in more than 600 sorties, a dramatic and fitting climax to the 10-year history of the USAF tactical airlift arm in Vietnam.

Other Applications of Tactical Airlift

Air Force transports performed numerous noncombat transportation roles during the war. Passengers, mail, perishable foods, and high value equipment were moved between aerial ports throughout South Vietnam. Such loads frequently originated at airfields served by Military Airlift Command and the principal seaports —Saigon, Da Nang, and the Qui Nhon-Nha Trang-Cam Ranh Bay complex. For routine bulk hauling within Vietnam, air transport remained secondary to the surface modes. An exception was the Army Special Forces logistic system, which depended primarily on airlift for the routine supply of its camps. The C-130 force also made overwater hauls between offshore points and fields in Vietnam, averaging 7,000 tons monthly in the peak year, 1966.

The war in Laos required substantial air transport, of which USAF helicopters based in north Thailand provided a part. Civilian contract firms were primarily responsible for fixed-wing transport in Laos. The 315th Air Division operated a passenger and air logistic service within Thailand, linking the principal Air Force bases there. In September 1965, a rotational C-130 detachment at Bangkok took on this role, replacing C-123's previously rotated from South Vietnam.

Casualty evacuations in South Vietnam were almost entirely by air. Army helicopters performed most battlefield evacuations, while USAF transports hauled between the 18 in-country hospitals, mostly located at C-130 airfields. Transports carried unrigged litters at all times for emergency evacuations. The 903d Aeromedical Evacuation Squadron, organized in 1966, provided flight medical personnel and operated a control center at Tan Son Nhut to monitor patient movements. Mobile casualty staging teams entered South Vietnam in early 1967, thereafter performing patient care at certain forward airheads. 315th Air Division C-130's and C-118's performed patient evacuations from Vietnam to offshore points. Specifically configured for patient evacuations, the C-118's were assigned to the 6485th Operations Squadron, based originally in Japan and later at Clark in the Philippines. In 1968 a C-118 detachment began operating at Cam Ranh Bay to support in-country patient movements. All-jet C-9's finally replaced the C-118's in 1972 as the PACAF specialized aeromedical evacuation force.

Late in 1965, the Air Force deployed a squadron of CH-3 helicopters to South Vietnam, each able to carry a 3-ton payload about 200 miles. The squadron performed a variety of tasks, including delivery of supplies to USAF radar and communication sites in South Vietnam, and occasionally joined Army and Marine units in air supply operations. Both the CH-3's and the Air Force UH-1's later deployed played major roles in special warfare operations in Laos, Cambodia, and remote areas of South Vietnam. Management remained outside the Common Service Airlift System (CSAS). Because of interservice agreements, Air Force operation of

184

1

transport helicopters was quite limited.

Techniques of air delivery were advanced. Introduced in 1966 was the container delivery system, which permitted supply drops from 600 rather than 1,000 feet. Thereafter, C-130's employed the system in all drops except for the heaviest items. Low-level extraction systems developed in the early 1960's proved useful for pinpoint aerial deliveries. One of these, the ground proximity extraction system (GPES), used a hook-and-cable arrangement which required prepositioning of an arrestor gear. The other, the low altitude parachute extraction system (LAPES), required a large extraction parachute and a long cleared space on the ground (often an old airstrip). The Air Force used both systems at Khe Sanh with mixed success.

For most airlifters, flight operations in Southeast Asia were an abrupt change from the methods taught and

(1-2) A U.S. Air Force HH-43 helicopter delivers supplies to allied troops in Vietnam, July 1970.

2

practiced in the United States. In peacetime flying, crews adhered to written regulations, regularly attended flying safety meetings, and practiced endlessly the mechanical techniques of instrument flight. In Southeast Asia, however, crewmen quickly learned to rely on their own wits and judgment. Prescribed criteria of ceiling and visibility were generally overlooked. Crews flew visually whenever possible, looked for breaks in overcasts, and stayed underneath low ceilings except when over hostile areas. Squadron commanders frequently had to curb the enthusiasm of their crews and caution them against unnecessary risks—a difficult message in view of the heady sense of mission accomplishment generally felt.

Special hazards existed at the forward airheads, where the fixed-wing transports shared crowded ground and air space with seemingly uncontrolled helicopters, trucks, pedes-

trians, and assorted hazards. Landings required the concentration of the entire crew to avoid other traffic, friendly artillery, and high terrain—all while maneuvering clear of clouds and setting up precision final approaches. Joint working groups set up in late 1968 belatedly addressed the hazardous conditions.

Beginning in 1970 the Air Force substantially reduced its airlift forces in the Pacific. Remaining by the end of 1971 were only five C-130, three C-7, and one C-123 squadrons; the 834th was inactivated in November. In 1972 the Caribou and C-123 wings went out of existence, leaving only four squadrons of C-130E's based in Taiwan and Thailand. On the other hand, the VNAF airlift force expanded from two squadrons in 1970 to eight in late 1972, including three C-7 and three C-123 squadrons. Two squadrons were equipped with C-130A's just before the 1973 ceasefire, making available the C-123's for the air forces of Laos, Thailand, and Cambodia.

Over the years between 1962 and 1973, the Air Force delivered more than 7 million tons of passengers and cargo within South Vietnam. By comparison, U.S. and British transports carried slightly more than 2 million tons during the Berlin airlift and about 750,000 tons during the Korean War. The Air Force lost 53 C-130's in the Southeast Asia war, more than half of them in 1967 and 1968. C-123 losses (including 1 spray aircraft) also totaled 53 and C-7 losses numbered 20. Of these 126 aircraft, enemy action accounted for 61, including 17 destroyed by sapper or shelling attacks. The other 65 were lost from "operational" causes, mainly associated with the difficult conditions at forward airstrips. All but 10 of the losses occurred in South Vietnam. Those airlift crewmen killed or missing numbered 269. In Vietnam, the USAF tactical airlift arm lived up to its proud history, adding a new, illustrious chapter.

Strategic Airlift

Chapter X

When the large-scale deployment of military forces to South Vietnam got under way in 1965, the Air Force's Military Airlift Command (MAC) found itself assigned the task of providing urgent transportation of personnel and certain supplies from the United States to Southeast Asia. U.S. reliance on strategic airlift stemmed from the fact that ship movements nearly half way around the world were slow and that the Republic of Vietnam at the time lacked suitable ports, roads, and railways to remove and distribute efficiently the materiel once it had arrived. It was not uncommon during the 1965-1966 force buildup for ships to wait in harbors for days or weeks to be unloaded. The airlift into Southeast Asia was not entirely new to the Military Airlift Command. As early as 1954, under its former designation as Military Air Transport Service, it carried some 500 wounded foreign legionnaires back to France and Algeria after the fall of Dien Bien Phu. However, the airlift to Southeast Asia that began in 1965 grew to proportions unequaled in the history of strategic airlift.

In 1965, to fulfill the demands placed upon it, the command had 34 squadrons: 21 C-124 Globemasters, 3 C-133 Cargomasters, 7 C-130 Hercules, and 3 C-135 Stratolifters. Only the C-124 and C-133 had been originally designed as cargo aircraft, and both were nearing obsolescence. The aging Globemaster served admirably as an intratheater cargo transport, but its speed and range were inadequate for intertheater operations. Thus, the C-124 normally required about 95 hours of flying time to go from Travis AFB, Calif., to Saigon and return—or, at the then-current utilization rates, slightly more than 13 days. The C-133 made fewer stops and carried more, but its speed was marginal for strateg-

ic airlifts. Moreover, flight safety modifications to the C-133 during early 1965 limited its utilization.

MAC had acquired both the C-130 and C-135 as interim aircraft, pending development and production of advanced jet transports such as the C-141 Starlifter—then on the assembly line but not yet operational—and the controversial C-5 Galaxy, which was still under development. The C-130's and C-135's helped take on the expanding strategic airlift work, although neither was entirely suited for the Southeast Asia job. The C-130 lacked true strategic airlift speeds and ranges; on the other hand, these features were quite adequate on the C-135 but its load capacity was insufficient, particularly for outsized cargo.

Unable to meet the mushrooming airlift demands with its own aircraft, MAC solicited the help of the Air Force Reserve and Air National Guard. They were equipped with C-97, C-119, C-121, and C-124 aircraft which were 12 to 15 years old, difficult to maintain, and capable of transporting no more than 10 tons at a time over the Pacific. Nevertheless, through their ongoing training program, the reserves provided an available airlift resource and, between 1 August 1965 and 30 June 1966, they carried 30,000 tons of cargo and 5,790 passengers to the Pacific area. Indeed, by October 1972 Air Force Reserve crews alone had made 1,294 trips into the war zone, during which they delivered 30,434 tons of cargo and 3,600 passengers. Perhaps even more important, by employing these reservists on some MAC stateside missions, the command was able to release more of its own aircraft for operations into Southeast Asia. The Air Force Reserve and Air National Guard took over some internal and near-offshore transport aeromedical

-141 transports at a west-n Pacific base. They ayed a key role in deliver-g men and supplies to outheast Asia.

evacuation and air airlift missions starting on 1 August 1965.

But as demand for airlift to support the war outstripped capacity, the Air Force turned to the commercial airlines. The President chose not to declare a national emergency and take control of the more than 180 commercial airliners that made up the Civil Reserve Air Fleet (CRAF). Instead, MAC relied on contract leasing of

these aircraft. The arrangement worked well as there was little to fear from enemy air activity.

A milestone in the modernization of the strategic airlift fleet occurred in April 1965 when the C-141 Starlifter became operational and then began flying to SEA in August. By 1967, the C-141 fleet had grown to more than 100, and in 1968 the 284th and last C-141 was produced. The Starlifter could

A C-5 Galaxy, the world's largest aircraft, made its first deliveries to South Vietnam in August 1971.

carry 67,620 pounds of cargo 4,000 miles or 20,000 pounds non-stop from California to Japan at speeds of 440 knots. By comparison, the C-124 could carry 50,000 pounds over a range of 1,000 miles or 25,000 pounds for about 2,300 miles at speeds of only 200 knots.

Fleet modernization received another boost in 1969 when the world's largest aircraft, the C-5 Galaxy, entered service. The Air Force received its first C-5 on 17 December 1969. Possessing unique cargo capabilities, the aircraft added much to MAC's airlift posture. The C-5 could carry 164,383 pounds over 3,000 miles at a speed of 450 knots. Perhaps its best feature was the giant cargo compartment, which accommodates equipment 120 feet long, 19 feet wide, and 13½ feet high. The C-5 could transport about 98 percent of the Army's equipment, including self-propelled howitzers, personnel carriers, and tanks. Had they been available, only 17 C-5's could have done the work of the 300 or more aircraft used each day in the 1948-1949 Berlin airlift. The C-5 made its first deliveries to South Vietnam in August 1971. In the months that followed, particularly in the spring of 1972, it played a major role in SEA strategic airlift. By mid-1973, MAC had 77 Galaxies ready for duty.

Bases and Routes

In responding to the urgent SEA requirements, the Air Force quickly found the base and route structure inadequate for the unusually heavy airlift traffic. Congestion quickly developed over routes into the theater. This was particularly true in South Vietnam, where all commercial inbound cargo and passenger flights processed through Tan Son Nhut. At this major South Vietnamese airfield, a huge cargo transshipment workload resulted and grew worse as the American military buildup increased. Soon the base had the highest air traffic density in the world.

Similar difficulties were encountered at en route stations throughout the Pacific area because of the tremendous flight surge. Pacific operations of MAC's 21st Air Force alone rose from 2,000 flying hours during January 1965 to more than 11,000 the following June. Overall, traffic to the Pacific grew from a monthly average of 33,779 passengers and 9,123 tons of cargo in fiscal year 1965 to 65,350 passengers and 42,296 tons of cargo in fiscal year 1967. Clark Air Base, the major Philippines terminal en route to South Vietnam, was particularly saturated.

To relieve congestion and speed cargo handling in South Vietnam, the United States initiated a vast construction program in that country. Dual runways were built at several existing bases and new air facilities added. This included new passenger terminals at Kontum, Qui Nhon, Tuy Hoa, Phu Cat, Da Nang, and Cam Ranh Bay. At Yokota Air Base, Japan, a passenger terminal capable of processing 35,000 personnel monthly opened in March 1969.

Aerial port backlogs also developed in the United States. In 1965 MAC's worldwide operations centered on several coastal aerial ports of embarkation (APOE's). Each served only specific destinations in the adjacent oceanic area. All passengers and cargo destined for SEA processed initially through Travis AFB, Calif., and it soon was congested.

As improved facilities became available, MAC increased its cargo routes between the United States and South Vietnam from 1 to more than 12, and passenger routes from 1 to more than 6. Many interconnecting routes were also established between the United States and numerous Pacific stations to and from the bases in Vietnam. The expansion of airlift services to these points reduced the transshipment

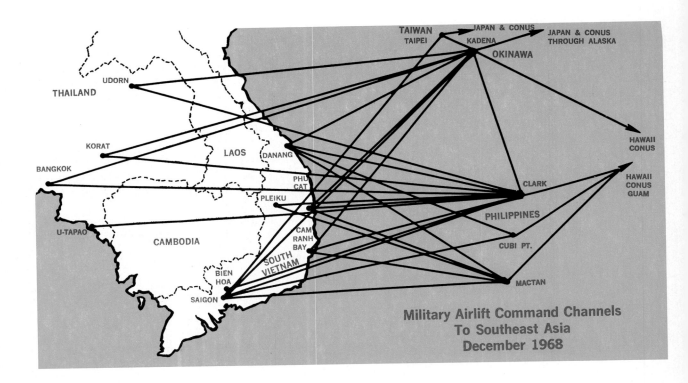

THAILAND
UDORN
KORAT
BANGKOK
U-TAPAO
LAOS
DANANG
PHU CAT
PLEIKU
CAMBODIA
CAM RANH BAY
SOUTH VIETNAM
BIEN HOA
SAIGON
TAIWAN
TAIPEI
JAPAN & CONUS
KADENA
OKINAWA
JAPAN & CONUS THROUGH ALASKA
HAWAII CONUS
CLARK
PHILIPPINES
HAWAII CONUS GUAM
CUBI PT.
MACTAN

Military Airlift Command Channels
To Southeast Asia
December 1968

workload that had contributed to the Tan Son Nhut congestion difficulties.

The Air Force removed or reduced bottlenecks at many of the en route bases by dispatching large numbers of MAC personnel to help out at the saturated or expanding stations. Other measures to ease traffic problems included securing approval to use Mactan Air Base in the Philippines, staging aircrews throughout the Pacific more efficiently, adjusting route patterns, bypassing saturated bases, and scheduling maintenance only at home bases. As examples of adjusting routes to the performance of the latest aircraft, the C-141 and C-5 did not need to land at Wake Island on their way from Hawaii to Southeast Asia, since flights on the "great circle" route between the United States and Southeast Asia operated via Elmendorf AFB, Alaska, and Japan.

On 1 April 1965, after a year of testing a concept of originating Pacific flights from the middle or eastern United States, the Air Force opened Kelly AFB, Tex., as a port of common-user service to western Pacific installations. Shortly thereafter, on 1 July, the APOE at McChord AFB, near the Army troop processing center at Fort Lewis, expanded to include passenger service to Japan and Korea. On 1 October Norton AFB, Calif., became an aerial port to provide cargo service to Okinawa and Vietnam.

The use of eastern U.S. bases as aerial ports for Southeast Asia began in April 1966, with cargo routes between Dover AFB, Del., and Clark and Tan Son Nhut Air Bases and between Charleston AFB, S.C., and Don Muang AB, Thailand. In May, passenger service from McGuire AFB, N.J., to South Vietnam also was initiated. These flights used the North Pacific route. On 1 January 1968 another aerial port in the interior, at Tinker AFB, Okla., began serving Guam and Thai bases directly, reducing cargo transshipments.

Lt. Gen. Tran Van Minh, commander in chief, Vietnamese Air Force, salutes Vietnamese student pilots on arrival at Keesler AFB in January 1972. Maj. Gen. Frank M. Madsen, Jr., USAF escorts him.

Improving the aerial ports through mechanization also helped relieve congestion and reduce transit times. The Air Force installed automated terminals at Travis in February 1965 and at McChord in early 1966. The automated system—463L Materials Handling Support System—included special vehicles to facilitate aircraft loading and unloading. Another effective measure to reduce in-transit down time of aircraft called for prepositioning crews at en route bases, thereby eliminating aircraft standdowns for crew rests. With standby crews at Hickam and Wake Island, for example, aircraft ground time decreased from 15 to 4 hours.

Coincident with the tremendous military expansion in Southeast Asia, the Secretary of Defense authorized the Air Force to increase the utilization rate of its aircraft incrementally. By 30 June 1966, this acceleration—appropriately named Fast Fly—saw aircraft utilization climb from a daily peacetime rate of 2.5 hours for troop carriers and 5 hours for air transports to approximately 4 and 8 hours, respectively. This had an important im-

(1) At Qui Nhon airfield the Air Force's 15th Aerial Port Squadron processed an average of 25,000 passengers per month. (2-3) Unloading U.S. Army helicopters from a C-5 Galaxy at Cam Ranh Bay. (4) Memorial service at Tan Son Nhut AB for U.S. soldiers killed in action. (5) The cavernous C-5A Galaxy cargo area after military supplies have been deposited at Cam Ranh Bay.

1

2

3

4

5

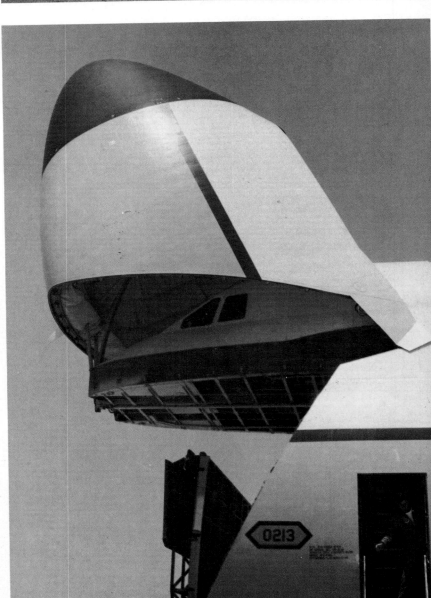

(1) An Air Force C-141 Starlifter at Bien Hoa AB, South Vietnam. (2-8) The strategic airlift in support of the war effort included the C-5 Galaxie, the largest transport in the world, the C-141 Starlifter, and the C-133 Cargomaster.)

8

7

pact on personnel, particularly on flight service and maintenance crews. Additional personnel were acquired from SAC units being discontinued and were put through a special training program.

To expedite the flow of critically required cargo from the aerial ports, the Air Force employed a series of priority designations: "999" identified the highest priority cargo; "Green Sheet" covered cargo to be moved ahead of older cargo of the same priority; and "Red Ball" (an airlift reference to the famous World War II truck express in Europe) tagged priority Army spare parts for inoperative combat equipment. The Military Airlift Command began its Red Ball Express on 8 December 1965, guaranteeing shipment within 24 hours of receipt at the APOE. The 1,000th Red Ball mission departed Travis on 1 May 1967.

MAC's primary responsibility involved the intertheater delivery of personnel and cargo, but it also performed numerous intratheater tasks. Before the Vietnam conflict, the Pacific Air Forces relied on its own tactical transports to move personnel and cargo to and from Japan, Okinawa, Taiwan, and the Philippines. The war in Southeast Asia, however, put a severe strain on PACAF's ability to operate the intratheater airlift system while also meeting tactical airlift requirements in South Vietnam. Whereupon, the Air Force decided that MAC should assume a major portion of the intratheater airlift load over routes previously supported by tactical airlift. Accordingly, Military Airlift Command established several new routes, extended others, and diverted aircraft in the theater for special assignments.

Intratheater cargo flights varied from the delivery of ammunition to Da Nang from Kadena to the movement of troops and equipment within South Vietnam. Altogether, MAC intratheater activity increased dramatically—from 53,198 tons of cargo and 175,539 passengers in 1965 to 117,465 tons and 254,000 passengers in 1966, and to 141,113 tons and 347,027 passengers in 1967. The largest increases occurred on the routes from Japan, Okinawa, and the Philippines to Southeast Asia.

1

(1) Aerial view of C-5 Galaxy, with viser raised at Cam Ranh Bay.

Airlifting Troops

The task of getting essential supplies, personnel, and units to Vietnam was a staggering one. In flying about 210,000,000 miles during 1967, MAC flew the equivalent of 8,750 aircraft around the world and carried sufficient troops to fill every manpower space in 85 Army infantry divisions. Military aircraft carried most of the cargo while chartered commercial airliners carried most of the passengers.

196

(2) Bulky cargo is removed from the C-5 by forklift, 1972.

sorties over a 26-day period and moving 3,000 troops and 4,700 tons of equipment some 6,000 miles to Pleiku by 23 January 1966. For a time, a C-141 or C-133 took off from Hickam every 3 hours. At the other end, aircraft unloaded with their engines running, enabling them to depart in an average time of 17 minutes instead of the planned 1 to 2 hours. Blue Light was completed 8 days ahead of schedule.

The Army required special airlift assistance again in late 1967 to move the remainder of the 101st Airborne Division from Fort Campbell, Ky., to Bien Hoa, Vietnam. Under the designation of Operation Eagle Thrust, MAC flew 10,355 paratroopers and 5,118 tons of equipment, including 37 helicopters, via 413 C-141 and C-133 flights between 17 November and 29 December —the largest single airlift of combat troops undertaken from the United States to a war zone to that time. Engine-running offloading procedures and the performance of support personnel enabled the aircraft to unload on the average of less than 7.5 minutes.

In February 1968, while still supporting a buildup of ground and air forces in Korea following the seizure of the USS *Pueblo*, MAC undertook the emergency movement of ground troops to South Vietnam to help stem the Communist Tet offensive. Involved were a brigade of the 82d Airborne Division at Fort Bragg, N.C., and a regiment of the 5th Marine Division at Camp Pendleton, Calif. Between 14 and 26 February, MAC successfully deployed more than 6,000 troops and almost 3,500 tons of equipment in 258 C-141 and C-133 flights. Fourteen reserve C-124 groups, which had not been recalled in January, also flew 158 support missions into Saigon.

In mid-1969 emphasis shifted to the return of units to the United States in accordance with the President's policy of gradual American withdrawal from Vietnam, beginning with 25,000

Not to be overlooked were the thousands of combat personnel flown by these aircraft to Honolulu and nine other cities in the Pacific area for rest and recuperation (R&R) leaves. The R&R flights began in fiscal year 1966 with 14,970 passengers. The numbers increased to 521,496 in 1967 and to 774,386 in fiscal year 1968.

On several occasions during the war, the Air Force was called on to undertake the deployment of major Army units under special conditions. The first of these, designated Operation Blue Light, came in response to the need to rush the 3d Brigade, 25th Infantry Division from Hawaii to Pleiku, Vietnam, to offset a buildup of Communist forces late in 1965 that threatened the area. The Military Airlift Command reacted quickly, flying 231 troops before 31 August. The Military Airlift Command carried out the redeployments through a series of operations called Keystone. In the first of these, MAC airlifted 15,446 of the 25,000 troops plus 47.5 tons of materiel. As the President directed other incremental withdrawals over the next several years, MAC responded accordingly.

In April 1972, after North Vietnam launched its spring offensive into South Vietnam, the Air Force dispatched the 49th Tactical Fighter Wing from Holloman AFB, N.M., to Takhli, Thailand (Operation Constant Guard). In support, MAC teamed up the C-5 Galaxy with the C-141 and commercial carriers and, starting on 6 May 1972, moved the wing's 3,195 personnel and 1,600 tons of cargo in only 9 days.

When the Communist offensive swept through the provincial capital of Quang Tri and moved southward, the U.S. Army turned to the Air Force to deliver more tanks and armored vehicles to the South Vietnamese. In response, the C-5 fleet airlifted 26 tanks —weighing about 1.6 million pounds —in 10 flights directly to Da Nang, including 6 which were delivered from a repair depot in the Pacific within 24 hours. Offloading averaged 32 minutes, and the tanks were in battle in a matter of hours.

Return of the POW's

As American participation in the war phased out, MAC devoted considerable airlift capacity to equipment being delivered to South Vietnamese forces. Following the peace agreements in January 1973, MAC turned its attention to the withdrawal of the remaining American military personnel and equipment from Vietnam. This task involved several thousand tons of equipment and more than 20,000 personnel.

One of the most dramatic airlift operations of the war—which captured the attention of millions of people

1

2

3

4

(1) An army truck is unloaded from a C-124 at a SEA base. (2) Unloading cargo from a C-5. (3) U.S. Army troops prepare to board a C-141 for the flight back to the United States. (4) A C-5 Galaxy takes off from Cam Ranh Bay.

A C-5 Galaxy takes off from Cam Ranh Bay.

around the world and brought to an end more than a decade of direct U.S. involvement in the conflict—was the return of American prisoners of war. Designated Operation Homecoming (see Chapter XXI), it consisted of three major phases: repatriating the prisoners and airlifting them to a processing center at Clark AB, continuing their homecoming journey to the United States, and then getting them to a hospital for a thorough medical examination.

Given the responsibility for airlifting the POW's from North Vietnam, the Military Airlift Command prepositioned several C-141's at Clark. Sparkling from the polishing given them and displaying red crosses on their tall tails, the Starlifters waited for the signal to take off for North Vietnam. Arrangements called for the release of the first 116 prisoners on 12 February, and three C-141's landed at Hanoi's Gia Lam airport one at a time, picked up the POW's, and returned them to Clark. North Vietnam released the remainder of the prisoners in 9 groups ranging in size from 10 to 108. In accordance with the schedules, C-141's picked up the prisoners during a 7-week period, with the last 67 leaving Hanoi on 29 March 1972.

At Clark, the repatriates underwent a medical examination and received individually tailored uniforms complete with appropriate insignia and ribbons. Boarding C-141's once again, they were whisked across the Pacific on the next and longest leg of their return to home and family. Upon their arrival in the continental United States, the returnees boarded C-9 Nightingale aeromedical aircraft and flew to 1 of 23 airfields serving 31 military hospitals nearest their homes. Completed with precision, the airlift portion of Homecoming drew praise for a flawless performance. This included a citation from the National Defense Transportation Association for undoubtedly the most popular airlift in the nation's history.

Chapter XI

Air Refueling

On 9 June 1964, four KC-135 jet tankers operating out of Clark AB in the Philippines under the nickname Yankee Team Tanker Task Force (TTF) provided inflight refueling over Da Nang to eight F-100 fighters on their way to strike Pathet Lao antiaircraft emplacements on the Plain of Jars. The KC-135's then loitered over southern Laos, ready to provide post-strike refueling as needed. After refueling two of the fighters, the KC-135's returned to Clark. They remained there until 15 June, then returned to Andersen AFB, Guam, where they rejoined the main body of the tanker task force supporting routine Tactical Air Command (TAC) deployments across the Pacific.

The Yankee Team refueling of 9 June was significant because it marked the first time that SAC tankers had directly supported combat operations in Southeast Asia. Also of interest was the fact that the receiving aircraft were fighters rather than B-52 bombers, the aircraft usually paired with the giant Stratotanker. The routine manner of performing the intricate aerial refueling in their unusual 9 June assignment also provided testimony to the proficiency that KC-135 crews and fighter pilots had attained in this technique.

Introduction of the KC-135 into the USAF inventory in 1957 provided significantly improved means of aerial refueling for SAC's bomber force. With it, refueling could be done at altitudes and speeds approaching or equalling those of the receiver aircraft. While refueling bombers was its primary mission, in 1959 the KC-135 was successfully tested with jet fighters and assigned to refuel TAC aircraft during some exercises and movements to and from overseas bases. In 1961, the Air Force designated SAC as single manager for the aerial refueling of its own and TAC forces.

Following the Gulf of Tonkin incident in August 1964, the Air Force ordered a deployment of 84 fighters from the United States to the western Pacific. They were supported by 48 tankers, some of which were quickly deployed to augment those already based at Andersen AFB, Guam, and Hickam AFB, Hawaii. By 15 August, after flying 172 refueling sorties, all deployed tankers returned to their home bases. At this time, the JCS directed reestablishment of the Yankee Team TTF in the Philippines to provide refueling support for SEA combat missions. Renamed Foreign Legion, the task force of eight KC-135's undertook its first operational refueling on 28 September.

In October 1964, when PACAF's obsolete KB-50 tankers were permanently grounded, SAC assumed responsibility for the PACAF air refueling requirements, with the Foreign Legion task force given the job. By the end of 1964, its KC-135's had flown 235 sorties, made 948 refuelings, and offloaded 11,900,000 pounds of fuel in western Pacific operations. To carry on this expanding task, the Air Force instituted a system wherein the aircraft and crews rotated with those at home on a regular basis.

The Foreign Legion force operated only until the end of the year, when the Air Force worked out a more permanent arrangement. Effective 12 January 1965, SAC organized the 4252d Strategic Wing at Kadena AB, Okinawa. It was assigned responsibility for operating and maintaining a tanker task force of about 15 KC-135's in support of tactical aircraft operations in Southeast Asia (nicknamed Young Tiger). As before, the task force consisted of aircraft and crews on tempo-

inflight refueling of the Phantom.

201

1

2

3

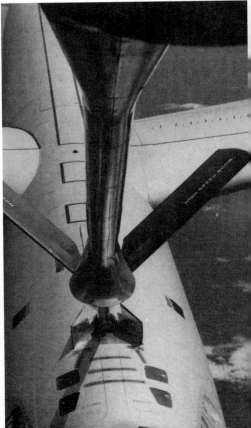

(1-3) Inflight refueling of B-52's. (4) An F-105 trails another in a refueling operation. (5) Refueling F-105's. (6) Refueling an F-4 Phantom. (7) Refueling an Air Force HH-3E helicopter over the Gulf of Tonkin by an HC-130.

rary duty, replaced periodically by others from the United States. The first Young Tiger inflight refueling occurred on 25 January 1965.

The 4252d soon developed a forward operating task force, designated Tiger Cub, at Don Muang Airport, Thailand. Early in March, this detachment, with four tankers acquired from the discontinued Foreign Legion force at Clark, began refueling combat fighters. The remaining Foreign Legion tankers were sent to Kadena.

In early 1965 a B-52 force also was deployed to Andersen for possible combat in Southeast Asia. Departing stateside bases on 17 February, the 30 bombers were refueled enroute by a tanker force of 38 KC-135's gathered in from 9 different air refueling squadrons and operating out of Castle AFB, Calif. Simultaneously with the bomber flight, an Arc Light tanker force, composed of the 904th and 913th Air Refueling Squadrons, was on its way to Kadena. These tankers performed no inflight refueling. Instead they carried about 30,000 pounds of cargo and passengers. This logistical role for the KC-135 would be repeated often within the Strategic Air Command as it airlifted personnel and supplies from one Pacific base to another or between them and the United States.

In mid-May, the 913th tankers returned to Barksdale AFB, La., along with the 2d Bomb Wing's B-52's. They were replaced at Kadena by KC-135's of the 7th Air Refueling Squadron, a subordinate unit of the 7th Bomb Wing which had joined the 320th at Andersen to form the Arc Light contingent. Thus, the pattern of maintaining Arc Light forces—bombers at Andersen and tankers at Kadena—was firmly established well before the bombing commenced. This mode of deployment would undergo several changes during the next few years. As the bomber and tanker forces grew, their basic elements consisted of "cadre units" to which were added aircraft called "augmentees." Both Young

Tiger and Arc Light tankers, although sent for different purposes, were organizationally placed under the 4252d Strategic Wing. And until the first B-52 bombing mission in June 1965, both sets of tankers were used to refuel tactical combat aircraft.

On 18 June, when 30 bombers took off from Andersen on their first bombing mission, 30 tankers left Kadena, arrived on schedule at the designated rendezvous northwest of Luzon, and refueled 27 bombers (two were lost in a mid-air collision and one did not take on fuel) on their way to South Vietnam. Refueling 30 bombers was accomplished without incident on 5 and 7 July, setting a pattern that continued for the next several months. Only the rendezvous point shifted occasionally to accommodate changes in weather. During October, the number of B-52's dispatched on missions began to vary, sometimes numbering as few as 15, and the refueling force was, of course, adjusted accordingly. Bomber destinations also influenced the number of tankers dispatched; obviously the closer the targets to Guam, the less fuel was required.

To transfer fuels from the tankers required two different techniques, depending on the type of aircraft being serviced. All bombers and some fighters, particularly those employed late in the war, had receptacles for the tankers' flying boom. To effect a hookup, the pilot of the receiver aircraft simply positioned himself behind and slightly under the tanker. The boom operator on the tanker then directed a 46-foot boom into the receiver's refueling receptacle, and the fuel transfer began. Several fighters used in the early years of the war, notably the F-100, were not equipped with boom receptacles and relied instead on the probe and drogue system. In this instance, the KC-135 used a drogue (a funnel-like device at the end of a flexible hose) which could be installed quickly on the boom. The latter was extended and maintained in a stable flight position, and the fighter aircraft then flew its probe into the drogue.

In addition to its boom operator, who was the only enlisted man on board, the KC-135 crew consisted of a pilot, co-pilot, and navigator. With such a small crew, the members performed some duties (flight engineer and loadmaster functions, for example) normally done by others on cargo aircraft. The pilot and co-pilot were responsible for fuel management—the distribution, balance, and offloading of the fuel. The navigator operated the electronic rendezvous equipment, and the boom operator assisted the navigator by making celestial observations with a periscope sextant.

Increasing Demands for Fuel

As bomber and fighter operations expanded, demand for inflight refueling grew. This, in turn, led to the idea of moving more KC-135's closer to the combat areas, particularly in view of the satisfactory Don Muang arrangement. Thereafter, and during the next 8 years, the Air Force stationed tankers at three additional Thai bases (Takhli, U-Tapao, and Korat) and at Ching Chuan Kang AB, Taiwan (commonly called CCK). The first of these expansions occurred in September 1965, when tankers moved to Takhli under the designation of King Cobra and supplemented those at Don Muang in refueling the Thai-based fighters. This had the beneficial effect of eliminating the long flights from Okinawa to the refueling areas over Thailand. By the end of 1965, there were about 55 tankers in the western Pacific: 40 at Kadena, 10 at Takhli, and 5 at Don Muang. During the year the tankers flew more than 9,200 sorties, conducted 31,250 refuelings, and transferred approximately 315,000,000 pounds of fuel.

On 2 June 1966, SAC organized the 4258th Strategic Wing at the U-Tapao

AB, then under construction in Thailand, to take over the Young Tiger job —refueling tactical combat aircraft— from the Kadena-based tankers of the 4252d. On 11 August, with the runway just completed, the first KC-135 landed at U-Tapao, then flew its first mission the same day. Throughout the remainder of the year—pending arrival of permanent ground personnel (flight crews normally were on temporary duty)—the U-Tapao tankers operated as a forward operating element of the 4252d. In late October, the Don Muang force ceased operations and its aircraft relocated to U-Tapao.

By the close of 1966, there were 75 KC-135's in the western Pacific. About 45 were at Kadena, primarily supporting Arc Light flights, although a few still flew tactical missions; another 20 were at U-Tapao, and the remainder were at Takhli, During the year, the tankers flew about 18,203 sorties, almost 11,000 of them in support of the fighters. More than 78,000 refuelings were effected in offloading more than 850,000,000 pounds of fuel.

On 1 January 1967, the 4258th Strategic Wing assumed full responsibility for the U-Tapao operations; a month later it assumed control of the Takhli tankers formerly belonging to the 4252d. The separation of refueling responsibilities was now complete. The 4252d at Kadena supported Arc Light bombers and the 4258th at U-Tapao and Takhli refueled the fighters. On occasion, however, the Kadena tankers furnished fighter support as required. Early in April, part of the B-52 Arc Light force began operating out of U-Tapao. These B-52's could normally complete their missions without inflight refueling.

At year's end, the tanker force numbered approximately 80—45 of them at Kadena, 30 at U-Tapao, and 5 at Takhli. Southeast Asia aerial refueling statistics during 1967 were again impressive, with approximately 22,891 sorties and more than 103,415 inflight transfers involving more than 1 billion pounds of fuel. Arc Light and other SAC support activities accounted for 9,180 sorties and 7,469 refuelings. The importance of the KC-135 to tactical operations was evident from the 13,711 sorties and 95,946 refuelings. In providing this support, one tanker ordinarily satisfied the needs of several fighter aircraft.

On 23 January 1968, North Korea seized the USS *Pueblo* in the Sea of Japan, and on 30 January the enemy launched the Tet offensive in South Vietnam. The United States responded to these crises by sending more B-52's to Andersen, others to Kadena, and increasing the number of fighters in the western Pacific, particularly in Korea. By mid-year, with demand for inflight refueling having reached an all time high, the tankers engaged in supporting operations had grown to more than 90, including 35 at Kadena, 40 at U-Tapao, and 15 at Ching Chuan Kang.

Although their primary job continued to be the refueling of the B-52's from Andersen, the Kadena tankers also supported PACAF flights in the northern Pacific areas and, after mid-February 1968, refueled B-52's launched from Kadena. Located closer to the target areas, these B-52's required fewer refuelings than those from Andersen. Normally, one tanker could service three Kadena bombers. As before, refueling for fighter combat operations came from U-Tapao, with Ching Chuan Kang now the second base. CCK entered the scene in February when the 4200th Air Refueling Squadron was activated with tankers formerly based at Takhli.

Concurrently with the tanker move to CCK, KC-135 radio-relay aircraft, operating since 1966 from U-Tapao, relocated there. Although these tankers had an emergency refueling capability and occasionally performed for that purpose, they were primarily responsible for operating a continuous radio link in the area of the Gulf of Tonkin. Through their radio contact

206

1

2

with tactical air control centers in Vietnam, these tankers served as airborne information and communication posts for American aircraft operating over much of Southeast Asia. In addition, as had been the case since the beginning of Arc Light, several KC-135's maintained an emergency strip alert on Andersen.

Southeast Asia refueling operations in 1968 broke all records, even though bombing of North Vietnam was halted during the year. During approximately 32,000 KC-135 sorties, more than 1.6 billion pounds of fuel was offloaded in more than 129,000 refuelings. As in previous years, tactical aircraft received most of the inflight support—18,667 sorties and 114,744 refuelings.

In 1969, KC-135 sorties dropped by more than 10 percent, to below 28,000, and fuel offloaded decreased to about 1.4 billion pounds while refuelings actually increased to 138,164, approximately 9,000 more than a year earlier. This apparent contradiction in increased fighter and decreased B-52 requirements stemmed from the gradual shift of bomber operations from Andersen to Kadena and U-Tapao. In fact, about 65 percent of the B-52 sorties originated at U-Tapao and normally required no aerial refueling.

During the next 2 years, as the American air campaign in Southeast Asia declined, air refueling activity dropped correspondingly. By mid-September 1970, all Arc Light operations were concentrated on U-Tapao, eliminating the requirement for air refueling support from Kadena. Late in 1970, fewer than 50 tankers were operating in the western Pacific: 30 at U-Tapao which refueled fighters and flew radio-relay missions, 15 at Kadena supported other requirements, and several continued on emergency strip alert at Andersen. Refueling operations dropped precipitously in 1970 to the lowest level in 5 years. Of approximately 19,540 sorties flown, more than 13,500 were devoted to fighter support and associated activi-

ties, while less than 6,000 assisted several types of strategic and related operations. The fighters accounted for about 82,000 individual refuelings, another 2,800 were specifically for B-52 bombing operations, and the remainder supported other strategic activities. Offloaded fuel in 1970 totalled 888,200,000 pounds.

In 1971, aerial refueling operations dropped again. In approximately 14,400 sorties, the KC-135's conducted 62,600 refuelings to offload 618,500,000 pounds. As usual, the preponderance of refueling activity—approximately 10,500 sorties and 61,000 refuelings—supported fighters. In November and December there was a noticeable increase in refueling as the Seventh Air Force conducted Operation Commando Hunt VII against growing personnel and materiel traffic on the Ho Chi Minh trail.

The 1972 Surge

The North Vietnamese invasion of South Vietnam during the spring and summer months of 1972 prompted expanded B-52 and tactical air operations and a concomitant surge in air refueling. The revival of Andersen as a B-52 base for these operations imposed greater demands on Kadena tankers. By the end of June, approximately 60 KC-135's, including the radio-relay aircraft which had relocated from U-Tapao, were based at Kadena. Closer to home, tactical requirements grew as additional fighter squadrons deployed into the western Pacific to support the South Vietnamese. During a 5-week period in April and May, TAC deployed nine squadrons to the area. Approximately 150 tankers supported these deployments on schedule with no fighter being delayed for lack of fuel.

Once in place, these fighters began combat operations requiring inflight refueling. U-Tapao soon had 45 tankers, but these proved insufficient to keep up with demand. Accordingly, in May and June, 70 additional KC-135's deployed to Clark and to three Thai bases—Don Muang, Takhli, and Korat —bringing to 115 the number of tankers supporting tactical operations. The KC-135 force remained at this level until October and November when several tankers were withdrawn from Don Muang, Korat, and Ching Chuan Kang AB (which replaced Clark in August).

In December 1972, when the United States resumed the large-scale bombing of North Vietnam, the tanker force increased again, to approximately 195. Major increases at Kadena supported the growing B-52 flights from Andersen. Other tankers were sent to Takhli and to a new detachment activated at Clark. In the 11-day bombing of Hanoi and Haiphong between 17-28 December, the tankers flew 1,390 sorties and made 4,625 inflight refuelings.

During 1972, the KC-135's flew about 34,700 sorties in Southeast Asia, some 2,700 more than in 1968, the previous high year. Approximately two-thirds supported tactical aircraft operations. The other third were devoted to SAC activities: B-52 bombing missions, reconnaissance flights, radio-relay sorties, and deployment flights to and from operational bases. The 115,272 refuelings (106,913 to fighters) were significantly below the levels of 1968 and 1969 but the fuel offloaded (more than 1.4 billion pounds) was second only to the record-breaking year of 1968.

With the suspension of bombing in North Vietnam and the resumption of peace negotiations, inflight refueling requirements decreased markedly. As a result, in late January 1973 many of the augmentee tankers including those at Clark returned to their home bases. In February, others returned home after being withdrawn from Takhli, Kadena, and Andersen.

The Air Force continued to retain more than 100 KC-135's in the western Pacific until U.S. participation in the war formally ended on 15 August

(1) Using model aircraft, these four officers demonstrate what may be the first tri-level air refueling in history, during which they saved six Navy aircraft and two Air Force F-104's. They are: (l. to r.) Maj. John H. Casteel, aircraft commander; Capt. Richard L. Trail, co-pilot; Capt. Dean L. Hoar, navigator; and MSgt Nathan C. Campbell, boom operator. (2) A fuel specialist with the 15th Air Base Wing checks a fuel sample for impurities.

1973. Approximately 50 were at Kadena, assigned temporarily to the 376th Strategic Wing, which had replaced the 4252d Strategic Wing in early 1970. A similar-sized force was on temporary duty with the 310th Strategic Wing Provisional, organized in June 1972 to handle the increased tactical air refueling mission at U-Tapao and the radio-relay aircraft that had returned in February 1973 after 10 months at Kadena. Several KC-135's remained on alert at Andersen.

During the last months of the war, between 1 January and 15 August 1973, the KC-135's flew 15,603 sorties. Approximately 6,900 supported SAC flights and the remainder tactical aircraft missions. In more than 67,000 refuelings, more than 726,000,000 pounds of fuel were dispensed.

In slightly more than 9 years in and around Southeast Asia, SAC tankers

An Air Force tanker refuels a flight of four F-105's heading for targets in North Vietnam.

Many fighter pilots departed successful hook-ups with a grateful "Thanks, tank, you can count this a save."

While most emergency refuelings involved USAF fighters, there were some with U.S. Navy aircraft. One such occasion on 31 May 1967 over the Gulf of Tonkin turned into perhaps the most complex and spectacular refueling ever accomplished. It started during the routine refueling of two F-104's when the tanker received word to intercept two Navy aircraft almost out of fuel. Periodically refueling the two F-104's that went along to provide MIG cover, the tanker successfully rendezvoused with the two Navy A-3 tankers, one with only 3 minutes of fuel (both had fuel aboard which they could transfer but could not use themselves). After taking on a small amount of fuel from the KC-135 the first Navy tanker pulled away and allowed the second A-3 to hook up. As this tanker took on fuel, two Navy F-8's came into the area for emergency refueling. One was so low on fuel that it could not wait for the A-3 tanker to complete its own refueling from the KC-135. It hooked up to the A-3 and began taking on fuel while the Navy tanker continued to draw from the KC-135. Concurrently with this unprecedented tri-level refueling, the first A-3 serviced the second F-8 and then returned to the KC-135 for additional fuel.

In the midst of this emergency, the KC-135 was informed of two Navy F-4's with insufficient fuel to return to their carrier. After refueling the two F-104's again, the KC-135 rendezvoused with the two F-4's and successfully refueled them. By this time, the KC-135's own fuel supply was so low that it could not return to its home base and had to land at an alternate base in South Vietnam, but not before again refueling the two F-104's. For this amazing series of life-saving refuelings, Maj. John H. Casteel and his crew received the 1967 Mackay Trophy, presented annually for the most meritorious USAF flight of the year.

provided almost 9 billion pounds of fuel, flew 194,687 sorties, and made 813,878 refuelings. Impressive as these statistics were, they fail to reflect the KC-135's real contributions to the overall USAF effort in Southeast Asia. Before the war, the KC-135 had demonstrated repeatedly that its availability could reduce by several days the movement of combat aircraft to forward operating locations. Its use for this purpose and in support of fighter and B-52 combat operations was vital to the conduct of the air war.

Not the least of its contributions was in saving fighter aircraft and the lives of their crews. Without the tankers, many fuel-starved fighters would have never returned to their bases. The refueling of these aircraft brought into being a new term, "aircraft save," which soon became common parlance among fighter and tanker crews.

Chapter XII

Tactical Reconnaissance

Throughout the war the Air Force relied heavily on its tactical reconnaissance force to provide vital target information. Initially, it had two squadrons of RF-101 reconnaissance aircraft in the western Pacific, one based at Misawa AB, Japan, another at Kadena AB, Okinawa. The twin-engine RF-101 Voodoo, which could carry a wide selection of aerial cameras for reconnaissance at all altitudes up to about 50,000 feet, was a proven, dependable aircraft. The Air Force also had available a few bomber, transport, and training aircraft which had been modified to fly reconnaissance missions. It was the RF-101, however, which served as the reconnaissance workhorse in the early years of the war.

The Air Force reacted to a Royal Laotian government request in early 1961 by sending an Air Force SC-47 aircraft with special cameras to photograph Pathet Lao and NVA installations. For almost 3 months it provided the only hard intelligence concerning these hostile forces. On 23 March 1961, however, this first Air Force "reconnaissance" aircraft in Southeast Asia was shot down over the Plain of Jars.

In April another Air Force plane—an RT-33 based at Udorn—resumed the reconnaissance sorties over Laos. Pilots of this aircraft flew over poorly mapped areas devoid of navigational aids or cultural features, often in poor weather, without weapons or fighter escort. Between 24 April and 10 May, when a negotiated ceasefire between the Laotian combatants halted the RT-33 flights, the aircraft brought back tangible evidence of Communist activity in northern Laos. The RT-33 sorties resumed from Don Muang Airport on 4 October, but again were halted on 7 November after the more modern RF-101's arrived in Thailand.

A South Vietnamese invitation to the United States to take part in an October 1961 Saigon air show provided the Air Force its first opportunity to deploy the Voodoo reconnaissance aircraft into Southeast Asia. Four RF-101's and a photo processing unit landed at Tan Son Nhut on 18 October, only to learn the air show had been cancelled. However, disastrous floods in the Mekong River delta provided a reason for the aircraft to remain in South Vietnam for some time. On 23 October the RF-101's flew over the Plain of Jars and photographed Soviet aircraft parachuting supplies to Pathet Lao and North Vietnamese forces at the Tchepone airfield. Other flights brought back additional photographs of Soviet involvement, as well as pilot reports of intensifying enemy AAA fire. On 21 November 1961, after 31 days of recording enemy activities with their cameras, the RF-101's departed Vietnam. They left behind the photo unit to complete processing of the accumulated film.

That same month the first elements of the Farm Gate detachment reaching Bien Hoa AB included among its aircraft four RB-26's. These modified, obsolete light bombers proved to be good reconnaissance platforms. Also, in November 1961, four RF-101's and a photo processing unit were deployed to Don Muang Airport, Thailand, to fly reconnaissance sorties over Laos and South Vietnam. When President Kennedy sent a task force into Thailand on

211

12 May 1962 to counter growing North Vietnamese aggressiveness, the RF-101's were placed under its control. USAF reconnaissance sorties over Laos, however, were intermittently halted because of indecision on the part of RLG officials. On 6 November 1962, after a year of RF-101 operations and more than 1,000 sorties, all reconnaissance over Laos was terminated.

Although the RF-101's and RB-26's were not allowed to fly over Laos, they continued photo missions over South Vietnam. Detouring southward around Cambodia, they photographed the southern portions of South Vietnam on nonstop sorties. To cover the northern provinces of South Vietnam, they had to stage through Tan Son Nhut where exposed film was turned over to the photo processing unit there, cameras were reloaded, and the aircraft refueled for a final sortie enroute back to Don Muang. These lengthy flights were largely eliminated when the reconnaissance task force moved to Tan Son Nhut in mid-December 1962.

As the number of U.S. advisers assigned to the South Vietnamese armed forces increased throughout 1962, the demand for aerial reconnaissance increased. Most were for photos of large areas, which required production of thousands of prints and created a tremendous workload for the small Tan Son Nhut photo unit. Pending construction of a larger facility, six semi-trailer photo vans were airlifted from Europe to South Vietnam to handle the film processing. To man the production unit, the 13th Reconnaissance Technical Squadron was organized at Tan Son Nhut on 18 April 1963.

On 15 April 1963, two RB-57E's were attached to the RF-101 force, bringing into the theater an infrared sensor capability and the first of the new panoramic cameras. Two additional Farm Gate RB-26's were modified at Clark AB for night photography, and two Cessna U-3B's were added in May

212

to serve as couriers for film, prints and intelligence reports to units throughout South Vietnam. The crash of two B-26's early in 1964, caused by structural fatigue, led to the withdrawal of all B-26's and RB-26's from the theater. This loss, however, was somewhat offset by the addition of two RF-101's to the task force.

Yankee Team

After a lapse of 18 months without tactical reconnaissance over Laos, U.S. and Laotian officials could only surmise the strength and disposition of much of the hostile forces in that country. When on 19 May 1964, Premier Souvanna Phouma approved a resumption of reconnaissance sorties over Laos, four RF-101's streaked low across the border to photograph segments of the Ho Chi Minh trail and key military installations on the Plain of Jars. Follow-up low-altitude Air Force and Navy reconnaissance sorties were ordered for the operation, nicknamed Yankee Team. On 21 May the United States announced that the Laotian government had asked for help in collecting information of the disposition of the Pathet Lao and other hostile forces, information that would be presented to the International Control Commission. In justifying the flights, U.S. officials cited repeated Pathet Lao and North Vietnamese violations of the Geneva agreements and Pathet Lao refusal to allow ICC access to its territory.

At the request of Vientiane officials, the northern portion of Laos had been avoided but in November 1964 certain targets were approved for strikes. Pathfinder RF-101's led F-100's to the targets and orbited until the strikes ended and then proceeded to photograph the bomb damage before returning to base.

Because the distance between Saigon and the Laotian target areas limited the photo time of the RF-101's, the

Air Force on 2 April 1965 deployed an RF-101 task force to Udorn. Initially intended for Yankee Team sorties, the force subsequently was authorized to fly over North Vietnam. Intensified enemy antiaircraft defenses and the threat of MIG interceptions for a time required a fighter escort for the RF-101's, a procedure that was dropped in favor of two-ship formations of Voodoos.

When the eastern portion of the Laotian panhandle was designated a separate operational area (Steel Tiger) in April 1965, the reconnaissance aircraft set about photographing roads, trails, and waterways in search of enemy targets. The area was further divided in December when General Westmoreland designated the southern half Tiger Hound and asked for frequent, detailed photography of infiltration targets and the use of infrared sensors to locate enemy bases. Army OV-1 Mohawk reconnaissance aircraft flew at night while Air Force units operated mostly during the day.

In March 1966 the Udorn task force was enlarged by the arrival of the 20th Tactical Reconnaissance Squadron and its 16 RF-101's from Tan Son Nhut. A detachment of 11 RF-4C's arrived in July and was absorbed into the 11th Tactical Reconnaissance Squadron, which deployed to Thailand in November with 10 more RF-4C's. All of the Thai-based reconnaissance units, including a new Reconnaissance Technical Squadron, were assigned to the 432d Tactical Reconnaissance Wing, organized on 18 September 1966.

When the Igloo White electronic sensor system was activated in Laos in 1967, the area where the acoustic and seismic sensors were to be implanted had to be photographed in detail so they could be put into the best locations. Sensor drops were likewise photographed so the exact position of each could be accurately plotted. Each significant signal return required visual or photographic evidence to prove the existence of a valid target before strikes were approved. RC-121 aircraft of the 533d Reconnaissance Wing flew orbits over Laos to relay signals from the sensors to the Thai-based infiltration surveillance center and to collect and analyze the signals as necessary.

North Vietnam

RF-101's were pathfinders for the F-100's taking part in the first Air Force strike against North Vietnam on 8 February 1965, leading the F-100's to the target and then orbiting until the last strike aircraft departed so they could photograph the damage. When the Rolling Thunder operations got under way, reconnaissance aircraft flew with or behind the strike force to photograph bomb damage. Subsequently, a separate reconnaissance program was set up to acquire photos for planning, targeting, and intelligence purposes. The RF-101's, which originally operated out of Tan Son Nhut, later flew almost all of their missions over North Vietnam from Thailand.

Shortly after the first Gulf of Tonkin incident in August 1964, SAC sent its drones to Southeast Asia and flew the first reconnaissance drone sortie in August. Launched from DC-130 aircraft, the strategic reconnaissance drones were intended to satisfy national intelligence requirements but also became a prime source of photos of portions of North Vietnam that were off limits to manned reconnaissance aircraft. SAC U-2 aircraft also began reconnaissance sorties over North Vietnam early in 1965, flying at altitudes well above antiaircraft fire and beyond the reach of enemy MIG's. In April 1965, a U-2 photographed the first SAM site in North Vietnam. Subsequently U-2 sorties monitored the development of additional sites. Because of its ability to fly largely undetected and beyond interceptor reach,

(1) Capt. Edward M. Greer checks the window glass over one of his aerial cameras before a mission. (2) Airmen load an aerial reconnaissance camera into the nose of an RF-101 at a base in South Vietnam. (3) A sentry guards a DC-130 launch aircraft carrying a remotely piloted vehicle which was employed as a reconnaissance vehicle over enemy territory. (4) These remotely piloted aircraft are launched from the mother ship in the background. (5) Fisheye lens view of Capt. Lawrence L. Champion, Det. 1, 460th Tactical Reconnaissance Wing, in the cockpit of an Air Force RB-57 prior to a mission. (6) An Air Force RB-57 reconnaissance aircraft. (7) Reconnaissance photo showing destruction of a North Vietnamese oil storage area. (8) On mission over North Vietnam, an Air Force pilot from the 432d Tactical Reconnaissance Wing, photographed a surface-to-air missile exploding in front of his RF-101 aircraft. (9) An RF-101 reconnaissance aircraft surprised North Vietnamese gunners out in the open as they sped to man their anti-aircraft positions the DMZ.

4

7

5

8

6

9

the U-2 could cross borders and surmount defenses almost with impunity, although the arrival of the Soviet SAM's portended a serious challenge.

During the 5-week halt of bombings north of the DMZ in early 1966, USAF reconnaissance over North Vietnam was intensified in an effort to determine what the enemy was doing. The photos obtained showed frantic enemy activity to repair roads, construction of new bridges, and a massive effort to move tons of supplies and equipment into Laos and the DMZ. During the bombing pause, North Vietnamese bumper-to-bumper convoys showed total disdain for the reconnaissance aircraft overhead.

Because of the areas over which they flew, reconnaissance aircraft generally suffered loss rates far higher than the strike aircraft. Thus, an RF-101 photographing an F-105 strike on the Thanh Hoa Bridge on 3 April 1965 was lost to enemy fire, one of the first such losses over the North. An RF-101 on a 26 January 1966 sortie over the Xuan Son Barracks was downed by ground fire, while two RF-101's on a 7 March 1966 mission northwest of Vinh disappeared without a trace. Losses in June 1966 included seven RF-101's, one RF-4C, and one RB-66, all to hostile antiaircraft fire.

In November 1965, two MIG-17's jumped two RF-101's east of Yen Bay, the first encounter with enemy fighters. While one RF-101 accelerated and completed its photo run, the other drew the attackers off before increasing his speed and leaving them behind. Four MIG's attempting another intercept later that month also found themselves outclassed by the speedy reconnaissance planes. It was not until the later models of the MIG showed up that the supersonic RF-101's lost their advantage.

For some time Air Force reconnaissance had revealed the North Vietnamese were dispersing and hiding their petroleum, oils and lubricants, even burying storage tanks in their river dikes. It was not until 29 June 1966, however, that the Air Force was authorized to launch its first strikes against the enemy's vital POL storage system. Once the bombing campaign began, additional RF-101 sorties were needed to photograph the bomb damage and keep abreast of the destruction of the storage facilities.

During 1965-1966 the North Vietnamese began unloading ships at Haiphong harbor at night to avoid Navy surveillance, whereupon the Air Force was assigned the mission of flying a photographic sortie over that busy port. Thus, on 28 February 1966 two Air Force RF-4C's used photoflash cartridges during a low-altitude dash across the busy harbor. This night photography revealed the North Vietnamese engaged in the intensive unloading of anchored ships and streets piled high with cargo that couldn't be moved because of bombed roads and rail lines.

When a U.S. bombing campaign against the rail lines in the North was launched early in 1967, the enemy concentrated antiaircraft weapons at rail yards and along key sidings to try to keep down the damage from American strike planes. The Air Force sent out daytime reconnaissance sorties which were flown at a low enough altitude to identify rolling stock by type and size, while night infrared missions were launched to discover and identify operating locomotives and active yards.

On 10-11 March the Air Force launched its first strike against the Thai Nguyen iron and steel complex, a symbol of North Vietnam's industrial growth. Post-strike reconnaissance photography showed damage to key buildings but analysts could not determine whether the plant was still operational. A low-altitude infrared reconnaissance sortie the following night proved that the coke oven, blast furnace, and power plant were in operation and there was hot slag in the dump area.

In 1967 Air Force RF-101's undertook photo surveillance of all North Vietnamese jet-capable airfields, monitoring the presence of MIG fighters, helicopters, and support aircraft. In September 1967, after a MIG-21 shot down one of the RF-101's, a decision was made to ban the Voodoo from all further missions over North Vietnam. The RF-101 squadron in Thailand was inactivated and replaced by a squadron of RF-4C's. The latter was a multisensor aircraft capable of speeds in excess of Mach 2. It carried a wide assortment of the most modern aerial cameras, side-looking radar, an infrared sensor, sophisticated all-weather navigation equipment, and a 2-man crew. All RF-101's remaining in the theater were redeployed to Tan Son Nhut for use over Laos and South Vietnam. By the end of 1967, only the RF-4C was flying tactical reconnaissance sorties over North Vietnam, augmented by low-altitude drones and U-2's over certain safe areas.

In late November 1967 air strikes against targets near Hanoi led to allegations by Hanoi that the bombing had damaged the Soviet embassy and other buildings in downtown Hanoi, which produced considerable worldwide publicity. In an effort to determine the extent and cause of the damage, special low-level reconnaissance missions were flown over the embassy area, resulting in the loss of two RF-4C's in 2 days.

South Vietnam

Reconnaissance over South Vietnam lacked the significant objectives characteristic of North Vietnam, but in many ways was more diversified. The intense antiaircraft defenses were missing but Viet Cong and NVA conventional weapons could be just as deadly.

In South Vietnam infrared imagery particularly gained popularity with Army units, who used it to find Viet Cong base camps and installations.

Photo interpreters gave priority to infrared film, passing significant intelligence to appropriate ground units by telephone or radio, greatly increasing the timeliness of the intelligence and permitting immediate reaction. For example, in April 1965 an RB-57 sortie south of Saigon discovered a well-defended Viet Cong base camp with arms factories, training areas, barracks, and a sampan base. Shortly thereafter, another infrared mission recorded the location of a Viet Cong regiment west of Da Nang. Infrared film also was used to set up an ambush for Viet Cong convoys.

When General Westmoreland was authorized to use B-52's over South Vietnam, tactical reconnaissance crews were given additional responsibilities. It became necessary to photograph each B-52 target box to make certain there were no temples, cultural monuments, and friendly personnel in the area beforehand. After each bombing, the target area had to be photographed again to assess the bomb damage. As the B-52 raids increased, this became a monumental task. In February 1966 the Air Force activated the 460th Tactical Reconnaissance Wing at Tan Son Nhut to manage the growing tactical reconnaissance workload in Southeast Asia. Its initial complement of three flying squadrons, a reconnaissance task force, and several support squadrons made it the largest wing in the war zone. Its seven types of aircraft also made it the most diversified.

One of these was the ageless C-47, which had been loaded with special equipment for radio direction finding to increase its versatility. Thus, on 21 November 1966 an RC-47 of the 360th Reconnaissance Squadron detected the position of a Viet Cong transmitter and passed the information to the appropriate Army unit. A FAC was diverted to the area, spotted an ambush being set up, called for strike aircraft, and had Army helicopters fire into the ambush position to alert an approaching Army convoy. The troops in the convoy ambushed the ambushers. The 360th, manned mostly by field grade veterans of World War II whose average age was well above 40, dubbed themselves "Antique Airlines" in honor of the dependable old RC-47 and the equally aged crews.

To relieve the tactical reconnaissance aircraft from covering larger areas and from the tedium of back-and-forth flight lines, USAF officials submitted several requests for mapping aircraft. There also was a need for cartographic quality photography throughout Southeast Asia, photography which was beyond the capability of the tactical reconnaissance aircraft. In July 1967 three specially equipped RC-130A mapping aircraft arrived in South Vietnam for a short stay that extended into many months as new mapping requirements continued to arise.

In 1967 Marine Corps positions south of the DMZ came under attack by North Vietnamese artillery hidden in the DMZ. Marine counterbattery fire proved ineffective because the enemy gun positions were well concealed. To pinpoint those positions, the Air Force began flying low-altitude reconnaissance missions over the area in September 1967. New high-acuity cameras and special infrared sensors were employed in an RB-57 aircraft to assist in the search, and artillery fire and air strikes were directed against those which were found. Although hostile fire diminished, the exact results of the counterbattery fire and air strikes were difficult to assess.

The year-end truce period in 1967 was followed by intensified reconnaissance activity throughout the war zone, including infiltration routes into South Vietnam and key Viet Cong base areas. Despite the large quantity of photography accumulated, the Allies had few indicators that the North Vietnamese and Viet Cong were about to launch a major offensive throughout South Vietnam. Most attention

was focused on an impending threat to the Marine Corps base at Khe Sanh, where General Westmoreland launched Operation Niagara. It involved a concerted intelligence effort to find, identify, and monitor NVA forces gathering in the vicinity of the Marine base. Aerial reconnaissance photos provided much of the required intelligence.

Despite poor weather conditions in the area, the RB-57's special high-acuity cameras quickly photographed all of the ground for 12 miles around Khe Sanh, revealing camouflaged positions, enemy supply dumps, bunkers, and similar intelligence information. Air Force RF-4C's and RF-101's also flew dozens of daily sorties to obtain more detailed photos from which the Marines could plot enemy trenches, gun emplacements, and other positions. Hundreds of sensors implanted around the base were monitored by Air Force EC-121 aircraft, which relayed the signals to the infiltration surveillance center in Thailand for computer processing and evaluation. The results were passed to the Marine defenders at Khe Sanh within minutes.

While much attention was being focused on the siege of Khe Sanh, the enemy launched a massive attack throughout South Vietnam. They assaulted Saigon, five other major cities, and dozens of provincial capitals, towns, villages, and military installations. The 460th Tactical Reconnaissance Wing was soon inundated by a flood of requests for aerial reconnaissance photos to help find enemy units, evaluate the damage to friendly cities and military installations, and determine the status of Allied lines of communication. Two Communist attacks on Tan Son Nhut on 31 January and 18 February, which destroyed eight reconnaissance aircraft and damaged many others, adversely affected the Wing's capability.

The combined demands of Khe Sanh and the enemy's nationwide Tet offensive placed an enormous burden on the already overextended reconnaissance support units. Seventh Air Force officials sought out every available photo interpreter from subordinate units and put out a call for more. From Air Force units around the world, photo interpreters were soon converging on Tan Son Nhut; the Army also sent every interpreter it could spare. A Niagara Task Force was quickly formed to insure the immediate exploitation of sensor products from the Khe Sanh sorties, provide rapid targeting of enemy positions, and assist in planning effective reconnaissance sorties. When Operation Niagara terminated successfully on 31 March, almost 1,400 reconnaissance sorties had been flown in less than 90 days. During that period Air Force cameras had exposed slightly less than 1 million feet of film, all of which was screened for target information.

The Post-Tet Era

When President Johnson announced that all bombing of North Vietnam "except in the area of the demilitarized zone" would end at 0800 on 1 April 1968, Saigon time, no mention was made of reconnaissance. After an initial period of indecision, U.S. officials also decided to restrict reconnaissance flights to the North Vietnamese panhandle south of Vinh. Photos taken of that area, however, showed that the North Vietnamese were redeploying missiles and antiaircraft guns into the panhandle, where they threatened the large number of reconnaissance and strike aircraft operating in a rather small air space.

Although tactical reconnaissance aircraft no longer flew over the northern portion of North Vietnam, other aircraft—including SR-71's, U-2's, and drones—brought back evidence of enemy efforts to repair and expand vital facilities, including damaged roads and rail lines. At Viet Tri, for example, the North Vietnamese were

repairing the thermal power plant and the nearby factories were being readied for production. Within 3 months after the partial bombing halt, 75 percent of North Vietnam's industrial installations were again in operation, its transportation network was carrying more freight than ever before, and all major airfields had been repaired and were being expanded to handle a growing MIG force.

The number of reconnaissance sorties over North Vietnam decreased after 1 April 1968, but there was no comparable decrease elsewhere. Within South Vietnam, enemy forces continued to harass allied lines of communication and military installations as American and South Vietnamese Army units slowly regained control of areas lost during Tet. Because fewer reconnaissance sorties were flown over North Vietnam, however, additional sorties became available for use in South Vietnam. Thus, when the enemy turned his attention once more to the A Shau Valley, frequent Air Force reconnaissance missions helped identify new targets for Army units engaged in Operation Grand Canyon and Buffalo. The week-long siege of the Kham Duc Special Forces camp in early May required a large number of reconnaissance sorties, many of them diverted from other assignments. In the Saigon area, reconnaissance crews continued to monitor enemy efforts to launch a new assault on the city.

In Laos, weather continued to be one of the controlling factors affecting reconnaissance operations. When the good weather returned to Laos in 1968, the Air Force initiated a new interdiction campaign. Selected targets, such as mountain passes, were photographed several times daily so that strike aircraft could keep them closed; roads leading into them were scanned for truck parks and storage areas.

President Johnson on 31 October 1968 ordered an end to all bombing of North Vietnam in order to speed a settlement of the war. American envoys in Paris, however, during their discussions with Hanoi's delegation, declared that the United States intended to continue reconnaissance flights. At first, the North Vietnamese insisted that reconnaissance was an act of war, but they later relented and accepted cessation of "all other activities that involve the use of force." SAC's reconnaissance vehicles continued to photograph North Vietnam as before, but a new tactical reconnaissance program was begun in the lower panhandle to "determine as soon as possible the reaction or intentions of the enemy with regard to a manned tactical reconnaissance program." When the North Vietnamese fired on the test missions, subsequent flights were accompanied by armed escort aircraft; however, two reconnaissance planes and one escort were lost to enemy fire within the first month. By the end of 1969 reconnaissance operations fell into a pattern: SAC's SR-71's covered the heavily defended areas of Hanoi and Haiphong and their environs, drones were used wherever they could be most effective, and the RF-4C's were restricted to the southern portion of the panhandle.

Reconnaissance Winds Down

Even as reconnaissance operations over North Vietnam continued following the complete bombing halt, the number of sorties decreased significantly towards the end of 1969. The allied ground incursions into Cambodia in 1970, however, led to a surge of reconnaissance activity, particularly infrared missions. The Air Force had sufficient resources on hand to satisfy all requirements. In July the number of sorties decreased after U.S. ground units withdrew.

The first reconnaissance force cut-

220

1

2

3

back came in March 1970 when an RF-4C squadron redeployed from Tan Son Nhut to Japan. In November the RF-101 squadron at Tan Son Nhut was inactivated, and one of the two RF-4C squadrons at Udorn redeployed to the United States. The departure of the RF-101's brought to an end 9 years of continuous combat operations in Southeast Asia by that aircraft. In August 1971, after flying reconnaissance missions in the theater for more than 8 years, the RB-57's also redeployed to the United States. One of them had accumulated more than 8,000 flying hours. Within a few days, the last RF-4C squadron in South Vietnam also returned to the United States, leaving only one tactical reconnaissance squadron with 24 RF-4C's at Udorn. Stripped of its squadrons, the 460th Tactical Reconnaissance Wing was inactivated on 31 March 1971

In September 1971 tactical reconnaissance flights over areas just north of the DMZ revealed a sharp increase in the number of North Vietnamese AAA weapons and missile sites. When the enemy began firing missiles at the reconnaissance aircraft, Seventh Air Force on 8 November launched protective reaction strikes on the gun positions and SAM sites near the Vinh and Quan Long airfields. A rash of ground attacks against U.S. bases in South Vietnam inspired renewed air strikes against targets in North Vietnam, beginning on 26 December 1971. Reconnaissance sorties were flown to assess bomb damage after each attack. Defense Secretary Melvin Laird charged that Hanoi had violated the understandings associated with the 1968 bombing halt, including the one concerning the U.S.-North Vietnamese agreement that unarmed reconnaissance aircraft did not involve the use of force.

In February 1972 NVA tanks and heavy artillery were photographed just north of the DMZ, and American officials received intelligence that Hanoi was planning another major invasion of South Vietnam. On 30 March the North Vietnamese launched a three-front attack on South Vietnam. The single RF-4C squadron was hard pressed to meet all of its commitments, but the South Vietnamese Air Force helped out wherever possible with its RF-5's.

When a U.S. air strike was directed against the famous Thanh Hoa Bridge on 27 April 1972, two RF-4C's and two F-4 escorts covered the target at high altitude and brought back word that the bridge had finally been dropped into the river after 7 years and hundreds of bombing sorties. Several enemy missiles were launched at the flight during the strike. North Vietnamese intransigence at the Paris peace conference triggered Linebacker II on 19 December 1972, an air offensive against targets in the Hanoi-Haiphong area, which also brought reconnaissance aircraft back to assess bomb damage. Two RF-4C's followed every strike element to photograph the resulting destruction. The film was processed at Udorn and rushed to Tan Son Nhut for exploitation for follow-up bombings. The sorties continued until the signing of the Paris agreements on 27 January 1973, which brought all combat operations over North Vietnam to an end.

Fighting in Laos officially ended on 16 February 1973, but the Air Force continued to fly reconnaissance sorties along lines of communication to maintain current data on enemy AAA positions, truck traffic, and storage areas. The RF-4C's also flew sorties over Cambodia to assess damage from B-52 and tactical aircraft bombing, and a few sorties were flown along the South Vietnamese border where Viet Cong and North Vietnamese forces were concentrated. All USAF operations ended on 15 August 1973. Between early 1961 and the halt of America's longest war, USAF reconnaissance crews had flown almost 650,000 tactical sorties.

Chapter XIII

Control of Strike and Defense Forces

As noted earlier, in the fall of 1961 the Air Force deployed a detachment from the 507th Tactical Air Control Group, Shaw AFB, S.C., to Tan Son Nhut, where it established a combat reporting center. Declared operational in October, the center took over responsibility for maintaining the primary control radars and directing air defense operations, i.e., scrambling and directing interceptor aircraft. It also performed routine air traffic control functions. In November 1961 additional elements of the 507th and the 5th Tactical Control Group also arrived in Vietnam. Early in 1962 they assisted in activating the joint USAF-VNAF Air Operations Center at Tan Son Nhut, adjacent to the combat reporting center. Rounding out the initial radar net were two combat reporting posts at Da Nang and Pleiku, each equipped with mobile search and height radars. Air Force personnel ran the Da Nang facility while the VNAF operated the Pleiku unit. The Air Operations Center became the heart of the tactical air control system, enabling air commanders to control and direct their strike forces.

Expanding the Radar Net

To provide coverage of the western air approaches to South Vietnam—from northeastern Cambodia and southern Laos—the Air Force in April 1962 moved a radar emplaced a year earlier at Don Muang to Ubon AB, where it provided a more favorable Thai location for detecting aerial activity in Laos, Cambodia, and South Vietnam. This installation not only greatly improved radar surveillance but also tied the air defense systems of Thailand and South Vietnam into a single coordinated whole. The installations at Tan Son Nhut, Da Nang, Pleiku, and Ubon provided high-altitude (above 5,000 feet) surveillance over South Vietnam. They also possessed a command and control capability and secure teletype circuits to radar and control units throughout South Vietnam and Thailand.

Except for a VNAF reporting post established at Ban Me Thuot in February 1963, the network remained essentially unchanged until April 1964 when more powerful radars were set up on Monkey Mountain near Da Nang and at Can Tho, which strengthened early warning and tactical air control operations. A few months later, the Air Force upgraded its Thai facilities, adding a combat reporting post at Udorn, thereby extending coverage over northeast Thailand and central Laos. The commissioning of several communication and navigation facilities in 1964 also benefited the air defense and tactical control systems.

One of the critical needs that grew out of the expanded forces was to enhance the tactical air control system. Although the network as of mid-1964 performed reasonably well, it became obvious that the ever-increasing military and commercial air traffic would soon overtax the system. In turn, this expansion made it imperative to build a single comprehensive system that could handle all U.S. and allied air operations, including air defense, tactical strikes, and air traffic control.

he flight line and control wer at Tan Son Nhut, 1964. to r.) two RF-101's, six 102's, and a B-66. ©N.G.S.

1

Coincident with the 1965 deployment of additional American forces to the area, the Air Force began to build the Southeast Asia Integrated Tactical Air Control System (SEAITACS). Established over a 2-year period, it consisted of four tactical air control centers (TACC's), two in South Vietnam and two in Thailand. Within South Vietnam, the focal point for all air operations was the TACC-South Sector (SS), which replaced the Air Operations Center at Tan Son Nhut in the summer of 1965. Like the AOC, the TACC-South Sector was manned by U.S. and VNAF personnel. Their job was to direct the air defense effort for South Vietnam, allocate air defense resources, and monitor all air movements within the air defense subsectors of a Mainland SEA Air Defense Region.

Acting for the Seventh Air Force commander in his capacity as Deputy Commander, MACV for Air Operations, TACC-South Sector had virtually complete responsibility for prosecuting the air war in South Vietnam.

Air Force officials in the Tan Son Nhut center planned, directed, and coordinated all allied tactical air operations in South Vietnam and achieved a remarkable ability to provide close air support to allied forces. American Army and Marine commanders repeatedly praised the air assistance provided them. For example, following Operation Paul Revere II, a 1st Cavalry Division (Mobile)/ARVN ground operation in the summer of 1966, Maj. Gen. John Norton, USA, wrote to General Momyer to praise "the outstanding combat support received." He noted that tactical air support requests, "both immediate and preplanned, were answered promptly and effectively; in every instance accuracy was excellent and target coverage complete." This letter was only one of many received by Seventh Air Force which acknowledged the contributions not only of USAF strike units but, indirectly, of the tactical air control system.

The TACC-North Sector became operational at Da Nang in November

(1) An Air Force mobile air traffic control team directed a C-123 to a safe landing on a small airstrip af Dau Tieng, South Vietnam. (2) A Troposcatter antenna, operated by the 1974th Communication Group, dominates a peaceful swampland scene near Don Muang Royal Thai AB, Thailand. (3) The Air Force Command Post Communications Center, operated by the 1876th Communication Squadron, Tan Son Nhut.

2

3

1966. Collocated with the combat reporting center at Monkey Mountain, it was responsible for the air defense of northern South Vietnam and for providing surveillance, warning, and limited control of air operations over North Vietnam and Gulf of Tonkin. The Thai-based tactical air control center was at Udorn. It served as an extension of the Seventh Air Force control center, controlling and coordinating USAF strike units in Thailand.

The Udorn facility was designated Alternate TACC-North Sector and—as its name implies—served as the backup to the main center at Da Nang for control of air operations over North Vietnam and Laos. In an emergency, Marine Corps air control radars could take over from the primary centers at Da Nang and Udorn in directing operations over North Vietnam or the Laotian panhandle.

The buildup of tactical air control centers in the mid-1960's was accompanied by a substantial expansion of radar facilities. To strengthen the control system, the Air Force added 9 radars to 12 already in its early warning net. South Vietnam received four, bringing its total to an even dozen. The other five were installed in Thailand, raising the total there to nine. Additional coverage was achieved by tying in the radars of the Marine Corps and the Navy's Carrier Task Force 77.

The Air Force also employed airborne combat command posts as command centers to control interdiction strikes in the Laotian panhandle and Route Package 1 in North Vietnam. These were C-130 aircraft equipped with a removable command communications module. The airborne command team consisted of approximately 12 personnel. Their ability to control air operations was amply demonstrated during the defense of the Marines at Khe Sanh in 1968. During the peak of the strike operations, C-130 command teams controlled approximately 850 aircraft per day.

The EC-121 Task Force

Another major USAF asset which enhanced Air Force operations in Southeast Asia was the ultra-sophisticated, electronic-laden EC-121D aircraft (code name College Eye). In effect a flying radar station and airborne control platform, the EC-121D possessed the AN/APS-95 search radar, IFF/SIF (Identification Friend or Foe/Selective Identification Feature), interrogation equipment, and a battery of communication gear. It became a key element in enabling successive Seventh Air Force commanders to exercise airborne control over tactical air operations. The range of its radar coverage and tactical air control extended over all of North Vietnam and the Gulf of Tonkin.

EC-121 operations began in Southeast Asia in the spring of 1965, after two F-105's were shot down by enemy MIG's while on strike missions over the North. From this incident—the first in which F-105's were lost in air combat—it became clear that early detection and warning of MIG flight activity were prerequisites to reducing aircraft losses. With the existing surface-based radar net unable to do the job, the Air Force brought in the EC-121's.

The EC-121 task force deployed to Southeast Asia early in 1965. It consisted of 5 aircraft, flight crews, and about 100 support personnel from the Aerospace Defense Command's 552d Airborne Early Warning and Control Wing at McClellan AFB, Calif. Its main support base was in Taiwan, but operations were generally flown from forward bases in South Vietnam or Thailand, originally Tan Son Nhut, later from Ubon, Udorn, and eventually Korat, where the task force finally found an in-theater home in October 1967. It was officially designated Detachment 1 (Rotational), 552d Aircraft Early Warning and Control Wing on 30 October 1968.

In performing what became their primary mission, College Eye airmen stationed themselves over the Gulf of Tonkin about 50 miles from Haiphong Harbor, flew elliptical orbits, and passed on information about North Vietnamese air activity. After Communist China charged in October 1965 and May 1966 that U.S. aircraft had violated its borders, the EC-121's took on the additional task of tracking and warning all American aircraft when they were approaching or appeared to be too close to the Chinese border. For this purpose, task force aircraft flew orbital patterns over Laos near the Plain of Jars.

The EC-121 crews undertook a number of other control duties. For example, from April 1965 to early 1966 and beginning again in late 1967, they controlled four fighters flying protective cover for unarmed support aircraft operating in the Gulf of Tonkin area. The EC-121's also (1) served as an airborne communications relay center through which aircraft returning from their targets could transmit strike results and position reports to the control center at Da Nang; (2) directed operations of fighter escorts, MIG combat patrols, C-130 flareships, and A-26 strike aircraft along the North Vietnamese-Laotian border; (3) provided rescue and navigational assistance in searches for downed pilots; and (4) frequently assisted fighters in finding tankers for emergency refuelings. In 1967 College Eye controllers also began actively directing USAF F-4 fighters to North Vietnamese MIG's.

Paradoxically, the EC-121's were called upon only three times to provide one of its basic services—early warning of enemy air attacks against South Vietnamese ground targets. The first occurred in October 1965 when intelligence reports indicated a possible IL-28 bomber attack on Da Nang. The second—and possibly most serious threat of the entire war—took place early in February 1968 when 4 IL-28's and 13 MIG's penetrated the DMZ. Upon entering the zone, the fighter escort broke off, some turning toward the Laotian border, the remainder flying out to sea. The four Beagles loitered in the DMZ area for almost an hour, then dropped below radar detection altitudes and departed. The third incident came in mid-June 1968 when an enemy helicopter threat appeared to be building up along the DMZ. In these three instances, night-flying College Eye crews were able to detect them and alert friendly ground forces.

Air Defense

Long before the EC-121's began providing early warning of potential enemy air operations against South Vietnam, the Air Force deployed interceptors to Thailand in 1961 to demonstrate America's resolve to support its SEATO allies and the beleaguered Kingdom of Laos. From that point on during the next several years, the Air Force kept a minimum of four aircraft on alert in Thailand.

In March 1962 USAF interceptors also were sent to South Vietnam after radars detected low-flying, unidentified aircraft along the Cambodian border. At the request of Saigon officials, the Air Force dispatched four F-102's to Vietnam from Clark AB. This deployment inaugurated a year-long series of rotations, with Navy EA-1F all-weather fighters alternating with the F-102's. Because the EA-1F was the slower aircraft, it proved better suited than the F-102 for low-speed, low-level interceptions. The two rotated every 6 weeks to Tan Son Nhut until May 1963, when base overcrowding and the low probability of an enemy air attack ended the deployments. Subsequently, a number of aircraft were kept at their home stations in an on-call status so as to permit a speedy flight to Vietnam if necessary.

During the summer of 1963, Thirteenth Air Force conducted a series of no-notice exercises to test the ability of the F-102's to deploy to Vietnam. They involved brief flights to Tan Son Nhut and Da Nang, which were continued through mid-1964 for training purposes. Occasionally during the early 1960's, allied radars detected unidentified, low-speed, low-altitude tracks in South Vietnam's airspace. They were presumed to be those of Communist aircraft engaged in the resupply of Viet Cong troops during hours of darkness, but some of the unidentified radar tracks also might have been caused by U.S. Army helicopters or even flocks of migratory birds.

Apart from sporadic radar returns and infrequent violations of South Vietnamese air space by Cambodian MIG's, no significant enemy air activity occurred through the 1960's, although the Gulf of Tonkin incidents in August 1964 had significant air defense ramifications. Not knowing whether the North Vietnamese attack signalled the start of a major military campaign, the Air Force quickly reinforced its alert forces. Within a week, 6 F-102's were on alert at Da Nang, 8 F-105's at Korat, and 18 F-100's were available at Da Nang and Takhli to fly escort. Air defense units stayed in a heightened alert status throughout the remainder of 1964.

Estimates of the air threat changed sharply in 1965, particularly in the spring when the North Vietnamese Air Force acquired the Soviet-built light bomber, IL-28 Beagle. For the first time, Hanoi possessed the potential to strike as far south as Saigon and into northeast Thailand. The deployment of larger numbers of American aircraft to a handful of South Vietnamese bases made such fields attractive targets. When the United States initiated air strikes against North Vietnamese military facilities in 1965, the possibility of enemy retaliation in the South obviously increased.

In this regard, the lack of low-altitude radar coverage was a problem. If the enemy chose an attack route

1

2

3

4

5

6

7

8

(1) A2C Douglas C. Christensen, seen through the plotting board on the EC-121D aircraft. The boards played a vital role in allowing crewmen to keep track of other aircraft in the area. (2) Control tower and helicopter area at Bien Hoa AB, 1 November 1964. (3) SSgt Eric M. Routkedge, a precision final controller, guides an aircraft to a safe landing during inclement weather at Dan Nang AB. (4) An Air Force F-100 Supersabre turns in making a strafing pass against an enemy force in the Mekong Delta of South Vietnam. (5) Aerial view of the Monkey Mountain radar site overlooking Da Nang AB and the city's harbor. (6) Tactical air navigation (TACAN) and power units were deployed to Binh Thuy AB, Vietnam, in 1965 by the 1st Mobile Communications Group at Clark AB, the Philippines. (7) 1st Lt. Lance D. Scalf, a weapons controller aboard an EC-121 aircraft, plots the locations of U.S. airstrikes over North Vietnam in November 1968. (8) TSgt James E. Johnson, a crewman aboard the EC-121D radar surveillance aircraft, checks his manuals as he prepares for a frequency "peak-up" of delicate equipment.

which exploited this weakness, the allies would receive little or no warning. It was estimated that Saigon might get an advance notice of 4 minutes; Da Nang, however, would have no more than 1 to 2 minutes to react. Given the closely parked, unreveted aircraft and their proximity to ordnance and POL storage, even one or two enemy aircraft could wreak havoc. One burning aircraft alone could trigger a holocaust under prevailing airfield conditions. Since command and control, radar, and communication systems were equally vulnerable, the creation of an adequate air defense system became a matter of urgency in 1965 and thereafter.

The number of aircraft committed to SEA air defense climbed gradually but steadily. Though still small, the air defense contingent tripled in size over the pre-1965 force. A round-the-clock alert was maintained by 12 F-102's—8 at Tan Son Nhut and 4 at Don Muang. For a period of nearly 6 months between October 1965 and the spring of 1966, F-102's and F-4C's performed alert duty at Da Nang on a 24-hour basis. The assignment of the F-4's marked the first operational use of these aircraft in an air defense role. As the war over North Vietnam intensified, the F-4's strike role took precedence and they were relieved of air defense duty, except during periods of tension when all fighters were alerted on a back-up basis. Beginning in late 1964, the U.S. Army also deployed surface-to-air Hawk missiles to Tan Son Nhut, Bien Hoa, Cam Ranh Bay, and Da Nang to help counter any enemy air attack on allied bases.

By the end of 1966 air defense forces had grown significantly both in South Vietnam and Thailand. At that

A view of Air Force tropo-scatter communication antennae at Monkey Mountain, South Vietnam.

maintaining alert aircraft at all times. Altogether, as many as 200 U.S. aircraft were available for air defense at the peak of the U.S. force buildup.

Air Traffic Control

One of the important functions performed by the allied air control system was that of traffic control. The first USAF team deployed to Southeast Asia for this purpose was an element of the 1st Mobile Communications Group, which arrived in Thailand on 15 February 1961 to assist in providing air route traffic control for the Thai Air Force. Subsequently, other teams deployed to the area to support the 2d Air Division, the Vietnamese Air Force, and other allied forces. In many instances in the early days, 1st Mobile Communications Group teams occupied control towers alongside Thai or Vietnamese personnel to facilitate local traffic handling of joint-usage airfields.

As the air forces in Southeast Asia grew, the problems of air traffic control mounted. During the early 1960's navigation throughout the area was based primarily upon nondirectional radio beacons. Existing fields lacked modern equipment to handle the upsurge in traffic. To help resolve the problem, the Air Force installed mobile radar approach control (RAPCON) units, mobile towers, and navigational aids at key locations. The nondirectional radio beacons were replaced or augmented as rapidly as possible with very high frequency omni-directional radio range equipment, tactical air navigation equipment, or a combination of both. Nondirectional beams at Da Nang, Qui Nhon, Binh Long, and Tan Son Nhut provided reporting and navigational reference points for enroute traffic. An additional beacon was placed on Phu Quoc Island, off South Vietnam's west coast, as a navigational aid for traffic routed around Cambodia—due to Phnom Penh restric-

In December 1967 a newly modified ground controlled approach radar unit went into operation. The new unit provided controllers with the capability of precision radar approaches on parallel runways at Tuy Hoa AB.

time, 22 F-102's were exclusively deployed for air defense: 12 on alert in South Vietnam (6 at Bien Hoa and 6 at Da Nang) and the other 10 in Thailand (6 at Udorn and 4 at Don Muang). Approximately 14 F-104's based at Udorn also had air defense duties as a secondary mission.

USAF air defense forces in Southeast Asia underwent little change in composition and location during 1967-1968. During those 2 years, the Air Force normally kept a minimum of 14 aircraft on 5-minute alert—4 each at Da Nang, Bien Hoa, and Udorn, and 2 at Don Muang. The remainder of the F-102 force was on 1-hour call. In addition, eight F-4C's stood alert at Cam Ranh Bay—one on a 15-minute basis and four others on 30-minute notice. Another two were on 15-minute alert at Da Nang. The U.S. Navy and Marine Corps augmented these forces by

tions of overflight of its territory.

The Republic of Vietnam, like all nations, exercised sovereign control of its airspace. Its Directorate of Civil Aviation delegated all South Vietnamese airspace control to its Saigon area control center, which in turn delegated authority to ground radar operators, who controlled landing approaches. Operations in subdelegated airspace were governed by letters of agreement between officials of operating facilities and the Saigon area control center. In July 1965 the Directorate formed an air coordinating committee in an effort to achieve closer coordination between civil and military agencies. Represented on this committee were U.S. Air Force, Army, and Marine Corps members and others from the VNAF, MACV, and the U.S. Civil Aviation Assistance Group. The U.S. Air Force and the Directorate of Civil Aviation jointly chaired the committee.

It resolved many problems, but rising air traffic, inexperienced personnel, cumbersome lines of authority, and the need to build an adequate air traffic control structure in the middle of a war complicated its job. A series of meetings was held in 1966 to discuss a variety of current problems, including terminal and enroute traffic control, equipment for navigation aids, point-to-point communications, and personnel training.

One important issue was the blocking or preemption of airspace as a result of impending artillery firing, special air operations, and naval gun fire. For example, when the B-52's began operations in the spring and summer of 1965, the need to block vast amounts of airspace had an unfavorable effect on enroute air traffic control. Navy amphibious operations and U.S. Army artillery fire also required airspace blocks. Naval operations were usually coordinated with the air component commander. In the Central Military District surrounding Saigon, 15 minutes prior to the firing

232

of artillery or mortar shells, the radar approach control facility at Tan Son Nhut advised all aircraft in the vicinity of the impending operations.

Because of artillery firings and blocked airspace, there were only three altitudes provided for aircraft departures at Tan Son Nhut: 7,000 feet, 9,000 feet, and 11,000 feet. At the same time, traffic was rapidly escalating. The arrival of the summer monsoons also caused difficulties, since precipitation cluttered the radar scopes, often rendering them useless when most needed. With nearly simultaneous operations being carried out by the Air Force, Army, Navy, VNAF, and civilian airlines, air traffic controllers at Bien Hoa, Tan Son Nhut, and Da Nang found themselves each handling more aircraft movements monthly than Chicago's O'Hare International Airport. During 1968 there were 4,779,647 aircraft movements (principally takeoffs and landings) controlled by towers manned partially by USAF personnel assigned to units of the 1964th Communications Group.

A number of steps were taken to maintain air safety. Since controllers of the South Vietnamese Directorate of Civil Aviation needed assistance, a U.S.-Vietnamese letter of agreement raised the status of USAF controllers to advisors with authority to take necessary steps to insure the safety of military flights. Previously, USAF controllers had only manned traffic control positions under the Vietnamese agency. In May 1966 the mobile radar approach facility at Tan Son Nhut became the first in Southeast Asia to receive a modification unit which provided additional surveillance radar scopes. With this equipment, operations at that facility were divided into sectors. During June-July 1966 the radar approach control units at Da Nang and Cam Ranh Bay also were modified. Similar actions were taken at other bases, increasing from three to five the number of control positions at each facility.

In February 1968 PACAF initiated a special project (Commando Indian) to create an air traffic regulatory system to handle heavy traffic between air bases. Under an agreement among the Directorate of Civil Aviation, MACV, and the VNAF, the Air Force created six air traffic regulation centers (ATRC's) as elements of the aircraft control and warning subsystem of the tactical air control system. The centers were located at existing control and reporting centers and posts, with which they were linked internally to enable coordination of data on aircraft movements. The last of these sites became operational in February 1969.

By mid-1969, the air traffic control centers were handling an average of more than 70,000 aircraft operations monthly, accounting for approximately 75 percent of the total traffic at the control and reporting centers and posts, thus permitting the weapon controllers there to concentrate on their primary duty of directing strike aircraft. Because of reduced flying starting in 1971, the weapon controllers were initially trained and then given responsibility for the traffic previously controlled by the ATRC's throughout Vietnam.

Control tower aircraft movements handled by USAF controllers decreased substantially after 1969. As American participation in the war ground down, the Air Force began transferring control towers, direct air support centers, and other communications facilities to the South Vietnamese. A final, orderly phaseout of remaining Air Force communications was carried out in January-March 1973. The 1964th Communications Group, whose mission had been to provide USAF telecommunications and air traffic control in Vietnam, terminated its operations on 23 March 1973. The 1974th Communications Group at Udorn continued to provide these services for USAF units remaining in Thailand.

Air Rescue

During the course of the war the Air Force's Air Rescue Service recovered several thousand U.S. and Allied fighting men who went down in jungles, mountains, and waters of Southeast Asia. The first USAF rescue team— three officers and three airmen—arrived in South Vietnam on temporary duty on 10 January 1962. Based at Tan Son Nhut, its mission was to organize a search and rescue (SAR) control center and network throughout the country. In April 1962 the 6-man cadre was designated Detachment 3, Pacific Air Rescue Center. Its first commander arrived on 2 July. The detachment initially had no aircraft and had to rely on U.S. Army advisors to provide their helicopters to assist in air rescue missions. Army personnel subsequently were assigned to the Tan Son Nhut control center and provided liaison between the Air Force and the Army.

In addition to not having its own aircraft, the detachment lacked most of the basic equipment needed for an effective SAR system. For example, in the early days of its operations the SAR center sent requests for help to operational units by bicycle—a method faster and more reliable than trying to use the existing Vietnamese telephone network. Its reliance on the Army and later the U.S. Marines for helicopter support also created problems because they were not configured for rescue missions. For example, in March 1963 an Army OV-1 aircraft went down near the top of a 6,000 foot mountain in II Corps. To reach the site, two Marine UH-34D helicopters attempted to insert a 4-man American-Vietnamese rescue team at the crash site. However, the Marine helicopters did not have a cable long enough to reach the ground through the high jungle canopy. When one descended to the jungle canopy, it suddenly lost power and crashed, killing an ARVN ranger who was on the hoist at the time. The aircrew managed to climb out of the wreckage moments before it erupted into flames. The copilot, however, was severely burned and died during the night. Subsequently, a second Marine helicopter attempting to land a Marine rescue team also lost power and crashed but the only injury was a sprained ankle. Eventually, the bodies of the Army OV-1 pilot, ARVN ranger, and Marine copilot, plus members of the American and Vietnamese rescue teams were extracted by helicopter.

It was clear that specialized aircraft and devices were needed to effectively operate over the jungle and mountainous terrain of Southeast Asia. In the early 1960's the only crash/rescue helicopters in the USAF inventory were the short-range (220 miles) HH-43 Huskies, operated by local base rescue (LBR) units in the United States and overseas. However, the HH-43 was considered inadequate for conditions in Southeast Asia. In June 1963 a more advanced helicopter, the CH-3 single-rotor cargo amphibian, made its first flight. It had a forward speed of about 150 miles per hour, an endurance of 4-1/2 hours, and range of approximately 500 miles. Impressed by its performance in November 1963, the Commander, Air Rescue Service, recommended to Headquarters USAF the purchase of the CH-3 in quantities. He reported that the Service was not equipped to do the job in Southeast Asia and that, by "utter default," Air Force combat crews were "made dependent upon ill-equipped and ill-trained. . .U.S. Army and Marine Corps helicopter resources diverted to accomplish our mission. . .Their no-

235

ble efforts have wrought confusion and even disaster when engaged in some attempts to prosecute Air Rescue Service missions."

In response, Headquarters USAF ordered a number of combat-modified CH-3's. But, pending their manufacture, the Air Force was forced to use the HH-43's. In March 1964 three USAF HH-43 units were transferred from the Philippines and Okinawa to Southeast Asia. In June 1964 the first temporary-duty contingent—two HH-43's and 36 personnel—was sent to Nakhon Phanom, Thailand. That same month the 31st Air Rescue Squadron at Clark deployed two HU-16 amphibian aircraft to Da Nang, South Vietnam, to provide rescue service for U.S. airmen downed in the Gulf of Tonkin. Two HU-16's from the 33d Air Rescue Squadron also were deployed to Korat Air Base, Thailand, to support USAF operations over that country and Laos.

On 20 October 1964 Detachment 4, Pacific Air Rescue Center, which was equipped with three HH-43F helicopters specifically modified for use in the theater, arrived at Bien Hoa, replacing a temporary duty unit deployed there

several months before. The modified HH-43's possessed heavy armor plating to protect the crews from hostile ground fire and 250-foot cables to facilitate rescues in high rain forest areas. The unit also had on hand HU-16 amphibian aircraft for use in sea rescue of downed pilots.

By 1 January 1965 five helicopter detachments were operating in the theater—at Bien Hoa and Da Nang, South Vietnam; and at Udorn, Nakhon Phanom, Takhli, and Korat in Thailand. However, only the Udorn and Nakhon Phanom detachments in Thailand operated solely in support of downed airmen. The others performed their normal local base rescue missions. The two detachments in South Vietnam flew aircrew recovery missions, although their "combat-modified" helicopters were extremely limited in range and loitering capability.

In January 1966, the Air Force activated the 3d Aerospace Rescue and Recovery Group at Tan Son Nhut to serve as the primary rescue agency in Southeast Asia. It took over the job of planning, organizing, coordinating, and controlling rescue operations

Capt. Leo F. Dusard, downed at sea after suffering an engine failure, climbs into the rescue sling of an HH-43 rescue helicopter after being forced to eject from his F-100 in the Gulf of Tonkin, December 1967.

from the Joint Search and Rescue Center at Seventh Air Force headquarters, Tan Son Nhut, and coordinating centers at selected operating locations. The group directed the activities of three rescue squadrons, the 37th at Da Nang, the 38th at Tan Son Nhut, and the 39th at Tuy Hoa. Later, the group operated a fourth squadron, the 40th at Udorn. Ten rescue detachments also were based throughout South Vietnam and four in Thailand.

While this dispersion of rescue units facilitated recovery of downed pilots over a wide area, there were many instances when helicopter crews found they were unable to reach grounded airmen due to the limited range of their aircraft. Looking for ways to extend their operations, rescue crews sought out clearings in the jungle for use as forward locations, where they could stockpile fuel and await calls for help many miles and minutes closer to a downed pilot. They also installed extra fuel tanks—initially a 150-gallon container, later as many as four 55-gallon drums—to gain additional operating time. To improve their ability to rescue crews shot down over North Vietnam, ordinarily far beyond their

reach, they also stored drums of fuel on mountain tops along the route north, enabling them to leapfrog from one to another.

The SAR Task Force

Other improvisations included employment of a SAR Task Force, or SARTAF. The basic rescue element for aircrew recovery missions after the 1965 force buildup, this task force subsequently developed a rescue formation involving a pair of helicopters, one flying high, the other low. The low aircraft would "go in" to make the recovery, while the high aircraft stood by to lend aid if required. Also, in 1965 rescue crews were provided high-flying USAF fighter cover to ward off MIG attacks. This fighter cover was known both as MIGCAP and Rescue Combat Air Patrol (RESCAP). In August 1965 Air Force A-1E Skyraiders also began escorting the rescue units. Coordination and control of all air elements involved was exercised by a fixed-wing rescue aircraft, itself a part of the SAR Task Force.

Typically, during a recovery operation, two A-1E's flew directly to the general search area and began a hunt

237

for the downed crew. Two other A-1E's escorted the helicopters to the area, flying above small-arms range. Reaching the target area, they circled until the first two A-1E's contacted the survivor by radio, located him, and determined whether he was in a hostile area. If he was, the fighters and escorting A-1E's attacked with bombs, rockets, and 20-mm cannon fire until the area was "neutralized" sufficiently for a helicopter to go in low for the recovery. The A-1E's orbited nearby but not directly over the downed pilot so as to avoid giving away his position. Although the HH-43's were poorly equipped for this rescue role, USAF crews performed it repeatedly. However, after accelerated tactical strike operations began over both North and South Vietnam, the number of downed airmen rose dramatically. Rescue detachments found they could not keep up with the number of calls for help, and it also became apparent that a more powerful, better-equipped helicopter was essential, especially if they were to operate deep in enemy territory.

In July 1965, the Tactical Air Command—many of whose crews were being shot down in enemy territory—loaned the Air Rescue Service two CH-3 cargo helicopters. However, it was not until November 1965 that there was a major improvement in air rescue capabilities, with the arrival in Southeast Asia of the first six HH-3E's. An updated version of the CH-3, the HH-3E was specifically modified for rescue operations. Its speed, endurance, and ceiling of approximately 10,000 feet were about the same as the CH-3, but auxiliary fuel tanks increased its range to about 640 nautical miles. Operating out of Udorn, Thailand, or Da Nang, South Vietnam, it could reach any point in North Vietnam and return to its home bases. When deployed to a forward location, its extended range enabled rescue crews to deploy near an area of aerial combat, where it could orbit ready for

an emergency deep within North Vietnam.

The HH-3E's communication equipment was compatible with all other allied aircraft operating in Southeast Asia, and it possessed an external variable-speed hoist with 240 feet of cable, stressed for 600-pound loads, and able to penetrate the jungle canopy. The new helicopter, along with its less powerful companion, the HH-3C, quickly became known as the Jolly Green Giant.

With these advanced helicopters, rescue crews were able to keep pace with the stepped-up tempo of the air war. Control of operations became more direct and responsive. Communications further improved when Udorn-based C-54's began flying as airborne command posts along the Thai frontier. HU-16 amphibians performed the same communications task over the Gulf of Tonkin. Old, slow, and limited like the CH-54 to low-altitude operations, the HU-16 had been in the inventory since 1949. However, it was able to make water landings in daylight and mild sea conditions and, by the end of 1965, had saved 70 people, 60 of them combat crewmembers.

Beginning in 1966, the amphibious HU-16's and other Air Rescue Services fixed-wing aircraft were replaced by the Lockheed HC-130 Hercules, an all-metal, high-wing, land-based amphibian tailored specifically for the global search and rescue mission. The Air Force contracted for the plane in 1963. With a top speed of approximately 340 knots and a range of more than 4,500 nautical miles, it could land easily on short runways or landing strips such as those usually found in advance-base operations. It obviously could not make vertical recoveries on land or water like the HU-16's, and could not commit its pararescue teams to jungle areas where parachutes would be caught in 150-foot trees or mountain slopes where jagged outcrops could spear a man. But the HC-130 could fly great distances over the oceans, find its objective with its electronic gear, and linger for a long, long time.

Over land, the HH-3E's began flying an increasing number of recovery missions as more of them entered the inventory. Despite its superiority over the HH-43, however, it still lacked the full capacity to loiter for lengthy periods over hostile territory. This was a serious problem since on deep penetration missions it was often necessary to loiter for a considerable time while escort and strike planes neutralized enemy areas. Also, when carrying a full load of fuel, the helicopter was unable to hover over mountain areas where many downed pilots deliberately guided their parachutes to avoid capture.

Recognizing this dilemma, the Air Rescue Service in 1964 proposed converting the HC-130 into an aerial tanker to provide an air-to-air refueling capability for the HH-3E. On long-range missions, this would enable the HH-3E to provide a complete land or water vertical recovery capability throughout the theater. With refueling, it could perform missions far beyond its normal range, enabling it to participate in extended SAR/recovery operations, to loiter indefinitely, and to return home.

The proposal was approved, and Air Force Systems Command experts immediately began working with the Rescue Service and industry to develop a workable mid-air helicopter refueling capability. A working system was devised and tried experimentally in 1965, was fully tested in 1966, and finally adopted in 1967 as the mainstay of air rescue operations. The first operational use of the aerial refueling technique involved an HH-3E helicopter which was assigned a Gulf of Tonkin orbit mission previously flown by an HU-16. With the help of two mid-air refuelings by an HC-130P, the HH-3E flew the 8-hour mission to successfully demonstrate its improved range and loiter capability. Thereafter, the HC-130/HH-3E team began flying daily operational missions.

Even as this important improvement was made in air rescue capabilities, the Air Force took steps to acquire a more powerful rescue helicopter. The result was the production and deployment in 1967 of the Super Jolly Green Giant—the HH-53B and its more capable sister, the HH-53C. Adapted from a Marine Corps helicopter, these new aircraft began flying rescue missions in late 1967. The HH-53 could carry 38 passengers, or 24 litter patients with 4 attendants, as well as its normal crew of 5. It could carry more than 7 short tons of dead weight, transport the cargo some 258 miles without auxiliary tanks, protect itself with three 7.62-mm miniguns, and fly at a top speed of 195 miles per hour. Besides having a complete air refueling system like the HH-3E, it had automatic flight control and engine anti-icing systems for all-weather flying. Altogether, the HH-53 was the largest, fastest, most powerful heavy-lift helicopter in the Air Force inventory. This team—along with a variety of other support aircraft—played a key role in the dramatic but unsuccessful effort to rescue American prisoners of war in the Son Tay prison camp near Hanoi the night of 20-21 November 1970 (discussed in Chapter IV).

Together with the older HH-3E, they were used extensively in Southeast Asia, while the Air Force continued working to improve their components. Advances were made in communications, navigation equipment, signaling devices used on and from the ground, fuel tanks to prevent explosions, and a fuel-dumping mechanism. In addition, the Air Force worked to develop a ground-fire warning device, a multichannel survival radio, better signals and flares, an improved jungle penetrator, a superior Doppler navigation system, more resistant armor plating, bullet-resistant windshields and sideview panels,

1

3

6

7

5

(1) An Air Force HH-43 helicopter approaches a jungle clearing in South Vietnam's "D" zone to pick up wounded American paratroopers. (2) An HC-130 refuels an HH-3E helicopter heading out on a rescue mission, accompanied by four A-1 Skyraiders to fly cover for the operation. (3) This Air Force painting depicts the rescue of Lt. Ken Thomas, whose plane went down in North Vietnam. (4) A U.S. Air Force gunner in an HH-43 helicopter prepares to give fire support during a 1966 rescue mission over Vietnam. (5) This air rescue crew plucked two Army flyers whose plane went down in South Vietnam. Shown checking map coordinates of the rescue site are (l. to r.): A1C Charles R. Ingulli, Jr., pararescueman; SSgt James Baldwin, flight engineer; and 1st Lt. John F. Kolar, rescue crew commander. (6) Maj. Carl B. Light (3d from l.) thanks an F-4 helicopter team which rescued him from the southern panhandle of North Vietnam in June 1968. The F-4's flew air strikes which enabled the helicopters to make the pickup. Shown (l. to r.): Maj. Don P. Olsen, rescue helicopter pilot; Sgt James A. Bowers, helicopter flight engineer; Lt. Col. Donald R. D'Amico, F-4 pilot and commander of the 480th Tactical Fighter Squadron; and Lt. Col. Charles R. Klinkert, an air rescue pilot. (7) Two A-1H's escort an Air Force HH-3 rescue helicopter during a mission in Southeast Asia. (8) Lt. Col. Robert F. Wilke, and A-1 pilot, 602d Fighter Squadron (Commando), surveys his damaged aircraft which was hit during a rescue mission over North Vietnam.

8

and electronic countermeasures to confuse enemy radars.

The Problem of Night Rescue

Normally, a survivor's chances of rescue from hostile territory were best within 15 minutes after landing; after 30 minutes, his chances declined sharply. The onset of darkness or bad weather forced suspension of all recovery activity until conditions again permitted a rescue attempt. The lull gave the enemy time to move into an area and capture the downed airman, or worse, to set a trap to blast the rescue helicopter from the skies when it returned in the morning or when the weather cleared.

In 1967, with night rescue growing in importance, the Air Force initiated a 3-year development program to acquire a system which would enable a rescue force to fly after sunset to any geographical point in any kind of weather, avoiding all obstacles. The Air Force also sought a system which would enable rescue crews to "see" with instruments on a moonless, starlit night, locate a downed airman approximately 5 miles away, establish and maintain a safe hover over him, and lift him out without giving away his location or that of the helicopter. These were extraordinarily difficult requirements, which American industry could only partially fill within the time and funds available.

Nevertheless, by March 1971 a limited night recovery system was produced and installed on five HH-53C's which became operational in Southeast Asia. These aircraft contained a low-light-level TV device which enabled the pilot to see on a cabin screen much more than he could out his window with the naked eye. In addition, infrared lights installed externally enabled crewmen equipped with night-vision goggles also to see outside. The aircraft also contained a semi-automatic approach-and-hover system to

This air rescue crew during an 11-day period saved 11 men wounded in combat. Shown in front (l. to r.): Maj. Harold Pickering, detachment commander; Sgt James A. Crawford, flight engineer; SSgt William L. Crawford, flight engineer; and Capt. Laurence W. Conover, rescue crew commander. In back row (l. to r.): A1C Ronald E. Sholes, pararescueman: A1C James L. Park, pararescueman; Capt. William J. Haugen, rescue pilot; Capt. Albert E. Tollefesen, rescue pilot; and Sgt Garry G. Harold, pararescueman.

help the pilot during a pickup. Night rescues with this interim system became possible, but only from lightly‘ defended territory, comparatively flat terrain, and in relatively good weather. Under these conditions it also was necessary for the survivor to have an infrared strobe light and be in an open area where he could be readily seen by a crewman with night-vision goggles.

Components under development

A fisheye lens view of A2C Roy E. Kelsey, 38th Aerospace Rescue and Recovery Squadron, who sits on a jungle penetrator as he prepares to be lifted to a hovering HH-43 helicopter during a practice mission in Vietnam.

third device, an electronic location finder (ELF), would enable the crew to pinpoint a survivor's exact position, even when under a jungle canopy, and come to a stable hover directly over it.

In 1973, the first two devices were still in the prototype test stage but the ELF had already been installed on HH-53's. In 1972 the latter device led to at least one rescue during a remarkable armed incursion into North Vietnam, which saved an F-4 crewmember, Capt. Roger C. Locher. His aircraft was shot down in May 1972 by a MIG-21 heat-seeking missile over North Vietnam while he was on his 407th combat mission. After parachuting safely into a valley, he tried without success to contact friendly aircraft by radio. During the next 23 days he hid some 8 miles from the MIG base at Yen Bai, living on fruits, nuts, and berries. He finally made contact with two USAF flights, which triggered a rescue attempt by a task force including HH-53 helicopters, A-1 fighters, an HC-130 command aircraft (which also refueled the helicopters), and F-4 and F-105 air cover. The initial rescue attempt on 1 June was driven off by enemy MIG's. However, the next day, with the help of the ELF, an HH-53 was able to locate him and pull him out with a jungle penetrator. Brought back to his base, Captain Locher declared: "There's no way to express my feelings. It's unbelievable. It's just a miracle."

It was one of many miracles brought about by the determination, endurance, and ingenuity of Air Force rescue crews, development agencies, and American industry. Together, they helped save 3,883 lives between 1964 and mid-August 1973. Of these, 2,807 were U.S. military: 926 Army, 680 Navy, and 1,201 Air Force. The rescuemen also saved 555 allied military men, 476 civilians, and 45 other unidentified persons. They also paid a high price. During the course of the war 71 U.S. rescuemen were killed and 45 aircraft destroyed.

which could transform this limited system into a full night recovery capability included an improved, virtually automatic Doppler navigation system which would take an aircraft to any point selected by the pilot. Another component was a radar system enabling the pilot to hug the ground at some 200 feet, safe from radar detection, automatically adjusting to the terrain and dodging obstructions. A

Logistics

Chapter XV

Long before the first combat aircraft deployed to Southeast Asia, personnel of the Air Force Logistics Command (AFLC) and other airmen were hard at work readying planes for training and combat. For example, beginning in 1961 maintenance crews began removing from "mothballs" many of the aircraft initially sent to South Vietnam. In many instances, the aircraft required modifications before being flown to the war zone. They included T-28's, SC-47's, and B-26's of the Farm Gate detachment which deployed to South Vietnam beginning in November 1961 and the C-123 Ranch Hand aircraft that followed early in 1962.

Upon reaching South Vietnam, the first USAF personnel to arrive found little in the way of adequate maintenance facilities. At several bases, lean-to or other temporary structures constituted the only roofed work areas. At other bases, buildings which had been built through the Military Assistance Program or those used by the French Air Force were available. One of the first challenges facing the Farm Gate crews was to set up a flightline supply and maintenance capability. To support them in this area, AFLC successfully developed, equipped, and shipped to Vietnam 24 mobile maintenance vans.

Aircraft deploying to Southeast Asia in the early 1960's carried within them 30-day mission support kits, which the Air Force periodically replenished from the United States. Initially, all other support came from USAF re-sources at Clark AB in the Philippines. This was not completely satisfactory because of the time required to fly in spare parts from Clark to the bases in South Vietnam and Thailand. Whereupon, in December 1962 the Air Force established Tan Son Nhut as a

main logistic base. A few months thereafter the Air Force ordered a return to normal supply procedures for its SEA units in lieu of the special aerial resupply system being used. Supply shortages, however, soon appeared with the result that NORS (Not Operationally Ready, Supply) rates climbed. On 13 August 1963 the Air Force reinstated a modified aerial resupply system and aircraft NORS rates improved.

Base Materiel

The beginning of air operations against North Vietnam in 1965 was followed by the deployment of thousands of additional men and planes to Southeast Asia. To house and support them, the Air Force established four new major air bases and expanded four others. To provide essential materiel for these bases, a major logistical effort—designated Project Bitterwine —got under way in mid-July 1965 under the aegis of a Logistics Activation Task Force established by AFLC. A few weeks later, however, the Secretary of Defense authorized still another sizable force buildup in the theater along with a further expansion of air facilities to include, overall, construction of 11 main bases and enlargement of 8 others. As a consequence, Project Bitterwine became the focus of one of the largest single Air Force logistic efforts undertaken since the Korean conflict.

Under Project Bitterwine, AFLC was responsible for determining, procuring, packing, and shipping all required materials for various bases in special packages—to be accomplished without resorting to the normal practice of

C William G. Simpson (l.) d A1C James H. Chester) line up a C-47 engine on mount as TSgt William C. arnes tightens a belt at eiku AB, South Vietnam.

245

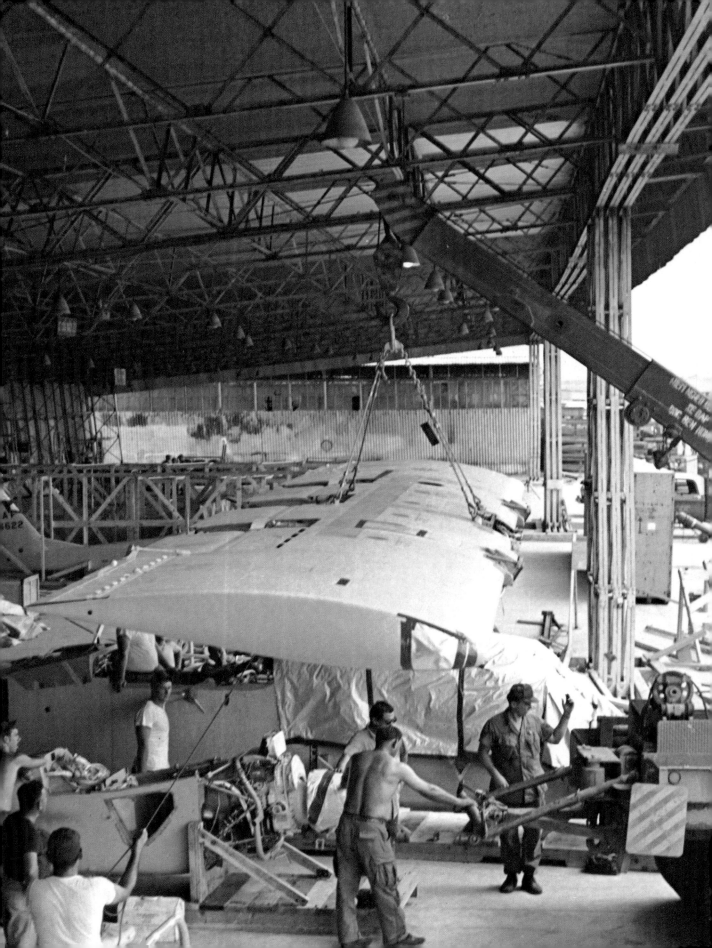

2

4

3

(1) The assembling of an Air Force OV-10 aircraft at Bien Hoa AB, August 1968. (2) Gen. John D. Ryan, PACAF commander-in-chief, discusses engine maintenance with Chief Master Sgt William F. Hair, noncommissioned officer in charge of the Tuy Hoa AB propulsion branch. (3) High priority cargo being loaded for dispatch to Southeast Asia. (4) Air Force Sgt Donald F. Clements (l.) and A1C Greg E. Sniegowski load a SUU-23/A gun pod at Phu Cat AB, Vietnam. (5) F-105 mechanics position a mobile console and power unit while munitions men watch.

(1) A C-123 transport downed by enemy ground fire in April 1969 is lifted by an Army CH-54 helicopter at Ben Tre, Vietnam. (2) A C-123 unloads aviation fuel at the An Khe airfield in South Vietnam. (3) Airmen prepare a missile for loading on an F-4 Phantom. They are (l. to r.): A1C Garry P. Mincer; Sgt Vernon E. Kisinger; A1C Lonnie J. Hartfield, and Sgt Phineas T. Berry. (4) Army armored vehicle exiting a kneeled C-5. It was among a number of tanks and armored cars sent to South Vietnam during the enemy's 1972 spring offensive. (5) An Air Force flight mechanic is silhouetted in the rear cargo doorway of a C-7A following an aerial resupply mission. (6) An airman loads napalm bombs prior to a combat mission.

249

preparing and processing the usual supply requisition forms. Each functional package was to contain equipment and supplies to support a particular base operation. A food service package, for example, contained all equipment needed to outfit and operate a base mess hall. The Bitterwine concept called for the base buildup to proceed in three distinct phases. First, so-called "Gray Eagle" kits containing housekeeping equipment to support 4,400 people in tent facilities were delivered to a new base. Next, temporary structures such as inflatable shelters and prefab buildings replaced the Gray Eagle installation. Finally, in the third phase, civilian contractors completed runway construction and built operational and support facilities and housing for a permanent base.

During the course of Project Bitterwine – which ran from mid-July 1965 to early 1967--the Air Force put together and shipped more than 1,500 functional packages. In toto, they contained 346,000 different items. Purchased and shipped at a cost of about $82 million, they permitted early air operations from four new bases in Vietnam—Cam Ranh Bay, Phan Rang, Tuy Hoa, and Phu Cat--and two in Thailand, Nakhon Phanom and U Tapao. They also were used to upgrade 13 others in those countries, Taiwan, and the Philippines.

The amount of supplies required in Southeast Asia increased tremendously as combat operations expanded. During the first 6 months of 1965, more than 56,000 tons of materiel was delivered by ship to South Vietnam and Thailand. Deliveries amounted to 592,554 tons in fiscal year 1966, to 1,155,719 tons in fiscal year 1967, and reached a high of 1,697,315 tons in fiscal year 1969. Air cargo deliveries grew commensurately--from 5,929 tons during the first 6 months in 1965 to more than four times that amount in fiscal year 1966. In fiscal year 1969 more than 48,000 tons of cargo were flown into the war zone.

The sheer volume of supply shipments to Southeast Asia--plus the total lack or general inadequacy of port, storage and handling facilities and accounting or sorting procedures, particularly at the forward bases—created immense problems and seriously complicated the operations of base and combat units. Many logistic organizations in the war zone simply were unable to cope with the vast amount of incoming materiel. Substantial portions of it were often unaccounted for, lost, or misplaced. In an attempt to overcome these problems, the Air Force recruited Rapid Area Supply Support (RASS) teams from among its military and civilian supply experts. These teams deployed to SEA for periods of 60 to 120 days and helped establish viable accounting, inventory, storage, and issue procedures and practices.

The first RASS team--consisting of 22 military personnel--departed for Clark AB on 23 June 1965 and returned to the United States 90 days later. Between January 1965 and the end of 1969, 138 teams (a total of 3,207 people, 2,271 of them civilians) visited 20 bases in the Fifth, Seventh, and Thirteenth Air Force areas and provided 293,063 man-days of expert assistance. Fifteen of the 20 bases were in South Vietnam and Thailand. The other five were in the Philippines, Taiwan, Okinawa, Guam, and Korea.

The Air Force also deployed special maintenance units—Rapid Area Maintenance (RAM) teams—to the theater to repair crash- and battle-damaged aircraft. A team normally consisted of 18 military or civilian personnel highly skilled in repairing aircraft. The first RAM team deployed in April 1965 to repair two crash-damaged F-105 aircraft. The teams subsequently repaired 885 aircraft which were returned to operational units, prepared another 88 for one-time flights to repair shops, disassembled and crated 126 for shipment to repair centers, and declared 29 irreparable and salvaged them for parts.

The value of these aircraft totalled more than 1.7 billion dollars. During the course of these activities, four RAM civilians were killed in South Vietnam and one seriously wounded as a result of enemy action.

Still another specialized logistic force dispatched to Southeast Asia by the Air Force was known as Rapid Area Transportation (RATS) teams. They helped to process backlogged priority cargo and trained Vietnamese civilians to do the work. Without their help, vital materials for isolated bases, outposts, and units would have been delayed or perhaps never received.

A fourth specialized unit, the Installation and Checkout (I&C) team, assisted with the installation and checkout of equipment in base maintenance shops, precision measurement laboratories (PMEL's), and computer facilities. Between 1966 and 1969, for example, the Air Force installed UNIVAC 1050-II computers at 17 bases. They enabled base supply and maintenance personnel to process requisitions in hours instead of days, and to control assets and forecast future requirements. The availability of these computers also allowed USAF personnel to employ normal Air Force supply or "pull" system practices.

Prime Beef and Red Horse

The Air Force resorted to other kinds of special organizations—one temporary and one permanent—to undertake minor construction, improvement, and repair of base facilities. Prime Beef (Base Engineering Emergency Force), the first of these, consisted of teams of about 25 men sent on TDY to Southeast Asia. In August 1965 the first three Prime Beef teams left for South Vietnam, where they erected dirt-filled steel-ribbed revetments to protect aircraft from enemy mortar and automatic weapons fire. By 15 February 1968, more than 40 teams—totalling more than 1,900 engi-

neers—had put in 120 days TDY in the combat area, performing urgent and emergency tasks of a base civil engineering nature. The Air Force eventually formalized the Prime Beef concept, forming teams and placing them on a stand-by basis for rapid deployment where they might be needed around the world.

The more permanent units were known as Red Horse (Rapid Engineer Deployable, Heavy Operations Repair Squadrons, Engineer) squadrons or, more precisely, civil engineering squadrons. The first two 400-man squadrons, activated late in 1965, deployed to Southeast Asia early in 1966 and initially engaged in construction of interim facilities such as combat centers, wing headquarters, and shops. Within a year, the Air Force had established, trained, and deployed a total of six Red Horse units to the war zone— five to South Vietnam and one to Thailand. At the peak of their activity, their total strength included 2,400 military men and more than 6,000 local nationals. Their work included digging wells to obtain potable water, quarrying and crushing stones for roads and runways, repairing damage caused by enemy standoff mortar attacks, constructing and upgrading operational facilities and housing, and doing a host of other jobs for which contract assistance was not readily available.

The rapid surge in requirements beginning in late 1964 and early 1965 led the Air Force to improve the flow of munitions to Southeast Asia. At the time, the supply line stretched from California through the Philippines to Southeast Asian depots. Commercial transport vessels under contract to the Military Sea Transportation Service (MSTS) carried the munitions destined for South Vietnam and Thailand to Subic Bay in the Philippines, where they were unloaded and hauled by truck to storage sites at Clark. The munitions were then hauled back to Subic Bay and loaded onto ships as requisitions came in from South Viet-

1

2

3

(1) Transport ships carrying construction materials and equipment to South Vietnam lay at anchor offshore while awaiting offloading at Tuy Hoa AB. (2) A bomb storage area at Da Nang AB, January 1966. (3) An A-1E Skyraider detachment operated out of Qui Nhon, South Vietnam in 1964-1965. (4) Saigon harbor served as a major port for the receipt of U.S. military equipment. (5) Offloading an OV-10 FAC aircraft at Saigon. (6) Bombs unloaded from a ship at Guam for use by B-52 bombers. (7) Using a fork lift, a loading crew places a cargo pallet aboard a C-130 transport at Tan Son Nhut. (8) 750-lb bombs are loaded on a B-52 at Andersen AFB, Guam.

4

7

5

6

8

nam and Thailand. Thus, the system consumed about 150 days in getting munitions from California to the forward bases in Southeast Asia.

To shorten the delivery cycle, Air Force logisticians again turned to special procedures, setting up Project Special Express. As originally established the project called for full-time assignment of MSTS vessels. These were loaded on the West Coast at scheduled intervals, moved to the Philippines to take on fresh water and provision, and then sailed to the coast of South Vietnam where they served as "floating warehouses." Then, as needed, munitions were unloaded onto U.S. Navy LCM (landing craft, medium) transports—manned by Air Force personnel—and taken to shore. Special Express reduced transit time by some 80 percent, from 150 to 30 days. The first Special Express vessel departed Concord Naval Weapons Station, Calif., on 25 April 1965 and arrived at Nha Be, South Vietnam, in mid-May. The number of ships involved in Special Express grew to 15 by May 1966.

Improved munitions, including 250- and 500-pound bombs, also were procured by the Air Force Logistics Command for the fighting units. It purchased in quantity a new fuze and warhead for the 2.75-inch rocket, an air-to-air weapon that was redesigned for air-to-ground strikes. Another item purchased was an aerial gun which fired at a rate of 6,000 rounds per minute, carried more ammunition than the gun it replaced, and was one-fourth the weight.

In 1967-1968 two new fuzes were added to the USAF munitions inventory, the FMU-26 for general purpose bombs, and the FMU-54—used with the Mau-91 retarding fin—which improved the low-level delivery of 750-pound bombs. In 1969 the 10,000-pound M-121 bomb, a veteran piece of ordnance developed during World War II, made its debut in Southeast Asia. Employed primarily to create in-

stant helicopter landing zones in dense jungle areas of Southeast Asia, it was dropped by C-130 transports or helicopters. Also, in the last year of the war, the Air Force began using newly developed "guided bombs" with great effect. They enabled strike aircraft to destroy a number of key North Vietnamese bridges which had withstood repeated attacks by conventional gravity bombs.

Modification of aircraft either at Air Force depots or contractor plants was another support function of importance to Air Force logisticians. Throughout the war, as operating shortcomings were found or appeal-

The Air Force Logistics Command initiated a "Special Express" system of ocean going vessels to carry numerous types of munitions to Southeast Asia.

254

(1) War munitions and supplies delivered to Andersen AFB, Guam. (2) Handling ordnance at Guam.

months later, faced with a long-term requirement to employ its huge bomber in a conventional bombing mode, the Air Force directed modification of other B-52's to permit them to carry 108 bombs at one time.

Modification and conversion of the aged C-47 into a gunship with three 7.62-mm miniguns on the port side of its fuselage provided added substance to the belief that this pre-World War II airplane was destined never to leave the skies. The first SEA missions in its new operational role were flown on 15 December 1964. Its successes thereafter led to the conversion of C-119 and C-130 aircraft into even more sophisticated gunships. They proved indispensable in defending isolated outposts and camps under enemy siege, in escorting truck convoys, and providing close air support to friendly forces.

How well the Air Force fared in fulfilling the materiel requirements of its operational units in a pipeline more than 10,000 miles in length can be illustrated in part by examining a statistical criterion used by the logisticians to evaluate performance. For example, there was the Not Operational Ready, Supply, or NORS rate data, maintained for each kind of operational aircraft. In the case of Arc Light B-52's, aircraft out of commission for lack of parts exceeded the Department of Defense standard of 5 percent during less than one-fifth of the period between October 1965 and the end of 1969. Of even greater significance, perhaps, was the fact that the Arc Light NORS rates were below the worldwide rates for more than half of the same period—some 29 months out of 51. The Air Force achieved a similar NORS rate success with the F-100.

The USAF logistical effort which got under way in 1961 and grew so tremendously after 1965 enabled the Air Force not only to support its combat forces at the end of a 10,000-mile pipeline but also America's allies in Southeast Asia.

ing technical innovations appeared, the Air Force would undertake modification of its aircraft.

For example, in 1963 the Air Force initiated an evaluation of the B-52 as a conventional bomb carrier. During the following year, the Air Force and the Boeing Aircraft Company conducted a series of tests to determine the feasibility and desirability of so modifying the B-52. Test results were encouraging and modification of the first 30 B-52F's began early in October 1964. These aircraft subsequently deployed to Andersen AFB, Guam, in February 1965 and, as noted earlier, flew the first B-52 strikes on 18 June. Two

255

Chapter XVI

Base Defense

In the Republic of Vietnam, the Air Force for the first time found itself flying combat missions from air bases which were repeatedly attacked by enemy ground forces. During previous conflicts, the Air Force had operated from relatively secure bases and had been free to concentrate exclusively on waging aerial warfare. But in the war without fronts that was fought in South Vietnam, U.S. and Vietnamese airmen found their bases and cantonments subjected to sudden enemy attacks, requiring a vigilant defense at all times.

When the first USAF crews arrived in South Vietnam in 1961, the VNAF installations where they became tenants did not appear to be in any danger. Indeed, during the first 3 years of Air Force operations, the Viet Cong ignored the bases. In the early 1960's, USAF officials also operated on the premise that any threat to men and planes would be of a clandestine nature. Thus, they gave their attention to traditional internal base security, e.g., requiring all personnel entering the facility to have identification badges and limiting them to their own work areas.

Lack of a clear understanding of the base defense responsibilities of ARVN and U.S. forces in Vietnam eventually became a problem. The job was tacitly acknowledged to be the Vietnamese Army's responsibility. ARVN troops were expected to provide area and local defense, while the Vietnamese Air Force handled internal airfield security. These arrangements were satisfactory up to the summer of 1964, when the first U.S. retaliatory air strikes were launched against North Vietnam following the Gulf of Tonkin incident. The latter apparently triggered the first enemy attack on Viet-

namese bases where large American units were located.

Thus at 0025 hours on 1 November 1964, the Viet Cong launched a stand-off mortar attack against Bien Hoa, a major USAF operating location northeast of Saigon. Using six 81-mm mortars emplaced less than 440 yards outside the northern perimeter of the base, Communist gunners fired between 60 and 80 rounds into the base and swiftly departed, undetected and unmolested. The damage inflicted was out of all proportion to the effort expended. Four American personnel were killed and 72 wounded. Five B-57 jet bombers were totally destroyed, eight sustained major damage, and seven others minor damage. Four USAF H-43 helicopters and three VNAF A-1H fighter bombers also were damaged. Only departure of one B-57 squadron from Bien Hoa the week before prevented even more extensive losses. This attack proved to be but the first of many launched against USAF facilities during the next 8 years.

The Enemy Threat

For the most part, the enemy planned, organized, rehearsed, and executed air base attacks in a highly professional manner. Initially, the Viet Cong conducted the raids. However, after suffering heavy casualties during the 1968 Tet offensive, they were increasingly supplanted by NVA personnel, who were better trained, equipped, and motivated. Both forces, however, responded to a single control, employed the same tactics, and used the same type of weapons and equipment.

In planning an attack, the enemy's first task was to collect maximum intelligence about a base. Special attention was given to allied defense forces, their organization, operation, equipment and morale, safeguards, fortifications, the attitude of the local population, and routes to and from the facility. Much of this intelligence was obtained from local sympathizers or agents living near or employed on the base. One of the more sensational examples of this type of espionage occurred at Tan Son Nhut where the enemy successfully recruited a lieutenant of the South Vietnamese Regional Forces, who worked in the Joint Operations Center at Tan Son Nhut and had access to the entire allied order of battle.

Specially trained military reconnaissance teams also were used to obtain additional information about a target. Under exceptional circumstances, personnel from such units were infiltrated into the base to gather vital information not otherwise obtainable. Several such incursions were thwarted at Bien Hoa and Phu Cat when security police detected and captured the infiltrators. Occasionally, the enemy would try to intercept radio and telephone communications seeking base defense intelligence. To locate and identify the type of allied weapons available and reaction time of artillery, the Communists would engage base defenders with sniper or harassing fires or small unit probes to provoke a response. Intelligence gathered in this fashion, combined with information on enemy manpower and materiel resources, became the basis for the plan of operation and organization of the attack force. Normally the proposed attack was extensively rehearsed beforehand. To preserve secrecy, participating troops were rarely told the identity of the target until the final approach march was under way.

The Communists conducted four types of operations against allied air bases: standoff attacks, sapper raids, mass attacks, and sabotage. The standoff attack, lasting from 1 to 20 minutes, was the most common, cost effective, and simple of the four operations, and allowed the attack force to evade defensive fire from the base. Through 1966 enemy standoff weapons consisted of 60-mm, 82-mm and 120-mm mortars plus 57-mm, 75-mm and 82-mm recoilless rifles. In February 1967 an attack on Da Nang AB marked introduction of 107-mm, 122-mm, and 140-mm rockets as the principal Communist standoff weapons, which gave the enemy additional flexibility and greater firepower.

Sapper raids against allied bases were initiated on 1 July 1965, also at Da Nang. The intent of these operations was to use small numbers of men to produce extensive materiel damage rather than casualties. Stealth, not firepower or numbers, was relied upon to penetrate perimeter defenses, reach the objectives, and place the explosive charges that were the basic sapper weapon. If all went well, the operation lasted no longer than 30 minutes. The mission was to hit and run, not to engage the enemy. The enemy sapper was not a guerrilla but a carefully selected, well trained, and highly disciplined combat engineer. The sapper standard of performance was illustrated by a February 1969 incident at Phu Cat. A wounded sapper captured by security police related that during the rehearsal for the attack, his company commander warned that anyone who jeopardized the success of the mission would be shot. Accordingly, when the prisoner detonated a trip flare, the commander shot him.

Mass attacks by multi-battalion forces with the goal of seizing and holding allied air bases were mounted on only one occasion against Tan Son Nhut and Bien Hoa as part of the Communist 1968 Tet offensive. It was one of the enemy's rare failures to achieve tactical surprise (see discussion below, pp. 265-269).

Sabotage, the technique most commonly associated with insurgent activity and originally considered the principal threat by American officials, was seldom employed against air bases. Indeed, the only truly noteworthy case of sabotage occurred on 8 February 1967 when the napalm bomb stockpile at Bien Hoa was exploded by devices of Soviet manufacture. How they were brought into the munitions storage area was never established. The previous day, however, when the devices were most likely emplaced, only 9 of 27 Vietnamese workers reported for duty, a circumstance which suggests that most had prior knowledge of the plan to destroy the stockpile. However, enemy activity of this nature was a minimal threat to base security. For example, during 1968—a year of intensive Communist operations—not a single incidence of actual or attempted sabotage was reported by a USAF installation.

Allied Defenses

Almost all USAF resources in South Vietnam were located on 10 major air bases. Six of them—Da Nang, Pleiku, Nha Trang, Bien Hoa, Tan Son Nhut, and Binh Thuy—were joint-use installations with the Air Force a tenant of the Vietnamese Air Force. The other four—Phu Cat, Tuy Hoa, Cam Ranh Bay, and Phan Rang—were constructed between 1965 and 1967 for use by the U.S. Air Force alone. The older bases were situated in urban areas where dense population provided ideal cover for enemy operations and prohibited or severely restricted defensive fire. These same bases usually were saturated with personnel and aircraft and thus presented attractive targets.

New bases, though less congested, were sited without much regard for defense considerations. Phu Cat, for example, overlapped three districts, thereby necessitating triple coordination of security operations with local officials. A universal and unending problem was the control of the dense

vegetation which concealed enemy movements and obscured fields of fire. Physical safeguards were either lacking or inadequate. A POL pipeline laid from the coast to Phu Cat couldn't be used because of sabotage and theft. Only at Da Nang, where the U.S. Marines installed perimeter barriers and lighting systems, was a satisfactory defense posture established. One feature of the Da Nang defense complex was unique. To detect and intercept enemy sapper and standoff forces, the Marines joined with ARVN troops to construct and man a 28-mile anti-infiltration barrier which enclosed the air base on the landward side.

The Air Force interpreted its base defense responsibilities in accordance with guidelines laid down by the Joint Chiefs of Staff. These provided that local air base defense was the responsibility of the local Air Force commander. On this basis, the Air Force took the position that its responsibility ended at the base boundary and that outside that line, the area ground commander was responsible for defense operations. But in the absence of a combined command structure, genuine coordination of area and local defense always was problematical. Again the notable exception was at Da Nang, where the dual responsibility of the Marine commander for both area and local defense resulted in the only truly unified base defense operation within South Vietnam. Thus, when the JCS rejected a proposal that U.S. ground forces be assigned to defend USAF bases in Vietnam, the Air Force in late 1965 began creating an organic base defense force, which ultimately grew to a strength of 5,000 personnel.

As this defense force accumulated combat experience and knowledge of enemy tactics, USAF officials came up with a three-zone base defense concept tailored to counter the Communist threat. Under this concept, static and mobile elements were deployed in

7

10

11

8

9

(1) Sgt David T. Hanson sets a trip flare along the perimeter of Hill 151 overlooking Phu Cat AB, South Vietnam, 1970. (2) A2C Bruce L. Hoffman examines the body of a Viet Cong infiltrator he had killed during an attempted attack at Tan Son Nhut AB, 1966. (3) Capt. D. Wise, chief of an explosive ordnance disposal team, disarms a Viet Cong Claymore land mine found during a perimeter sweep of the Tan Son Nhut AB. (4) U.S. and Vietnamese security troops stand on alert at Tan Son Nhut behind a sandbag bunker on the base perimeter. The Americans are (l. to r.): A1C Major Wingfield and A1C Douglas M. Terry, both members of the 6250th Air Police Squadron, 1966. (5) In July 1967 the Viet Cong attacked Da Nang AB with rockets. This aerial view of the parking ramp shows damage done to aircraft located there. (6) Members of the 377th Security Police Squadron at Tan Son Nhut take up positions to repulse Viet Cong infiltration of the base. (7) Despite direct hits by enemy rockets launched during the enemy 1968 Tet offensive, this Bien Hoa AB bunker—completely surrounded during a 7-hour attack—remained in allied hands. (8) Air Force Lt. Col. Eugene J. Kelly (l.) and Army Sgt Lorenzo Beckwith inspect a captured Soviet rocket launcher, part of a Communist cache found near Bien Hoa AB. (9) An enemy mortar attack on Tan Son Nhut in April 1966 demolished this Vietnamese Air Force C-47. (10) This USAF sentry dog, Nemo, returned to the United States from Vietnam in July 1967 to a hero's welcome. The previous December, while on patrol at Tan Son Nhut, he detected four Viet Cong infiltrators, who opened fire and hit both the dog and his handler, A1C Robert A. Throneburg. Throneburg commanded Nemo to charge. The powerful German shepherd, despite a head wound, killed two of the intruders. (11) An enemy mortar and rocket attack in February 1968 destroyed a C-47 transport at Tan Son Nhut.

a sectorized defense in depth, which was designed to contain and destroy any enemy forces that penetrated the base. The outermost zone consisted of a complex of barriers, mines, lights, flares, and observation points. The intermediate zone contained bunkers manned by armed USAF security police and was patrolled by mobile security alert teams and sentry dogs. A final protective line—including barriers, lights, bunkers, and foot and mobile patrols—was maintained at the boundaries of areas containing essential combat resources, e.g., aircraft, munitions, fuel. Heavily armed and mobile quick reaction teams were kept on standby alert to reinforce any part of the system.

The key to USAF base defenses was the individual security policeman, uniformly young, inexperienced and untrained in the weapons and skills of ground combat, but also alert, enthusiastic, and completely reliable. The valor with which he responded to the enemy challenge and the stoicism with which he endured the mind-numbing daily routine of his unglamorous calling quite properly evoked commendations from the highest quarters. His efforts more than any others accounted for success of the USAF base defense mission.

The organization of the 10 security police squadrons deployed to South Vietnam differed little from that of their counterparts at home. It consisted of three flights, each permanently assigned to one of the three 8-hour shifts. By January 1966 it was customary to employ 50 percent or more of the security force on the 2000-0400 hour shift, the high threat period. To offset the loss of continuity resulting from the 1-year tour and to promote detection of indicators that might precede an enemy attack, most security policemen were retained in stabilized duty assignments in a single sector. The closest approximation to a tactical element to emerge from this non-tactical organization was the 13-man quick reaction team, an ad hoc reserve formation analogous to an infantry squad. Available as auxiliary U.S. defense forces were select personnel drawn from other combat support group units and from tenant U.S. Army organizations. At Da Nang this arrangement was essentially reversed: USAF security policemen augmented U.S. Marine base defense forces.

Beginning in 1966 these ground elements were increasingly supplemented by aerial components of all U.S. forces and VNAF which flew reconnaissance, illumination, and fire support missions in a base defense role. Among the most successful applications of air power to base defense was the Rocket Watch which between 1968-1970 was largely responsible for deterring, detecting, or suppressing standoff attacks in the Saigon-Tan Son Nhut-Bien Hoa area.

Even as the Air Force began building up its air base security police squadrons, the enemy continued their successful standoff attacks. Thus, on 13 April 1966 Tan Son Nhut was hit by one of the most intensive and destructive assaults of the war. Late the preceding day, a Communist attack force numbering about 90 men moved undetected to preselected firing positions located about half a mile outside the base perimeter. There they placed at least three 75-mm recoilless rifles and ten 81/82-mm mortars at three sites. Then, within a span of 13 minutes beginning at 0027 hours they fired no less than 245 rounds into the base. Its mission accomplished, the force withdrew without sustaining a single casualty.

Seven Americans and two South Vietnamese died that night and 184 U.S. personnel were wounded. One USAF C-123 and 2 VNAF C-47 aircraft were destroyed; 29 USAF aircraft of various types were damaged; a fuel storage tank containing 420,000 gallons of gasoline was set ablaze and destroyed; and 34 USAF vehicles were destroyed or damaged.

There was no reliable tactical warning. Vietnamese and U.S. forces alike showed their incapacity to cope with enemy standoff attacks even on the doorstep of the capital. Fragmented ARVN external defense elements never made contact with the enemy. U.S. reaction forces failed to place ordnance on the enemy mortar positions, hence the battery of ARVN 105-mm howitzers it supported never went into action. Also, the need to obtain prior South Vietnamese clearance for ground and air units to engage enemy forces actively assaulting allied installations contributed to the failure to engage the attackers.

Remedial actions subsequently focused on Tan Son Nhut. Prodded by USMACV, the Vietnamese Joint General Staff reorganized its external defense forces to centralize control in the VNAF wing commander, who was designated the commander of Tan Son Nhut "sensitive area." In this latter capacity, he also was vested with authority to approve fire missions. The sensitive area concept became a standard pattern for air base defense. But only at Tan Son Nhut was the commander authorized to clear fires on his own authority. Elsewhere, detailed coordination with frequently unresponsive district and province chiefs remained the rule.

After the 13 April attack, a USAF AC-47 gunship began flying nightly airborne alerts in the Bien Hoa-Tan Son Nhut area. Also, U.S. Army gunships on ground alert were assigned revetted parking space away from the heliport. All American and Vietnamese defense forces were directed to integrate their activities by the publication of a single combined plan. However, the guiding principle was not allied unity of command but coordination and cooperation.

These actions did not prevent Tan Son Nhut from being hit again during the early morning hours of 4 December 1966 by the largest sapper raid to date and the first since the 1 July 1965

sapper attack on Da Nang described above. The first indication the base was under attack came at 0110 hours when a USAF sentry dog handler reported unidentified personnel on his post in the interior of the base. Subsequent investigation and prisoner interrogation disclosed that the sapper raiding party consisted of 2 support platoons totalling 58 men and 1 assault platoon with a strength of 34. All belonged to parent main force battalions operating from a Communist stronghold about 11 miles southwest of Tan Son Nhut. Two days earlier members of this force had been told of the attack and briefed on the target with the aid of "sandtable studies." Their objective was the destruction of Allied aircraft "to prove the Viet Cong were winning and to heighten the morale of VC soldiers and cadres."

Departing their base in the early evening of 2 December 1966, the platoons arrived at a friendly village some 6 miles west of the base early the next morning. There they remained unreported for 15 hours, then departed for Tan Son Nhut which they reached at midnight. The assault platoon cut through three barbed wire fences undetected by a nearby Vietnamese guard post and entered the base followed by an unknown number of men from the support platoons. While advancing southward toward the aircraft parking ramp on the far side of the main runway, they were fired on by the USAF security police who had responded to the alarm of the sentry dog handler. At this point the assault platoon split into two groups which continued toward the ramp by different routes. Thirteen sappers were killed when they came within range of a security police machinegun position at the close-in boundary of the parking area.

The other group of sappers was not detected until it had reached the ramp. Supported by mortar fire they inflicted minor damage before they were driven off by security police, close-in sentries, and patrols. Leaving behind one dead, the sappers withdrew along their entry route. Thirty minutes had elapsed since they were first detected. By 0210 reaction forces of security police and tenant U.S. Army troops had been deployed in accordance with contingency plans. A security blocking force was across the enemy withdrawal route near the opening cut in the perimeter fence. To reopen the escape route for their comrades, elements of the support platoons engaged the security police with automatic weapons, rocket propelled grenades, and hand grenades. With support from Army gunships, the security police maintained their position and returned intensive fire. Failing in their effort, the enemy support elements withdrew, abandoning the remnants of the sappers trapped inside the base.

The U.S. Army countermortar radar located the off-base mortar sites and directed counterfire by ARVN artillery and USA gunships. Illumination was furnished by USAF AC-47 gunships which expended 490 flares between 0120 and 0650 hours. At no time did South Vietnamese internal security forces engage the enemy. At daybreak four more enemy troops were sighted and taken prisoner; no other survivors were found. Thereafter, the base returned to normal operation until 2021 hours 4 December 1966 when security police killed nine more enemy sappers who had concealed themselves in the dense vegetation.

In this action 3 USAF security police were killed and 15 wounded. ARVN forces lost three killed and four wounded. Twenty U.S. aircraft sustained minor damage estimated to total $64,230. Five security police vehicles were destroyed. Communist casualties were 28 killed. Four prisoners and a sizable quantity of enemy weapons and munitions were taken. In the words of the USMACV Combat Operations Log, the 4-5 December 1966 engagement was one in which "the

brunt of a highly successful ground operation [was] borne by the U.S. Air Force with close air support furnished by the U.S. Army."

In the early spring of 1967 the Communists began using a new weapon which substantially increased the problems of air base defense. It was unveiled at 0310 hours 27 February when Da Nang was subjected to another standoff strike. In this attack fifty-six 140-mm rockets hit the base proper while eight others fell in an adjacent village. The operation, lasting less than 60 seconds, killed 11 U.S. personnel and wounded 125. Thirteen aircraft and various facilities were damaged. In the Da Nang village 35 people were killed and 50 wounded.

This was the first Communist use of rockets in South Vietnam. A detailed account of the organization and execution of the attack was obtained from captured prisoners. The firing positions, located nearly 9,000 yards southwest of the base, were selected by a skilled and well-trained team on the afternoon of 26 February. Concurrently, the rockets were brought in by porters and rivercraft to the launch site, arriving at 2300 hours. Some 4 hours later, upon completion of final site preparation and weapon assembly, the rockets were fired. The rounds were fuzed at the super-quick setting which provided maximum shrapnel effect and the greatest damage to aircraft. Although more than 500 enemy troops were involved in this attack, the operation was not compromised.

This use of rockets, which during 1967 came to include 107-mm and 122-mm varieties, gave the Communists more firepower and flexibility since these weapons had a greater range and could be fired remotely and simultaneously in large numbers from crude improvised launchers. In response to this threat, the Air Force increased its AC-47 gunship fleet by 50 percent—from 22 to 33 aircraft— and expanded and accelerated construction of aircraft revetments and personnel shelters.

The 1968 Tet Offensive

The most sensational of all enemy operations mounted against U.S. bases during the war were the multi-battalion attacks on Tan Son Nhut and Bien Hoa during the 1968 Tet offensive. By launching this major offensive during the festivities celebrating the Vietnamese lunar new year, the enemy clearly hoped to achieve maximum tactical surprise. In this he was disappointed. A variety of sources—captured documents, prisoners, and defectors—all indicated the Communist intention to attack population centers and military installations. Accordingly, the Americans and Vietnamese concentrated maneuver battalions around Saigon in expectation of a Tet attack. In a message released the morning of 30 January 1968, USMACV cancelled the Tet truce, ordered resumption of full-scale military operations, and directed all installations and air bases to assume a maximum security posture. However, the allies did not anticipate the true magnitude of the impending offensive. At Bien Hoa the enemy committed two infantry battalions and one reinforced infantry company; at Tan Son Nhut, one sapper and four infantry battalions. In each case, North Vietnamese troops were a sizable percentage of the attacking force.

The enemy infiltration into the area surrounding Saigon and the two air bases was facilitated by the increased number of holiday travelers and by the jungle terrain. Except for the few radial roads emanating from Saigon, the city is bounded on the north, west, and east by a combination of paddies, jungles and swamps interlaced by waterways. These waterways provided excellent avenues for clandestine approach to the capital and its environs. In crossing this terrain, Communist units that engaged Bien Hoa, Tan Son Nhut, and other targets in the Saigon area made normal tactical marches over established routes, through established base camps and known base areas. These troops were held in assembly areas 9 to 12 hours marching distance from their targets for the coordinated assault. Apart from avoiding detection on approach, enemy units attacked their targets overtly, preceded or accompanied by supporting fires and supplementary attacks.

Thus, at approximately 0300 hours 31 January 1968 Bien Hoa was hit by 35 rounds of 122-mm rocket and 10 rounds of 82-mm mortar fire. Almost simultaneously a sentry dog handler near the southeast perimeter reported the base was being penetrated. Approaching from the southeast an enemy force estimated at eight companies breached the perimeter at four points but was thwarted in a fifth attempt by fire from U.S. Army gunships. A concrete pillbox located directly in the path of the main penetration force became a center of resistance. Unable to capture this bunker, which remained in security police hands throughout, the attackers were caught in a crossfire when they bypassed it in an effort to reach the flight line without delay. By 0400 hours the enemy penetration was halted just east of the flight line complex by security police and augmentee blocking forces vigorously supported by Army gunships. Consequently, the enemy force never reached the aircraft parking area, its prime objective.

At dawn on 31 January 1968 there were only three centers of enemy resistance: a revetted engine test stand, the dearming pad, both east of the flight line complex, and an estimated reinforced squad located near a penetration point on the eastern perimeter. A counterattack by security police and other security personnel cleared the test stand and, supported by 57-mm recoilless rifle fire, subsequently regained control of the dearming pad.

(1) An Air Force sentry and his German shepherd watch an Air Force F-4C Phantom jet land at Cam Ranh Bay. (2) An Air Force security alert team checks a sentry dog post for possible enemy activity. Shown (l. to r.): Airmen First Class Freeman Tilden, Francis A. Jasinski, Joseph A. LeBlanc. On far right is A1C Leon E. Senecal, with his sentry dog, Rex. (3) An enemy attack on Qui Nhon AB destroyed a number of U.S. aircraft including this A-1E Skyraider. (4) Remains of the hulk of what was an Air Force C-130A aircraft destroyed by enemy rockets at Da Nang, 1967. (5) An Air Force sentry, silhouetted in the light from a search beacon, mans a perimeter post on the outskirts of Da Nang AB. (6) An Air Force security policeman and his sentry dog silhouetted against the setting sun at Phan Rang AB.

1

2

3

4

5

6

Supported by Army gunships, a final sweep of the field to the eastern perimeter terminated all enemy resistance on base at 1640 hours. Damage from enemy standoff weapons included 2 USAF aircraft destroyed and 20 damaged. Air Force casualties totalled 4 killed, 26 wounded. Enemy losses inside the air base were 139 killed and 25 taken prisoner. In the Bien Hoa area enemy losses were 1,164 killed and 98 captured.

That same day, one of the most significant air base battles of the war was fought at Tan Son Nhut. The strength of the enemy force, his tactics, and post-battle investigations indicated the Communists intended to overrun and occupy the base. The capture of Tan Son Nhut along with Headquarters MACV, Seventh Air Force, VNAF, and the adjoining South Vietnamese Joint General Staff compound could well have been the key to Communist seizure of Saigon.

The attack on Tan Son Nhut, coordinated with other strikes into Saigon and its environs, commenced at 0320 hours 31 January 1968 when enemy forces initiated probes at various points around the entire perimeter. The main assault was concentrated against the southwest perimeter midway between Gate No. 051 and a concrete pillbox, Bunker 051, the latter manned by USAF security police. Following a barrage of grenades and mortar rounds, sappers who had approached the perimeter along National Highway No. 1 in a Mabretta taxi, detonated a Bangalore torpedo to breach the fence line. This opening became the entry port for Communist troops into Tan Son Nhut. A last transmission was received from Bunker 051 at 0344 hours. Shortly thereafter, all defenders having been killed, the position was overrun and converted to an enemy strongpoint.

At approximately 0600 hours the attack reached its high water mark, enemy forces having penetrated eastward 650 yards into the base where they established a north-south line about 330 yards in length. At that point the attackers were halted and contained by a blocking force of USAF security police and personnel from tenant Army units supported by fire from helicopter gunships. After some delay due to unsatisfactory radio communications, friendly artillery and mortars were cleared to engage the enemy on the western perimeter. When three VNAF-controlled light tanks were committed in an effort to dislodge the enemy from Bunker 051, two were immediately destroyed by rocket-propelled grenades and the third forced to retire. In time the U.S. blocking force was augmented by two ARVN airborne companies.

Between 0630 and 0800 hours two troops of U.S. cavalry and one battery of U.S. 105-mm artillery arrived on the scene after fighting their way along Highway No. 1 from their base camp at Cu Chi, 18 miles northwest of Tan Son Nhut. All friendly forces launched a coordinated counterattack forcing the enemy to fall back from the base. Much of the fire cover for this withdrawal came from Bunker 051 which remained in enemy hands until it was successfully assaulted and taken by USAF security police elements at 1210 hours. At 1217 hours the breach in the western perimeter was closed and secured. Fighting on the east and southeast perimeter continued until 1300 hours when those areas also were declared secure, bringing the engagement to a successful conclusion. The performance of ARVN air base defense forces showed little improvement. A Combat After Action Report noted that a number of the South Vietnamese personnel assigned to static perimeter defense positions in the vicinity of the enemy penetration deserted their posts.

Friendly casualties included 4 USAF security police, 19 U.S. Army, and 32 South Vietnamese troops killed. Eleven Air Force security police, 75 U.S. Army troops, and 79 Vietnamese

An Air Force sentry and his dog.

PACAF to monitor all information on enemy activities within an 18-mile radius of each air base. This procedure reduced but did not eliminate the problem of timely and well defined tactical warning.

The USAF concept of close-in internal security was sufficiently discredited to be replaced in South Vietnam by a PACAF concept of local base defense applicable to the type of threat encountered in an insurgent environment. Since air base defense training conducted in the United States and South Vietnam appeared to be inadequate, Seventh Air Force undertook to provide its own instruction at a Heavy Weapons and Small Unit Tactics School. In the materiel area, armored cars, armored personnel carriers, heavier weapons (81-mm mortars, 90-mm recoilless rifles, .50-cal. machineguns), and a four-channel, non-tactical radio net were added to the security police equipment inventory.

The 1968 Tet offensive also pointed to the need for a mobile, in-country base defense contingency force that could be deployed quickly to any facility where the threat was particularly grave or where security force effectiveness was critically reduced by prolonged duty in advanced alert status. At the urgent request of Seventh Air Force, Headquarters USAF accelerated activation of security forces to provide the desired defenses. Three combat security police squadrons were formed and rotated this duty in South Vietnam between April 1968 and March 1971 when, due to force withdrawals and related defense budget reduction, the program was scrapped. During the 2 years that followed, the bulk of USAF units departed the area. As for Air Force base defense forces, they had reached peak strength and effectiveness in 1969. Repeatedly proven in combat, the 10 security police squadrons that were the core of the defense effort had earned a memorable and distinguished place in USAF annals.

were wounded. Thirteen U.S. aircraft received minor damage from standoff weapons. Enemy forces lost 962 personnel killed and 9 taken prisoner.

The successful defense of Bien Hoa and Tan Son Nhut was attributed chiefly to the advanced tactical warning which triggered the mobilization and deployment of U.S. air base defense forces. Even so, the allied failure to estimate accurately the true scale of the Communist effort meant that these anticipatory countermeasures did not provide any margin for safety. To avert a repetition of this predicament, security police units were directed by

Chapter XVII

Medical Support

The first Air Force medical officer sent to South Vietnam arrived on 4 December 1961, several weeks after the first Farm Gate aircraft reached that country. He was Maj. George Haworth, brought in from the Air Force Academy and initially detailed to the American Dispensary in Saigon. This facility was operated by the U.S. Military Assistance Advisory Group and manned by doctors from the U.S. Army, Navy, Air Force, and State Department. Early in 1962 Major Haworth was reassigned to the MAAG's Air Force Section and later to 2d ADVON and its successor, 2d Air Division.

In May 1962 Haworth became commander of the first USAF medical facility in South Vietnam. Located at Tan Son Nhut, it consisted of a tactical hospital of 14 tents and 36 beds flown in from Thailand. An interim facility, it was subsequently replaced by a 10-bed Class A dispensary and, in October 1962, designated the 6220th USAF Dispensary. Its staff consisted of five doctors, one dentist, and one veterinarian under the command of Haworth. A sixth USAF doctor was assigned to the Saigon dispensary. The Air Force also had deployed to Bien Hoa and Da Nang medical teams consisting of one USAF officer and three enlisted men to provide medical support to Air Force personnel there.

Soon after the first USAF C-123's arrived at Tan Son Nhut, the Air Force opened an aeromedical evacuation control center on the base manned by two technicians from the Japan-based 9th Aeromedical Evacuation Squadron. One C-123 was kept on 24-hour alert to respond to emergency requests for evacuation, while others stowed two unrigged litters aboard for emergency use. Beginning in November 1962, the center scheduled weekly

C-123 aeromedical evacuation missions between the U.S. Army's 8th Field Hospital at Nha Trang and Tan Son Nhut. Other C-123's flying resupply missions to South Vietnamese outposts frequently evacuated the sick and wounded to Saigon. In March 1962 C-130's began evacuating patients from South Vietnam to Clark AB in the Philippines, and in May they began weekly flights between Clark and Tan Son Nhut. Subsequently, the Air Force also established a C-130 route into Thailand, using an aeromedical evacuation control center at Don Muang. During the next 2 years, as U.S. units became more deeply involved in combat, the number of American casualties and evacuation flights from the theater rose.

Following the August 1964 Gulf of Tonkin incident, PACAF's 1st Medical Service Wing at Clark AB ordered several squadron medical elements from Japan and Okinawa to Southeast Asia. Element 1, Detachment 1—consisting of a captain, sergeant, and two airmen —departed Yokota AB, Japan, on 7 August for Bien Hoa to support B-57 squadrons which had arrived there the previous day. Medical Element 1 remained at Bien Hoa 15 months and won commendation for its conduct and care of casualties suffered during the devastating 1 November 1964 Viet Cong standoff mortar attack on the base. It was replaced in November 1965 by another element of Detachment 4, 1st Medical Service Wing, based at Kadena AB, Okinawa.

On 7 August 1964 Squadron Element 2 also departed Yokota for Korat, Thailand, to support an F-105 squadron deployed there. The same day, the 1st Medical Service Wing dispatched a third element from Naha AB, Okinawa, to Bien Hoa. Because of

ded serviceman is car-
down a ramp at an Air
base where he will be
italized until he recovers
his wounds.

the lack of office space, this element was forced to operate out of a South Vietnamese dispensary. During its brief tour ending on 27 October 1964, the unit treated 226 patients. It also instituted a program of malaria prophylaxis whereby all USAF personnel were required to take 0.5 grams of chloroquine each week. Medical personnel dispensed the tablets in dining halls and crew briefing rooms.

In 1965 malaria was the major medical problem facing American forces in Vietnam, its incidence rising to the point where it was a significant military problem as well. Prior to 1965, malaria attack rates among Americans were negligible. But as large numbers of newly-arrived U.S. Army and Marine troops began moving into the countryside for combat, the rates rose to 8 and 16 per 1000 a year—with a sharp increase to 73 per 1000 in September, 98 in October, and a further increase to more than 100 in November.

On the other hand, the Air Force did not have a serious malaria problem. In 1963 there were no cases among Air Force personnel in Vietnam; in 1965 there were less than 15. The likeliest explanations, aside from the fact that there were fewer USAF personnel in South Vietnam compared to Army and Marine troops, were that the former were on duty at fixed bases in relatively secure areas where mosquito and other malaria control measures were easier to implement than in the field and jungle areas. Also, most airfields were located in the flat lowlands or coastal areas of South Vietnam where there was much less malaria than in the foothills and plateau areas where ground troops operated.

But Air Force personnel did begin to suffer from an upsurge of chronic sinusitis and other common respiratory diseases, attributable in part to the extremely wet and extremely dry seasons. During the monsoon season, humidity was very high; personnel could be drenched several times daily from the frequent showers and/or through excessive perspiration. In the dry season, heavy wind-blown dust resulted in irritation of mucous membranes. The nature of military operations also required personnel to be in almost constant motion—by air and, increasingly, by surface travel. Thus, changes from wet to dry seasons could be experienced in a single day by personnel travelling from north to south or vice versa. In air travel, there was the added factor of rapid cooling as the perspiring individual took off from a super-heated runway and rose to altitude. Dysentery and parasitic infections also were fairly common in the early years of USAF operations.

In the post-1965 period of rapid growth of U.S. forces in Southeast Asia, the Air Force opened up two Class "A" dispensaries and three Class "B" dispensaries, bringing the latter total to eight. Where more substantial inpatient care was required, Air Force physicians transferred their patients to U.S. Army hospitals at Saigon, Nha Trang, and Korat; the U.S. Navy station hospital in Saigon; the naval hospital supporting U.S. Marine Corps operations near Da Nang; the USAF hospital at Clark; and to others as needed. Specialist consultation in internal medicine was available at the 33d USAF Dispensary at Tan Son Nhut. The U.S. Navy hospital in Saigon provided surgical and neuro-psychiatric consultation. A U.S. Army neurosurgeon served at the Cong Hoa military hospital, Saigon. An additional neuropsychiatrist, an orthopedic surgeon, a pathologist, and a radiologist were available at the U.S. Army 8th Field Hospital, Nha Trang.

Recognizing the importance of preventive medicine, the 2d Air Division Surgeon's Office inspected base water supplies to insure adequate chlorination. Initially, insect and rodent control was inadequate because of shortages of equipment and supplies. During the 1965 force buildup nearly all installations in Vietnam and Thailand found it difficult to obtain insecticides and rodenticides through supply channels. The surge in new personnel overtaxed troop quarters, while construction of additional facilities lagged behind requirements. At one point the 2d Air Division Veterinary Service warned that the inflow of troops was overtaxing existing dining halls. The quality of food served, although not comparable to that prevailing in the United States, was satisfactory. Because of lack of refrigeration, one of the Air Force's biggest food problems in 1965 was the delivery of perishable items to remote sites fast enough to keep them from spoiling.

In both Vietnam and Thailand the Dental Service provided routine examination, emergency treatment, including fillings and limited prosthetic maintenance and repair, and established an oral health program. At Tan Son Nhut, the Air Force dental facility initially consisted of two small dental operating rooms. One contained a wall-mounted X-ray, and the other a small bench for prosthetic work and repair. At Da Nang, where Air Force personnel numbered more than 2,000 by the end of June 1965, one dental officer and two technicians provided care in a dental van.

Facilities and Supplies

In 1965—as the combat casualties increased—USAF medical personnel realized they needed additional dispensaries, casualty staging units, and hospitals in the theater. Because there was a shortage of construction materials in South Vietnam and existing building methods were too slow, the Air Force in April 1966 decided to procure prefabricated, modular type buildings for use as medical facilities at Da Nang (100-bed casualty staging facility) and Takhli, Thailand (10-bed dispensary). The destination of the latter was subsequently changed to U-Tapao, Thailand. A contract for the

manufacture of these two modular medical facilities was awarded to an Idaho firm. They were designed and engineered at the Mobile Air Materiel Area, Brookley AFB, Ala., based upon concepts provided by the Surgeon General, Headquarters USAF. Both facilities were completed in 59 days.

The first facility package arrived at the port of Da Nang in mid-August 1966, the U-Tapao package at Sattahip, Thailand, in early September. Both were in operation by late November 1966. This represented 8 and 10 months, respectively, from the start of the initial design effort. By mid-1969, the Air Force had assembled and put into use 19 prefabricated module medical facilities.

The standard prefab unit was 10 feet wide by 40 feet long, with several modules joined together side-to-side to form the medical facility. These buildings contained electrical systems, water supplies, waste plumbing, air conditioning, heat, finished interiors, vinyl tile floors, conductive floors where necessary, and adequate lighting. Casework, sinks, lavatories, toilets, tubs, and showers were installed. Full utility support, such as steam and electric generators, hot water heaters, fuel storage tanks, and electrical switching gear came with the package, plus a utility building to put them in. The completed facility included waiting rooms, nurses' stations, diet kitchens, dining areas in larger facilities, treatment rooms, laboratories, pharmacy, administration and supply area, operating rooms, X-ray rooms, wards, ancillary service areas, and corridors.

The modular-erected facility enabled the Medical Service to expand fast enough to handle the growing patient load. Starting with its eight Class "B" dispensaries for outpatient care only and two Class "A" dispensaries with 16 beds, the Air Force by June 1969 added one 200-bed hospital at Cam Ranh Bay and five more Class "A" dispensaries with 62 beds.

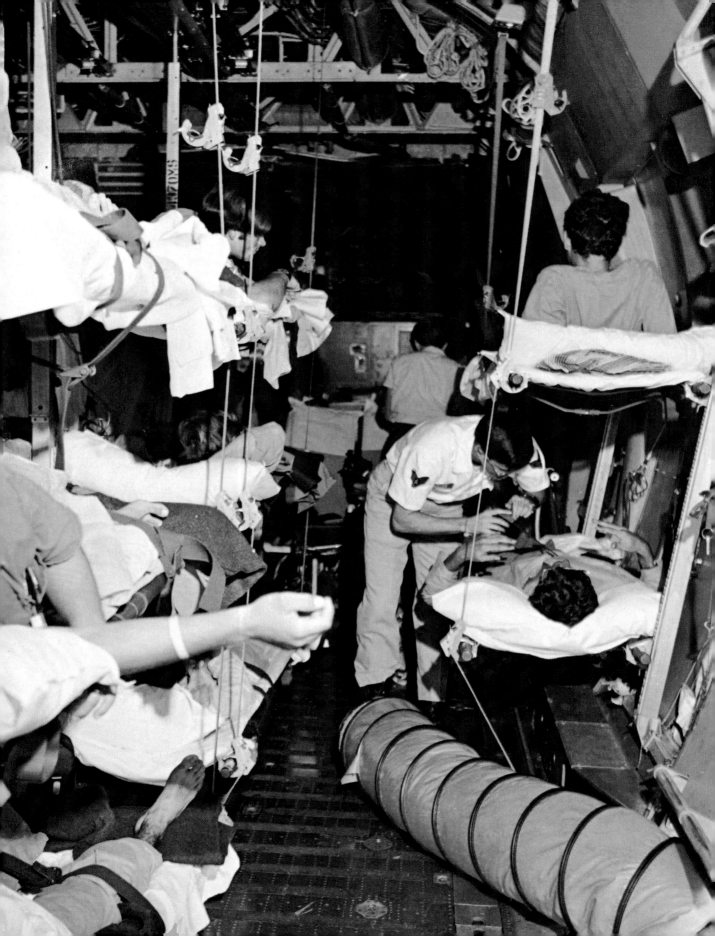

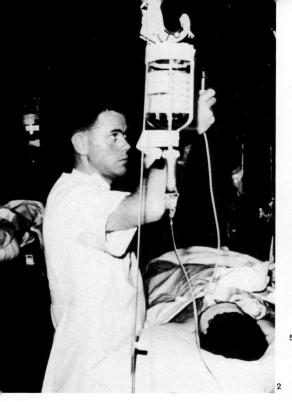

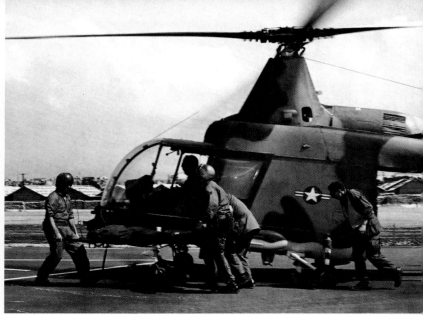

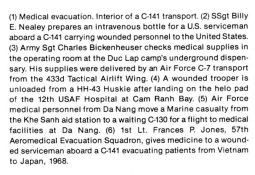

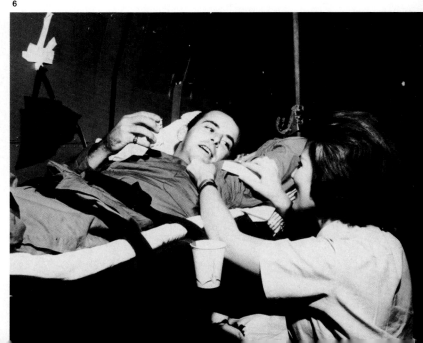

(1) Medical evacuation. Interior of a C-141 transport. (2) SSgt Billy E. Nealey prepares an intravenous bottle for a U.S. serviceman aboard a C-141 carrying wounded personnel to the United States. (3) Army Sgt Charles Bickenheuser checks medical supplies in the operating room at the Duc Lap camp's underground dispensary. His supplies were delivered by an Air Force C-7 transport from the 433d Tactical Airlift Wing. (4) A wounded trooper is unloaded from a HH-43 Huskie after landing on the helo pad of the 12th USAF Hospital at Cam Ranh Bay. (5) Air Force medical personnel from Da Nang move a Marine casualty from the Khe Sanh aid station to a waiting C-130 for a flight to medical facilities at Da Nang. (6) 1st Lt. Frances P. Jones, 57th Aeromedical Evacuation Squadron, gives medicine to a wounded serviceman aboard a C-141 evacuating patients from Vietnam to Japan, 1968.

Offshore medical facilities at Clark and Tachikawa Air Base, Japan, also were expanded by 100 beds. During 1967-1968 the number of inpatient facilities in the war zone rose substantially. And by 30 June 1969 the Air Force was operating a medical complex in Southeast Asia which consisted of 3 hospitals, 12 Class "A" dispensaries, 2 Class "B" dispensaries, and 5 aeromedical staging facilities. At the time of the 1965 buildup, the medical supply account at Clark had the responsibility for medical materiel support for all USAF medical units in the Philippines, Taiwan, and Southeast Asia. As the war escalated and the medical establishment began expanding rapidly, the demands placed upon the Clark medical supply account exceeded the manning, inventory and facility capabilities available. Consequently, shortages of medical supplies somewhat hampered medical operations in the war zone.

Under the impact of the additional workload, warehousemen, key punch operators, and officers handling the Clark Air Base medical supply account soon found themselves working overtime to get supplies in and out as fast as possible. But there were significant delays in obtaining supplies from the continental United States. It was not unusual for a shipment of medical supplies destined for Clark to remain in the hold of a cargo ship lying for weeks at anchor off each of several Vietnamese ports before war materiel was partially unloaded so the vessel could proceed to Manila. This logistical problem increased pipeline time for medical materiel to get to Clark by an additional 60 days in October 1965 and as much as 75 days in November. Due to stringent limitations on air shipments, only the most essential items were airlifted to Clark. Anything less than an emergency shipment was usually sent by sea.

Distribution of medical supplies from Clark to South Vietnam and Thailand, on the other hand, was not a

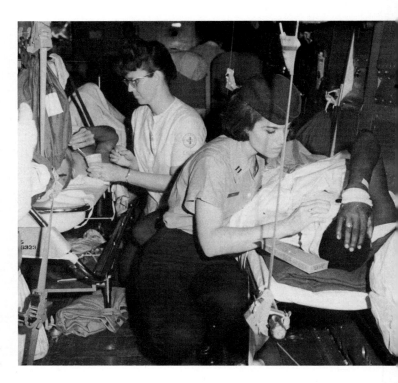

major problem. It was accomplished by a large fleet of USAF transports, whose routes and frequency of flights normally insured that supplies arrived at intended destinations within several days to 2 weeks. To speed sea deliveries of medical supplies to South Vietnam, a priority effort was made to install improved port-handling equipment to help reduce pipeline time. The initiation of port-to-port cargo hauls also helped. For example, a ship destined for Cam Ranh Bay was loaded in the United States with cargo solely destined for that port.

In 1966, the Air Force relieved the Clark medical supply account of responsibility for the entire area and set up separate medical supply accounts in South Vietnam, Thailand, and Taiwan for support of medical units in those countries. In July 1966, the medical supply account at Cam Ranh Bay took over the job of resupplying all USAF medical units in South Vietnam. In January 1967 two other accounts were established at U-Tapao airfield, Thailand, and Ching Chuan Kang AB,

Two nurses, one of them from the American Red Cross, attend wounded servicemen enroute to the United States.

Patients await loading aboard a C-130 Hercules transport at Qui Nhon.

Taiwan. The addition of these accounts essentially eliminated most of the medical support problems encountered in 1965.

The significance and tempo of the medical supply operation in Southeast Asia and vicinity is best illustrated by the chart on page 279.

The volume of medical supplies issued during 1968 by the account at Cam Ranh Bay alone exceeded the total issued by bases in most major commands. In addition to medical supplies, the accounts at Cam Ranh Bay and U-Tapao issued very large amounts of equipment in 1967 and 1968. They also were involved in handling of approximately $1.2 million of supplies and equipment shipped direct from the United States to Vietnam and Thailand.

Aeromedical Evacuation

During the war only 1 percent of all U.S. personnel wounded in Southeast Asia died after reaching a medical fa-

cility. This was a substantial improvement over the survival rate during the Korean War and World War II, and was primarily attributed to speedy aeromedical evacuation. In Korea, where fewer than 15 percent of the wounded were evacuated by helicopter, the death rate was 2.5 percent. During World War II, when no tactical aircraft were made available to fly casualties from the battlefield, the rate was 4.5 percent.

The key to saving lives was to get the patient to an adequate medical facility as quickly as possible. Once there, other medical innovations—such as the use of frozen whole blood, artificial kidney and blood volume machines, and an ultrasonic device that locates shell fragments deep within the body by sonar—helped lower the death rate. For example, almost immediately after the early morning Viet Cong attack on Pleiku airfield on 7 February 1965, local aircraft began evacuating the wounded to the Army's field hospital at Nha Trang. Some 4 hours later, Detachment 4, 9th Aeromedical Evacuation Squadron at Clark, received a request for service. At 0800 hours a C-130 departed the Philippines for Nha Trang, where it was met by a medical flight crew of one nurse and one aeromedical evacuation technician from Detachment 6, 9th Aeromedical Evacuation Squadron, Saigon. At 1300 hours this medical flight crew left Nha Trang for Clark with 21 patients, all casualties.

The next day another C-130 flew from Clark to Vietnam to evacuate another 31 litter patients from Saigon and Nha Trang. All but 4 of the 31 were victims of the enemy attack of the previous morning. The medical flight crew—one nurse and two aeromedical evacuation technicians—provided extensive inflight care to 12 who were in serious condition. The crew administered chest and abdominal suction and intravenous fluids. With the medical personnel checking each patient

1

(1) 1st Lt. Billy G. Priddy, a male flight nurse with the 9th Aeromedical Evacuation Squadron, keeps a watchful eye on the condition of wounded Marines during a flight from a Vietnam battlefield to Da Nang, 1966. (2) A wounded trooper is queried aboard an Air Force evacuation aircraft at Da Nang. (3) The large container rolling into the open tail and ramp doors of a C-130 provides a complete operating room and X-ray facility. This unit, a doctor, and a staff of corpsmen were moved to Quang Tri airfield from its previous location at Lai Khe. (4) Air Force Sergeants Daniel Beste and Garry Bolyard handle medical stock at a Thai base.

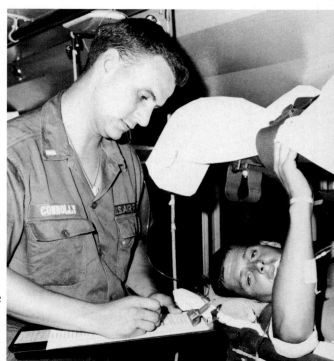

2

3

4

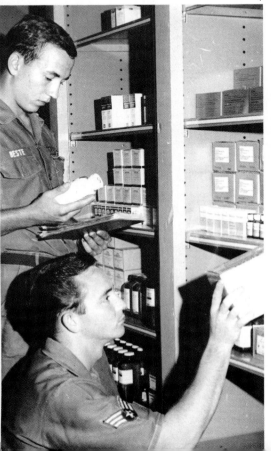

1ST MEDICAL SERVICE WING

CLARK AIR BASE, PHILIPPINES

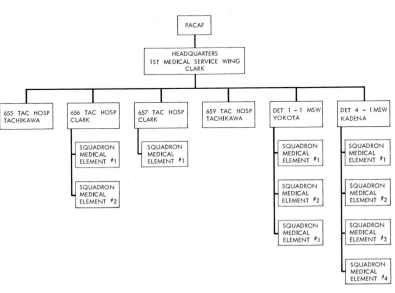

```
                              ┌──────────┐
                              │  PACAF   │
                              └────┬─────┘
                    ┌──────────────────────────────┐
                    │         HEADQUARTERS          │
                    │   1ST MEDICAL SERVICE WING    │
                    │            CLARK              │
                    └───────────────┬───────────────┘
```

655 TAC HOSP TACHIKAWA	656 TAC HOSP CLARK	657 TAC HOSP CLARK	659 TAC HOSP TACHIKAWA	DET 1 – 1 MSW YOKOTA	DET 4 – 1 MSW KADENA
	SQUADRON MEDICAL ELEMENT #1	SQUADRON MEDICAL ELEMENT #1		SQUADRON MEDICAL ELEMENT #1	SQUADRON MEDICAL ELEMENT #1
	SQUADRON MEDICAL ELEMENT #2			SQUADRON MEDICAL ELEMENT #2	SQUADRON MEDICAL ELEMENT #2
				SQUADRON MEDICAL ELEMENT #3	SQUADRON MEDICAL ELEMENT #3
					SQUADRON MEDICAL ELEMENT #4

279

throughout the flight, all arrived at Clark without serious deterioration of their condition. By 14 February the squadron had completed the evacuation of all casualties of the Pleiku attack.

The demand for aeromedical evacuations rose steadily with the increase of combat casualties. To handle the increased patient load, the Air Force deployed TDY personnel to the theater to augment the 9th Aeromedical Evacuation Squadron and authorized an increase in Clark's bed capacity from 40 to 250 beds. Patient movements within Southeast Asia and from there to offshore hospitals rose from 3,719 in December 1965 to 21,-474 in May 1968. Evacuation of patients from the theater to the United States by the Military Airlift Command increased from 1,085 in December 1965 to 5,401 in May 1968.

In South Vietnam nearly all battlefield casualties were evacuated to rear areas by U.S. Army UH-1 helicopter ambulances, each able to carry six litter patients. At the peak of combat operations in 1968, the Army operated 116 of the air ambulances. Air Force helicopters occasionally assisted in battlefield evacuations, the H-43 air rescue helicopter being particularly useful in bringing out casualties from deep jungle areas. Otherwise, thousands of casualties were moved in-country by a variety of USAF transports—including C-130's, C-123's, and C-7's. In January 1968, C-118's of the 6485th Operations Squadron were assigned to fly in-country aeromedical evacuation missions, freeing the C-130's to carry combat cargo missions during the Communist Tet offensive. Based at Cam Ranh Bay, the C-118's flew scheduled aeromedical evacua-

Members of an Air Force C-123 aircrew and a medic rush a wounded airman to a hospital in Saigon. He is SSgt Richard G. Benton, shot through the arm during a paradrop mission north of Saigon. Others shown (l. to r.): A1C Carl W. Larson, Capt. Donald J. Haney, unidentified Vietnamese soldier, and A1C Donald E. Delahunt, February 1966.

280

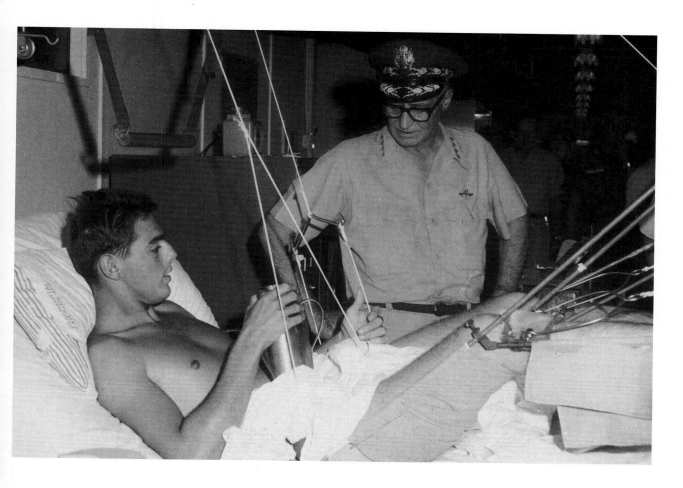

tion missions four times a week, serving Pleiku, Qui Nhon, Nha Trang, Tuy Hoa, Phu Cat, and Phan Rang. One C-118 at Clark flew four missions a week to Chu Lai, Da Nang, Qui Nhon, and Nha Trang and terminating at Cam Ranh Bay.

Committing aircraft specifically for aeromedical evacuation became one of the main features of medical support in South Vietnam. Working with medical agencies and the 834th Air Division, the 903d Aeromedical Evacuation Squadron provided scheduled service throughout the country. From July 1967 through January 1968, patient movements averaged 5,813 per month; from February through June the average was 9,098 per month. Almost 11 times each day requirements were called in, missions set up, medical crews picked up, cargo offloaded, planes reconfigured, and pa-

tients evacuated—almost always on a short notice or no notice basis. Equally important, about 11 times each day aeromedical evacuation requirements disrupted the programmed cargo and passenger commitments of the airlift agencies.

The 1968 Communist Tet offensive produced large numbers of military and civilian casualties and required four to five unscheduled aeromedical evacuation flights each day and occasionally eight. To keep up with the demand, a C-130 assault aircraft operated a daily round-robin shuttle from 0900 to 1700 hours. This aircraft averaged from 125 to 158 patients per day, most of them recent Marine and Army battle casualties. To handle patients during late afternoons and evenings, another C-130 operated a regular nightly round-robin. This aircraft averaged 40 to 60 patients per flight. Both

MAJOR AEROMEDICAL EVACUATION ROUTES

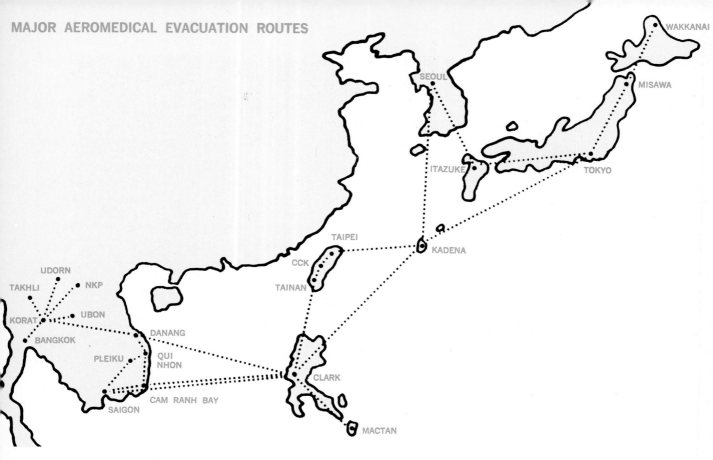

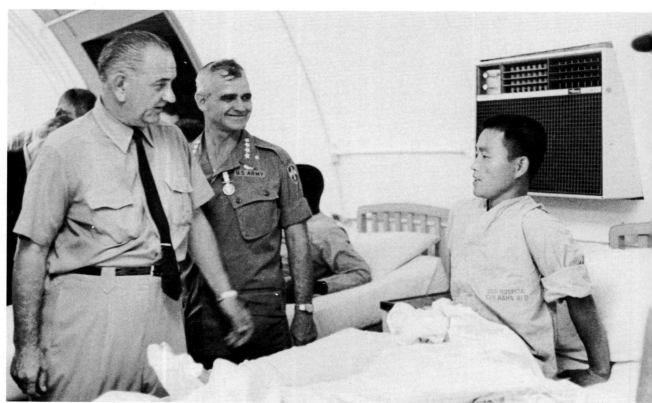

aircraft operated into forward sites such as Dong Ha, Quang Tri, and Hue/Phu Bai, and evacuated patients to Da Nang. Occasionally, after its second round-robin the aircraft further evacuated the patients to Qui Nhon, Phu Hiep, Nha Trang, or Cam Ranh Bay when Da Nang was saturated. An average of 2.4 aircraft per day were used in I Corps to support aeromedical evacuation requirements. In February 1968 more than 10,770 patients were evacuated on 330 flights.

The heavy and continuous fighting in the provinces around Saigon during the early months of 1968 also produced many casualties requiring evacuation. To handle these patients, an aircraft began flying 7 days a week from Tan Son Nhut servicing Cu Chi, Bien Hoa, Vung Tau, Binh Thuy, and terminating at Cam Ranh Bay. Following the 1968 surge of casualties, the Air Force increased the number of flight nurses in the Far East from 314 to 409. In February the Air Force transferred 20 nurses from a MAC C-141 evacuation unit at McGuire AFB, N.J., to Yokota, Japan, increasing the number there to 62. Twenty MAC nurses also were sent to Yokota on 90 days TDY. When their time expired, they were replaced by another 30 stateside nurses. Twenty of the latter were members of an Air Force Reserve Unit, the 34th Aeromedical Evacuation Squadron, Kelly AFB, Tex., activated in May 1968. The other 10 were transferred from other USAF hospitals. After its recall to active duty, the 34th deployed to Yokota and flew more than 1,200 aeromedical evacuations from Southeast Asia to the United States plus about 1,000 others from Japan to stateside hospitals.

Throughout the war the Military Airlift Command played a vital role in evacuating thousands of casualties from the theater to the United States. From a small force of one squadron and a detachment which it operated in mid-1964, MAC expanded the system by 1968 to one aeromedical evacuation group, three squadrons, and five detachments. The monthly average of evacuated patients rose from 342 in August 1964 to 8,956 in 1968. As indicated, the principal evacuation redistribution centers in the Pacific were Clark and Yokota. Mid-Pacific flights transited Guam, Wake, or Hawaii or went directly from Yokota to Travis AFB, Calif. In August 1966 MAC also inaugurated evacuation flights from Vietnam to the eastern part of the United States via Yokota and Elmendorf.

The introduction of C-135, C-141, and C-9 aircraft made MAC's aeromedical airlift more responsive than in previous wars. In 1965 the C-141 replaced the C-135 as the principal intertheater evacuation aircraft. On 15 July it flew its first long distance air evacuation mission in the Pacific area. The C-141's advantages included high speed, long range, and a larger cabin capacity able to handle 60 litter patients, 100 ambulatory patients, or a combination of both. Approximately 6,000 C-141 air evacuation missions were flown within the Pacific and from the Pacific area to the United States between July 1965 and December 1972. The C-9, the Air Force's newest theater aeromedical evacuation aircraft, flew its first operational mission in Southeast Asia on 15 March 1972. Overall, the Military Airlift Command evacuated a total of 406,022 patients, including 168,832 battle casualties between 1965 and 1973. The airlift was accomplished with a perfect flying safety record.

President Johnson (l.) and General Westmoreland greet a wounded Vietnamese soldier hospitalized at Cam Ranh Bay.

Military Civic Action

The Air Force not only fought a tenacious enemy in Southeast Asia but also participated in a program of civic action to assist friendly governments in the theater to gain the support of their rural populations. This civic mission had its origins in a Defense Department task force report to President Kennedy, dated 27 April 1961, which proposed a number of military and economic steps the United States might take to help counter North Vietnam's drive to overthrow the government of South Vietnam. Two days later the President approved the task force recommendations, one of which called for setting up civilian and military civic action teams to help the peoples of Southeast Asia to raise their standards of living.

Although the Air Force did not form civic action teams in South Vietnam in the early 1960's as had the U.S. Army, its Farm Gate crews began providing direct aid to the Vietnamese within days of their arrival in the country. Beginning in January 1962, Air Force C-123's began delivering relief supplies and other necessities to Vietnamese communities cut off by monsoon floods or Communist insurgents. The role of the C-123's was graphically described by Col. Benjamin S. Preston, the Air Force commander at Da Nang. In his 1964 end-of-tour report, he wrote:

> . . .I came to realize how much these little people looked forward to the stops by our C-123 aircraft. Our airlift system has revolutionized the way of life of these people; particularly the outpost people who depended upon us for resupply. The daily shuttle run between Da Nang and Tan Son Nhut. . .has become famous to Vietnamese and us alike as the only way most of them can travel north or south. Sometimes it breaks down enroute to Nha Trang, Qui Nhon, Quang Ngai, or Hue Fue Bai, and it becomes a community project to load, unload, handle block and tackle, etc., and try to get it going again. I guess it comes closer to the old Western Overland Stage than anything else I can think of . . . .
>
> I watched our crews at work, and the way they handled themselves in helping people, reassuring children and ancient old peasant couples, laughing and joking, sweating and cursing, but acknowledging the human dignity of the individual all the while made me realize that they were some of Mr. Lodge's best possible ambassadorial representatives.

The use of Air Force transports contributed greatly to Saigon's administrative control of its territory. Flying in and out of some 100 airfields throughout Vietnam, the C-123's provided a vital line of communication which helped maintain the nation's viability in times of extreme distress.

Beginning in the early 1960's, Air Force officers and enlisted men also became personally involved in a variety of assistance projects. For example, since there was an acute shortage of trained physicians in Vietnam (in 1970 there were only 1,300 doctors for more than 17 million people), Air Force medical officers and dentists volunteered their talents and days off to orphanages and leprosariums in the vicinity of their bases. USAF veterinarians also assisted nearby villagers to set up disease-prevention programs including purification of their water supplies. Many enlisted men contributed their time and personal funds to help the many orphans in Vietnam, and during New Years holidays, joined with the Vietnamese Air Force personnel to distribute toys to the children. At Bien Hoa AB, USAF crews contributed $1,500.00 in personal funds for distribution to needy Vietnamese.

Assisted by a Vietnamese woman, Air Force Sgt. Craig . Wenzel inspects a drinking well at a village near Phan Rang AB, South Vietnam, 1971.

285

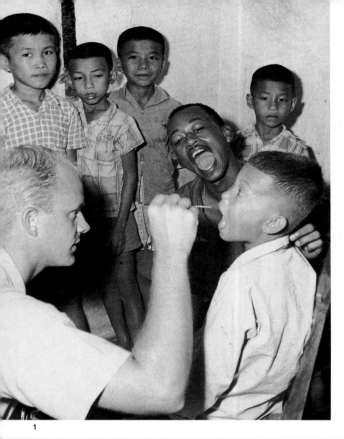

1

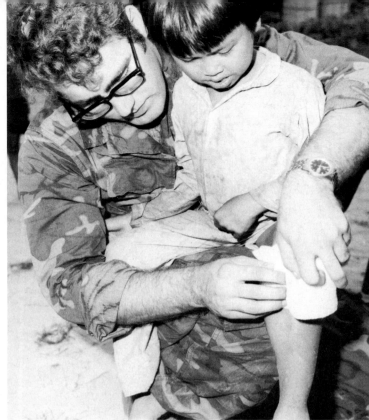

2

3

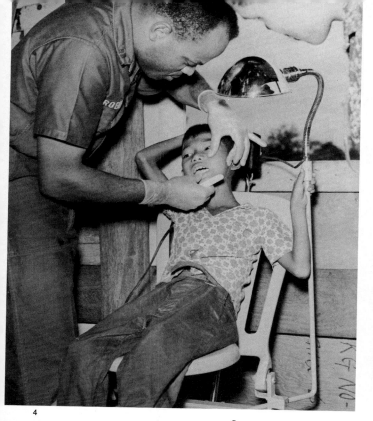

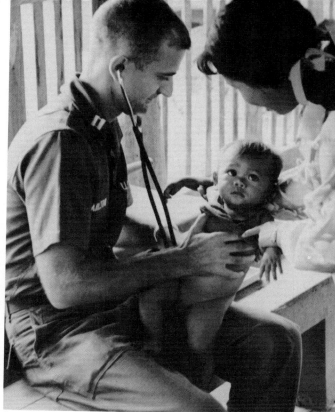

4

5

6

7

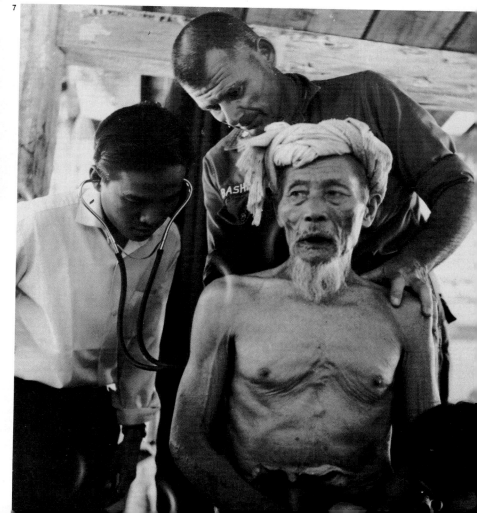

(1) Capt. Drew D. Whiteside (l.) looks for cavities in a young Vietnamese patient's mouth. A1C Ivory Herbert, Jr., a dental technician urges the boy to open wide. (2) A medical corpsman of the 466th USAF Dispensary, Da Nang, attends to the needs of a local Vietnamese child. (3) 2d Lt. Kathleen M. Sullivan treats a Vietnamese child during Operations Med Cap, a U.S. Air Force civic action program. (4) Capt. Robert Robinson, general dental officer, 388th Tactical Dispensary, Korat Royal Thai Air Base, examines the teeth of a young boy from a nearby village. (5) The leg of this Vietnamese child became infected after he had be scalded by hot water. A1C Arthur D. Krull (l.) and a fellow Air Force Reserve medic remove bandage in preparation for more extensive treatment. (6) Capt. Thomas K. Carlton, Jr., a general medical doctor with the 388th Tactical Dispensary, Korat, examines a child from a nearby village. (7) Maj. Jack D. Bashaw, an Air Force doctor at the Cam Ranh Bay Air Base hospital, examines a patient from a nearby village, June 1966.

Funding the Program

Most of these humanitarian activities were undertaken on an ad hoc basis, and it was not until President Johnson put the full weight of the U.S. government behind civic action in 1966 that the program picked up substantial momentum. In a message to Congress, he said he would "give new stress to civic actions programs through which local troops would build schools and roads and provide literacy training and health service." Substantially, a special fund was set up for the use of U.S. civilian and military agencies in Southeast Asia to support such projects.

In the last half of 1966 planning for the program went into high gear, after MACV issued a directive establishing procedures for U.S. and free world military units in Vietnam to obtain working funds. Initially Seventh Air Force was allotted 200,000$VN to finance projects by bases or units too small to qualify for their own funds. The first such project for which funds were allotted helped repair and rebuild a road between the hamlet of Trang Sup and the provincial capital of Tay Ninh. It was begun as a joint venture of the United States Agency for International Development (USAID) and the U.S. Army Special Forces, which contributed 50,000$VN out of a total 75,000$VN cost. USAID asked the Air Force unit in Tay Ninh province—the 617th Tactical Control Squadron—to finance the remaining 25,000$VN. Seventh Air Force headquarters authorized the expenditure and transferred the money to the squadron. Bases allotting their own civic action funds (100,000$VN each) were Bien Hoa, Cam Ranh Bay, Da Nang, and Nha Trang. Tan Son Nhut was allotted 200,000$VN.

In July 1966 General McConnell emphasized the importance of the Vietnamese pacification program and the "tremendous potential for civic action and assistance" that could be provided by "indigenous air forces." He suggested establishment of a civic action assistance council in Southeast Asia to advise Air Force commanders and to coordinate and expand their civic action activities. Second to combat operations, he said, "our efforts in this area are the most valuable contributions we can make to the defeat of the Communist insurgency. . . ."

Responding to McConnell's guidance, Seventh Air Force during the summer of 1966 organized a civic action coordinating group within its headquarters. On 6 October it published a regulation requiring the establishment of "Civic Action Councils" within both Headquarters Seventh Air Force and all USAF bases in Vietnam. On 8 October it issued a second regulation defining the responsibility of each base commander and outlining objectives and reporting procedures which would govern civic action projects. The same day, all base commanders were directed to use the capabilities and energies of USAF units to implement "a positive civic action program" geared to the ongoing Vietnamese revolutionary development program.

Immediately, personnel requisitions were made to obtain full-time civic action officers and noncommissioned officers at each base in Vietnam. Funds to finance their various projects were allotted to base commanders. In October information about the program was provided in a civic action "Notebook." Subsequently, Seventh Air Force published a *Civic Action Newsletter* which provided information on projects under way at various bases, their successes, and problem areas. On 10 November 1966 the Seventh Air Force Civic Action Council was convened for its first meeting by the Chief of Staff, Brig. Gen. Franklin A. Nichols. Council members discussed funding problems, ways to further encourage VNAF participation in the programs, and the use of the command's "civic action airlift."

On at least one occasion, the civic action program enabled USAF and VNAF officials to thwart a planned Viet Cong mortar attack on Binh Thuy AB in the fall of 1966. Some months before, USAF/VNAF civic action personnel had gone into several hamlets on the southern perimeter of the base to offer their help in various ways. Among the projects they supported were construction of community washhouses, schools, and latrines. One USAF and two VNAF doctors and four VNAF and two USAF medical assistants also made weekly visits to the villages to treat the sick and distribute food supplements and clothing to poor inhabitants. These civic actions won over several hamlet residents, as the following Seventh Air Force report to PACAF makes clear:

> In early October the VC moved into one of the perimeter hamlets in preparation for a mortar attack against the air base planned for 12 October. At great risk to their own lives, several residents of the hamlet involved reported the attack plans to the VNAF and USAF security police at the base. With sufficient warning the security police moved into the hamlet a couple of days prior to the planned attack capturing mortars and ammunition, thus preventing the. . .attack. The security police attributed this "save" to the excellent rapport established with the local populace and the newly won support of the local people to the GVN and to the continuous fine efforts of the military civic action program at Binh Thuy.

This incident, however, apparently energized the Viet Cong, who began to shell Binh Thuy on a regular basis. Thus, the Viet Cong did manage to hit the base with several mortar rounds, but the damage was minor due to the fact they had been forced to set up their positions 7 kilometers away, well beyond the perimeter hamlets. Although intelligence reports about Viet Cong activities in the base environs also progressively improved, the enemy managed to hit Binh Thuy at least

once a month during the first half of 1965.

On the other hand, relations with South Vietnamese villagers were occasionally exacerbated by accidents of war. For example, on 1 July 1966 a 3d Tactical Fighter Wing aircraft accidentally bombed the village of Tan Uyen, about 10 miles north of Bien Hoa AB, killing 8 Vietnamese and injuring 40 and substantially destroying the village marketplace. Base medical personnel immediately sped to the scene along with U.S. Army advisers and Vietnamese province officials to help evacuate the wounded. However, the villagers were openly hostile to the first Americans who appeared, even shouting at one officer. In the weeks that followed, Viet Cong agents used the incident to stir up the peasants against the government and the United States.

However, the early and continuing massive effort to ease the villagers' plight by volunteers from the 3d Tactical Fighter Wing was able to partly offset the Communist effort. Within 24 hours they began to repair the damaged village structures. Emergency supplies were distributed through Vietnamese province officials and, with the help of U.S. Army advisers and Vietnamese officials, the Wing legal officer compiled a list of the injured and dead for solatium payments. Within 2 weeks market stalls and several houses were rebuilt, roofs were repaired, and other assistance provided. As a climax to the successful rehabilitation of the village and its inhabitants, a "Country Fair" was staged there in August.

Medical Services

One of the most effective of all American civic action projects during the war was the medical and dental care provided to the people. For example, in November 1966 local South Vietnamese militia requested the aid of USAF medical and dental personnel to accompany them in a "clear and

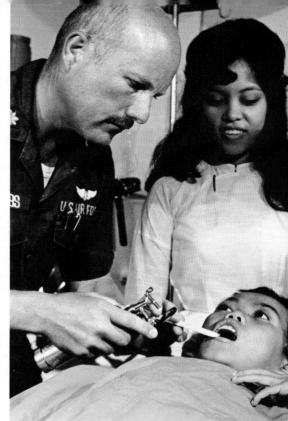

1 2

3

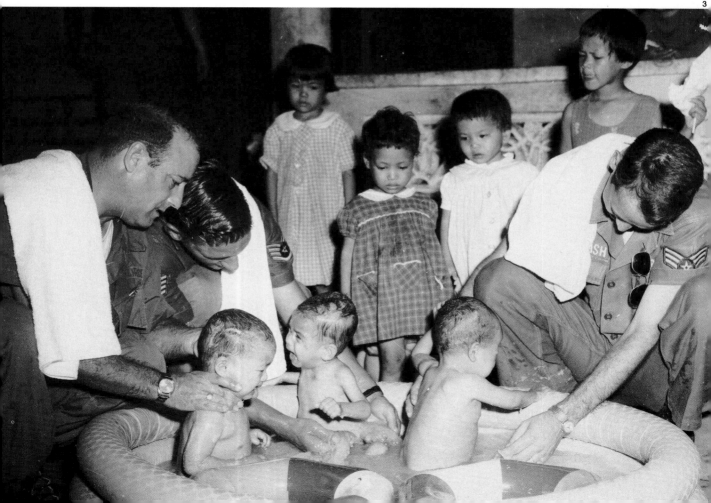

4

6

5

(1) Students are taught English at the 20th Street School and Protestant Orphanage at Can Tho City. This class was instructed by Col. Delbert J. Light, Chief of the Air Force Advisory Team Seven based at Binh Thuy AB. (2) Maj. Thurman Dabbs, a National Guard flight surgeon, examines a Vietnamese youngster brought from a refugee camp to the Tuy Hoa AB hospital, 1968. (3) Youngsters from the Tan Mai Orphanage in the village of Tan Hiep exercise their lungs as they receive their weekly baths from three Air Force sergeants of the 1877th Communications Squadron, Bien Hoa, AB. They are (l. to r.): SSgts Anthony R. Scarlett, Walter S. Hornat, and Sgt Ben E. Shipwash. (4) The Air Force airlifted two anaesthetized elephants from Ban Dou to Chu Lai, Vietnam, where they were put to work assisting South Vietnamese workers in the logging industry. (5) An Air Force plane drops rice and medical supplies to residents of a small Thai village isolated by rising flood waters on the Nam Bae Wang river. Some 300 bags of rice were delivered to the village. (6) Medics of the 366th USAF Dispensary prepare to depart for a village, accessible only by boat, to provide medical care and treatment to the Vietnamese. (7) USAF Chaplain (Capt.) Donald J. Sheeband, and Father Joseph Hien, leader of the village complex of Dai An-Thai Hung, look on as a villager uses a tractor donated by Americans to the farmers, 1968.

7

hold" operation in the Nhon Trach area of Bien Hoa province, which had been under enemy control for many years. After the local military moved in and cleared out the Viet Cong, they secured the hamlets, and then escorted the USAF medical teams into the area where they set up a clinic in a local home. Many of the people had not seen a doctor in several years and some had not seen a dentist in their entire lifetimes, so that the impact of the visit was great. The hamlet chiefs made the doctors promise to return again to treat their people. When news of the "painless" dentist spread through the sector being cleared, people from distant hamlets infiltrated through Viet Cong-held areas for treatment.

Between 1966-1968 the medical civic action program expanded steadily into all hamlets, villages, and autonomous city areas contiguous to Seventh Air Force bases. From an occasional trip into the countryside in 1966, Seventh Air Force medical and dental personnel expanded their volunteer assistance to the Vietnamese to the extent that more than 60,000 medical, dental, and immunization treatments had been provided by the fall of 1968. Whenever possible, they were accompanied by VNAF medical personnel. On these visits, dental personnel distributed soap, toothbrushes, and toothpaste.

In Thailand, the Air Force also fielded mobile medical teams in seven politically sensitive areas in the northeast part of that country, which faced the potential subversive threat from Communist terrorists. In 1966, with the deployment to Thailand of the 606th Air Commando Squadron, the unit organized a Civic Action Branch to serve as part of the country team headed by the U.S. ambassador. This branch later was redesignated a Civic Actions Section and finally a Civic Actions Center. In 1967 it was manned by 84 officers and enlisted personnel—most of them physicians, medical

technicians and dentists—who were assisted by 12 Thai interpreters. They worked closely with Thai officials at all levels of government, from the Ministry of Health down to remote village medical centers, treating some 10,000 patients each month.

In 1967 they initiated a unique Floating Mekong Medical Clinic in an effort to reach tens of thousands of people in remote villages who were completely isolated from the outside world during the rainy season. Conceived by civic action personnel, the waterborne clinic was coordinated and approved by the Royal Thai government. A commercial river boat was leased by the government and renovated into a medical facility. The boat was staffed by one physician (on a rotational American-Thai basis), one dental technician, one U.S. medical technician, and three Thai "sanitarians." Areas and specific villages to be visited were selected by Thai provincial health officers. The floating clinic proved a great success, was the pride and joy of Air Force personnel and Thai government officials, and greatly benefited the rural people along its route.

USAF physicians and dentists also lived and worked in a number of medical centers where they held daily sick call in the mornings and went out in the afternoons—with the help of Thai military and public health officials—to visit surrounding villages on a scheduled basis. Approximately 350 villagers were treated during these visits. On some visits to remote villages, the Americans were acompanied by a Thai sanitarian and midwife, a Royal Thai Army doctor, and occasionally a small armed escort. In the countryside USAF dental technicians also undertook to promote a preventive dental program. For example, during the first 3 months of 1968 they distributed 18,000 toothbrushes and toothpaste to school children in northeast Thailand and instructed them in the proper use. The only problem was how to provide a continuing supply of toothpaste.

When the latter ran out, the brushes were discarded.

Air Force veterinarians gave a great deal of attention to rabies, a prevalent disease among thousands of stray dogs in Thailand, which caused 300 reported human deaths each year and an estimated unreported death toll ranging as high as 1,200. Although rabid dogs were greatly feared by the Thais, proposals to destroy them were opposed by the government because of Buddhist sensitivity to killing man or beast. An abbot at one of the monasteries offered an alternative solution, which was adopted. He advised the Americans to set out both poisoned and unpoisoned meat for the dogs. Thus, according to the abbot, the decision of life or death would not be the responsibility of the government. If Buddha decided a dog should die, he would lead it to the poisoned meat. If he determined the animal should live, he would direct it to the unpoisoned bait. By the end of 1968 this approach eliminated some 3,000 strays. More than 30,000 other dogs were immunized against rabies.

Tet Recovery Activities

The Communist Tet offensive of January-February 1968 was the crucible for the civic action program in South Vietnam. The widespread damage and destruction and large refugee problem it caused galvanized both Vietnamese and Americans to combine their efforts to promote a rapid recovery. Seventh Air Force civic action units constituted an available resource to coordinate the USAF effort, which was marked by a further outpouring of voluntary contributions of money, goods, and thousands of man-hours of precious free time. The Vietnamese Air Force played an important role during these recovery operations.

Before the emergency recovery program ended, Seventh Air Force civic action personnel had provided assistance to about 60,000 refugees, 3,400 of whom were airlifted to new locations. They also delivered 132 tons of commodities and other supplies to needy people, rebuilt or repaired more than 6,000 homes, provided medical care to 23,741 Vietnamese, immunized 23,021, provided dental care to 4,287, and contributed $24,-798.00 to local relief projects. In addition, they expended $85,481.00 in appropriated funds for the recovery program.

By late summer and the early fall of 1968 the Air Force was able to resume its normal civic action projects, including agricultural development and improved education and social welfare. In the agricultural area, Da Nang AB civic action personnel in September 1968 provided the farmers of Con Dau hamlet a mechanical rice threshing machine. The device consisted of a drum with attached wire spokes. Driven by a large foot pedal, it was both simple to operate and maintain. This machine threshed rice twice as fast as the traditional hand flailing method, was approximately 99 percent effective in removing all rice grains from the stalks without damage (as opposed to 80 percent by the flailing method), and partially separated the rice grains from the chaff, reducing this portion of the operation considerably. The rice thresher was owned and maintained by the hamlet. Individual farmers were authorized to use it one-half day during the harvesting period.

The thresher arrived just in time for the harvest season and a semi-emergency condition resulting from a recent monsoon, which knocked the tops of the stalks into the flooded paddies. The only way to save the rice was to cut it quickly (and slightly prematurely), dry it and thresh it. The hamlet did this on a cooperative basis. The rice thresher enabled the farmers to thresh their crops in approximately one-half the normal time. USAF civic action personnel later arranged to purchase additional threshers for other hamlets in the Da Nang area.

In Bien Hoa province, in the summer of 1968, base personnel enlisted the aid of the Air Force chaplain and his congregation to assist a recently formed "Farmers Cooperative" in the hamlets of Dai An and Xa Thai Hung. A 9-horsepower Kobota garden plow, with four interchangeable attachments, was purchased from the church collections and formally presented to the cooperative. Father Joseph Hien accepted the tractor on behalf of all the residents. Selected farmers of the two hamlets were provided basic instruction in the operation of the plow.

Air Force personnel at Pleiku AB, working with local Montagnard village officials, initiated several farm instruction programs. Using surplus lumber obtained from the base dump, they taught the Montagnards how to build animal shelters, chicken coops, and grain storage bins. After obtaining vegetable seeds from the United States, they helped in the planting of more than eight acres of vegetables by Montagnard villagers. They also assisted the people to build dams, spillways, irrigation systems, wells, and rice-drying platforms.

Throughout the war Air Force personnel contributed funds, labor and materials to Vietnamese schools and orphanages. For example, in the summer of 1966 the need for school furniture in Bien Hoa elementary schools came to the attention of the local AID officials and members of the 3rd Tactical Fighter Wing. Since lumber for furniture was in short supply, the Wing donated used bomb fin crates from its dump, delivering them to the schools with the help of the Vietnamese Air Force. USAF technicians showed AID representatives and school carpenters how to disassemble the crates and reassemble them to make suitable and attractive (when

painted) desks and benches. News of the Bien Hoa school furniture program quickly spread to outlying districts, which requested "bomb fin crate" furniture to equip 14 classrooms. Again, VNAF and USAF personnel delivered the crates and local school carpenters were taught how to make the furniture.

In the fall of 1968 USAF personnel furnished wire, electrical fixtures, and other materials to build Do Vinh elementary school in Phong Dinh province, a library at Cong Thanh high school in Bien Hoa province and three blackboards for the Tay Do School in Phong Dinh. They also furnished lumber, nails, paint, and wire screen to build five dormitories at the II Corps National Police Academy and a library and visitors lounge at the Highland Junior Military Academy in Pleiku province. In addition, they contributed 60,000$VN to the Phu Yen public administration library to purchase books.

One of the interesting civic action projects supported by the Air Force was known as "Dollars for Scholars." Financed by funds donated by organizations and individuals in the United States as well as USAF personnel in Southeast Asia, it provided needy and deserving youth, money for school tuition. Local school principals and teachers, assisted by area officials, determined student eligibility and made the selections. By the end of 1967 more than 700 students were being helped by the "Dollars for Scholars" project. In the view of one Vietnamese school principal, these scholarships had hampered Viet Cong efforts to recruit teenagers.

Throughout the war and against the background of natural disasters and the ravage of war, Americans at home generously donated food, clothing, money, toys, and other materials to orphanages, religious institutions, schools, and villages. For example, between April and September 1967, Seventh Air Force civic action person-

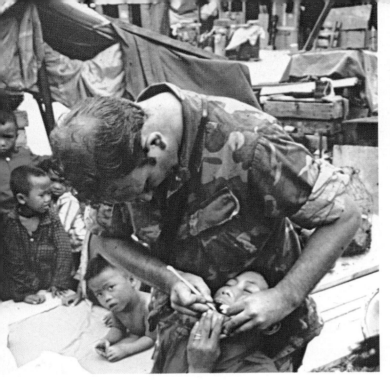

An Air Force dentist on a medical visit to To Cau village examines the teeth of a Vietnamese woman.

1970 and 96 percent in 1971. Similarly, the percentage of Vietnamese-supplied material rose from 20 percent in 1969 to 48 percent in 1971. Vietnamese man-days and expenditures on agricultural, public works, and refugee rehabilitation projects also rose accordingly. This situation in part reflected the steady withdrawal of U.S. forces from South Vietnam which was initiated by President Nixon in the summer of 1969.

During these latter years, however, USAF personnel continued to play a significant civic action role. One project they became involved in was the resettlement of Truong Long village in Phong Dinh province in 1970. Four years earlier, all residents of the village fled to more secure areas when the Viet Cong moved in. As enemy-occupied territory, the Truong Long area became a free fire zone. In 1970, Saigon decided to restore Truong Long and station a military post there for security. Former residents were located in refugee centers and agreed to return with the help of the government. USAF civic action personnel provided the construction materials that enabled the villagers to rebuild their houses and to reestablish a market place, two hamlet offices, a school, and other buildings.

In 1970 Seventh Air Force civic action medical teams also expanded their services into 22 districts and 3 provinces which had not previously been supported, despite the danger of possible enemy ambushes. The effectiveness of the Air Force medical teams was noted in a captured Viet Cong document:

> The enemy [Americans] behaved kindly to the people to win their heart. They carried the people's children in their arms, washed and changed their clothes. . .those who were wounded were given thorough medical treatment. . .although the people knew the enemy was dishonest, they seemed to appreciate the treatment and compared them with those performed by our civil health teams.

nel distributed 32,650 pounds of food, 21,000 pounds of clothing, 83 cartons of toys and playground equipment for orphanages, more than 3,000 cots, 2,365 pounds of soap, and cash totalling $34,000.00 and 1.4 million Vietnamese piasters.

In October 1968 President Thieu announced the start of an accelerated military pacification campaign to extend his government's control throughout South Vietnam. As part of this campaign, he emphasized civic action "as a means to win the people." In gearing its activities to this new pacification program, Seventh Air Force doubled the civic action funds provided to air base commanders who were authorized to approve projects costing up to $1,000 to respond faster to Vietnamese needs. Planning and managing the various civic action projects was done by Vietnamese officials, with Air Force personnel and equipment being used only when there was no alternative available.

Thus, during 1969 the Vietnamese supplied 72 percent of the labor on USAF-supported civic action projects. That figure increased to 80 percent in

295

Chapter XIX

Training and Manning the Combat Force

During the first few years of combat support operations in South Vietnam, the Air Force manned its small contingent of fighting units in that country without difficulty. Following the Gulf of Tonkin incident of August 1964 and the start of Rolling Thunder operations in March 1965, however, the Air Force found itself facing a demand for substantially larger combat forces in the theater. Until units could be deployed on a permanent basis, the Air Force turned to extensive use of temporary duty personnel, drawn mostly from Pacific Air Forces resources, who served up to 179 days (most averaged 120). By July 1965, approximately 42 percent of the 17,900 USAF personnel in South Vietnam were there on TDY. Between November 1965 and February 1966, the Tactical Air Command, one of the primary sources for expansion, sent 14,000 men and 23 fighter, 4 reconnaissance, and 8 C-130 squadrons to Southeast Asia or the western Pacific. During that same period the Air Force also reassigned another 18,000 officers and airmen from other commands to the war zone.

The Pilot Deficit

Even as the 1965-1966 force buildup got under way, the Air Force found itself short of flying personnel. The problem surfaced at an awkward time, as large numbers of World War II-trained pilots were nearing the end of their military careers (more than 13,000 left the service between July 1964 and July 1967) and new pilot production was at a low ebb as a result of ac-

tions taken in 1957 to reduce the number of pilots trained. Under a Congressional mandate to cut back its pilot force in light of the changing USAF force structure—that is, the introduction of intercontinental ballistic missile squadrons—the Air Force reduced undergraduate pilot training from a post-Korean War high of 5,726 graduates in fiscal year 1957 to 1,300 in fiscal year 1962. Ironically, in that year the first combat units were dispatched to South Vietnam.

The shortage quickly became apparent. Headquarters USAF initially required all deploying squadrons to have a minimum of 1½ aircrews per tactical aircraft, but lack of enough rated personnel soon caused the Chief of Staff to cut the requirement to 1.25 aircrews. The lack of pilots was further compounded by two other decisions made by the Chief of Staff in November 1965 and February 1966. He directed that combat tours in Southeast Asia be limited to 1 year or a specified number of mission sorties, and that USAF members not be required to serve an involuntary second SEA tour until other similarly qualified members had served a tour. These decisions in the long term enabled many more officer and enlisted personnel to acquire combat experience. They also produced extensive manpower turbulence and turnover within combat units throughout the war.

As one of its first steps to increase the number of rated officers, Headquarters USAF late in 1965 directed TAC and the Air Training Command to expand pilot and crew training. At the time, TAC conducted combat crew fighter and reconnaissance replace-

Air Reserve technician, 5th Tactical Air Training hool, instructs a student a simulated C-130 cockpit.

ment training at five bases. To meet the new requirements, TAC converted combat-ready wings into replacement training units (RTU's) and combat crew training wings (CCTW's). Within a short time, all operational wings were deeply involved in a massive training effort conducted at nine bases. By 31 December 1966, this TAC training program had produced 1,842 fighter and reconnaissance aircrewmen, 1,017 troop carrier flying personnel, and 1,486 airmen assigned to special air warfare units.

During the same period Air Training Command also felt the heavy burden of the war. Responsible for undergraduate pilot training, ATC had a special problem in that it took a great deal of time to obtain trainee candidates for the flight course, which itself lasted 53 weeks. In 1965 ATC's pilot production capability also was limited by the capacity of eight training bases. On the other hand, ATC got a significant boost in July 1965 when it acquired the first of 171 T-41's (Cessna 172F) for primary pilot training. Civilian contractors provided 30 hours of T-41 flight training at civilian airfields near ATC bases, which eased runway and airspace problems and increased pilot production at each base.

After completing primary training, each student received 90 hours of flight training in the T-37 (instead of the usual 132 hours) and 120 hours in the supersonic T-38 (reduced from 130 hours). Despite the reduced flight training time, it was soon apparent that ATC's eight bases were insufficient to handle the growing pilot training load. Consequently, Headquarters USAF authorized ATC to institute USAF pilot training at two other bases —Randolph AFB, Tex., and Columbus AFB, Miss. Meanwhile, during the fall of 1967 ATC introduced a new method for controlling T-37 and T-38 takeoffs, thereby relieving runway and air traffic congestion at some bases. At those equipped with Category VI radar, ATC permitted simultaneous use of three parallel runways, with aircraft spaced 3 minutes between launches, one from the T-37 runway and one from the overflow runway. Even at bases with only two runways, the 3-minute launch was used.

Meanwhile, however, the accelerated American air offensive against North Vietnam caused F-105 and F-4 pilots to complete their tours earlier than expected, thus exacerbating the shortage. A study group headed by Maj. Gen. Jack J. Catton in the fall of 1966 looked into this problem and recommended a number of short- and long-term measures to provide 9,400 flight personnel for Southeast Asia over a 21-month period beginning 1 January 1967. After reviewing these proposals, General McConnell on 18 October directed action be taken on many of them. One of his more significant decisions was to turn to the major air commands for pilots serving in "behind the line" administrative or other non-flying positions. Some 3,000 pilots subsequently were identified by name and withdrawn from these organizations. Many were older pilots who required retraining and found themselves going through TAC's combat crew or replacement training schools. General McConnell also ordered a 30 percent reduction in the number of officers attending professional military schools; advanced the phaseout dates of certain SAC and ADC squadrons, freeing their personnel for retraining and reassignment; retained Reserve officers scheduled for retirement for another year; withdrew, effective 1 January 1967, all USAF advisers below the grade of colonel with Air National Guard and Air Force Reserve units; substituted navigators for pilots in the F-4 rear seat*; and expanded ATC's undergraduate pilot training program.

In 1971, based on experience obtained from several years of combat

---

*Although the substitution of navigators for pilots helped alleviate the pilot shortage, it had the reverse effect on navigator manning.

and on the need to reduce expenditures, the Air Force decreased the length of undergraduate pilot training from 53 to 48 weeks and cut the amount of actual flying time from 240 to 208.5 hours. ATC accomplished this in part by providing 16 instead of 30 flying hours in the T-41, a period deemed sufficient to identify students lacking the aptitude to go on to jet training. The command obtained the remainder of the savings by eliminating five flights from the T-37 and seven flights from the T-38 portions of the course.

These actions helped to alleviate the shortage of fixed-wing pilots, but other measures were necessary to fulfill rising helicopter pilot requirements in Southeast Asia. In 1965 there were about 700 helicopter pilots in the Air Force engaged primarily in flying rescue, recovery, mapping, and charting missions, in supporting SAC missile sites, and in assisting humanitarian relief operations. To maintain the helicopter force, ATC graduated about 60 pilots a year through a special undergraduate course that included instruction in both fixed- and rotary-wing aircraft. They underwent 120 hours of training in the T-28, another 70 hours of rotary wing transition in the H-19, and 35 hours of specialized flying in the H-21, H-43, or CH-3 helicopters—altogether a total of 43 weeks.

Presuming a sizeable growth in its helicopter inventory, the Air Force determined that it would need to almost double the number of pilots. To expand the undergraduate helicopter training program, ATC dropped the T-28 phase and transferred it from Randolph to Sheppard AFB where it could use the jet undergraduate pilot training pipeline. However, the training still consumed 43 weeks.

In an effort to shorten training time, the Air Force in December 1965 requested, and the Secretary of Defense approved, taking experienced fixed-wing pilots and converting them to helicopter pilots. ATC set up a 12-week conversion course during which students received 70 hours of rotary-wing training in the H-19 and either the H-43 or CH-3. The first students entered the new course in April 1966 and graduated 3 months later. In September 1966, as the pilot shortage continued, Headquarters USAF directed ATC to concentrate all helicopter training efforts on the 12-week course. Since undergraduate helicopter trainees received 105 hours of rotary-wing flight time and conversion students only 70 hours, it was possible to increase production significantly by relying on experienced fixed-wing pilots as the source of supply for helicopter training.

Thus, where ATC previously trained 60 helicopter pilots in 43 weeks, it could now produce 90 in 12 weeks with no increase in training resources. There was another dividend. By eliminating undergraduate helicopter students from the fixed-wing undergraduate course, ATC could train 60 additional jet pilots annually with the same training facilities.

Overall, during the 6 years between fiscal 1965 and 1971, the period of expanding combat activity, ATC trained 22,948 pilots of all types. In the last years of the war, even as combat gradually wound down, the training bases produced another 10,250 pilots.

Airlift and Special Operations Crews

Another important training effort in 1965—producing replacement crews for Southeast Asia airlift units—was a TAC responsibility. Before 1965, TAC had annually trained about 400 C-130 crews (pilot, copilot, navigator, flight engineer, and loadmaster as a unit). In the late summer of 1965, as combat requirements rose, Headquarters USAF directed TAC to expand the rate of training to 480 crews for 1966.

To handle this larger training load,

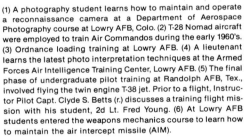

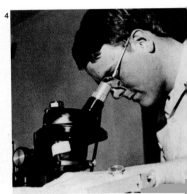

(1) A photography student learns how to maintain and operate a reconnaissance camera at a Department of Aerospace Photography course at Lowry AFB, Colo. (2) T-28 Nomad aircraft were employed to train Air Commandos during the early 1960's. (3) Ordnance loading training at Lowry AFB. (4) A lieutenant learns the latest photo interpretation techniques at the Armed Forces Air Intelligence Training Center, Lowry AFB. (5) The final phase of undergraduate pilot training at Randolph AFB, Tex., involved flying the twin engine T-38 jet. Prior to a flight, Instructor Pilot Capt. Clyde S. Betts (r.) discusses a training flight mission with his student, 2d Lt. Fred Young. (6) At Lowry AFB students entered the weapons mechanics course to learn how to maintain the air intercept missile (AIM).

DEPARTMENT
of
AEROSPACE MUNITIONS
TRAINING

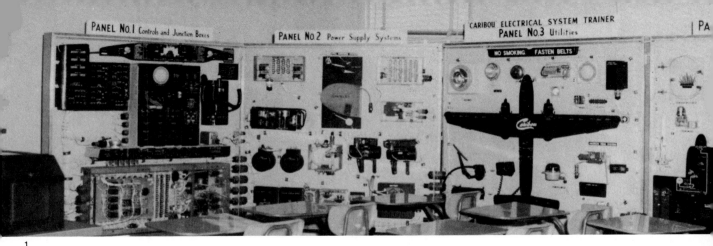

PANEL NO. 1 Controls and Junction Boxes   PANEL NO. 2 Power Supply Systems   CARIBOU ELECTRICAL SYSTEM TRAINER PANEL NO. 3 Utilities   PA

NO SMOKING FASTEN BELTS

1

PANEL N...Supply Sy...   CARIBOU ELECTRICAL SYSTEM TRAINER PANEL NO. 3 Utilities   PANEL ...Power Plant...

NO SMOKING FASTEN BELTS

2   3

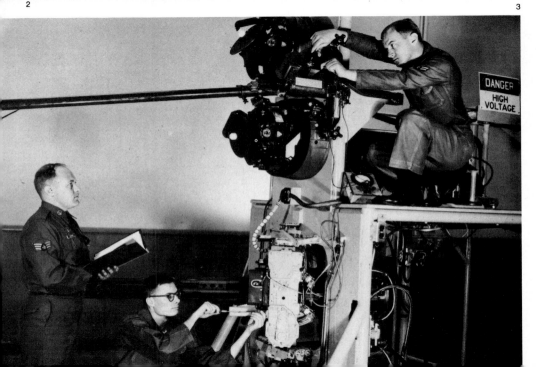

DANGER HIGH VOLTAGE

(1) A C-7A Caribou transport Electrical System Training Aid. (2) Caribou crewmen study the C-7's electrical systems training aids at Sewart AFB, Tenn. (3) Students learn to adjust the controlling radar system in the Bomber Branch of Lowry's Department of Avionics Training.

TAC transferred 42 pilots and flight engineer instructors and 24 aircraft from its operational force to the 4442d Combat Training Group (later Wing) at Sewart AFB, Tenn. The number of instructors soon grew to 146 pilots, 63 navigators, 84 flight engineers, and 84 loadmasters, who manned five TAC replacement training units established in November 1965 within five airlift wings. These RTU's were based at Forbes AFB, Kan.; Lockbourne AFB, Ohio; Pope AFB, N.C.; Dyess AFB, Tex., and Sewart.

Phase I of C-130 crew training began in December 1965 and included navigators and loadmasters only; the rest of the crew joined in the training during Phase II. At the time, few TAC pilots had qualified to operate C-130's into short, unimproved fields, a basic necessity in Southeast Asia. Consequently, TAC emphasized instruction and practice in landings and takeoffs from such types of fields. Within a year, TAC had trained 500 C-130 replacement crews. After completing this initial task, the command inactivated the Forbes and Dyess units and kept the other three for on-going replacement training.

TAC also trained replacements to man C-123 squadrons, the first elements of which had arrived in South Vietnam as early as January 1962. As the inventory of aircraft and the scope of operations increased, the command in late 1965 established the 4410th Combat Crew Training Wing at Hurlburt AFB, Fla., to provide replacements. By 30 June 1966, it had graduated and made available for SEA duty almost 600 aircrewmen (252 of them pilots).

Training crews for the Air Force's third tactical transport, the C-7A Caribou, got under way in 1966, after the Army Chief of Staff agreed in April to turn the airplane over to the Air Force. In preparation for the actual transfer, TAC organized the 4449th Combat Crew Training Squadron at Fort Benning, Ga., as a component of its 4449th Wing. Beginning in May, Army instructors provided a 3-week course to squadron personnel slated to train USAF pilots and flight engineers in the operation of the C-7. The first class of USAF students began training at Fort Benning in June 1966, but later classes met at Sewart. By 30 June 1967, TAC had trained sufficient crews—479 Caribou pilots, copilots, and flight engineers—to enable them to operate the six Caribou squadrons in Southeast Asia.

The task of training replacement crews for a host of other tactical aircraft—such as the 0-1, 0-2, 0V-10, U-10, A-1E, A-26, C-47, and A-37—also fell to TAC. As the war continued, the command's capabilities grew to encompass two wings which operated training facilities at Hurlburt AFB, Fla.; England AFB, La.; Holly Field Navy Auxiliary Air Station, Fla.; and Forbes AFB, Kan. Replacement crewmen to operate this myriad of airplanes gradually increased over the mid- and late 1960's. For example, 1,620 crewmen were trained in fiscal year 1966; 3 years later, the figure had grown to more than 2,880.

Technical Training

During the early years of the war, the shortage of maintenance personnel became a manpower problem second only to the aircrew deficit. With the tours of aircraft mechanics and other maintenance men also limited to 1-year tours, the Air Force found it necessary to provide for a continuous flow of airmen technicians to Southeast Asia. Consequently, the training of aircraft, engine, radar, and other specialists became a priority matter and, on 28 October 1965, Headquarters USAF directed TAC and ATC to undertake an expanded program for this purpose.

Representatives of the two commands and the Air Staff held two conferences on the subject during November and December 1965 at Randolph AFB, Tex., and Langley AFB, Va. They concluded that TAC should provide most of the aircraft maintenance replacements through expanded on-the-job training (OJT) on its own bases. The conferees rejected an alternate proposal to transfer aircraft to ATC technical training centers for the same purpose. ATC supported TAC by expanding field training detachments at 16 TAC bases.

TAC was expected to provide half of the maintenance replacements for Southeast Asia with other commands supplying the remainder. But since many airmen in the latter group would lack current qualification or would have no actual experience on TAC aircraft, TAC and ATC jointly undertook another improvisation. Such personnel would be sent to TAC bases in a temporary "enroute to SEA" duty status and receive job-oriented flight line proficiency training as well as specialized instruction. The airmen would get 4 hours of classroom instruction from the ATC detachment and 4 hours of proficiency training from TAC personnel daily during the TDY period, expected to average about 30 days.

Initially, highest priority was given to training approximately 1,800 maintenance personnel to augment TAC units deployed to Southeast Asia in November 1965. Soon after the deployment, it became evident that 25 to 35 percent more maintenance men per squadron were needed to support the high level of combat. This special training effort got under way in January 1966 on an emergency basis. By May, more than 1,800 had completed the course and could serve with maintenance crews of the F-100, F-105, F-4C, RF-4C, RB-66, or C-130 aircraft.

In April 1966, the urgency of the second phase of replacement training was underlined by PACAF's request for 4,813 maintenance personnel between July 1966 and May 1967. Concurrently, Headquarters USAF noted that additional units would deploy to Southeast Asia between May 1966 and April 1967. This expanded combat force meant that ATC and TAC would have to train 3,237 technicians to support the additional units. The requirement was subsequently modified because most of the deploying units obtained "filler" personnel several months before they left.

As demand for replacements increased during 1966, TAC suffered a steady decline of skilled personnel and had to depend more and more on semi-skilled maintenance men. To ease this pressure on TAC, Headquarters USAF raised to 55 percent the number of replacement trainees withdrawn from other commands and sent through the "enroute" course. TAC on-the-job training doubled in 1966—from 16,711 airmen in January to 32,355 by December. The airmen soon overloaded housing and messing facilities and, at one point, some enroute personnel undergoing TDY training lived off base and were transported daily to and from the maintenance shops and flight lines. Replacement training eased somewhat after PACAF agreed to accept semi-skilled personnel to meet one third of its requirements.

Maintenance training was but one aspect of a vast technical training effort which began in the summer of 1965. In July Headquarters USAF decided to recruit 88,000 new airmen, most of whom would require specialized technical training in such areas as communications, electronics, supply, munitions, and avionics. By the spring of 1966 the Air Force had raised its fiscal year 1966 recruitment target to 107,000 personnel. To handle these large numbers, ATC placed the five technical training centers—Chanute AFB, Ill.; Keesler AFB, Miss.; Lackland and Sheppard AFB's in Texas; and Lowry AFB, Colo.—on 6-day, round-the-clock operations.

A problem that ATC faced in taking on this large training burden was a

1

2

(1) TSgt N.D. Newson discusses simulator lessons and training progress, procedures, techniques, and study assignments in updating Royal Australian Air Force crewmen who served under the Australian Task Force in Vietnam. (2) Students in the Undergraduate Pilot Training Course at Randolph AFB, Colo. receive classroom instruction prior to starting flight training. (3) Conventional Weapons Branch instructors. Department of Aerospace Munitions practice loading ordnance on an F-105 at Lowry AFB, Colo. (4) This realistic C-130 simulator interior was used to train flight personnel. (5) At the Armed Forces Air Intelligence Training Center. Lowry AFB, an instructor discusses briefing techniques to a class of intelligence operations students. (6) TSgt Scholen, 304S Field Training Detachment, explains the construction and function of the C-7A propellers and components at Sewart AFB, Tenn.

3

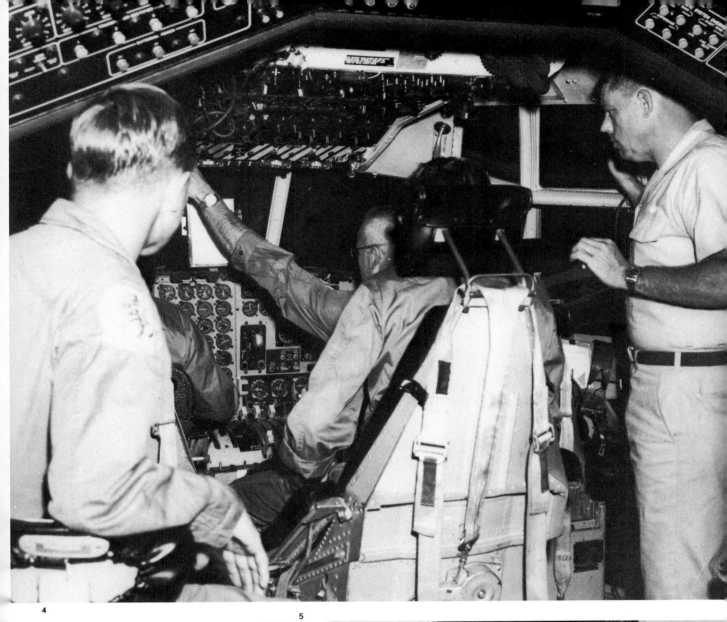

4

5

6

shortage of about 7,000 instructors. As a partial solution, ATC identified former instructors and had them reassigned to the training centers. Headquarters USAF gave priority to manning the ATC instructor force, but combat demands for experienced personnel in Southeast Asia soon forced ATC to use recent school graduates. As a result, at the height of the 1965-1967 Southeast Asia buildup, 25 percent of the instructors were recent graduates of their training centers.

By the end of June 1966, ATC technical centers had graduated 145,000 students and, with the major bottleneck broken, ATC soon returned the centers to a 5-day week. Thereafter, ATC maintained normal operations with minor exceptions. In 1968, for example, Lowry went to a 6-day-a-week schedule to training 4,000 munition specialists, more than double the number trained before January 1968.

Officer Recruitment

Recruitment of adequate numbers of officers for the expanding Air Force brought with it several difficulties which the Air Training Command undertook to resolve. One stemmed from the location of the Officer Training School (OTS) on Lackland AFB, which was soon overcrowded and without enough classroom and housing facilities due to the tremendous surge in airman basic military training which also was conducted there. During 1965, OTS commissioned 2,596 college graduates, of which 332 were former enlisted men who had passed through the Airman Education and Commissioning Program. Under this program, the Air Force sent airmen with high scholastic aptitude, particularly in science and engineering, to college for up to 24 months. After obtaining a degree, they received military training at the Lackland school to earn their commissions as second lieutenants.

As the pace of combat quickened, the Air Force raised its requirement for OTS officers to 7,781 in fiscal year 1967. To meet this goal in the face of existing facility shortages, ATC added a half-day to the school week, reduced the course time from 60 to 54 days, and increased the number of classes each year from 8 to 10. OTS production was at a high the next year, when 7,383 officers were commissioned. Thereafter, as requirements were satisfied, the course reverted to the normal 60-day, 5-day-a-week schedule. Between 1 July 1966 and 1 July 1970, the Officer Training School commissioned 26,582 new officers.

Another important source of officers during the war was the Air Force Reserve Officers Training Corps (AFROTC) which commissioned 26,853 college graduates between July 1966 and July 1970. In 1966 AFROTC training was offered at 177 colleges and universities. As the conflict proceeded in Southeast Asia, the growth of antiwar sentiment throughout the nation caused a number of colleges and universities to first challenge the academic rank, credit, and departmental status of the AFROTC units on their campuses and then, in some cases, to eliminate them entirely. On the other hand, some non-participating educational institutions invited the Air Force to establish units on their campuses. In 1970, AFROTC operated at 174 colleges and universities.

Survival Training

In late 1961 the Air Force required all flying personnel at wing level and below who were involved in counterinsurgency operations to complete a

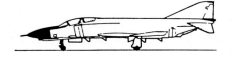

basic survival, escape, and evasion course. The first class of 134 students to undergo instruction in the 21-day course met at Stead AFB, Nev., on 23 November. During the next 3 years additional hundreds received survival training at Stead preparatory to their departure for South Vietnam and Thailand.

As the pace of air operations in Southeast Asia quickened, Headquarters USAF in January 1965 directed PACAF to establish a jungle survival school to train aircrew members enroute to the war zone. At the time the only course for such training was at the Tropic Survival School, Albrook AFB, C.Z. The Jungle Survival School began operation at Clark on 12 April with a 4-man instruction team detailed from Stead for 120 days. Initially set for 6 days, the course was soon reduced to 5 days. By late June, a permanent instructor cadre was in place.

The school's original goal was to train 720 per year. The surge in combat operations after mid-1965 caused the training goal to be increased. In 1967 the school graduated 6,734 students at Clark, while its mobile training teams instructed another 1,582 in South Vietnam and Thailand. Even these measures proved inadequate, and in 1968 more than 11,000 personnel completed the jungle course.

Meanwhile, with Stead AFB scheduled to close in 1966, the Air Force shifted the survival training course to Fairchild AFB, Wash., where a class commenced training on 27 June. In January 1966, prior to the move, the course was reduced from 21 to 18 training days. It included academic and operational training in basic survival, escape, and evasion. On 1 November 1966 the Air Force made another important change by shifting TAC's Sea Survival School from Langley AFB, Va., to Homestead AFB, Fla. The new school location enabled TAC to train aircrews year round, whereas training at Langley was limited to 7 months. Some cooler temperatures during the 5 coldest months were unendurable. Tactical fighter and reconnaissance crews destined for the war zone received priority for this training.

In July 1967 the Air Force reduced the Fairchild survival course to 13 days for SEA-destined personnel by eliminating the field training phase. This was done because the PACAF Jungle Survival School provided field training in the Philippines. Two additional days were saved in 1968 by eliminating unarmed combat training. The number of graduates of the Fairchild school grew steadily, with 10,164 completing the course during fiscal year 1970. Budgetary and manpower limitations subsequently led to smaller training classes, but they obviously reflected the reduced levels of combat in the war zone.

During the course of its strenuous efforts to increase and maintain the strength of its combat forces, the Air Force built up to a peak in March 1969 of 97,551 officers and airmen in the war zone—60,785 in South Vietnam and 36,766 in Thailand. After peaking in 1969, personnel strength in South Vietnam declined fairly steadily, almost in a direct line until only 7,608 officers and airmen were there on 31 December 1972. By March 1973, there were none. The Thailand-based force also began a decline from its 1969 peak strength, slipping downward at a steady rate except for a 5-month period begining in March 1972, when Hanoi launched its massive invasion of South Vietnam. The North Vietnamese attack led to the return of additional USAF units (about 13,800 men) to Thailand, from where they resumed air attacks against the Hanoi-Haiphong area. After this latest enemy offensive, a substantial USAF force stayed on in Thailand after the formal cease-fire agreement was signed in Paris in January 1973, ending U.S. combat operations in both South and North Vietnam.

Chapter XX

Vietnamization

From the beginning of U.S. involvement in Southeast Asia, Washington officials undertook to strengthen South Vietnam's armed forces so they could deal with their Communist opposition themselves. Thus, shortly after his inauguration President Kennedy approved a buildup of the Vietnamese armed forces along with an increase in the size of the U.S. Military Assistance Advisory Group. In the case of the Vietnamese Air Force, the Defense Department was authorized to replace its obsolete American-supplied aircraft with better aircraft—A-1's, T-28's and H-34's.

When the Farm Gate detachment arrived at Bien Hoa in November 1961, Vietnamese airmen were in the process of activating their first T-28 squadron. In January 1962, as noted earlier, Farm Gate instructors began training 25 Vietnamese pilots to fly the T-28 in methods of day and night operations. The training effort went well and, in the spring of 1962, the first T-28 squadron was declared operational. When a second squadron was activated, Farm Gate pilot instructors again helped with its training. The Vietnamese proved to be apt pupils and soon were flying combat strikes in their new aircraft. By mid-1962, the Vietnamese Air Force had grown to a force of about 5,700 officers and airmen with an operational inventory of 140 aircraft.

As the VNAF buildup continued, the Air Force found itself carrying a heavy training burden both in Vietnam and the United States. Thus, Air Training Command dispatched several mobile detachments to South Vietnam to instruct VNAF personnel how to maintain and operate the new aircraft. For example, in May 1962 it sent a 45-man team to Vietnam for 6 months TDY to teach Vietnamese maintenance personnel the intricacies of the T-28. Other mobile training teams taught VNAF personnel RT-28 reconnaissance procedures and others how to fly the U-17A, an off-the-shelf Cessna aircraft provided South Vietnam under the military assistance program. In the spring of 1963 TAC dispatched 20 USAF L-19 pilots to Vietnam to augment VNAF liaison squadrons so that Vietnamese pilots could begin upgrade training in the A-1E.

By mid-1963 approximately 1,800 Vietnamese airmen out of a total VNAF strength of 7,736 personnel were students, most of them pilots. Of that number, 459 were being trained in the United States. One hundred fourteen attended U.S. Army and Navy training courses since several of the new aircraft in their inventory came from those services.

The Language Problem

Throughout the war the language barrier was a factor that inhibited all U.S. training programs. In early 1962 the Farm Gate detachment—to partly resolve the problem—produced an English-Vietnamese list of basic words for voice communications. Vietnamese airmen studied this as part of their curriculum at the VNAF FAC school at Tan Son Nhut. Also, in October 1962, the Air Force instituted an 8-week language school for Vietnamese airmen in training at Hurlburt Field, Fla.

In July 1963, in a further effort to overcome the language barrier, the Air Force dispatched a 5-man English language training detachment to Vietnam, which it later augmented with five more instructors. These men helped organize three English lan-

aj. George T. Bennett, viser to the 524th Squad- (VNAF), checks a target p with a VNAF pilot at en Hoa AB.

309

guage schools in South Vietnam, two of them operating on two 6-hour shifts per day. One school was located in Saigon, the others at Tan Son Nhut and Nha Trang. By 31 January 1964, a total of 994 Vietnamese students had begun language training and 514 had completed the course.

Subsequently, VNAF personnel sent to the United States for pilot training were required to complete a 15-week English language course at Lackland Air Force Base, Tex. The Lackland school—later assigned to the Defense Language Institute—became the first stop for thousands of Vietnamese airmen trained in the United States. To facilitate the training effort both in Vietnam and the United States, the Air Force also began translating a number of its on-the-job training publications into the Vietnamese language. In South Vietnam, the Air Force used both uniformed and civilian contractor personnel in the OJT program until such time as Vietnamese noncommissioned officers were qualified as instructors. However, the language barrier was never entirely overcome and remained a problem which handicapped all USAF training efforts throughout the war.

As the buildup of the Vietnamese Air Force continued, it reached a December 1964 strength of 10,592 personnel. They manned four tactical fighter squadrons, four helicopter and four liaison squadrons, two troop carrier squadrons, plus other miscellaneous units. In 1965 modernization was accelerated when the single-seat A-1H attack planes and the two-seat A-1G began replacing the VNAF's T-28's. The A-1's were faster and carried a larger bomb load. The transition to the A-1's was completed by April 1965. During the year the VNAF O-1 liaison fleet more than doubled in size, going from 37 in January to 84 in December. Its U-17 inventory rose from 25 to 46 aircraft. In all, during the year, the VNAF acquired 108 additional aircraft, a 38 percent increase over the previous year.

310

3 © N.G.S.

Throughout 1965 Air Force training efforts were aimed at increasing the number of VNAF fighter, helicopter, and liaison pilots, while also producing mechanics, communication specialists, and other support personnel. A substantial portion of this growing training took place in Vietnam, with 1,232 VNAF personnel completing OJT and 320 language training in 1965. The Air Force continued to make extensive use of ATC field training detachments and mobile teams (including one from the U.S. Navy), and civilian contract technical service personnel. The last-mentioned group, assigned to the Air Force Advisory Group in Vietnam, taught a variety of technical subjects to the Vietnamese, e.g., engines, communications, and radio navigation aids. At Bien Hoa, the 6251st Combat Support Wing, USAF, provided VNAF pilots A-1 transition training, while the 19th Tactical Air Support Squadron taught Vietnamese

airmen to fly the O-1F. A U.S. Marine element provided H-34 helicopter upgrade training for Da Nang-based VNAF helicopter pilots.

As the air war escalated, South Vietnamese officials—particularly the new Premier, Nguyen Cao Ky (he continued to head the VNAF)—pressed the United States to provide Vietnam with jet aircraft. They argued that the North Vietnamese, Cambodians, and Thais already possessed jet aircraft. American officials subsequently approved their request, and on 9 August 1965 the first of four B-57's were turned over to the Vietnamese Air Force. Transition training was begun in the Philippines and initially involved 6 pilots, 4 navigators, 4 maintenance officers, and 16 aircraft mechanics. By year's end, four combat-ready VNAF crews began flying training missions with the Air Force B-57 unit at Da Nang.

Meanwhile, the Air Force Advisory

311

1

2

3

4

5

(1) VNAF students in a classroom at Sheppard AFB, Tex. (2) Vietnamese officers were trained on oscilloscope sets, its chief use being to serve as an indicator in a radar set. (3) VNAF pilot, Lt. Van Lich Hien, prepares for a mission in his A-1 Skyraider at Bien Hoa AB. (4) An A-37A light ground attack aircraft (in foreground) was turned over to the VNAF in October 1970. (5) Maj. Dang-Duy Lac, commander of the VNAF 524th Squadron makes a final adjustment in his equipment, while Lt. Col. Walter V. Woods, 604th SOS commander, starts up the A-37 engine. (6) Air Force TSgt Bruce A. Miller, a 604th Special Operations Squadron aircraft maintenance technician, shows a VNAF mechanic how to install a canopy safety clamp.

6

Group studied other options to provide the VNAF an additional jet capability. It focused on the F-5, a new jet aircraft which the Air Force had sent to South Vietnam in October 1965 to begin combat field tests. The Advisory Group recommended, and Secretary McNamara approved, conversion of one A-1 squadron to F-5's. Thirty-two VNAF pilots departed in August to begin F-5 conversion training at the Combat Crew Training Center, Williams AFB, Ariz. Ten of these men, however, were first required to take 9 weeks of language training before entering flight training.

In December 1966, after the first F-5 crews returned from combat crew training in Arizona, an F-5 training detachment arrived at Bien Hoa to continue VNAF pilot training in the jet. The following month 10 USAF noncommissioned officers and a civilian contract engineer were dispatched to Vietnam to provide further training to F-5 officers and airmen. By the spring of 1967 the Vietnamese had flown hundreds of training sorties in their new jet aircraft. On 1 June, at a formal VNAF-USAF ceremony held at Bien Hoa, the planes were officially turned over to the 522d VNAF Fighter Squadron, which immediately began flying combat sorties.

In 1967 USAF personnel also assisted the Vietnamese to modernize their transport fleet. VNAF C-47 officers and airmen were sent to the United States to begin transition training in the C-119. After completing ground courses at Lackland and Sheppard Air Force Bases, they were sent to Clinton County AFB, Ohio, the Air Force's C-119 training center. There they were taught engine and airframe maintenance by ATC's 614th Field Training Detachment and C-119 crewmen of the Air Force Reserve. The first seven VNAF C-119 crews—six pilots, eight copilots, and seven flight engineers—returned home in September 1967. They were followed to Vietnam in October by an Air Force C-119G detach-

314

1

2

3

4

(1) An Air Force captain briefs a Vietnamese airman prior to flying a gunship mission. (2) A VNAF gunner performs maintenance on a UH-1's miniguns at Binh Thuy AB, South Vietnam. (3) A Vietnamese student checks out a night observations scope at Phan Rang AB as his instructor, Capt. William H. King, looks on. (4) With Capt. Jim Downs looking on, a Vietnamese navigator in a flare plane radios defenders below to learn the location of enemy troops.

ment, which continued their training there. By mid-March 1968, more than 200 Vietnamese airmen had completed all C-119 training.

Air Force modernization plans also called for converting three VNAF A-1 fighter squadrons to A-37 jets and one C-47 squadron into an AC-47 gunship unit. During 1967 the Vietnamese Air Force assigned 103 pilots to three squadrons scheduled to receive the A-37's. On 1 January 1968 the first squadron to receive the A-37's stood down to prepare for the conversion, and the following month the first 18 pilots departed for the United States to begin transition training. In May, an A-37 mobile training detachment arrived at Nha Trang to begin maintenance training.

Actual squadron conversion began in November 1968 with delivery of the first A-37 jets from the United States. By May 1969 the full complement of 54 A-37B jets was on hand and assigned to the 524th, 520th, and 516th Fighter Squadrons. The first A-37 jet squadron was declared operationally ready in March 1969, the last one in July. During 1969 VNAF personnel strength grew to about 29,000 officers and airmen, an increase of more than 5,000 over the previous year.

Shortly after becoming President in January 1969, Mr. Nixon announced that one of the primary goals of his administration would be to end U.S. combat in Southeast Asia while simultaneously strengthening South Vietnam's ability to defend itself. In March Secretary of Defense Melvin R. Laird, after visiting officials in Saigon, ordered an accelerated "Vietnamization" program aimed at turning over combat operations to the South Vietnamese. In May Mr. Laird informed the Joint Chiefs that Vietnamizing the war was the Defense Department's highest priority. In June 1969, after conferring with South Vietnamese officials on Midway Island, the President announced plans to withdraw the first U.S. troops from South Vietnam. In

3

(1) VNAF students in a classroom at Sheppard AFB, Tex. (2) Vietnamese Air Force Captains stand at attention before the first of 40 A-37 jets were turned over to the VNAF in October 1970. (3) Aboard a VNAF UH-1 helicopter gunship, a Vietnamese gunner fires a minigun during a training mission in South Vietnam. An Air Force adviser, Sgt Isidro Arroyo, Jr., looks on. (4) Two VNAF crewmen check out the Forward-Looking Infrared (FLIR) sensor system. Their instructors were members of the 17th Special Operations Squadron at Phan Rang AB, South Vietnam. (5) An Air Force staff sergeant, member of an air weather unit, instructs a VNAF airman in plotting weather maps.

4

5

support of this action, the South Vietnamese requested further assistance for Vietnamization. Among other things, they asked for F-4 Phantoms, C-130 transports, and air defense missiles.

In August 1969 Secretary Laird directed the JCS and the services to prepare plans and programs to develop a South Vietnamese capability to cope successfully with a combined Viet Cong/NVA attack. In response, the Air Force began intensive planning on ways to speed the Vietnamization program. A joint Seventh Air Force-USAF Advisory Group Ad Hoc Committee was established in South Vietnam for that purpose. In Washington, an office for the Special Assistant for Vietnamization was organized within Headquarters USAF on 3 November 1969 to monitor all actions concerning transfer of Air Force combat responsibilities to the Vietnamese Air Force.

Integrated VNAF Training

An important innovation in the Vietnamization program took place in 1970 with the start of on-the-job integrated training conducted by USAF C-123 operational crews for their South Vietnamese counterparts. The project was undertaken when it became clear to the Air Force that the VNAF airmen would be completing C-123 combat crew training in the United States about 9 months before activation of the first VNAF C-123 squadron. To maintain VNAF pilot proficiency in the interim, the Air Force decided to integrate the Vietnamese airmen into USAF C-123 units in Vietnam, pending transfer of those aircraft to the VNAF. This was a reversal of the 1962 assignment of 30 U.S. Air Force pilots (the "Dirty Thirty") as crewmen flying with VNAF C-47 transport units. The ensuing on-the-job training by USAF C-123 crews gave Vietnamese pilots current operational experience, reduced the

need to train them in the United States, and also lessened Air Force C-123 pilot requirements in South Vietnam.

The idea of both integrated and OJT training for VNAF officers and airmen subsequently was adopted at all bases where Vietnamese and American air units were collocated. Conventional OJT methods were used with courses tailored to fit VNAF requirements. Special emphasis was given to training the Vietnamese in base support operations, a subject not previously given high priority. Individual skill upgrading resulted from this integrated program but it was designed primarily to achieve VNAF self-sufficiency as soon as possible. By 31 January 1970, more than 900 trainees were enrolled in this integrated training program. By mid-year, more than 1,-240 officers and airmen were being taught more than 30 different specialties at Bien Hoa, Nha Trang, Binh Thuy, Pleiku, Da Nang, and Tan Son Nhut. Many of the VNAF airmen were trained in security, fire protection, weather, communications/electronics, air traffic control, and civil engineering.

Meanwhile, Secretary Laird approved further increases in VNAF strength—to 35,786 officers and airmen in 1970 and 44,712 in 1972 to support a VNAF force of 34 squadrons. To support this major expansion, the Vietnamese Air Force was completely restructured. It emerged in 1970 with 5 air divisions, 10 tactical wings, 5 maintenance and supply wings, and 7 air base wings. The VNAF Air Logistics Wing was transformed into an Air Logistics Command, equipped with a modern computer and given control of all VNAF inventory assets. Also with the help of ATC, the Vietnamese began expanding their Nha Trang Training Center, which was the location of six military schools and the English Language School. In the military schools, all instructors were Vietnamese.

To further speed VNAF self-sufficiency, 243 Vietnamese technicians were sent to the United States in 1970 to be trained as instructors to serve in the Nha Trang schools. This training consisted of a basic mechanics course tailored to their specific needs, instructor training, and follow-on training in ATC classrooms or with ATC field training detachments. The first instructor course began in March 1970. By mid-1971 more than 5,500 Vietnamese instructors had graduated and returned to Vietnam, while another 1,330 remained in training in the United States. In addition to this program, the Air Force sent ATC mobile training teams to Nha Trang to teach 37 specialized skills. The Air Force Advisory Group also provided teams at each VNAF base to assist the Vietnamese wherever possible.

During 1971 the VNAF flew more combat sorties in Vietnam than the U.S. air arms combined—63 percent of all such missions. This constituted a 69.8 percent increase over the VNAF's 1970 operations. In September 1971 the Air Force transferred a second AC-119G gunship squadron to the VNAF. During the year the VNAF transport fleet was increased to five squadrons following turnover of three USAF squadrons of C-123's. In addition, 3 C-119's were added to the 16 already being flown by the Vietnamese. In November, the VNAF took control of the direct air support centers at Pleiku, Bien Hoa, and Da Nang. By year's end, the Vietnamese also were solely responsible for operating air navigation facilities at eight bases—Binh Thuy, Ban Me Thuot, Bien Hoa, Nha Trang, Da Nang, Chu Lai, and Phu Cat.

Meanwhile, a plan was adopted to phase out most Vietnamese training in the United States. As part of this plan, the Air Force turned its attention to translating technical orders into Vietnamese and building training aids so that all instruction could be performed in South Vietnam. Additional mobile training teams were sent to Southeast Asia equipped with specially built training aids to expedite the teaching of VNAF maintenance personnel.

The partial success of Vietnamization of the air war was demonstrated during North Vietnam's 1972 spring invasion of the south. Responding to the enemy attack, the VNAF began flying the first of more than 20,000 strike sorties, which helped blunt the North Vietnamese advance. VNAF transports carried more cargo and troops than ever before, while fighters, gunships, and helicopters provided close air support to ARVN ground forces. In March and July, the VNAF activated its first C-7A Caribou squadrons and subsequently also acquired its first C-130 Hercules transports. The first VNAF C-130 instructor aircrew took its final check in December 1972.

The turnover of all training programs to the Vietnamese continued throughout 1972. English language training went from an almost entirely USAF effort to an almost entirely VNAF responsibility. In May 1972 the VNAF established a communications and electronics school at Bien Hoa. Also, with the aid of USAF mobile training teams, the VNAF took over maintenance training for the C-130, T-28B, and other aircraft systems. An AC-119K mobile training team started cross-training VNAF AC-119G and C-119G aircrews and maintenance crews into the AC-119K.

By December 1972 the Vietnamese Air Force had almost doubled in size over its June 1969 strength. From an organization of about 29,000 men, 20 squadrons, and an inventory of 428 aircraft in 1969, it had grown to 42,000 officers and airmen (with another 10,000 in training), organized into 49 squadrons equipped with about 2,000 aircraft (22 different types). In terms of numbers of aircraft, it had emerged as the fourth largest Air Force in the world—behind Communist China, the United States, and the Soviet Union.

Chapter XXI. American POW's and Operation Homecoming

On 23 January 1973 Dr. Henry Kissinger, Assistant to the President for National Security Affairs, and Special Adviser Le Duc Tho of North Vietnam reached agreement in Paris to end the war in Vietnam and restore the peace. Four days later the four major combatants—the United States and South Vietnam on the one side and North Vietnam and Viet Cong (the Provisional Revolutionary Government of the Republic of South Vietnam) on the other—signed the cease-fire agreement. It required the release of all American prisoners of war held by the Communists simultaneously with withdrawal of all U.S. forces from South Vietnam, these actions to be completed within 60 days.

For the nearly 600 POW's the 27 January agreement meant freedom after many years of captivity in North Vietnamese, Viet Cong, Laotian, and Chinese prison camps. Three hundred and twenty-five were USAF personnel, mostly combat pilots. Two were Korean war aces—Lt. Col. James L. Kasler and Col. Robinson Risner—who had spent 6½ and 7 years in captivity, respectively. A third Air Force pilot, Col. John P. Flynn, who was shot down in October 1967, was the senior American POW in North Vietnam. Promoted to brigadier general while in captivity (to protect him against harassment, no announcement was made), Colonel Flynn helped to organize and command the "4th Allied POW Wing" in the last years of the war.

USAF officials did not have much information about the prisoners' living conditions or their treatment during the early years of their captivity. What was known was not encouraging. As early as 25 June 1965, Hanoi radio reported that the Viet Cong had executed Sgt. Harold G. Bennett, an adviser to an ARVN unit, who was captured on 29 December 1964, in retaliation for the execution of Communist terrorists by the Saigon government. In August 1965—after Hanoi radio broadcast the tape-recorded statements of two recently captured Air Force pilots praising their captors for their "humane" treatment—fears were expressed that they had been tortured. These fears eventually were confirmed.

Beginning in late 1965 and during the next 7 years, the U. S. government worked to bring international pressure to bear on Hanoi to insure that the rights of the prisoners under terms of the 1949 Geneva Convention were being observed. Although North Vietnam had signed the convention in 1957, it announced that captured American pilots were not entitled to POW status. According to Hanoi, there had been no formal declaration of war between the United States and North Vietnam (the Geneva convention made no such distinction) and the pilots were "criminals" who could be convicted "under the principles established by the Nuremburg war crime trials."

In its efforts to ease the plight of the POW's, the Johnson administration solicited the assistance of the Interna-

1

(1) Newsmen swarm around Ambassador Averell Harriman (see arrow), who headed the U.S. delegation to the preliminary peace talks, after emerging from a meeting with French Foreign Minister Couve de Murville at the Quai d'Orsay, in May 1968. (2) Dr. Henry A. Kissinger (l.) and Hanoi's senior representative Le Duc Tho (r.) are shown during a break in the Paris talks on a cease-fire, November 1972. In the center is Tho's interpreter. (3) A group of wives and relatives of U.S. prisoners of war held in North Vietnam conferred with Secretary of Defense Melvin R. Laird in his office in April 1970. (4) Secretary of State William Rogers signed the Vietnamese Peace Agreement in Paris, 27 January 1973. Shown on his right is Under Secretary Designate of Political Affairs, Ambassador William J. Porter.

2

3

4

(1) President Nixon at a White House ceremony presented awards for gallantry to four men who participated in the U.S. raid on the Son Tay POW camp near Hanoi in November 1970. Shown (l. to r.): Air Force Brig. Gen. LeRoy J. Manor, overall commander of the raiding party; Air Force TSgt LeRoy M. Wright, Army SFC Tyrone Adderly; and Col. Arthur D. Simons, the Army Ranger leader of the unsuccessful rescue effort. (2) An aerial view of the Hoa Lo prison in Hanoi where many U.S. prisoners were held. (3) Navy Lt. Cmdr. R. A. Stratton in his prison cell. (4) 1st Lts. J. R. Shivley (l.) and 1st Lt. R. A. Abbott, USAF (r.). (5) Capt. Murphy N. Jones, USAF. (6) Seaman D. B. Hegdahl, USN. (7) Lt. Cmdr. H. A. Stafford, USN.

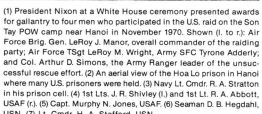

tional Red Cross and friendly nations to use their influence in obtaining proper treatment. On 29 April 1966, at the request of the White House, the State Department established a Committee on Prisoner Matters which included representatives from several Department of Defense agencies. On 10 May the President designated W. Averell Harriman as his Special Representative and Ambassador to negotiate an exchange of prisoners. The United States also asked the Soviet Union to intervene with North Vietnam to allow Red Cross representatives to visit the POW's, but Moscow referred the Americans to Hanoi.

Hanoi Threatens "War Crimes" Trials

During the early summer of 1966, following increased U.S. air strikes against oil facilities in the Hanoi-Haiphong area, North Vietnam initiated a propaganda campaign leading to the scheduling of "war crime" trials for the captured airmen. As part of this campaign, 52 American POW's handcuffed in pairs were paraded through the streets of Hanoi while agitated crowds stoned, beat, and reviled them. On 7 July 1966 Hanoi radio read depositions from several pilots (they had been tortured) denouncing American war operations and asking for Vietnamese "forgiveness." On 12 July two East European Communist press agencies reported that 60 American military men would be brought to trial later in the month or in early August.

The United States took North Vietnam's plans for war crime trials seriously. President Johnson made no public threats but warnings about his reaction should the trials actually take place were soon dispatched around the world. In Washington, 19 senators who strongly opposed Johnson's Vietnam policies on 15 July issued "a plea for sanity" to Hanoi. Violence against the captured Americans, they warned,

would "incite the public demand for retaliation swift and sure." The next day Sen. Richard B. Russell, chairman of the Senate Armed Services Committee, warned that North Vietnam would be made "a desert" if the trials were held. Sen. George D. Aiken predicted "complete destruction of North Vietnam" if the POW's were killed. The *New York Times* reported that there was little doubt that "Lyndon Johnson's reaction would be severe."

These warnings had a salutary effect on Hanoi, which abruptly ceased its propaganda campaigns about the trials. Its treatment of the captured airmen, however, remained severe. Their lot included torture—ranging from being trussed up by ropes and hung on rafters to being beaten severely by prison guards or having their fingernails pulled out. Some POW's were tortured to persuade them to meet with American antiwar and other visiting delegations and recite dictated statements about their "humane" treatment. Many prisoners—especially senior officers—were placed in solitary confinement for years and fed a bare subsistence diet. Except in certain serious cases, medical care was minimal. Mail privileges were nonexistent for most prisoners. During the Christmas season of 1966, 457 of 467 packages sent to them by their families were returned with the stamp: "Refused by the Postal Authorities of Vietnam."

During 1967 the U. S. government continued its search for ways to persuade Hanoi to allow Red Cross representatives to visit the prison camps in the North. The South Vietnamese government cooperated by opening its camps for Viet Cong and North Vietnamese prisoners to inspection by the International Committee of the Red Cross and allowing mail privileges. Still Hanoi refused to budge. On 26 July 1967 the Department of Defense established a Prisoner of War Policy Committee. Chaired by Paul C. Warnke, Assistant Secretary of Defense (International Security Affairs), it had the job of coordinating all POW matters and planning the eventual recovery and repatriation of the prisoners.

Information about the living conditions and treatment of POW's held by the Viet Cong in jungle camps in South Vietnam or Cambodia came to light from the infrequent successful escapee or from the American captive occasionally released by the enemy for political purposes. Living conditions were extremely primitive, with many POW's succumbing to disease and starvation.

In the case of North Vietnamese camps, the first authoritative information became available in February 1968, when Hanoi released three American pilots shot down 4 to 6 months earlier. They were Lt. Col. Norris M. Overly, USAF; Capt. John D. Black, USAF; and Lt. (jg.) David P. Matheny, USN. The North Vietnamese announced their impending release on 27 January, noting that they would be handed over to the U. S. National Mobilization Committee to End the War. Two of its members—the Rev. Daniel Berrigan and Dr. Howard Zinn —flew to Hanoi, where the release took place on 16 February.

The entire affair may have been a North Vietnamese ploy related to the 1968 Tet offensive, launched on 31 January. If, as seems likely, the enemy thought that the 3-man release might ward off U. S. retaliatory strikes in the Hanoi-Haiphong area, they were correct. In Washington, Assistant Secretary Warnke—serving as a member of a working group created by the newly designated Secretary of Defense, Clark Clifford, to prepare new military recommendations for the President— argued against JCS proposals for such bombings. He recommended that the existing bombing ban "should be continued pending the return of the 3 American PWs."

When the three released captives reached the United States several weeks later, U. S. officials learned for the first time that many of the American POW's were in prison camps in the Hanoi area. The airmen also identified 40 men as prisoners who had been listed as missing in action. Citing their testimony, Warnke argued that heavy and "indiscriminate" attacks in the Hanoi area "would jeopardize the lives of these prisoners and alarm their wives and parents."

Subsequently, the President on 31 March 1968 announced a halt to all bombing of North Vietnam (except for the area immediately north of the DMZ) and invited Hanoi to begin peace talks in Paris. The North Vietnamese accepted and, in May 1968, the first meetings got under way in Paris. Apparently, in an effort to further encourage an end to all bombings of North Vietnam, in August 1968 Hanoi released three more captured pilots, all members of the Air Force and recent captives. They were Maj. James F. Low, a Korean War ace shot down in December 1967; Maj. Fred N. Thompson, captured in March 1968; and Capt. Joe V. Carpenter, captured in February 1968. Turned over to members of the U. S. antiwar movement in Hanoi on 18 July, they were escorted back to the United States.

During the waning months of the Johnson administration in late 1968, little progress was made in the Paris talks. The next major event affecting the POW's involved the efforts of the new administration of President Richard M. Nixon, who took office in January 1969. Within days of his inauguration, the President sent Ambassador Henry Cabot Lodge to Paris to head the U.S. delegation to the peace talks. Mr. Lodge very early proposed to the North Vietnamese the release of POW's held by both sides as part of any peace agreement. Hanoi, however, demanded that the United States end its support of Saigon. As the talks deadlocked over this issue, the administration in early 1969 abandoned quiet diplomacy in dealing with the

2

(1-2) POW's were driven to the Gia Lam Airport preparatory to their turnover to American officials. (3) Col. Emil J. Wengel, USAF greets Maj. Hubert K. Flesher (l.), who was shot down on 2 December 1966. (4) Happy former POW's after boarding a C-141 transport taking them back to the United States. (5) The end of a long journey for Army Sgt. Edward W. Williams, greeted by close relatives at Scott AFB, Ill. (6-7) Welcome signs greet returned POW's.

4

1

3

5

6

7

1

2

3

6

4

(1-8) Scenes of homecoming.

7

5

8

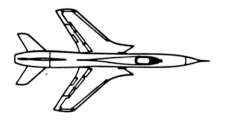

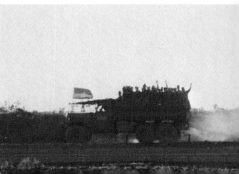

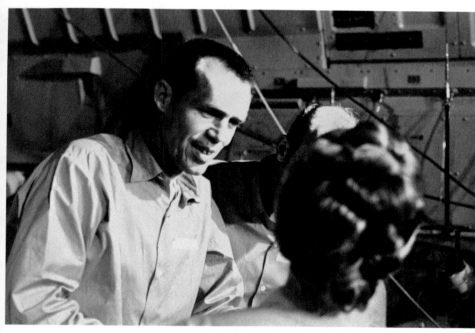

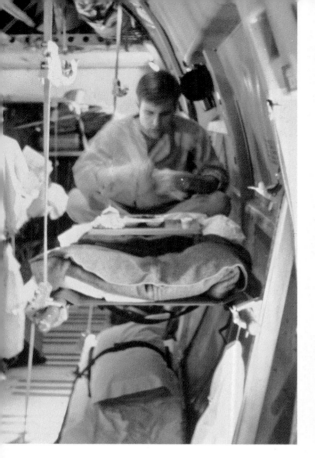

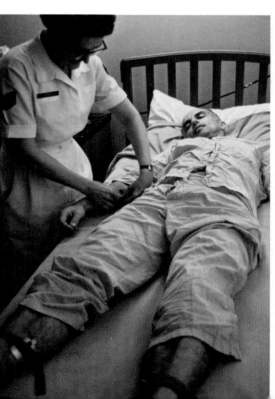

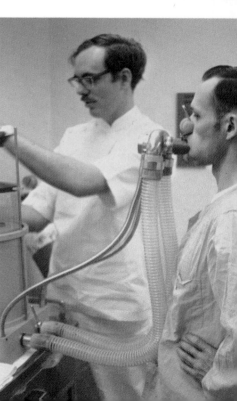

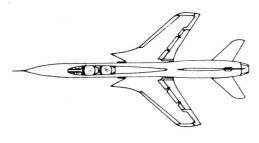

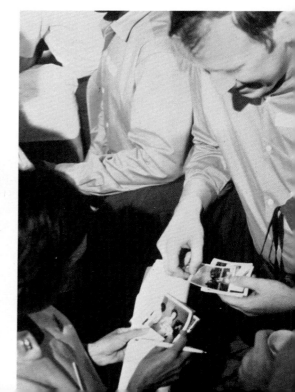

POW issue and proposed discussing it "openly, candidly, forcefully, and repeatedly." In the dozens of meetings with the North Vietnamese during 1969, the Americans repeatedly brought up the subject. They cited "disturbing evidence" that the prisoners were being held "in solitary confinement and being subjected to physical and mental duress." They repeatedly proposed a prisoner exchange, repatriation of the sick and wounded, and inspection of the camps by impartial outsiders. They pressed the North Vietnamese for lists of all POW's so that their families could know "who is dead and who is alive."

Although it rejected all these proposals, Hanoi on 3 July 1969 announced that "in recognition of the American Independence Day," it would release a third group of prisoners. They were: Capt. Wesley L. Rumble, USAF, a captive 15 months; Seaman Douglas Hegdahl, imprisoned more than 2 years; and Lt. Robert F. Frishman, USN, a prisoner for about 20 months. Prior to their turn-over to another U. S. antiwar group in Hanoi on 18 July, the North Vietnamese warned Lieutenant Frishman not to cause them any "embarrassment" since they would retaliate against those left behind. The other POW's, however, had urged him to speak out about their ill-treatment when he got home.

He did several weeks later, with the encouragement of the administration. On 3 September 1969, Frishman and Hegdahl held a press conference at the Bethesda Naval Hospital, during which the lieutenant reported that POW's had been beaten, tortured, placed in solitary confinement, provided minimal medical care, and otherwise mistreated. Frishman, for example, almost lost his injured right arm, which became shorter than his left arm for lack of adequate medical aid. Based upon these statements and other available information, the U. S. government on 13 September report-

ed to the International Conference of the Red Cross meeting in Istanbul, Turkey, on Hanoi's gross violations of the Geneva Convention.

The publicity about the harsh treatment had a galvanizing effect on the families of the prisoners. Starting in September-October 1969, delegations of wives and relatives of POW's descended on the North Vietnamese delegation in Paris to plead for information about their men. The spectacle produced widespread headlines and television coverage and adversely affected North Vietnam's position in the eyes of the world. On 12 November the United States also took its case to the United Nations General Assembly, where it denounced Hanoi's torture and treatment of the prisoners and its refusal to allow mail privileges to the POW's.

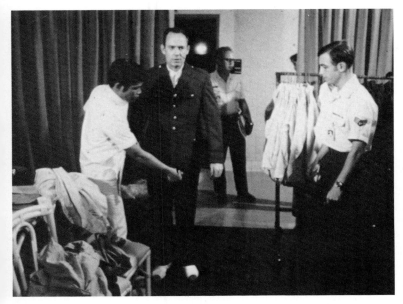

These events finally produced a North Vietnamese reaction. Responding to the unfavorable publicity, Hanoi requested members of the American peace movement to form a "Committee of Liaison With Families of Servicemen Detained in North Vietnam" to transmit letters from the POW's to their families in the United States. Subsequently, on 14 December 1969, North Vietnamese prison officials suddenly directed the POW's: "Everyone will write home for Christmas." There followed a dramatic change in the number of letters sent and received. For example, in the 4½ years ending in January 1969, American families had received only 620 letters from 103 prisoners. During the next 11 months, the number climbed to 940 from 294 writers, most of the additional 320 letters being written in November and December. Of those,

191 came from new writers, whose fate for the most part had remained unknown to their families. This was an important break-through for the prisoners and was followed by noticeable improvement in their living conditions.

The administration continued to hammer away at the POW issue in various forums. In early 1970 both houses of Congress adopted a resolution expressing concern about the prisoners' fates. During the summer, President Nixon appointed Col. Frank Borman (he and two companions orbited the moon in December 1968) as his Special Representative on Prisoners of War. Borman traveled to 14 countries (including the Soviet Union) seeking assistance in persuading Hanoi to exchange American prisoners for the thousands of captured North Vietnamese troops. Although the trip was unsuccessful, it helped to focus the spotlight on the plight of the POW's. After his return to the United States in September 1970, Colonel Borman reported to a joint session of Congress on his efforts.

In October the National League of Families of American Prisoners and Missing in Southeast Asia held its first annual convention in Washington, D.C., attended by more than 450 family members. The League grew out of the activities of a group of wives on the West Coast in 1966. In November the U.S. government received—via the antiwar Committee of Liaison—the first news from Hanoi about the death in captivity of six POW's. The committee also turned over a North Vietnamese list of 339 American captives, which included 4 new names.

In late November 1970—as a direct result of the daring U.S. raid on the Son Tay prison camp west of Hanoi— the North Vietnamese evacuated all outlying prisons and brought the POW's—352 of them—to the Hoa Lo prison (Vietnamese for "hell hole" but usually called the "Hanoi Hilton" by the POW's). This consolidation opened a new era for the prisoners. For the first time they were placed in large open-bay rooms housing 20 to 50 men, enabling them to organize to a greater extent than ever before. Their senior officers, although still kept in isolation by the North Vietnamese, were able to issue policy guidance and directives to the younger men via a variety of clandestine communication methods and maintained effective command of the "4th Allied POW Wing" despite efforts to halt this activity.

During 1971-1972 perhaps the most important influence on Hanoi—and the final peace settlement—was President Nixon's state visits to North Vietnam's major military suppliers—Communist China in February 1972 and the Soviet Union in May. Within months after Dr. Kissinger's secret trip to Peking in July 1971 which led to arrangements for the President's trip to China, a North Vietnamese delegate at Paris offered to release all POW's if the United States promised to withdraw all its forces from Vietnam by a fixed date. The proposal became the foundation for reaching a final agreement between Kissinger and Tho in 1972. There were several setbacks and interruptions in their negotiations, including Hanoi's major offensive in the spring of 1972 to seize territory in South Vietnam and defeat the Saigon government. The heavy bombardment of Hanoi and Haiphong in December 1972—following Hanoi's procrastination over the settlement—apparently was a factor leading to the 27 January 1973 agreement and set the stage for Operation Homecoming, the return of all American prisoners.

Planning the POW Recovery

Operation Homecoming plans, refined over a period of several years, called for each returning POW to remain in medical channels from the time he returned to American control

until he had completed all post-captivity processing in a hospital in the United States. Representatives of the Office of the Secretary of Defense, the military services, and the State Department attended the final planning conference, held in Honolulu, Hawaii, during August 1972. Among the attendees were physicians, surgeons, lawyers, escorts, consular officials, chaplains, public affairs officers, and others. The Commander, 9th Aeromedical Evacuation Group (PACAF), was appointed overall aeromedical evacuation coordinator for the recovery operation.

The operation was divided into three phases. First, there was to be the initial reception of prisoners at three release sites: prisoners held by the Viet Cong were to be flown to Saigon by helicopter; those in North Vietnam, the majority of the prisoners, would be released at Hanoi; and finally, three American POW's held in China—two U.S. pilots and a CIA agent imprisoned during the Korean War—would be set free at Hong Kong. All would be flown to Clark AB in the Philippines for the second phase of the operation—processing through the Joint Homecoming Reception Center. Then the POW's would fly to 1 of 31 military hospitals

in the United States for detailed medical assistance and processing, the third phase of the operation.

In late September 1972 a realistic rehearsal for Operation Homecoming took place after North Vietnam released three more American POW's: Maj. Edward K. Elias, USAF; Lt. Norris A. Charles, USN; and Lt. Markham L. Gartley, USN. Their release gave Homecoming personnel the opportunity to exercise and refine their procedures. The 9th Aeromedical Evacuation Group, for example, responded five times, sending a C-9A aeromedical aircraft to potential release sites, including Vientiane, Laos.

On 27 January 1973, as specified in the cease-fire agreement, North Vietnam and the Viet Cong provided the United States with a list of 578 American POW's of whom 556 were military personnel and 22 civilians. On 1 February the "Lao Patriotic Front" provided the names of nine other American prisoners—seven military and two civilians. Finally, an additional POW in Viet Cong hands also was reported, bringing the total of American personnel to be released to 588. The Communist side also listed nine non-U.S. personnel: two West Germans, two Canadians, two Filipinos, two Thais, and one South Vietnamese. The total number of Americans returning home—including the three released by China—was 591.

Under provisions of the cease-fire agreement, POW's were to be released simultaneously with the withdrawal of American troops, at approximately 15-day phased intervals. The first release took place almost on schedule and was followed by another North Vietnamese "good will" release a few days later. When the North Vietnamese fell behind the release schedule, the President ordered a halt in American force withdrawals from the South to make clear the importance the United States attached to prompt and full compliance with the agreement. North Vietnam responded by releasing additional prisoners, the last of them on 29 March. In the South, Saigon officials released 26,508 North Vietnamese and Viet Cong prisoners while the Communist side released about 5,000 South Vietnamese POW's.

For the American people the return of the nation's captured military men was a moment of tears and joyous celebration as they watched the arrival of their servicemen at Clark and then at air bases throughout the United States. A State Department official, Frank A. Sieverts, Special Assistant to the Deputy Secretary of State for Prisoner of War/Missing in Action Matters, told a congressional committee in May 1973 of being at Hanoi's Gia Lam airport on 12 February and his joy when the first group of POW's arrived there for their flight to freedom. He said:

> The guards ordered the men off the bus. Suddenly, the senior American officer of the group took command away from the guards and gave the orders for the men to march in formation to the release point. The guards tried to intervene but fell back. It was clear then that, despite the grim experience of their captivity, our men had endured and prevailed. They deserve our thanks and commendation.

Key Air Force Leaders During the War in Southeast Asia

Secretaries of the Air Force

Eugene M. Zuckert .... 24 Jan 1961-
                                    30 Sep 1965
Harold Brown .... 1 Oct 1965-
                                    14 Feb 1969
Robert C. .... 15 Feb 1965-
   Seamans, Jr.   14 May 1973
John L. .... 15 May 1973-
   McLucas (Act)   18 Jul 1973
John L. McLucas .... 19 Jul 1973-

Chiefs of Staff of the Air Force

Gen. Curtis E. .... 30 Jun 1961-
   LeMay   31 Jan 1965
Gen. John P. .... 1 Feb 1965-
   McConnell   31 Jul 1969
Gen. John D. Ryan .... 1 Aug 1969-
                                    31 Jul 1973
Gen. George S. .... 1 Aug 1973-
   Brown   30 Jun 1974
Gen. David C. Jones .... 1 Jul 1974-

Under Secretaries of the Air Force

Joseph V. Charyk .... 28 Jan 1960-
                                    1 Mar 1963
Brockway McMillan .... 12 Jun 1963-
                                    30 Sep 1965
Norman S. Paul .... 1 Oct 1965-
                                    30 Sep 1967
Townsend Hoopes .... 2 Oct 1967-
                                    3 Feb 1969
John L. McLucas* .... 17 Mar 1969-
                                    18 Jul 1973
James W. Plummer .... 20 Dec 1973-

Commanders in Chief, Pacific Air Forces

Lt. Gen. Emmett .... 1 Aug 1959-
   O'Donnell, Jr.   31 Jul 1963
Gen. Jacob E. .... 1 Aug 1963-
   Smart   31 Jul 1964
Gen. Hunter .... 1 Aug 1964-
   Harris, Jr.   31 Jan 1967
Gen. John D. Ryan .... 1 Feb 1967-
                                    31 Jul 1968
Gen. Joseph J. .... 1 Aug 1968-
   Nazzaro   31 July 1971
Gen. Lucius D. .... 1 Aug 1971-
   Clay   30 Sep 1973
Gen. John W. .... 1 Oct 1973-
   Vogt, Jr.   30 Jun 1974
Gen. Louis L. .... 1 Jul 1974-
   Wilson, Jr.

---

*McLucas served in this post through 19 December 1973 in addition to serving as Secretary of the Air Force.

Commanders, Seventh Air Force

Organized at Tan Son Nhut AB, RVN, 1 April 1966. Replaced 2d Air Division.

Lt. Gen. Joseph H. Moore	1 Apr 1966-30 Jun 1966
Gen. William W. Momyer	1 Jul 1966-31 Jul 1968
Gen. George S. Brown	1 Aug 1968-31 Aug 1970
Gen. Lucius D. Clay, Jr.	1 Sep 1970-31 Jul 1971
Gen. John D. Lavelle	1 Aug 1971-6 Apr 1972
Gen. John W. Vogt, Jr.	7 Apr 1972-30 Sep 1973
Lt. Gen. Timothy F. O'Keefe	1 Oct 1973-

Commanders, Seventh/Thirteenth Air Force

Organized 6 January 1966 at Udorn AB, Thailand as 2/13 Air Force. Redesignated 7/13 Air Force April 1966. Redesignated 13 Air Force ADVON in late March 1973.

Maj. Gen. Charles R. Bond, Jr. (Dep Cmdr)	6 Jan 1966-31 Mar 1967
Maj. Gen. William C. Lindley, Jr.	1 Jun 1967-31 May 1968
Maj. Gen. Louis T. Seith	1 Jun 1968-31 May 1969
Maj. Gen. Robert L. Petit	1 Jun 1969-5 Mar 1970
Maj. Gen. James F. Kirkendall	15 Apr 1970-11 Oct 1970
Maj. Gen. Andrew J. Evans, Jr.	12 Oct 1970-30 Jun 1971
Maj. Gen. DeWitt R. Searles	1 Jul 1971-8 Sep 1972
Maj. Gen. James D. Hughes	9 Sep 1972-19 Apr 1973

Commanders, Eighth Air Force

Moved, without personnel or equipment, from Westover AFB, MA to Andersen AFB, Guam on 1 April 1970. Replaced 3d Air Division. Moved without personnel or equipment, to Barksdale AFB, LA on 1 January 1975.

Lt. Gen. Alvan C. Gillem, II	1 Apr 1970-12 Jul 1970
Brig. Gen. Leo C. Lewis	13 Jul 1970-31 Jul 1970
Lt. Gen. Sam J. Byerley	1 Aug 1970-13 Sep 1971
Lt. Gen. Gerald W. Johnson	14 Sep 1971-30 Sep 1973
Lt. Gen. George H. McKee	1 Oct 1973-29 Aug 1974
Maj. Gen. Charles F. Minter, Sr.	30 Oct 1974-31 Dec 1974

Division, Wing, and Group Commanders

2d ADVON

Established by Thirteenth Air Force on 15 November 1961 with four numbered detachments, three located in South Vietnam, and one in Thailand. Inactivated October 1962; replaced by 2d Air Division.

Commanders, 2d Air Division

Organized 8 October 1962. Discontinued 1 April 1966; replaced by Seventh Air Force.

Brig. Gen. (Later, Maj. Gen.) Rollen H. Anthis	*8 Oct 1962-19 Dec 1963*
Brig. Gen. Milton B. Adams	*20 Dec 1963-C. 20 Jan 1964*
Maj. Gen. (Later, Lt. Gen. Joseph H. Moore	*C. 21 Jan 1964-2 Apr 1966*

*Anthis also wore a second hat as Chief, Air Force Section, MAAG, Vietnam.

Commanders, 3d Air Division

Activated at Andersen AFB, Guam on 18 June 1954. Inactivated 31 March 1970. Replaced by 8 AF. Activated at Andersen AFB, Guam on 1 January 1975.

Brig. Gen. Harold W. . . . . . 2 Jul 1963-
Ohlke   16 Jul 1965
Maj. Gen. William J. . . . . . 16 Jul 1965-
Crumm   7 Jul 1967
Maj. Gen. Selmon W. . . . . . 8 Jul 1967-
Wells   5 Jun 1968
Lt. Gen. Alvan C. . . . . 6 Jun 1968-
Gillem, II   31 Mar 1970
Maj. Gen. Charles F. . . . . . 1 Jan 1975-
Minter, Sr.   10 Aug 1975
Maj. Gen. Thomas F. . . . 20 Aug 1975-
Rew   17 Aug 1976

17th Air Division (Prov)

Activated 1 Jun 1972 at U-Tapao Afld, Thailand, attached to 8 AF (SAC). Inactivated 1 January 1975.

Brig. Gen. Frank W. . . . . . 1 Jun 1972-
Elliott, Jr.   5 Jun 1972
Brig. Gen. Glen R. . . . . . . 6 Jun 1972-
Sullivan   1 Feb 1973
Brig. Gen. Billy J. . . . . 2 Feb 1973-
Ellis   12 Oct 1973
Brig. Gen. James S. . . . . 13 Oct 1973-
Murphy   4 Aug 1974
Brig. Gen. George D. . . . . 5 Aug 1974-
Miller   31 Dec 1974

57th Air Division (Prov)

Activated 1 June 1972 at Andersen AFB, Guam, attached to 8 AF (SAC). Inactivated 15 November 1973.

Brig. Gen. Andrew B. . . . . 1 Jun 1972-
Anderson, Jr.   14 Jan 1973
Brig. Gen. John W. . . . . . 15 Jan 1973-
Burkhart   Oct 1973
Brig. Gen. Edgar S. . . . . . . Oct 1973-
Harris, Jr.   15 Nov 1973

315th Air Division

Activated 25 January 1951, Tachikawa AB, Japan. Inactivated 15 April 1969.

Brig. Gen. Theodore . . . . 31 Aug 1963
G. Kershaw
Brig. Gen. Richard H. . . . . 1 Sep 1963-
Ellis   15 Jun 1965
Col. Lester R. . . . . 16 June 1965-
Ferris, Jr. (Interim)   12 Jul 1965
Col. Charles W. . . . . 13 Jul 1965-
Howe   25 Jul 1968
Col. Robert D. . . . . 26 Jul 1968-
Brown   15 Apr 1969

834th Air Division

Organized 25 October 1966 at Tan Son Nhut AB, RVN.

Brig. Gen. William G.
Moore, Jr. . . . . 11 Nov 1967
Brig. Gen. Hugh E. . . . . 12 Nov 1967-
Wild   28 Nov 1967
Brig. Gen. Burl W. . . . . 29 Nov 1967-
McLaughlin   22 Jun 1969
Brig. Gen. John H. . . . . 23 Jun 1969-
Herring, Jr.   1 Dec 1971
Brig. Gen. Eugene W. . . . . . . 24 Jan 1972-
Gauch, Jr.

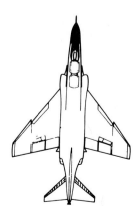

3d Tactical Fighter Wing

Arrived at Bien Hoa AB, RVN, 8 November 1965. Inactivated 15 March 1970. Activated 15 March 1971.

Col. Robert A. .... 8 Nov 1965-
Ackerly   31 Oct 1966
Col. Richard C. .... 1 Nov 1966-
Catledge   29 Sep 1967
Col. George W. .... 30 Sep 1967-
McLaughlin   4 May 1968
Col. Homer K. .... 5 May 1968-
Hansen   31 Mar 1969
Col. Howard M. .... 1 Apr 1969-
Lane   10 Apr 1970
Col. William E. .... 11 Apr 1970-
Charlson   Unkn
Col. Abner M. .... 11 Mar 1971-
Aust, Jr.   20 May 1971
Col. Clement D. .... 20 May 1971-
Billingslea (Temp)   6 Jun 1971
Col. Abner M. .... 7 Jun 1971-
Aust, Jr.   16 Nov 1971
Col. Charles A. .... 17 Nov 1971-
Watry   4 Oct 1972
Col. Paul A. .... 5 Oct 1972-
Kattu   18 Nov 1973
Col. Harry W. .... 19 Nov 1973-
Schurr

8th Tactical Fighter Wing

Organized at Ubon AB, Thailand, 8 December 1965.

Col. Joseph G. .... 8 Dec 1965-
Wilson   29 Sep 1966
Col. Robin Olds .... 30 Sep 1966-
                                22 Sep 1967
Col. Robert V. .... 23 Sep 1967-
Spencer   4 Jul 1968
Col. Charles C. .... 5 Jul 1968-
Pattillo   7 May 1969
Col. Donald N. .... 8 May 1969-
Stanfield   5 May 1970
Col. David J. .... 6 May 1970-
Schmerbeck   1 Oct 1970
Col. Lloyd R. .... 2 Oct 1970-
Leavitt, Jr. (Temp)   3 Oct 1970
Col. Larry M. .... 4 Oct 1970-
Killpack   18 May 1971

Col. James A. .... 19 May 1971-
Young   27 Feb 1972
Col. Carl S. Miller .... 28 Feb 1972-
                                24 Nov 1972
Col. Francis A. .... 25 Nov 1972-
Humphreys, Jr.   24 Jan 1974
Col. Tom M. .... 25 Jan 1974-
Arnold, Jr.

12th Tactical Fighter Wing

Arrived Cam Ranh Bay AB, RVN, on 8 November 1965.
Moved to Phu Cat AB, RVN, 31 March 1970. Inactivated at Phu Cat AB, RVN, 17 November 1971.

Col. Levi R. Chase .... 8 Nov 1965-
                                17 Oct 1966
Col. Jones E. Bolt .... 18 Oct 1966-
                                19 Mar 1967
Col. Joel D. .... 20 Mar 1967-
Thorvaldson   8 Apr 1967
Col. Woodard E. .... 9 Apr 1967-
Davis, Jr.   4 Apr 1968
Col. Floyd White .... 5 Apr 1968-
                                6 Apr 1969
Col. Ramon R. .... 7 Apr 1969-
Melton   30 Mar 1970
Col. Harry B. .... 31 Mar 1970-
Trimble   12 Apr 1970
Col. Larry M. .... 13 Apr 1970-
Killpack   3 Oct 1970
Col. Ralph S. Parr .... 4 Oct 1970-
                                18 Feb 1971
Col. Richard H. .... 19 Feb 1971-
Schoeneman   3 Oct 1971
Col. Albert L. .... 4 Oct 1971-
Melton   17 Nov 1971

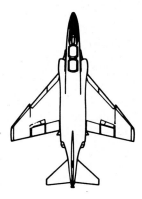

14th Air Commando Wing

Organized at Nha Trang AB, RVN, 8 March 1966. Redesignated 14th Special Operations Wing, 1 August 1968. Moved to Phan Rang, 15 October 1969. Inactivated 30 September 1971. Redesignated 14th Flying Trng Wg 22 March 1972. Activated 1 June 1972 at Columbus AFB, Miss.

Col. Gordon F. Bradburn	9 Apr 1967
Col. Forrest L. Rauscher	10 Apr 1967-16 Nov 1967
Col. John M. Patton	17 Nov 1967-2 Jun 1968
Col. Conrad S. Allman	3 Jun 1968-4 Mar 1969
Col. William K. Bush	5 Mar 1969-1 Sep 1969
Col. Clyde S. Cherry	2 Sep 1969-2 Apr 1970
Col. William H. Fairbrother	3 Apr 1970-12 Sep 1970
Col. Alfred F. Eaton	13 Sep 1970-13 Mar 1971
Col. Mark W. Magnan	14 Mar 1971-12 Sep 1971
Col. Malcolm L. Nurnberg	13 Sep 1971-30 Sep 1971

31st Tactical Fighter Wing

Arrived Tuy Hoa AB, RVN, 25 December 1966. Redeployed back to the United States, 15 October 1970.

Col. Warren R. Lewis	28 Nov 1966-6 Dec 1967
Col. William J. Evans	7 Dec 1967-2 May 1968
Col. Abner M. Aust, Jr.	3 May 1968-7 Feb 1969
Col. Cuthbert A. Pattillo	8 Feb 1969-7 Aug 1969
Col. William B. Yancey, Jr.	8 Aug 1969-14 Jun 1970
Col. Gilbert D. Hereth	15 Jun 1970-15 Oct 1970

35th Tactical Fighter Wing

Organized Da Nang AB, RVN, 8 April 1966. Moved to Phan Rang AB, RVN, 10 October 1966. Inactivated 30 June 1971 at Phan Rang.

Col. Franklin H. Scott	8 Apr 1966-9 May 1966
Col. Allan P. Rankin	10 May 1966-9 Oct 1966
Col. George S. Weart	10 Oct 1966-27 Feb 1967
Col. James A. Wilson	1 Mar 1967-31 Jan 1968
Col. Herndon F. Williams	1 Feb 1968-22 Sep 1968
Col. Frank L. Gailer, Jr.	23 Sep 1968-8 Aug 1969
Col. Walter T. Galligan	9 Aug 1969-9 Jun 1970
Col. Walter C. Turnier	10 Jun 1970-31 Dec 1970
Col. Cregg P. Nolen, Jr.	1 Jan 1971-30 Jun 1971

37th Tactical Fighter Wing

Organized at Phu Cat AB, RVN, 1 March 1967. Inactivated 31 March 1970.

Unkn	1 Mar 1967-5 May 1967
Col. Raymond C. Lee, Jr.	6 May 1967-14 May 1967
Col. Edwin A. Schneider	15 May 1967-14 May 1968
Col. Leroy J. Manor	15 May 1968-31 Mar 1969
Col. Harry B. Trimble	1 Apr 1969-31 Mar 1970

43d Strategic Wing

Activated 1 April 1970 at Andersen AFB, Guam, assigned to 8 AF (SAC) and later attached to Air Division Provisional, 57 during existence of latter. Replaced 3960th Strategic Wing.

Col. Lawrence E. Stephens . . . . 1 Apr 1970-30 Jun 1970

Col. Glenn R. Dunlap . . . . 1 Jul 1970-28 Apr 1972

Col. William P. Armstrong . . . . 28 Apr 1972-14 Jun 1972

Col. James H. McGrath . . . . 16 Jun 1972-30 Nov 1972

Col. James R. McCarthy . . . . 1 Dec 1972-1 Jun 1973

Col. Morris E. Shiver . . . . 1 Jun 1973-Aug 1973

Col. Lawton W. Magee . . . . Aug 1973-15 Nov 1973

Col. James R. McCarthy . . . . 15 Nov 1973-15 Jun 1974

Col. Andrew Pringle, Jr. . . . . Jun 1974-Jun 1975

Col. Donald C. Bass . . . . Jun 1975-Mar 1976

56th Air Commando Wing

Organized at Nakhon Phanom AB, Thailand, 8 April 1967. Redesignated 1 August 1968 as Special Operation Wing.

Col. Harry C. Aderholt . . . . 8 Apr 1967-18 Nov 1967

Col. Roland K. McCoskrie . . . . 19 Nov 1967-6 Nov 1968

Col. Edwin J. White, Jr. . . . . 7 Nov 1968-30 May 1969

Col. Patrick M. Fallon (Temp) . . . . 31 May 1969-4 Jul 1969

Col. Edwin J. White, Jr. . . . . 5 Jul 1969-4 Oct 1969

Col. Samuel E. Crosby, Jr. . . . . 5 Oct 1969-7 Aug 1970

Col. Edward J. Walsh, Jr. . . . . 8 Aug 1970-14 Jul 1971

Col. Jack A. Robinson . . . . 15 Jul 1971-16 Jun 1972

Col. Norbert L. Simon . . . . 17 Jun 1972-30 Nov 1972

Col. Robert E. Wayne . . . . 1 Dec 1972-29 Jun 1973

Col. William B. Owens . . . . 30 Jun 1973-14 Sep 1973

Col. Ralph H. Bowers, (Temp) . . . . 15 Sep 73-25 Sep 1973

Col. Charles E. Woods . . . . 26 Sep 1973-22 Jun 1974

72d Strategic Wing (Prov)

Activated 1 June 1972 at Andersen AFB, Guam, attached to Air Division Provisional, 57. Inactivated 15 November 1973.

Col. Kenneth M. Holloway . . . . 1 Jun 1972-8 Oct 1972

Col. Thomas F. Rew . . . . 8 Oct 1972-16 Mar 1973

Col. Thomas W. Sherman, Jr. . . . . 16 Mar 1973-16 Apr 1973

Col. Nathaniel A. Gallagher . . . . 16 Apr 1973-15 Nov 1973

307th Strategic Wing

Activated 1 April 1970 at U-Tapao AB, Thailand, assigned to 8 AF (SAC) and attached to Air Division Provisional, 17 while the latter was in existence. Replaced 4258th Strategic Wing. Inactivated 30 September 1975.

Brig. Gen. Woodrow A. Abbott . . . . 1 Apr 1970-4 Jul 1970

Brig. Gen. John R. Hinton, Jr. . . . . 5 Jul 1970-4 Jul 1971

Brig. Gen. Frank W. Elliott, Jr. . . . . 5 Jul 1971-31 May 1972

Col. Donald M. Davis . . . . 1 Jun 1972-10 Feb 1973

Col. Bill V. Brown . . . . 11 Feb 1973-20 Aug 1973

Col. Frank J. Apel, Jr. . . . . 21 Aug 1973-9 Apr 1974

Col. Ernest J. Stirman . . . . 10 Apr 1974-31 Dec 1974
Brig. Gen. George D. Miller . . . . 1 Jan 1975-21 Jan 1975
Col. Ernest J. Stirman . . . . 22 Jan 1975-5 Mar 1975
Col. Caryl W. Calhoun . . . . 6 Mar 1975-30 Sep 1975

310th Strategic Wing (Prov)

Activated 1 June 1972 at U-Tapao AB, Thailand, attached to Air Division Provisional, 17. Inactivated 1 July 1974.

Col. James R. McCarthy . . . . 1 Jun 1972-13 Jun 1972
Col. William L. Nicholson, III . . . . 14 Jun 1972-5 Dec 1972
Col. Stanley C. Beck . . . . 6 Dec 1972-12 Jun 1973
Col. Robert T. Herres . . . . 13 Jun 1973-7 Sep 1973
Col. Vernon R. Huber . . . . 15 Sep 1973-20 Nov 1973
Col. Richard J. Smith . . . . 21 Nov 1973-1 Jan 1974
Col. Earl T. O'Laughlin . . . . 2 Jan 1974-21 Mar 1974
Col. Donald N. Webster . . . . 22 Mar 1974-1 May 1974
Col. Lavern E. Williams . . . . 2 May 1974-1 Jul 1974

315th Tactical Airlift Wing

Organized as 315th Air Commando Wing, Troop Carrier, on 8 March 1966 at Tan Son Nhut AB, RVN. Moved to Phan Rang AB, RVN, on 15 June 1967. Redesignated 315th Air Commando Wing on 1 August 1967. Redesignated 315th Tactical Airlift Wing on 1 January 1970.

Col. George L. Hannah, Jr. . . . . 8 Mar 1966-22 Jun 1966
Col. Robert T. Simpson . . . . 23 Jun 1966-18 Nov 1966

Col. Vernon W. Froehlich . . . . 19 Nov 1966-8 Aug 1967
Col. Bill M. Richardson . . . . 9 Aug 1967-19 Nov 1967
Col. Robert D. Brown . . . . 20 Nov 1967-7 Jun 1968
Col. Noble F. Greenhill, Jr. . . . . 8 Jun 1968-18 Jul 1968
Col. John W. Pauly . . . . 19 Jul 1968-9 Jun 1969
Col. Leslie J. Campbell, Jr. . . . . 10 Jun 1969-26 May 1970
Col. Charles S. Reed . . . . . . 27 May 1970-30 Jan 1971
Col. Kenneth T. Blood, Jr. . . . . 31 Jan 1971-18 Nov 1971
Col. Ray C. Staley . . . . 19 Nov 1971-31 Mar 1972

355th Tactical Fighter Wing

Based at Takhli AB, Thailand, 8 November 1965 to 10 December 1970. Replaced 6235th Tactical Fighter Wing. Inactivated 10 December 1970.

Col. William H. Holt . . . . 8 Nov 1965-3 Aug 1966
Col. Robert R. Scott . . . . 4 Aug 1966-1 Aug 1967
Col. John C. Giraudo . . . . 2 Aug 1967-29 Jun 1968
Col. Michael C. Horgan . . . . 30 Jun 1968-26 Jun 1969
Col. Heath Bottomly . . . . 27 Jun 1969-14 Jun 1970
Col. Clarence E. Anderson, Jr. . . . . 15 Jun 1970-10 Dec 1970

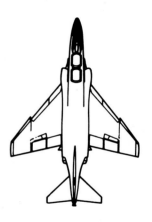

366th Tactical Fighter Wing

Arrived at Phan Rang AB, RVN 20 March 1966; moved to Da Nang 10 October 1966. On 27 June 1972 transferred to Takhli AB, Thailand. On 1 November 1972 transferred to Mt. Home AFB, ID.

Col. George S.
Weart .... 9 Oct 1966
Col. Allan P. Rankin .... 10 Oct 1966-
19 Mar 1967
Col. Jones E. Bolt..... 20 Mar 1967-
26 May 1967
Col. Robert W. .... 27 May 1967-
Maloy   18 Dec 1967
Col. Clifford H. .... 19 Dec 1967-
Meier   16 Jan 1968
Col. Paul C. Watson .... 17 Jan 1968-
2 Jan 1969
Col. (Later BG) John .... 3 Jan 1969-
W. Roberts   30 Sep 1969
Col. Joseph C. .... 1 Oct 1969-
Secino   18 Sep 1970
Col. Daniel C. .... 19 Sep 1970-
Perry   17 Feb 1971
Col. John R. .... 18 Feb 1971-
Spalding, Jr.   6 Jul 1971
Col. Julian D. .... 7 Jul 1971-
Sawyer   21 Mar 1972
Col. George W. .... 22 Mar 1972-
Rutter

374th Troop Carrier Wing

Organized 8 August 1966. Redesignated 374th Tactical Airlift Wing 1 August 1967. Based at Ching Chuan Kang AB, Taiwan.

Col. John R. Neal .... 8 Aug 1966-
15 Jun 1967
Col. Russell D. .... 16 Jun 1967-
Crane   24 Jan 1969
Col. (Later BG) Kelton ..... 25 Jan 1969-
M. Farris   10 Jul 1970
Col. Noble F. .... 11 Jul 1970-
Greenhill, Jr.   31 May 1971
Col. Andrew P. .... 1 Jun 1971-
Iosue   17 May 1973
Col. James I. .... 18 May 1973-
Baginski

376th Strategic Wing

Activated 1 April 1970 at Kadena AB, Okinawa. Replaced 4252d Strategic Wing.

Brig. Gen. Alan C........ 1 Apr 1970-
Edmunds   1 Sep 1970
Col. Jack A............. 2 Sep 1970-
Weyant   30 Aug 1972
Col. Dudley G........ 30 Aug 1972-
Kavanaugh   9 Sep 1974
Col. Raymond L........ 10 Sep 1974-
Horvath   30 Sep 1977

388th Tactical Fighter Wing

Organized at Korat AB, Thailand, 8 April 1966; replaced 6234th Tactical Fighter Wing.

Col. Monroe S. .... 8 Apr 1966-
Sams   Aug 1966
Brig. Gen William S. .... Aug 1966-
Chairsell   31 Jul 1967
Col. Edward B. .... 1 Aug 1967-
Burdett   17 Nov 1967
Col. Jack C. .... 18 Nov 1967-
Berger   21 Nov 1967
Col. Neil J. .... 22 Nov 1967-
Graham   18 Jan 1968
Col. Norman P. .... 19 Jan 1968-
Phillips   23 Jun 1968
Col. Paul P. .... 24 Jun 1968-
Douglas, Jr.   14 Dec 1968
Col. Allen K. .... 15 Dec 1968-
McDonald   10 Jun 1969
Col. John A. Nelson .... 11 Jun 1969-
4 Dec 1969
Col. James M. .... 5 Dec 1969-
Breedlove   29 Jun 1970
Col. Ivan H. .... 30 Jun 1970-
Dethman   31 Jul 1970
Col. Irby B. .... 1 Aug 1970-
Jarvis, Jr.   25 Jul 1971
Col. Webb .... 26 Jul 1971-
Thompson   14 Dec 1971
Col. Stanley M. .... 15 Dec 1971-
Umstead, Jr.   4 Aug 1972
Col. Richard E. .... 5 Aug 1972-
Merkling   24 Jan 1973

Col. Mele .... 25 Jan 1973-
   Vojvodich, Jr.   30 Jun 1973
Col. Robert K. .... 1 Jul 1973
   Crouch

405th Tactical Fighter Wing

Activated 9 April 1959 at Clark AB, Philippines.

Col. Edward P. .... 5 Feb 1968-
   McNeff   9 Jan 1970
Col. Walter J. .... 10 Jan 1970
   Brown   31 May 1971
Col. James E. .... 1 Jun 1971-
   Tilton   31 Dec 1971
Col. John R. Geyer .... 1 Jan 1972-
                     5 Jun 1972
Col. Henry C. .... 6 Jun 1972-
   Gordon   Mar 1973

432d Tactical Reconnaissance Wing

Organized at Udorn AB, Thailand, 18 September 1966.

Col. Robert W. .... 18 Sep 1966-
   Shick   17 Sep 1967
Col. Victor N. .... 18 Sep 1967-
   Cabas   3 Sep 1968
Col. Wendell L. .... 4 Sep 1968-
   Bevan, Jr.   6 Jun 1969
Col. Darrell S. .... 7 Jun 1969-
   Cramer   27 Jul 1970
Col. David S. .... 28 Jul 1970-
   Mellish   25 Nov 1970
Col. Lloyd R. .... 26 Nov 1970-
   Leavitt, Jr.   2 Apr 1971
Col. Lyle E. Mann .... 3 Apr 1971-
                   28 Oct 1971
Col. Charles A. .... 29 Oct 1971-
   Gabriel   14 Jun 1972
Col. Scott G. Smith .... 15 Jun 1972-
                 18 Mar 1973
Col. Robert W. .... 19 Mar 1973-
   Clement

460th Tactical Reconnaissance Wing

Organized at Tan Son Nhut AB, RVN, 18 February 1966. Inactivated 31 August 1971.

Col. Edward H. .... 18 Feb 1966-
   Taylor   Jan 1967
Col. Robert G. .... Jan 1967-
   Williams   20 Dec 1967
Brig. Gen. Robert J. .... 21 Dec 1967-
   Holbury   7 Jul 1968
Col. Leslie J. .... 8 Jul 1968-
   Westberg   27 May 1969
Col. Hal L. .... 28 May 1969-
   Fitzpatrick   20 Jun 1969
Col. Harry M. .... 21 Jun 1969-
   Chapman   30 Apr 1970
Col. James E. .... 1 May 1970-
   Tilton   14 Apr 1971
Col. Dale L. .... 15 Apr 1971-
   Flowers   31 Jul 1971
Col. Jerome F. .... 1 Aug 1971-
   O'Malley   31 Aug 1971

463d Troop Carrier Wing

Constituted 463d Troop Carrier Wing (M), 1 December 1952. Redesignated Troop Carrier Wing (Assault), 1 October 1962; Troop Carrier Wing (M), 15 May 1965; Troop Carrier Wing, 8 December 1965; 463d Tactical Airlift Wing. 1 August 1967. Inactivated at Clark AB, Philippines, 31 December 1971.

Col. Arthur E. .... 17 Oct 1964-
   Aenchbacher   6 Nov 1966
Col. Lopez J. .... 7 Nov 1966-
   Mantoux   6 Dec 1967
Col. Thomas A. .... 7 Dec 1967-
   Twomey   11 Apr 1968
Col. Marion F. .... 12 Apr 1968-
   Caruthers   8 May 1969
Col. Charles S. .... 9 May 1969-
   Wolfe   1 Jul 1970
Col. John R. Geyer .... 2 Jul 1970-
                 1 Sep 1971
Col. Stewart Young .... 2 Sep 1971-
               31 Dec 1971

483d Tactical Airlift Wing

Organized at Cam Ranh Bay AB, RVN, 15 October 1966, as 483d Troop Carrier Wing. Inactivated May 1972.

Col. Paul J. Mascot	4 Nov 1966-7 Oct 1967
Col. William H. Mason	8 Oct 1967-29 Sep 1968
Col. Wilbert Turk	30 Sep 1968-3 Sep 1969
Col. Keith L. Christensen	4 Sep 1969-22 Mar 1970
Col. Abbott C. Greenleaf	23 Mar 1970-10 Apr 1971
Col. Rodney H. Newbold	11 Apr 1971-24 Feb 1972
Col. Duane H. Erickson	25 Feb 1972-15 May 1972

553d Reconnaissance Wing

Based at Korat AB, Thailand, 31 October 1967. Inactivated 15 December 1970.

Col. Gus Weiser	31 Oct 1967-30 Jun 1968
Col. John W. Emis	1 Jul 1968-7 Jul 1968
Col. Henry L. Timmermans	8 Jul 1968-31 Jun 1969
Col. Ted H. Ostendorf	1 Jul 1969-6 Dec 1969
Col. John W. Mitchell	7 Dec 1969-10 Dec 1970
Col. Robert A. Sloan	11 Dec 1970-

633d Special Operations Wing

Organized at Nakhon Phanom AB, Thailand, 15 July 1968. Inactivated 15 March 1970.

Col. George P. Birdsong, Jr.	15 Jul 1968-24 Apr 1969
Col. Samuel D. Berman	25 Apr 1969-15 Mar 1970

3960th Strategic Wing

Activated at Andersen AFB, Guam 1 April 1955, assigned to 3d Air Division. Underwent short-lived changes of designation to Air Base Wing and Combat Support Group. Inactivated 31 March 1970, replaced by 43d Strategic Wing.

Col. Edward C. Unger	Apr 1964-21 Jul 1964
Col. Edward D. Gaitley, Jr.	22 Jul 1964-9 Jul 1965
Col. Joseph J. Semanek	10 Jul 1965-11 Jul 1967
Col. James M. Smith	12 Jul 1967-6 Jul 1969
Col. Lawrence E. Stephens	7 Jul 1969-31 Mar 1970

4133d Bombardment Wing (Prov)

Activated at Andersen AFB, Guam 1 February 1966. Turned over its combat mission to 43d Strategic Wing and inactivated on 1 July 1970.

Col. William T. Cumiskey	1 Feb 1966-31 Mar 1966
Col. Harold J. Whiteman	1 Apr 1966-12 Jun 1966
Col. Albert H. Schneider	13 Jun 1966-20 Sep 1966
Col. Willard A. Beauchamp	21 Sep 1966-27 Sep 1966
Col. Earl L. Johnson	28 Sep 1966-28 Feb 1967
Col. Mitchell A. Cobeaga	1 Mar 1967-30 Oct 1967
Col. Robert E. Brofft	31 Oct 1967-28 Mar 1968
Col. Madison M. McBrayer	29 Mar 1968-31 Aug 1968
Col. Robert E. Blauw	1 Sep 1968-25 Sep 1968
Col. Robert E. Brofft	26 Sep 1968-20 Mar 1969

Col. Robert E. . . . . 21 Mar 1969
   Blauw   19 Sep 1969
Col. Raymond P. . . . . . . 20 Sep 1969
   Lowman   29 Sep 1969
Col. Howard P. . . . . 30 Sep 1969
   McClain   24 Mar 1970
Col. Harold E. . . . . 25 Mar 1970
   Ottoway   Jun 1970
Col. William P. . . . . Jun 1970-
   Armstrong   1 Jul 1970

4252d Strategic Wing

Organized and activated, 12 January 1965, at Kadena AB, Okinawa. Inactivated, 1 April 1970. Replaced by 376th Strategic Wing.

Col. Holly W. . . . . 12 Jan 1965-
   Anderson (Acting)   17 Feb 1965
Col. (Later, Brig. Gen.) . . . 18 Feb 1965-
   Morgan S. Tyler, Jr.   18 Jul 1967
Col. (Later, Brig. Gen.) . . . . 19 Jul 1967-
   Eugene A. Stalzer   3 Aug 1969
Brig. Gen. Alan C. . . . . 4 Aug 1969-
   Edmunds   31 Mar 1970

4258th Strategic Wing

Activated at U-Tapao AB, Thailand, 2 June 1966 to 1 April 1970. Replaced by 307th Strategic Wing.

Capt. Ralph W. . . . . 2 Jun 1966-
   Ingram   20 Jul 1966
Col. John W. Farrar . . . . 21 Jul 1966-
                  30 Jun 1967
Col. Alex W. . . . . 1 Jul 1967-
   Talmant   4 Aug 1968
Brig. Gen. Richard . . . . 5 Aug 1968-
   M. Hoban   10 Jul 1969
Brig. Gen. Woodrow . . . . 11 Jul 1969-
   A. Abbott   31 Mar 1970

6234th Tactical Fighter Wing

Organized at Korat AB, Thailand, 5 April 1965. Discontinued 8 April 1966. Replaced by 388th Tactical Fighter Wing.

Col. William D. . . . . 5 Apr 1965-
   Ritchie   13 Dec 1965

Col. Monroe S. Sams . . . . . . 14 Dec 1965-
                  8 Apr 1966

6251st Tactical Fighter Wing

Organized at Bien Hoa AB, RVN, 8 July 1965. Discontinued 18 February 1966.

Col. Philip Brooks . . . . 8 Jul 1965-
                  20 Nov 1965

6252d Tactical Fighter Wing

Organized at Da Nang AB, RVN, 8 July 1965. Discontinued 8 April 1966.

Col. Franklin H. . . . . 8 Jul 1965-
   Scott   8 Apr 1966

3d Aero Rescue & Recovery Group

Organized 8 January 1966 at Tan Son Nhut AB, RVN.

Col. Arthur W. . . . . 8 Jan 1966-
   Beall   31 Oct 1966
Col. Albert P. . . . . 1 Nov 1966-
   Lovelady   5 Oct 1967
Col. Paul E. Leske . . . . 6 Oct 1967-
                  19 Sep 1968
Col. Hollon H. . . . . 20 Sep 1968-
   Bridges   16 Jun 1969
Col. Rayvon . . . . 17 Jun 1969-
   Burleson   16 Aug 1969
Col. Malcolm C. . . . . 17 Aug 1969-
   Frazee   16 Jul 1970
Col. Frederick V. . . . . 17 Jul 1970-
   Sohle, Jr.   17 Oct 1970
Col. George C. . . . . 18 Oct 1970-
   Pinyerd   Unk
Col. Warner A. . . . . Unk-
   Britton   12 Jan 1972
Col. Cecil N. . . . . 13 Jan 1972-
   Muirhead, Jr.   Unk
Col. Herbert R. . . . . Unk-
   Zehnder   16 Dec 1973
Col. Richard F. . . . . 17 Dec 1973-
   Burdett   Unk

315th Troop Carrier Group

Organized at Tan Son Nhut AB, RVN, 8 December 1962. Redesignated 315th Air Commando Group, 8 March 1965. Inactivated 8 March 1966.

Col. Thomas B. .... Mid-June 1964-
   Kennedy   14 Jun 1965
Col. David T. .... 15 Jul 1965-
   Fleming   22 Jun 1966
Col. George L. .... 23 Jun 1966-
   Hannah, Jr.   8 Mar 1966

504th Tactical Air Support Group

Organized at Bien Hoa AB, RVN, 8 December 1966. Inactivated at Tan Son Nhut, 15 March 1972.

Col. Carl E. Taylor .... 8 Dec 1966-
                         5 Mar 1967
Col. Clyde W. Strain .... 6 Mar 1967-
                     22 Nov 1967
Col. James M. .... 23 Nov 1967-
   Fogle   7 Mar 1968
Col. Robert L. .... 8 Mar 1968-
   Herman   3 May 1968
Col. William I. .... 4 May 1968-
   Williams   26 Mar 1969
Col. Andrew J. .... 27 Mar 1969-
   Chapman   11 Feb 1970
Col. Guy E. .... 12 Feb 1970-
   Hairston, Jr.   14 Oct 1970
Col. Andrew P. .... 15 Oct 1970-
   Iosue   23 Feb 1971
Col. Fleetwood .... 24 Feb 1971-
   Pride, Jr.   10 Jun 1971
Col. Patrick G. .... 11 Jun 1971-
   Long   15 Mar 1972

505th Tactical Control Group

Activated, 8 November 1965 at Tan Son Nhut AB, RVN. Inactivated 26 February 1973.

Col. Charles L. .... 8 Nov 1965-
   Daniel   Unk

Col. James L. Price .... Jan 1967-
                     15 May 1967
Col. Delbert R. .... 16 May 1967-
   Smyth   17 Apr 1968
Col. Emanuel A. .... 18 Apr 1968-
   Pelaez   6 Apr 1969
Col. Lewis R. Smith .... 7 Apr 1969-
                     27 Mar 1970
Col. William P. .... 28 Mar 1970-
   Lehman   23 Jul 1971
Col. Paul L. Park .... 24 Jul 1971-
                     Unk
Col. Robert A. .... Unk-
   Coffin   28 Feb 1973

552d Airborne Early Warning Task Force

552d Airborne Early Warning and Control Wing (Air Defense Command), designated Big Eye Task Force, 4 April 1965. Redesignated College Eye Task Force, 1 March 1967.

Col. Gus Weiser .... 4 Apr 1965-
                     30 Jun 1965
Col. James Q. .... 1 Jul 1965-
   McCall   27 Jul 1966
Lt. Col. Waldo W. .... 28 Jul 1966-
   Peck   14 Aug 1967
Lt. Col. Harold T. .... 15 Aug 1967-
   Knutty   25 Sep 1967
Col. Ross Davidson .... 26 Sep 1967-
                     12 Sep 1968
Col. James L. .... 13 Sep 1968-
   McCall   8 Sep 1969
Col. Floyd M. .... 9 Sep 1969-
   McAllister   22 Sep 1970
Col. Milton E. .... 23 Sep 1970-
   McEwen   (1972)
Lt. Col. Elliott .... (1972-1973)
   Powers
Col. Harold P. .... (1973)
   Knutty (Interim)
Col. Richard E. .... (1973)
   Williams

1964th Communications Group

Organized at Tan Son Nhut AB, RVN, 1 May 1962, as 1964th Communications

Squadron. Redesignated 1964th Communications Group on 1 October 1962. Moved to Ramstein AB, FRG, on 27 March 1973.

Lt. Col. Kenneth .... 1 May 1962-
  Keyte   19 Apr 1963
Lt. Col. John M. .... 20 Apr 1963-
  O'Reilly   27 Oct 1963
Col. Gilbert H. .... 28 Oct 1963-
  Bertie   1 Dec 1964
Col. Erwin F. .... 2 Dec 1964-
  Matelski   6 Jan 1965
Col. Lewis L. .... 7 Jan 1965-
  Bradley, Jr.   19 Jan 1966
Col. Charles Y. .... 20 Jan 1966-
  Shultz, Jr.   9 Dec 1966
Col. Louis A. .... 10 Dec 1966-
  Raeke, Jr. .... 31 Aug 1967
Col. James M. Neff .... 1 Sep 1967-
                               1 Aug 1968
Col. Howard R. .... 2 Aug 1968-
  McKendrick   8 Jul 1969
Col. Ivey J. Lewis .... 9 Jul 1969-
                               14 Mar 1970
Col. Joseph H. Weeks ..... 15 Mar 1970-
                               5 Jul 1970
Col. Robert E. .... 6 Jul 1970-
  Sadler   Apr 1971
Col. Forrest K. .... Apr 1971-
  Looney   1972

1974th Communications Group

Organized at Korat AB, Thailand, 1 November 1965. Moved to Udorn AB, Thailand, on 1 April 1968.

Lt. Col. Charles R. .... 1 Nov 1965-
  McMahan   20 Dec 1965
Lt. Col. Dirk Duys .... 21 Dec 1965-
                               28 Jan 1966
Col. George C. .... 29 Jan 1966-
  Kougias   6 Jan 1967
Lt. Col. Joseph A. .... 7 Jan 1967-
  Bailey   13 Jan 1967
Col. Albert J. Brown .... 14 Jan 1967-
                               11 Dec 1967
Col. Robert P. .... 12 Dec 1967-
  Baumann, Jr.   14 Nov 1968
Col. Joseph H. Weeks ..... 15 Nov 1968-
                               21 Aug 1969
Col. Robert A. .... 22 Aug 1969-
  Bourcy   24 Jul 1970
Col. John M. Bolger .... 25 Jul 1970-
                               6 Jul 1971
Col. William R. Yost .... 7 Jul 1971-
                               2 Jul 1972
Col. Theodore F. .... 3 Jul 1972-
  DeMuro   19 Jun 1973
Col. Richard A. .... 20 Jun 1973-
  Goldfogle   6 Jun 1974
Col. Ben P. Lee .... 7 Jun 1974-

Air Force Recipients of the Medal of Honor

On 10 March 1966, Major Bernard F. Fisher took off in an A-1E Skyraider from Pleiku, South Vietnam, to fly a routine bombing and strafing mission. Soon after taking off, he was diverted to Ashau where a Special Forces camp was under heavy attack by 2,000 North Vietnamese troops.

Arriving over the area, Major Fisher found four Skyraiders, which had also been diverted, circling over a dense cloud cover. He led his wing man and two of the other A-1E's down through a hole in the overcast. As they flew down a valley leading to the camp, the pilots were informed that it was being overrun by the enemy.

The A-1E's were making strafing runs against the attacking troops when one of the aircraft was hit by ground fire. The pilot crashlanded on the airstrip at the camp, and ran from his burning plane to seek refuge down an embankment. With enemy troops all around him, it appeared certain that he would be captured before a rescue helicopter could reach him.

Major Fisher, quickly realizing his fellow pilot's predicament, made a perilous landing on the airstrip. The steel planking runway was torn up and littered with debris. As he taxied under fire, Major Fisher saw the downed pilot dashing from his hiding place. The A-1E stopped and he clambered aboard. Dodging shell holes and debris, Major Fisher took off safely despite many hits on his aircraft by small arms fire.

The Medal of Honor awarded to Major Fisher for this daring rescue was presented to him by President Lyndon B. Johnson at the White House on 19 March 1967.

Major Bernard F. Fisher

Captain Hilliard A. Wilbanks

On 24 February 1967, Captain Hilliard A. Wilbanks, a forward air controller, was dispatched in an unarmed 0-1 Bird Dog aircraft to assist in an operation against enemy forces attacking near Dalat, South Vietnam.

While flying reconnaissance for a South Vietnamese Ranger Battalion, Captain Wilbanks discovered hostile units concealed on two hilltops. He promptly called in helicopter gunships by radio and alerted the Rangers advancing into the area.

Realizing that their ambush was being compromised, the enemy reacted with a barrage from mortars, machine guns, and automatic weapons. Captain Wilbanks received much of this fire as he marked the enemy positions with white phosphorus rockets for the gunships. He himself opened fire with an M-16 rifle that he carried in his plane when he spotted forward Ranger squads that were pinned down and about to be overrun. Firing out of the side window of his 0-1, Captain Wilbanks distracted the enemy troops and momentarily slowed their advance.

The outnumbered Rangers were afforded a chance to withdraw as the attackers diverted their fire against the low-flying aircraft. Despite the hits being scored on his plane, Captain Wilbanks persisted in covering the withdrawal. On his third pass, he was severely wounded and crashed in the battle area. The Rangers managed to rescue Captain Wilbanks from the wreckage of his plane, but he died while being evacuated to a hospital.

For his heroic support of the Rangers, Captain Wilbanks was posthumously awarded the Medal of Honor. The presentation was made to his widow by Secretary of the Air Force Harold Brown at the Pentagon, Washington, D.C. on 24 January 1968.

On 10 March 1967, Captain Dethlefsen flew on a mission against the steel works at Thai Nguyen some fifty miles north of Hanoi, North Vietnam, with three other F-105 Thunderchief pilots. Their task was to go in ahead of a strike force of fighter-bombers and attack the surface-to-air missile (SAM) complex, antiaircraft guns, and automatic weapons ringing the target.

On the first pass against these defenses the F-105 flight leader was shot down and his wing man was forced to withdraw with severe battle damage. Captain Dethlefsen decided to continue the attack on his own. As he maneuvered, he evaded an intercepting MIG-21 by flying into heavy enemy antiaircraft fire but his F-105 was seriously damaged.

Captain Dethlefsen nonetheless made repeated strikes with his wing man against the defense positions, even after they became obscured by the smoke and dust of the exploding bombs being dropped by the fighter-bombers. The bombing completed, the strike force withdrew but the two F-105's remained over the target.

Evading a second MIG, Captain Dethlefsen was diving through the obscuring haze to locate the missile complex when he was again hit by flak. Making a final dive bombing attack and a strafing run with 20-mm cannon fire, Captain Dethlefsen effectively destroyed two missile sites before leaving for home in his battered F-105

For this action, Captain Dethlefsen was awarded the Medal of Honor. The presentation was made at the White House by President Lyndon B. Johnson on 1 February 1968.

Captain Merlyn H. Dethlefsen

Major Leo K. Thorsness

On 19 April 1967, Major Leo K. Thorsness piloted an F-105 Thunderchief on a combat mission over North Vietnam. He was flying with a strike force sent out to suppress surface-to-air missile (SAM) sites.

Acting with his electronic warfare officer, Major Thorsness first detected one site as it was about to launch an attack and destroyed it with a Shrike missile. Almost immediately, another site was discovered. Major Thorsness flew through heavy antiaircraft fire to score direct hits on the site with cluster bombs.

On this second strike Major Thorsness' wingman was hit and the two crew members bailed out. As he circled the descending parachutes, a MIG-17 appeared in the area. Major Thorsness promptly dived but his shots missed the enemy fighter. Attacking again, he closed rapidly to pour 20-mm cannon fire into the MIG. Just as he pulled up sharply to avoid a collision, he saw the fighter go into a tight spin and crash.

Major Thorsness then had to leave because he was low on fuel. While searching for a KC-135 Stratotanker, he learned from the Search and Rescue Center that two helicopters were waiting for an escort before attempting a rescue of the downed crew. Major Thorsness flew back alone, spotting four MIG-17's as he neared the bailout area. He immediately attacked and damaged one of the enemy aircraft with a long burst of cannon fire. He drew the others away by diving and flying close to the ground until they gave up pursuit.

Although now critically short of fuel, Major Thorsness advised another F-105 to fly to the nearest tanker when the crew reported that it would have to bail out unless their aircraft could be quickly refueled. He then diverted to a forward base where he landed with only a 10-minute supply of fuel remaining.

Major Thorsness was awarded the Medal of Honor for his deeds of extraordinary heroism on this mission. Only 11 days later he was shot down over North Vietnam and held prisoner for nearly 6 years. Following his release, Major Thorsness received this highest decoration for valor from President Richard M. Nixon at the White House on 15 October 1973.

Shortly before midnight on November 8, 1967, Captain Gerald O. Young, the commander of a HH-3E rescue helicopter, was dispatched to evacuate the survivors of a U.S. Army reconnaissance team. The soldiers were surrounded and about to be captured in enemy-held territory in the Laotian Panhandle. Two helicopters had already been lost trying to rescue them.

Captain Young and his crew were flying as backup for another helicopter on this night operation. The first aircraft managed to pick up three members of the team before extensive battle damage forced it to withdraw. The commander of the craft advised Captain Young that intense enemy fire made the rescue of two soldiers left behind all but impossible. Accompanying gunships were also running low on fuel and ammunition.

Intent on completing the evacuation, Captain Young guided his helicopter down into the flare-lit darkness, touching down on a slope not far from the two soliders. Both wounded, they were loaded aboard under heavy attack with enemy troops closing in. As it moved forward for takeoff, the helicopter was fired on at point blank range. It plunged downward and crashed in flames in an upside down position.

Captain Young dropped out of a cockpit window and rolled down the slope, his parachute afire. Although badly burned, he beat out the flames and gave aid to another crew member, a sergeant, who had also escaped. He then tried to reach the burning helicopter but was driven back by the intense heat. When enemy troops approached the crash scene, he led them away from the wounded sergeant hidden in the underbrush.

At dawn, Captain Young reached a clearing and helped to pinpoint his

Captain Gerald O. Young

position for searching aircraft with flares and radio signals, but he broke contact when he realized that he was being used as bait by enemy gunners in the area. He again concealed himself in the dense foliage and continued to evade throughout the day despite the mounting pain of his burns. After 17 hours, Captain Young was finally rescued by a helicopter that he attracted with his radio and by firing tracers with his revolver. He then immediately informed his rescuers of the position of his fellow crew member.

For his heroism in this action, Captain Young was awarded the Medal of Honor. It was presented to him by President Lyndon B. Johnson on 14 May 1968 at the Pentagon, Washington, D.C.

Lieutenant Colonel Joe M. Jackson

On 12 May 1968, Lieutenant Colonel Joe M. Jackson, commander of an unarmed C-123 transport aircraft, flew from Da Nang to Kham Duc, South Vietnam, on an emergency mission. A Special Forces camp at Kham Duc was being overrun by enemy forces. They had taken the forward outpost and were in complete control of the airstrip. Located in a valley, the airstrip was surrounded on all sides by mountainous terrain.

While orbiting over the battle area Colonel Jackson learned by radio that in the evacuation of the camp by air a three-man Combat Control Team had inadvertently been left behind. Another C-123 transport was ahead of Colonel Jackson in the traffic pattern. The aircraft landed successfully on the airstrip littered with debris, including a wrecked helicopter, but failed to evacuate the team.

Colonel Jackson then descended rapidly from 9,000 feet and made an assault landing on the strip under heavy enemy fire. After he stopped, a rocket fell in front of the transport. A dud, it bounced harmlessly toward the nose of the plane without exploding. Colonel Jackson had landed near the spot where the three men had been reported to be hiding. With the team safely on board, he quickly took off under a mortar barrage and intense automatic weapons fire from the surrounding hills. After landing at Da Nang the crew found that not a single bullet had touched their aircraft during the enire flight.

Colonel Jackson was awarded the Medal of Honor for rescuing the three-man team. The presentation was made by President Lyndon B. Johnson at the White House on 16 January 1969.

On 1 September 1968 Lieutenant Colonel William A. Jones, III, led a flight of four A-1H Skyraider aircraft on an escort mission. The flight was accompanying two helicopters sent out to rescue the pilot of an F-4 Phantom downed about twenty miles northwest of Dong Hoi, North Vietnam.

Arriving over the area, Colonel Jones made several low passes across a valley to find the pilot and pinpoint enemy gun positions. On one pass he felt an explosion beneath his aircraft and his cockpit was filled with smoke. After the smoke cleared, he continued his search and finally spotted the downed pilot near a towering rock formation. Enemy gunners occupying a position near the top of the formation opened fire on the propeller-driven Skyraider.

Lieutenant Colonel William A. Jones, III

Colonel Jones realized that the gun position had to be destroyed before a rescue could be made and that strikes against it would endanger the survivor unless his location was known. He himself attacked with cannon and rocket fire while relaying the pilot's location by radio. While making his second pass, Colonel Jones' aircraft was hit and his cockpit was set ablaze. He sought to eject but the damaged extraction system only jettisoned the canopy without pulling him from the cockpit. At the same time his transmissions to the rescue force were being blocked by repeated calls from other aircraft that he bail out.

Before the fire died out Colonel Jones was badly burned and his radio transmitters were disabled. He chose to return to base to report the downed pilot's exact location. Despite his se-

vere burns he landed his damaged aircraft safely, and insisted on passing on the vital information before receiving medical treatment. The downed pilot was rescued later that day.

The Medal of Honor was awarded to Colonel Jones for his selfless heroism, but he died in an aircraft accident in the United States before it could be presented to him. His widow received the decoration from President Richard M. Nixon at the White House on 6 August 1970.

First Lieutenant James P. Fleming

On 26 November 1968, First Lieutenant James P. Fleming and four other UH-1F helicopter pilots were returning to their base at Duc Co, South Vietnam, for refueling and rearming when an emergency call for help was received from a Special Forces reconnaissance team.

The home bound force—two gunships and three transport helicopters—immediately changed course and sped to the area without refueling. The six-man Special Forces team was pinned down by a large, hostile force not far from a river bank. As the gunships descended to attack the enemy positions, one was hit and downed. The remaining gunship made several passes, firing away with its miniguns, but the intense return fire from enemy machine guns continued. Low on fuel, the helicopters were being forced to leave and return to base.

Lieutenant Fleming, piloting the only remaining transport helicopter, descended over the river to evacuate the team. Unable to land because of the dense foliage, he hovered just above the river with his landing skids braced against the bank. The lone gunship continued its strafing runs, but heavy enemy fire prevented the team from reaching the helicopter. The leader advised Lieutenant Fleming by radio to withdraw.

After pulling away, Lieutenant Fleming decided to make another rescue attempt before completely exhausting his fuel. He dropped down to the same spot and found that the team had managed to move closer to the river bank. The men dashed out and clambered aboard as bullets pierced the air, some smashing into the helicopter. The rescue craft and the gunship then returned safely to Duc Co, arriving with their fuel tanks nearly empty.

For this miraculous rescue, in which not a single life was lost, Lieutenant Fleming was awarded the Medal of Honor. He received this highest decoration for valor at the White House from President Richard M. Nixon on 14 May 1970.

On 24 February 1969, Airman First Class John L. Levitow flew on a combat air patrol over South Vietnam as the loadmaster of an AC-47 Dragonship. The gunship was patrolling in the vicinity of Tan Son Nhut, when the Army Post at nearby Long Binh came under mortar attack. The aircraft was diverted to aid in the defense of the post.

Firing its miniguns at the enemy, the gunship knocked out two mortar positions, but further firings were observed a few kilometers away. As the AC-47 flew in that direction, a mortar shell fell on the top of its right wing. A brilliant explosion shook the aircraft violently and the fuselage was riddled by thousands of shell fragments.

Airman Levitow and another crew member were standing near the open cargo door at that moment, dropping parachute illumination flares. The explosion knocked both of them to the floor, and a flare that they were handling was tossed inside the cargo compartment. Spewing toxic smoke, the activated magnesium flare was due to separate explosively from its canister and ignite within seconds.

Although stunned and wounded by shrapnel, Airman Levitow moved forward in the compartment and flung himself on the flare to keep it from rolling. He then dragged himself and the flare back toward the cargo door and tossed it out. The flare ignited just as it cleared the aircraft.

Airman Levitow was awarded the Medal of Honor for his selfless heroism that saved his fellow crew members and the gunship. The presentation was made by President Richard M. Nixon at the White House on 14 May 1970.

Airman First Class John L. Levitow

Captain Steven L. Bennett

On 29 June 1972, Captain Steven L. Bennett, a forward air controller, was flying an OV-10 Bronco on an artillery adjustment mission near Quang Tri City, South Vietnam. A Marine gunfire spotter occupied the rear seat of the lightly armed reconnaissance aircraft.

After controlling gunfire from U.S. naval vessels off shore and directing air strikes against enemy positions for approximately 3 hours, Captain Bennett received an urgent call for assistance. A small South Vietnamese unit was about to be attacked by a much larger enemy force. Without immediate help, the unit was certain to be overrun. Unfortunately, there were no friendly fighters left in the area, and supporting naval gunfire would have endangered the South Vietnamese.

They were between the coast and the enemy.

Captain Bennett decided to strafe the advancing soldiers. Since they were North Vietnamese regulars, equipped with heat-seeking SAM 7 missiles, the risks in making a low-level attack were great. Captain Bennett nonetheless zoomed down and opened fire with his four small machine guns. The troops scattered and began to fall back under repeated strafing.

As the twin-boomed Bronco pulled up from its fifth attack, a missile rose up from behind and struck the plane's left engine. The explosion set the engine on fire and knocked the left landing gear from its stowed position, leaving it hanging down. The canopies over the two airmen were pierced by fragments.

Captain Bennett veered southward to find a field for an emergency landing. As the fire in the engine continued to spread, he was urged by the pilot of an escorting OV-10 to eject. The wing was in danger of exploding. He then learned that his observer's parachute had been shredded by fragments in the explosion.

Captain Bennett elected to ditch in the Gulf of Tonkin, although he knew that his cockpit area would very likely break up on impact. No pilot had ever survived an OV-10 ditching. As he touched down, the extended landing gear dug into the water. The Bronco spun to the left and flipped over nose down into the sea. His Marine companion managed to escape, but Captain Bennett, trapped in his smashed cockpit, sank with the plane. His body was recovered the next day.

For sacrificing his life, Captain Bennett was posthumously awarded the Medal of Honor. The decoration was presented to his widow by Vice President Gerald R. Ford on 8 August 1974.

On 26 August 1967, Major Day was forced to eject from his aircraft over North Vietnam when it was hit by ground fire. His right arm was broken in three places, and his left knee was badly sprained. He was immediately captured by hostile forces and taken to a prison camp where he was interrogated and severely tortured. After causing the guards to relax their vigilance, Major Day escaped into the jungle and began the trek toward South Vietnam. Despite injuries inflicted by fragments of a bomb or rocket, he continued southward surviving on only a few berries and uncooked frogs. He successfully evaded enemy patrols and reached the Ben Hai River where he encountered United States artillery barrages. With the aid of a bamboo log float, Major Day swam across the river and entered the demilitarized zone.

Major George E. Day

Due to delirium, he lost his sense of direction and wandered aimlessly for several days. After a number of unsuccessful attempts to signal United States aircraft, he was ambushed and recaptured by the Viet Cong, sustaining gunshot wounds to his left hand and thigh. He was returned to the prison from which he had escaped and later was moved to Hanoi after giving his captors false information to questions put before him. Physically, Major Day was totally debilitated and unable to perform even the simplest task for himself. Despite his many injuries, he continued to offer maximum resistance. His personal bravery in the face of deadly enemy pressure was significant in saving the lives of fellow aviators who were still flying against the enemy.

Major Day continued in internment by the North Vietnamese until his release on 14 March 1973. He was awarded the Medal of Honor for his personal bravery by President Gerald R. Ford on 4 March 1976.

Captain Lance P. Sijan

On 9 November 1967, while on a flight over North Vietnam, Captain Sijan ejected from his disabled aircraft and successfully evaded capture for more than 6 weeks. During this time, he was seriously injured and suffered from shock and extreme weight loss due to lack of food. After being captured by North Vietnamese soldiers, Captain Sijan was taken to a holding point for subsequent transfer to a Prisoner of War camp. In his emaciated and crippled condition, he overpowered one of his guards and crawled into the jungle, only to be recaptured after several hours. He was then transferred to another prison camp where he was kept in solitary confinement and interrogated at length.

During his interrogation, he was severely tortured; however, he did not divulge any information to his captors. Captain Sijan lapsed into delirium and was placed in the care of another prisoner, Lieutenant Colonel Robert Craner, to care for him. During Captain Sijan's intermittent periods of consciousness until his death, he never complained of his physical condition and, on several occasions, spoke of future escape attempts. Due to his extreme weakness, adverse living conditions, insufficient clothing, and an inadequate diet, Captain Sijan contracted pneumonia on 18 January 1968. Removed from his cell on 21 January 1968, he died at the Hoa Lo prison camp, as reported by his Vietnamese captors.

The Medal of Honor was presented to his parents on 4 March 1976 by President Gerald R. Ford.

Vietnam War Aces

Capt. Charles D. DeBellevue,
USAF
6

Lt. Randy Cunningham,
USN
5

Lt. William Driscoll,
USN
5

Capt. Jeffrey S. Feinstein,
USAF
5

Capt. Richard S. Ritchie,
USAF
5

USAF Air Munitions Consumption WW II, Korea, and Southeast Asia

(Cumulative through period shown)

Million Tons

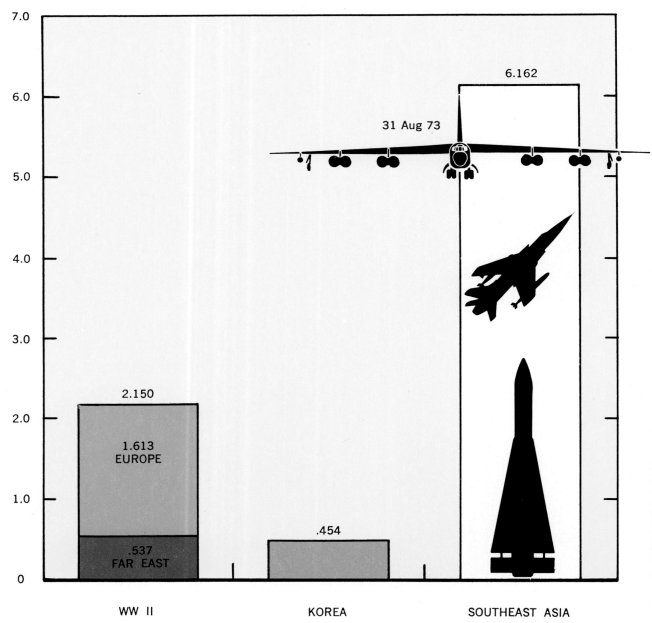

Source: USAF Southeast Asia Summary, 28 Sep. 73, p. 18

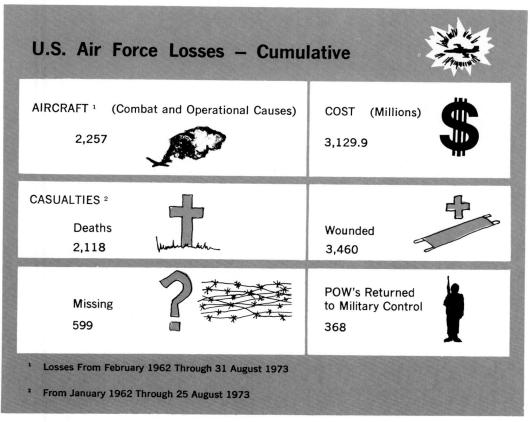

U.S. Air Force Losses — Cumulative

AIRCRAFT [1] (Combat and Operational Causes)	COST (Millions)
2,257	3,129.9

CASUALTIES [2]	
Deaths 2,118	Wounded 3,460
Missing 599	POW's Returned to Military Control 368

[1] Losses From February 1962 Through 31 August 1973

[2] From January 1962 Through 25 August 1973

Sources: USAF Southeast Asia Summary, 28 Sep 73, p. 18
Southeast Asia Review, Final Issue, 31 May 74, pp. 12, 25

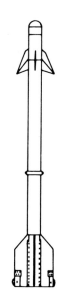

Glossary of Terms and Abbreviations

AAA	antiaircraft artillery	FAC	forward air controller
AB	air base		
AD	air division	GPES	Ground Proximity Extraction System
ADVON	advanced echelon		
AFB	Air Force Base		
AFLC	Air Force Logistics Command	I&C	installation and checkout
AFROTC	Air Force Reserve Officer Training Corps	ICC	International Control Commission
AFSC	Air Force Systems Command	IFF/SIF	Identification Friend or Foe/ Selective Identification Feature
AID	Agency for International Development		
ALCC	Airlift Control Center		
ALO	air liaison officer	JCS	Joint Chiefs of Staff (U.S.)
ANG	Air National Guard	JGS	Joint General Staff (South Vietnamese)
AOC	Air Operations Center		
APOE	Aerial Port of Embarkation		
ARVN	Army of Republic of South Vietnam	LAPES	Low-Altitude Parachute Extraction System
ATRC	air traffic regulation center	LBR	local base rescue
		LCM	landing craft, medium
BLU	bomb, live unit	LOC	line of communication
		LORAN	long-range electronic navigation
CAP	combat air patrol		
CBU	cluster bomb unit (anti-personnel weapon)	LS	Lima Site - Temporary aircraft landing sites in Laos
CCC	Combat Control Center	LZ	landing zone
CCK	Ching Chuan Kang (AB, Taiwan)		
CCTW	combat crew training wing	MAAG	Military Assistance Advisory Group (U.S.)
CIA	Central Intelligence Agency (U.S.)	MACV	Military Assistance Command, Vietnam (U.S.)
CIDG	Civilian Irregular Defense Group	MAF	Marine Amphibious Force
		MAC	Military Airlift Command
CINCPAC	Commander in Chief, Pacific	MSTS	Military Sea Transportation Service
CINCPACAF	Commander in Chief, Pacific Air Forces		
COSVN	Central Office for South Vietnam (Vietnamese Communist headquarters)	NCP	National Campaign Plan (South Vietnamese)
		NLF	National Front for the Liberation of Vietnam
CRAF	Civil Reserve Air Fleet		
CRP	control and reporting post	NORS	not operationally ready, supply
CSAS	Common Service Airlift System	NSC	National Security Council (U.S.)
CTZ	Corps Tactical Zone		
DASC	Direct Air Support Center	NVA	North Vietnamese Army
DMZ	demilitarized zone	NVAF	North Vietnamese Air Force
ECM	electronic countermeasure	OJT	on-the-job training
ELF	electronic location finder	OSD	Office of Secretary of Defense
EW	electronic warfare	OTS	Officer Training School

PACAF	Pacific Air Force	USAF	United States Air Force
PACOM	Pacific Command	USAID	United States Agency for International Development
PMEL	Precision Measurement Equipment Laboratory	USMACV	U.S. Military Assistance Command, Vietnam
POW	prisoner of war		
Prime Beef	base engineering emergency force	VNAF	Vietnamese Air Force (South Vietnam)
R&R	rest and recuperation		
RAM	rapid area maintenance		
RAPCON	radar approach control		
RASS	rapid area supply support		
RATS	rapid area transportation support		
Recce (Recon)	reconnaissance		
Red Horse	rapid engineering deployment and heavy operational repair squadron, engineering		
RESCAP	rescue combat air patrol		
RLAF	Royal Laotian Air Force		
RLG	Royal Laotian Government		
RTU	replacement training unit		
RVNAF	Republic of Vietnam Armed Forces		
SAC	Strategic Air Command		
SAM	surface-to-air missile		
SAR	search and rescue		
SARTAF	SAR Task Force		
SAW	special air warfare		
SEA	Southeast Asia		
SEAAS	Southeast Asia Airlift System		
SEAITACS	Southeast Asia Integrated Tactical Air Control System		
SEATO	Southeast Asia Treaty Organization		
TAC	Tactical Air Command		
tac	tactical		
TACC	Tactical Air Control Center		
TACC(NS)	Tactical Air Control Center, North Sector		
TACC(SS)	Tactical Air Control Center, South Sector		
TACS	Tactical Air Control System		
TDY	temporary duty		
TFW	tactical fighter wing		
TTF	Tanker Task Force		
USA	United States Army		

Photo Credits

The Office of Air Force History is indebted to various government agencies, private organizations, and individuals who kindly provided photographs to illustrate this book. They include: the USAF Still Photo Depository, 1361st Audiovisual Squadron, Aerospace Audio-Visual Service, Military Airlift Command; the White House, U.S. Information Agency, U.S. Army, Navy, and Marine Corps; Maj. Thomas A. Dwelle, Capt. Keith Grimes, Donald W. Randle, Brig. Gen. A.R. Brownfield (USA, ret.), Maj. Donald J. Kutyna, and others. The Office is particularly indebted to the National Geographic Society for permission to use several color and black and white photos dealing with the war. The bold face numbers listed below refer to pages, numbers within parenthesis indicate photo numbers, with the source identified, such as AF (Air Force), USA (U.S. Army), U.S. Marines, etc.

6 (1-2), Ministere des Armées "AIR"; (3), AF; **7** (4-5, 7), AF; (6), DD Eisenhower Library; **8**, source unk; **9**, AF; **10**, UPI; **11**, JFK Library; **12-13**, AF; **14**, AF; **22-23**, AF; **25**, source unk; **26** (1), AF, (2), Dwelle; **27**, AF; **30**, (1), AF, (2), U.S. Army, (3) AF Art Collection; **31**, (4) Dwelle; (5-7), AF; **33**, Dwelle; **36**, AF; **38**, (1), U.S. Army; (2), AF; (3) N.G.S.; **39** (1-3), AF; **40**, AF; **41**, source unk; **42** (1-3), U.S. Army; (2), AF; **43**, (4), U.S. Army, (5), USIA; (6-8), AF; **44**, source unk; **51**, AF; **54**, (1), AF, (2), AF Art Collection; **55**, (3-5), AF; **58**, (1), U.S. Army, (2) source unk; (3), Dwelle; **59**, (4) U.S. Marines, (5) source unk, (6), U.S. Army; (7-8), U.S. Army; **60**, AF; **62**, (1), U.S. Army, (2), AF, (3), Dwelle; **63**, (4) source unk; (5-7), AF; **64**, source unk; **65**, AF; **66** (1), AF Art Collection, (2), U.S. Army; (3), AF; **67**, (5-6), U.S. Army; (7-8), AF; **68**, AF; **71**, Kutyna; **72**, (1-3), AF; **73**, (4-7), AF; **74**, AF; **75**; **76**, (1-2), Kutyna; (3), AF, (4), AF Art Collection; **77**, (5-10), AF; **80**, (1-2), AF; **81**, (3-4), AF; **82**, AF; **83**, AF; **84**, (1-3), AF; **85**, (4-8), AF; **86**, (1-4), AF; **87**, (5-7), AF; **88-89**, AF; **90**, (1-2). source unk; (3-5), AF; **91**, (6-8), AF; **92**, AF; **94**, AF, (1-5), AF; **97**, (1-4), AF; **98**, (1-4), AF; **99, 100**, AF; **102**, (1), AF Art Collection; (2), AF,; **103** (3-4), AF; **106**, AF; **107**, AF; **110**, (1), source unk, (2), U.S. Army, (3), AF; **111**, (4), source unk; (5), source unk; (6), AF; **112**, AF; **116**, (1-8), AF, **117**, (3-4), AF; **118** , AF; **119**, AF; **120**, AF; **124**, (1, Capt Ray De Arrigunaga, (2) Lt Col Billy Keeler; (3), Keeler; **125**, (4), AF, (5-6), Capt Donald W. Randle; (7), Keeler; **128**, (1-2), Capt Keith Grimes; **129**, (3-4), Keeler; (5), N.G.S.; (6) Col. John S. Wood, Jr.; (7), DOD; (8) Arrigunaga; **132**, Keeler; (1-2); **133**, Keeler; **134**, Grimes; **135**, N.G.S.; (4), Keeler; (5), Arrigunaga; **136**, AF; **138** (1-2), U.S. Army, (3) AF; **144-145**, U.S. Army; **146**, (1), ARVN; (2), U.S. Army; (3) source unk; (4) source unk; **147**, (1) source unk; **148**, AF; **152-153**, AF; **154-155**, AF; **158-159**, AF; **163-164** (1-7), AF; (8) U.S. Army; **164-165**, AF; **168**, AF; **172**, (1-4, 7), AF; (5), N.G.S.; **173** (8-10), AF; **176**, AF; **177**, AF; **178** (1-3) AF; **179** (4-8), AF; **180**, AF; **181** (2-3), AF; (4), U.S. Army; **182-183** (1-3), AF; **184**, AF; **186**, AF; **188**, AF; **191**, AF; **193-194**, AF; **195**, AF; **196**, AF; **197**, AF; **198-199**, AF; **200**, AF; **202-203**, AF; **206**, AF; **208**, AF; **209**, AF; **210**, AF; **214** (1-2), AF; (3) Teledyne Ryan Aeronautical; **215**, (4), Teledyne; (4-9), AF; **220**, AF; **222**, N.G.S.; **224**, AF; **225**, AF; **229**, AF; **230-231**, AF; **232**, AF; **234**, AF; **236**, AF; **237**, AF; **240**, (1-2), AF, (3) AF Art Collection; **241**, AF; **242-243**, AF; **244**, AF; **246**, AF; **247**, AF; **248**, AF; **249**, AF; **252**, (1-2), AF; (3) Dwelle; **253**, AF; **254**, AF; **255** (1-2), AF; **256**, AF; **260**, AF; **261**, AF; **266-267**, AF; **269**, AF; **270**, AF; **274**, AF; **276**, AF; **277**, AF; **278**, AF; **279**, (1-2), AF; **280** (3), AF; (4), Sgt. Arlin J. Frerich; **281**, AF; **282**, AF; **286-287**, AF; **290-291**, AF; **295**, AF; **296**, AF; **297**, AF; **300-301**, AF; **304-305**,

The Scenes shown on these pages were taken in Southeast Asia by U.S. Air Force photographers serving with the 1365th Photo Squadron, 600th Photo Squadron, and 601st Photo Squadron, all assigned to the Air Force's Aerospace Audio-Visual Service, Military Airlift Command.

Index

Radar systems and nets
ARVN: 15, 225
enemy stikes against: 126
strikes against: 70, 74 - 75, 79, 98
in Thailand: 223, 225
U.S.: 11, 15, 71, 75, 105, 108, 118 - 119, 151, 157, 175, 182, 223 -233, 298
Radio sets: 15, 239
Railways
enemy construction and repair: 82, 219
strikes against: 3, 70, 74, 79 - 83, 86, 95, 98, 155 - 166, 216
Ranch Hand detachment: 12, 245
Randolph Air Force Base: 298 - 300, 303 - 304
Ranger units, ARVN: 19 - 20, 58, 166
Rangoon: 3
Rapid Area Maintenance (RAM) teams: 250
Rapid Area Supply Support (RASS): 250
Rapid Area Transportation (RATS) teams: 251
Rapid Engineer Deployable, Heavy Operations Repair Squadrons, Engineer (Red Horse): 251 - 255
Ratley, Lonnie O.: 147
Raven detachment: 123, 130
Recoilless rifle fire assaults: 265
Recoilless rifle fire assaults, enemy: 143, 262
Reconnaissance, ground
enemy: 258
U.S.: 45, 51, 104 - 108, 115, 150
Reconnaissance missions, aerial: 12 - 13, 17 - 18, 24, 32, 47, 57, 61, 70 - 71, 79, 83, 89, 92, 101, 104 - 105, 109, 114, 119, 130, 135, 208, 211 - 221, 262
Reconnaissance Technical Squadron, 13th: 212
Reconnaissance Wing, 553d: 350
Recruiting programs: 303, 306
Red Ball Express: 196
Red Horse (Rapid Engineer Deployable, Heavy Operations Repair Squadrons, Engineer): 251 - 255
Refrigeration facilities: 273
Refueling operations and techniques: 71, 104, 114, 149, 156, 161, 201 - 209, 226, 239, 241
Refugees, evacuation and care of: 125, 133, 176, 293, 295. See also Resettlement programs
Regional Forces, RVN: 258
Repair systems and forces. See Maintenance, supply and support forces
Replacements
pilots: 75
training: 298, 302 -306
Republic of China: 3 - 4, 44
Republic of Korea: 40, 42, 44, 197, 206, 250
Republic of Vietnam
air operations over: 217 - 221
airspace control: 232
armed forces buildup: 309
emigration from North: 8, 101
enemy infiltration and assaults: 34, 51 - 67, 69, 83 - 88, 91 - 99, 109, 207, 221
first major U.S. combat action: 41
independence proclaimed: 8
manpower deployments and strength in, USAF: 5, 13, 18 - 19, 21, 40 - 41, 52, 64, 169, 235, 251
physicians, ratio of: 285
political crises: 25 - 28, 34 - 35
troop rotation program, U.S.: 170, 297
troop units in, deployments and withdrawals: 28, 40, 56, 61 - 67, 109, 197 - 198, 297, 309, 315 - 318, 339
troop units in, periodic strength: 40, 44, 49, 52, 307
work force: 295
Republic of Vietnam Air Force
Air Force details to: 18
air operations by: 69 - 70, 114 - 119, 142 - 147, 169, 221, 309, 314, 319

aircraft deployments to, inventories and withdrawals: 9, 11 - 13, 16 - 17, 25, 27 - 29, 32, 34, 40, 44, 64 - 65, 94, 119, 161, 169 - 171, 185, 187 - 188, 201, 207 - 208, 211, 217, 221, 223, 226 - 227, 236, 245, 309, 311, 314 - 315, 317, 319
in air-ground operations: 44, 114 - 119
in civic actions: 293-294
combat efficiency: 65
command, control and coordination : 263
expansion and organization: 11, 18 - 19, 29, 32, 64, 169, 185, 310, 318 - 319
personnel strength, periodic: 309 - 310, 315, 318 - 319
pilot training: 15, 27, 169, 191, 309-319
sorties, number flown: 25, 64-65
security measures: 257
training programs: 4, 8 - 9, 11, 16 - 17, 64, 309 - 319
1st Fighter Squadron: 15
2d Fighter Squadron: 15
516th Fighter Squadron: 30, 315
520th Fighter Squadron: 315
522d Fighter Squadron: 314
524th Fighter Squadron: 315
716th Reconnaissance Squadron: 18
Republic of Vietnam Army
airborne units: 268
combat efficiency: 24, 41, 268
combat operations: 18 - 25, 114 - 119, 150
establishment: 8
expansion, organization and strength: 8, 11, 18, 27
leadership and morale status: 24 - 25, 27, 37, 94, 115
materiel losses: 27, 64, 116
1st Division: 21, 161
2d Division: 21
5th Division: 16, 24, 28, 45
7th Division: 20, 24
9th Division: 24, 27, 35
21st Division: 19, 25 - 27
22d Division: 24
25th Division: 24, 151
32d Ranger Battalion: 28
33d Ranger Battalion: 35
Republic of Vietnam Marine Corps: 24, 26, 35, 58
Republic of Vietnam Navy: 18, 143
Rescue Combat Air Patrol (RESCAP): 237
Rescue missions. See Search-and-rescue missions
Reserve components: 109, 187, 283, 298, 314
Reserve Officers Training Corps: 306
Resettlement programs: 295. See also Refugees, evacuation and care of
Respiratory ailments: 272
Rest and recuperation leaves: 197
Ridgely, Edward, USA: 42
Risner, Robinson: 321
Ritchie, Richard S.: 95, 97
Road systems
construction and repair: 251, 288
enemy construction and repair: 79, 82, 92, 117, 131, 216, 219
strikes against: 74, 83, 104 - 105, 109 - 112, 142, 216
Roberts, Thomas S.: 75
Robinson, Robert: 287
Roca, Blas: 10
Rocket assaults: 55
Rocket assaults, enemy: 52, 58, 63, 125, 143, 156, 258, 261, 264 - 265
Rocket launchers, enemy: 261
Rocket ridge: 164
Rocket Watch: 262
Rockets: 254
Rogers, William: 323

Rolling Thunder operation: 69-71, 74-89, 92, 101, 123, 213, 297
Rosecrans, R.P., Jr.: 121
Roosevelt, Franklin D.: 3
Rostow, Walt W.: 12
Rotation program: 170, 297
Route 1: 268
Route 4: 127
Route 5: 127
Route 7: 127, 130 - 131
Route 9: 114, 157
Route 12: 101, 105
Route 14: 164
Route 19: 40
Route 23: 101, 105
Route 61: 127
Route 121: 101
Route 911: 105
Route packages: 79, 108, 225
Routledge, Eric M.: 229
Rumble, Wesley L.: 336
Ruses: 82
Rusk, Dean: 140. See also State, Department of
Russell, Richard B.: 326
Russia. See Soviet Union
Ryan, John D.: 39, 247. See also Chief of Staff, USAF

S

Sabotage, enemy: 258 - 259
Safety measures: 233
Sage, Rex R., USA: 57
Saigon: 3 - 4, 8 - 13, 16, 18 - 19, 25, 27 - 28, 30, 35, 45, 49, 56 - 58, 63, 104, 141, 174, 177, 183, 197, 212, 218 - 219, 227, 230, 232, 252, 262, 265 - 269, 271 - 272, 277, 283, 310, 338
Saigon air show: 211
Sam Houston operation: 49
Sam Neua province: 121, 123, 127
Sam Thong: 131
Sapper raids, enemy. See Demolition operations, enemy
Saravane: 125
Sattahip: 273
Scalf, Lance D.: 229
Scarlett, Anthony R.: 291
Scholen, T/Sgt: 304
Schools, assistance to: 294
Schools, RVNAF: 309 - 319
Scott Air Force Base: 328
Sea of Japan: 56, 206
Seamans, Robert C.: 39
Search-and-destroy operations: 41, 44, 151, 171, 174
Search-and-rescue missions: 44, 55, 63, 75, 89, 118, 167, 177, 226, 235 - 243
Secretary of the Air Force. See Seamans, Robert C.: Zuckert, Eugene M.
Security measures and systems: 141, 257 - 259, 262, 269
Security Police Squadron, 377th: 261
Senate, U.S. See Congress
Senecal, Leon E.: 266
Sensor devices: 57, 92, 109, 111, 118, 212 - 213, 218 - 219, 239
Sewart Air Force Base: 301-302, 304
Shank, Edwin G., Jr.: 29
Shark, David B.: 257
Sharp, U. S. Grant, USN: 32, 69, 79, 137. See also Pacific Command
Shaw Air Force Base: 11, 223
Sheeband, Donald J.: 291
Sheppard Air Force Base: 299, 303, 313 - 314, 317
Shipping
cargo tonnages delivered: 250
supply flow and transit time: 251 - 254, 276

☆ U.S. GOVERNMENT PRINTING OFFICE : 1984 O - 459-488 : QL 2